Autodesk Fusion 360 CAD Project Workbook

A Step-by-Step Guide to 3D Modeling, Assemblies, and 2D Drafting

Merrick Vane

Autodesk Fusion 360 CAD Project Workbook

Published by: Merrick Vane
merrickvane99@gmail.com

Preface

Autodesk Fusion 360 has changed how we approach design and manufacturing. By combining 3D CAD, CAM, and simulation into a single cloud-based platform, it allows anyone from a garage hobbyist to a professional engineer to design complex products. However, learning a professional-grade software tool can feel overwhelming when you stare at a blank digital canvas.

This workbook removes that barrier.

Rather than overwhelming you with dense theory and endless menus, this book is built entirely around practical application. You will learn by doing. You will start with basic shapes and progress systematically through multi-part assemblies and formal engineering drawings. By the time you finish the final project, you will possess the foundational skills required to model your own original ideas confidently.

Who This Book is For

This workbook is designed for complete beginners who want a structured, hands-on introduction to mechanical design. Whether you are an aspiring engineer, a product designer, a 3D printing enthusiast, or a student preparing for official Autodesk certification, this guide will provide the exact steps you need to succeed. You do not need any prior 3D modeling experience to complete these projects.

How to Use This Workbook

You must treat this book as an active training manual, not passive reading material. You should sit at your computer with Fusion 360 open and follow the instructions click-by-click.

- **Sequential Learning:** You should complete the tutorials in order. Early projects (like the hex bolt or pawn) teach fundamental tools like Extrude and Revolve. Later projects (like the mechanical vise) rely heavily on those early skills.
- **Save Your Work:** You must save your files frequently into your cloud Data Panel, as later assembly chapters will require you to insert parts you modeled in earlier chapters.

Software Updates

Because Fusion 360 is a cloud-connected software, Autodesk updates the interface regularly. While the exact location or icon of a specific tool may shift slightly after this book's publication, the core parametric workflows and fundamental commands taught here remain consistent.

Getting Started with Autodesk Fusion 360

Autodesk Fusion 360 is a three-dimensional engineering platform that integrates computer-aided design (CAD), computer-aided engineering (CAE), and computer-aided manufacturing (CAM) into a single environment. The application operates on Windows and macOS. It utilizes a cloud-based data management architecture to store project files, enabling users to access native design data across multiple devices and collaborate with distributed teams in real time.

Various engineering and manufacturing sectors utilize Fusion 360, including consumer product development, automotive component fabrication, medical device engineering, and industrial machinery manufacturing. The platform primarily supports solid parametric modeling. Mechanical engineers use it to define dimension-driven components and build structurally constrained multi-part assemblies, while machinists use it to program CNC toolpaths, configure nesting layouts, and prepare files for additive manufacturing.

Because these distinct tools operate within one shared workspace, the user can advance a solid model from initial 3D geometry to final production code without relying on external file translation or secondary CAD applications.

Workspaces in Fusion 360

Fusion 360 is organized into workspaces. Each workspace focuses on a specific discipline, while sharing the same central model.

Design workspace

The Design workspace is the primary environment for part and assembly creation. It contains commands for sketches, solid features, surface features, sheet metal parts, direct edits, and component relationships.

SOLID Tab

This is the primary tab and the starting point for standard mechanical modeling.

- The **Create** panel contains the Create Sketch command, which is used to draw two dimensional profiles. These profiles are converted into **three-dimensional** geometry with commands such as Extrude, Revolve, and Sweep.
- The **Modify** panel contains feature editing commands such as Fillet, Chamfer, and Shell. It also contains direct face editing commands such as Press Pull, which modify geometry without returning to the original sketch.

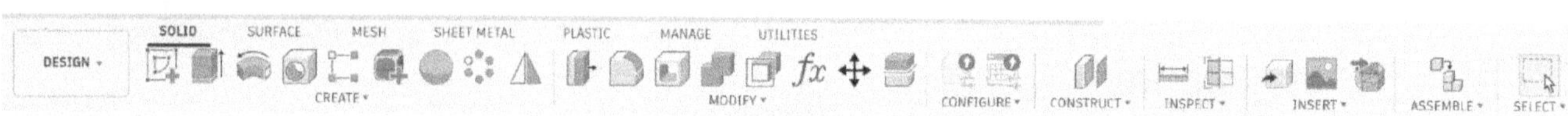

SURFACE Tab

The SURFACE tab is used to create and edit zero thickness geometry. The Create and Modify panels include commands such as Extrude, Patch, Trim, and Stitch. These commands are used to define complex exterior form and then close the surface set into a solid body when required.

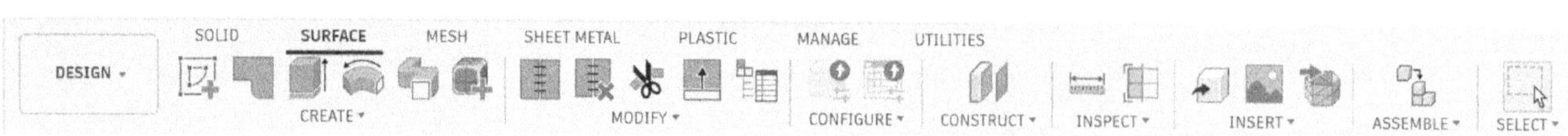

MESH Tab

The MESH tab is used for polygon based geometry, usually imported from scan data or STL and OBJ files. The Prepare and Modify panels contain commands for repair, smoothing, reduction, and conversion of mesh geometry for later editing.

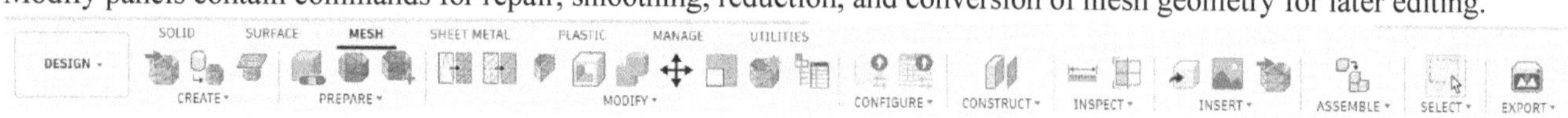

SHEET METAL Tab

The SHEET METAL tab is used for parts manufactured from bent sheet stock. The Create panel generates flanges instead of standard solid extrusions and maintains constant thickness and bend radius. The tab also contains commands for flat pattern generation for cutting and forming operations.

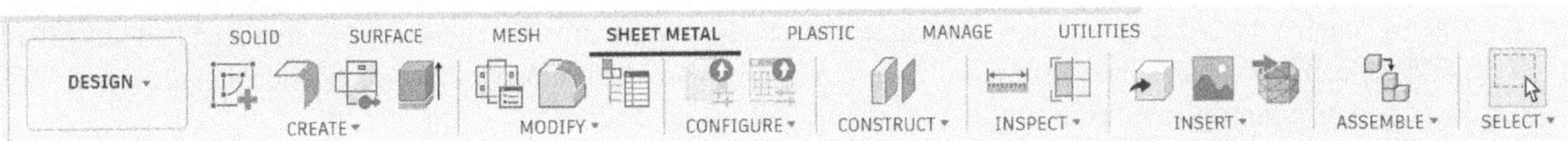

ASSEMBLY Tab

The ASSEMBLY tab is used to define relationships between components. The Relationships and Motion panels are used to position components and control rotation, sliding, and other mechanical movement.

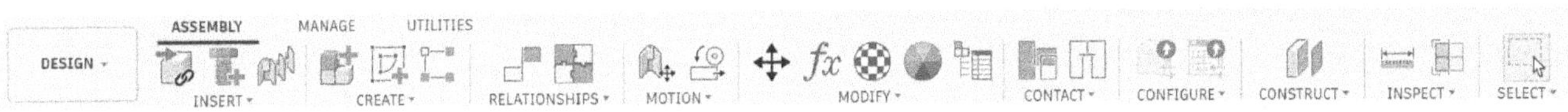

UTILITIES Tab

The UTILITIES tab contains supporting commands rather than geometry creation commands. The Make panel prepares the model for printing, the Inspect panel contains measurement and analysis commands, and the Add Ins panel manages scripts and extensions.

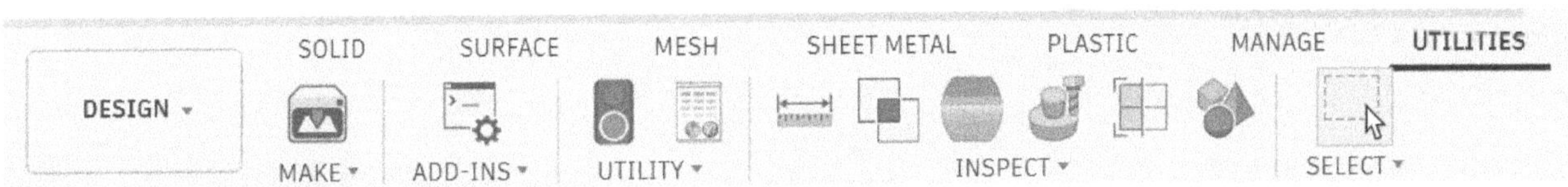

Drawing workspace

The Drawing workspace is used to create **two-dimensional** engineering documentation. It contains commands for orthographic views, isometric views, dimensions, tolerances, parts lists, and title block data.

The DRAWING Tab

The DRAWING tab contains the main drafting commands.

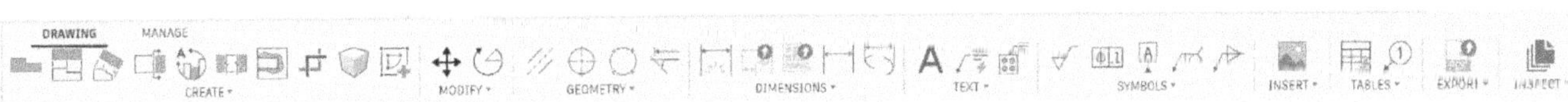

- Create Panel: Creates the drawing layout. You place a Base View first, then generate projected, section, and detail views.
- Modify Panel: You use these tools to manage sheet space. This panel allows you to move, rotate, or delete existing views and annotations to prevent clutter and maintain drawing clarity.
- Geometry Panel: You apply these tools to establish drafting references before adding dimensions. You place Center Marks on circular holes and apply Centerlines to indicate the symmetrical axes of shafts or cylinders.
- Dimensions Panel: You use this section to define the physical scale of the model. You select edges or points to apply linear, angular, radial, and diametric measurements directly to the drawing views.
- Text Panel: You use this panel to manage alphanumeric data. You can place general manufacturing notes, point out specific features with leader text, and populate the title block with metadata such as your name, part number, and revision date.

- Symbols Panel: You apply these tools to define strict manufacturing limits. You use this section to place Geometric Dimensioning and Tolerancing (GD&T) markers, Datum Identifiers, and Surface Texture requirements directly onto model edges or dimensions.
- Insert Panel: You use this panel to import external graphical assets. This is most commonly used to embed a company logo image directly into the drawing sheet.
- Tables Panel: You utilize this section to document assembly components. You generate an automated Parts List (Bill of Materials) that extracts data from your 3D design, and you use the Balloon tool to tag individual parts in the drawing views so they match the table.
- Export Panel: You use this final step to output the completed drawing. You can export the document as a PDF for printing and sharing, or as a DWG/DXF file for use in legacy 2D CAD systems.
- Inspect Panel: You use this utility to measure the exact distance between points directly on the 2D sheet space to verify layout accuracy.

The MANAGE Tab

You use the Manage tab to synchronize your 2D document with the 3D design. If you modify the 3D model, you click the update icon here to automatically sync your drawing views, dimensions, and parts lists to the new geometry.

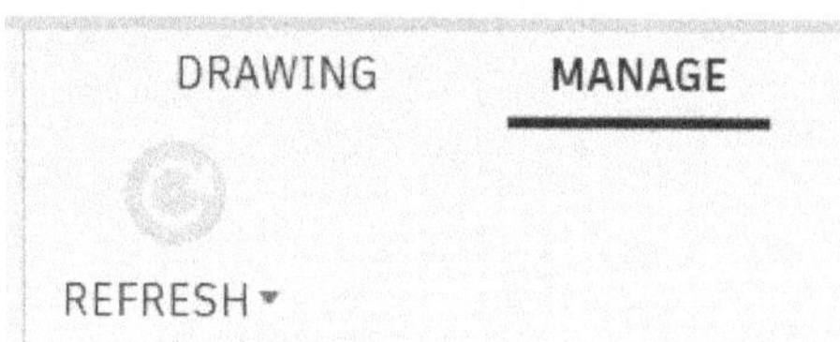

Manufacture workspace

The Manufacture workspace contains tools for defining setups and toolpaths for milling, turning, drilling, cutting, and additive manufacturing.

Simulation workspace

The Simulation workspace runs studies such as static stress, modal, thermal, and shape optimization to evaluate how a design behaves under loads and constraints.

Additional workspaces support rendering, animation, generative design, and electronics, allowing visual presentations, motion studies, optimized forms, and circuit board layouts to be developed from the same model.

For a new learner, the Design workspace is the foundation. Once sketches, features, and assemblies are comfortable, drawings, manufacturing operations, and simulation studies can be added naturally.

Parametric modeling in Fusion 360

Fusion 360 uses parametric modeling as its primary method for creating and editing geometry. In a parametric model, the shape is controlled by parameters: dimensional values, geometric constraints, feature options, and relationships between components.

In practice, this means:

- Sketches are defined by dimensions and constraints. A line can be set to a specific length, aligned horizontally or vertically, or fixed equal to another line.

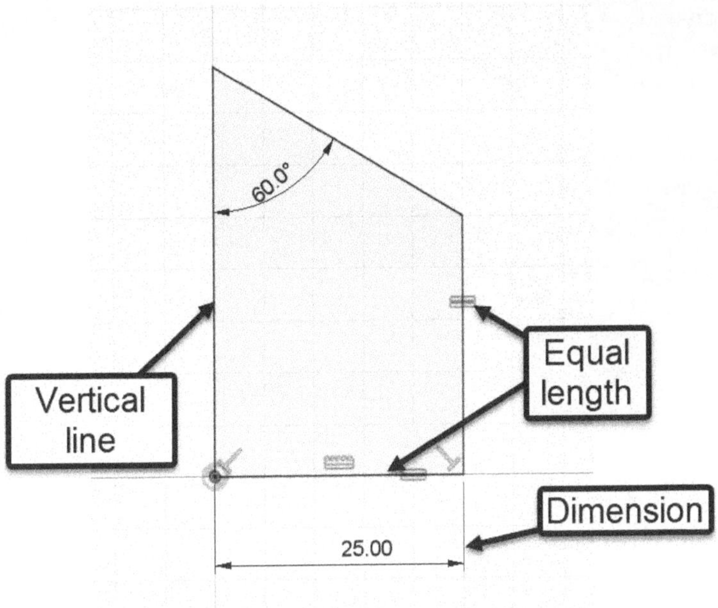

- Features such as extrusions, revolves, chamfers, and fillets are driven by numerical inputs. Changing a value in a dialog or parameter table adjusts the feature and any geometry that depends on it.

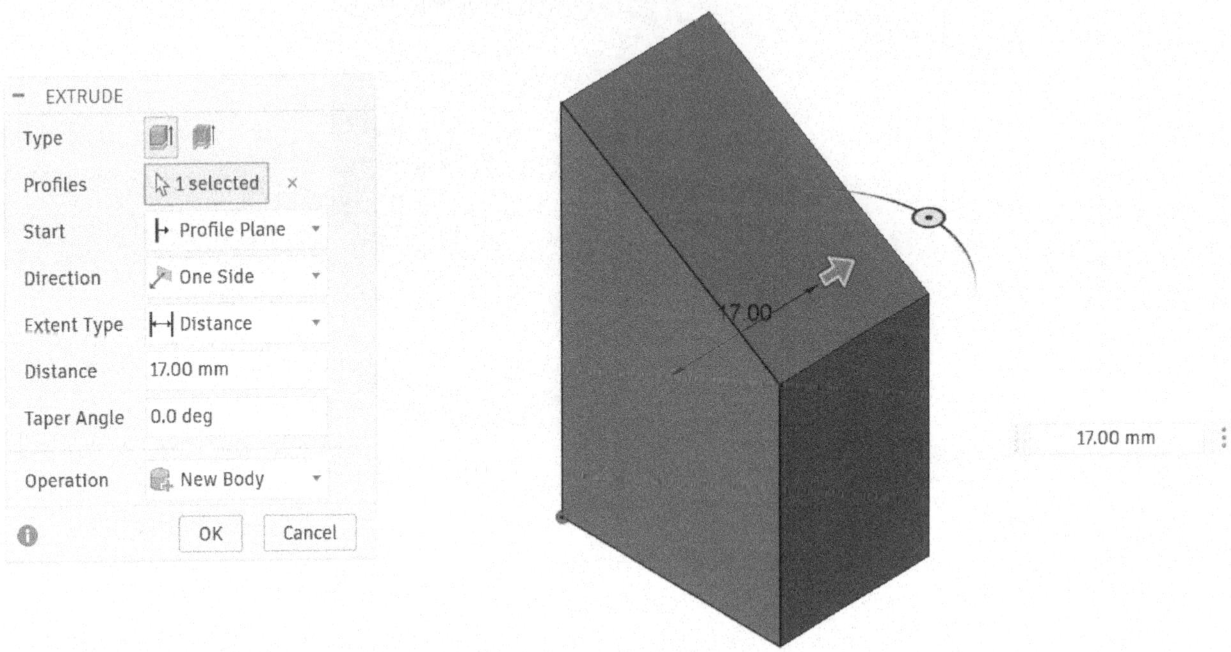

- Parameters can be named and stored in a dedicated parameter table. For example, a design might define parameters called WIDTH, HEIGHT, and THICKNESS. Any feature dimension linked to these names will update automatically when the values change.

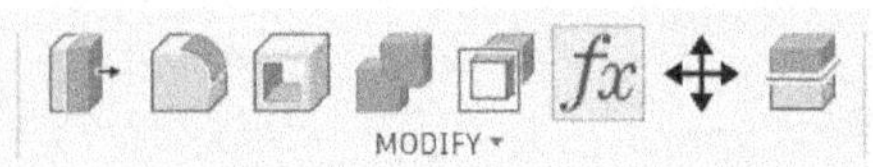

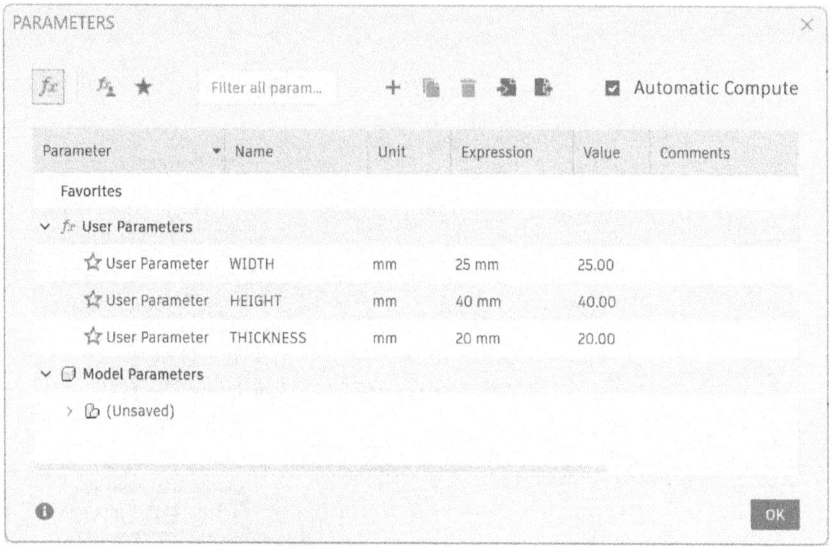

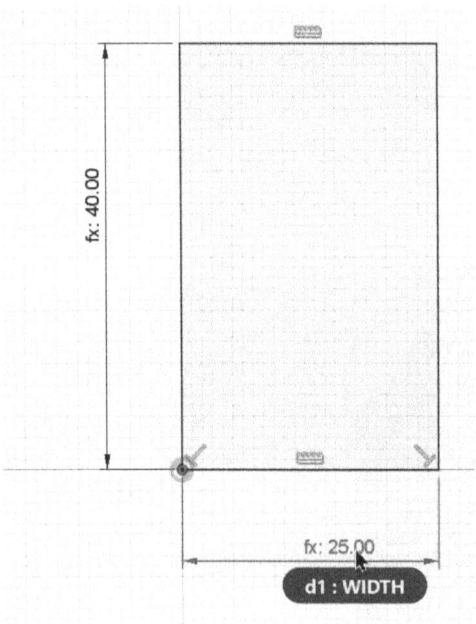

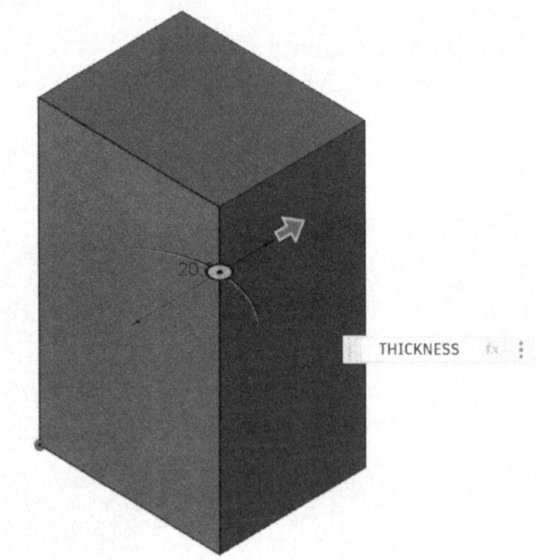

- Assemblies use joints, contact relationships, and motion limits to capture intent between components. When a driving parameter changes, connected parts update while satisfying these relationships.

This approach has several advantages. Design updates can be applied by editing a small set of key parameters instead of manually redrawing shapes. Families of related parts can be created by varying parameter values. Production drawings and toolpaths stay synchronized because they reference the same underlying model.

Files, projects, and document types

You manage your data in Fusion 360 through cloud projects, design documents, and an internal file structure rather than relying on many separate file types.

Projects: You use a project as a shared container to store your design files, drawings, manufacturing setups, and related documents. You can keep projects private or share them with collaborators.

Design documents: You use design documents as either single parts or as master assemblies. You create your components in separate files and insert them into a main assembly document. This creates a linked relationship that lets you reuse parts across different designs and keeps your main assembly file lightweight.

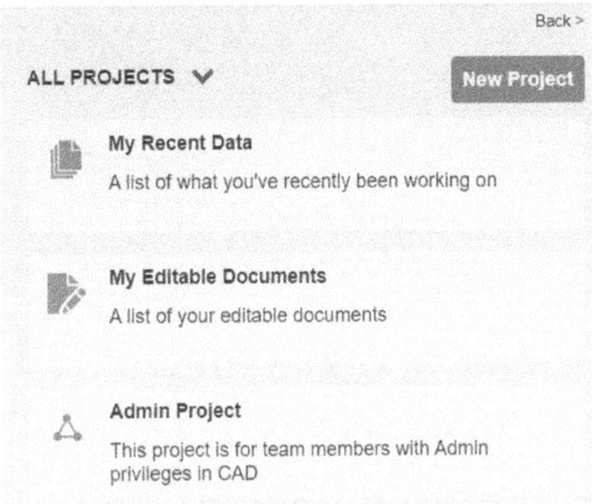

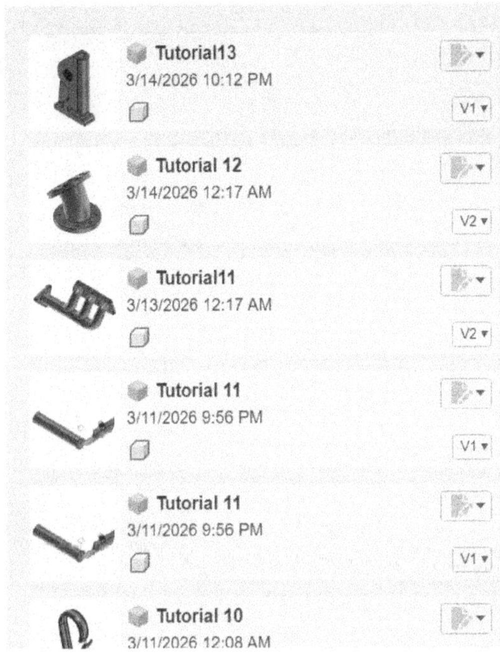

The Browser: You use the Browser panel to view all your components, bodies, sketches, construction geometry, and reference elements organized in a tree structure. When you activate a component here, you focus your operations and visibility strictly on that part of the design.

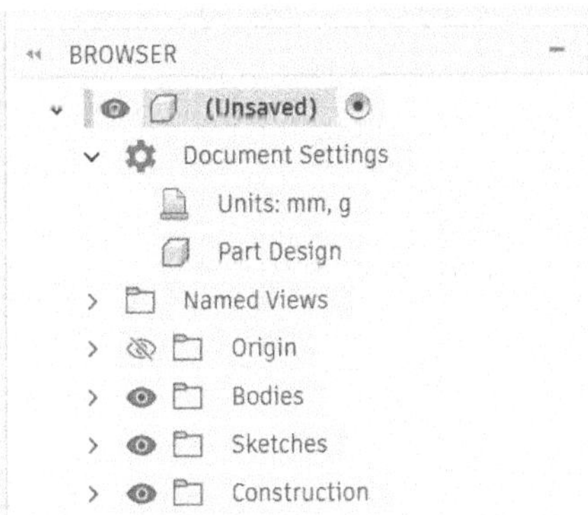

Drawings: You store 2D drawings as separate documents that link directly back to your 3D files. You can generate sheets for your complete assembly or for your individual component files. When you change the 3D model, you update the drawing to reflect those exact modifications.

Manufacturing and simulations: You save your manufacturing setups, toolpaths, simulations, and animations directly within the active design file. You can apply these to a single component file for machining, or to the master assembly file to test mechanical motion and contact.

You use this structure to keep all related product information grouped together while maintaining a clear separation between your 3D model, your 2D documentation, and your downstream manufacturing processes.

Interface and navigation

The Fusion 360 interface is designed around a central canvas with surrounding controls that give access to tools, data, and navigation.

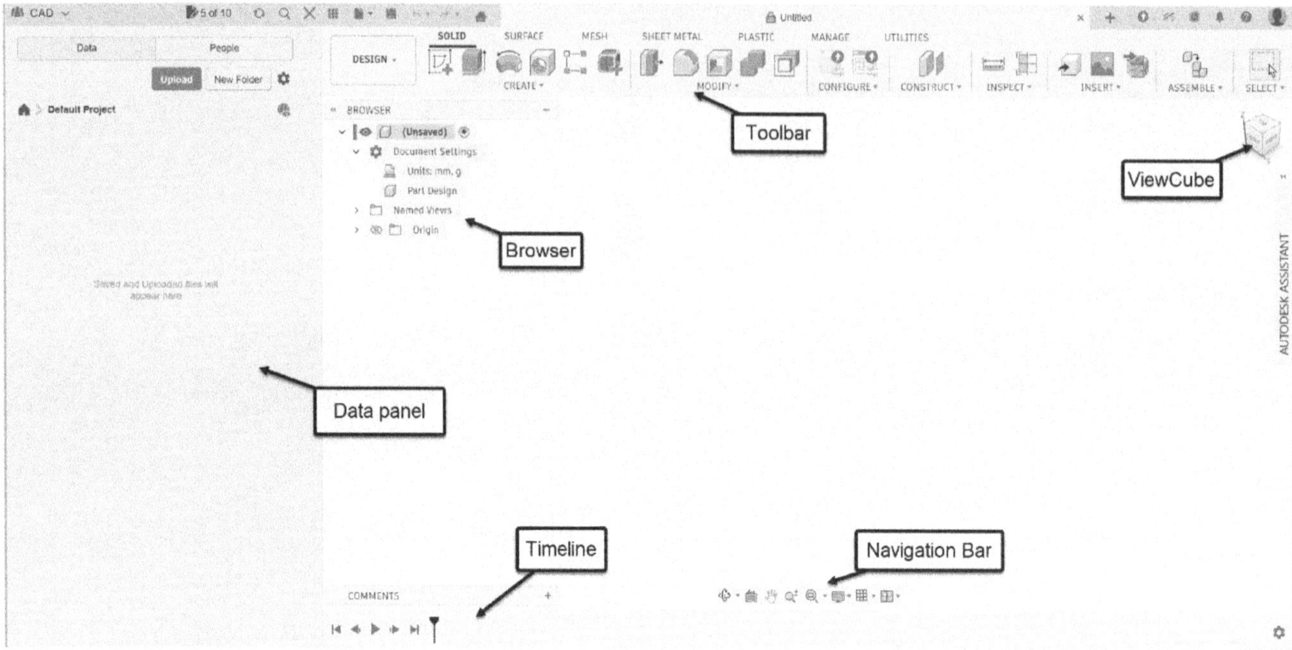

The Data Panel

You use the grid icon in the top-left corner to open the Data Panel. This is your cloud-based file manager. You use it to navigate between different project folders, invite collaborators to your team, open existing 3D models, and create entirely new designs. Because your files are stored in the cloud, you must use this panel instead of a traditional local Windows or Mac file browser to manage your Fusion 360 documents.

The Toolbar

You use this toolbar at the top of the screen as your primary command center. The tools visible here automatically change depending on which workspace you select (e.g., Design, Drawing, Manufacture). Within the Design workspace, you navigate through tabs (Solid, Surface, Sheet Metal) that contain distinct panels (Create, Modify, Assemble). You click these icons to execute actual modeling operations like extruding sketches, applying fillets, or generating assembly joints.

The Browser

You use the Browser on the left side of the screen as your project's table of contents. It lists every element you create in a hierarchical tree structure. You use this panel to organize your file: you can click the "eye" icons to hide or show specific bodies, activate specific components to isolate your workflow, and manage the underlying origin planes and construction axes that anchor your design.

The ViewCube

You use this interactive, 3D cube in the top-right corner to orient your camera precisely. As you model, you can click specific faces of the cube (like "Top" or "Front") to snap your camera to a flat, 2D orthographic view. You can click the corners of the cube to snap to standard 3D isometric angles, or you can click and drag the cube itself to freely rotate the model. You also use the small home icon next to the cube to instantly return your camera to the default starting position.

The Navigation Bar

You use the toolset at the bottom center of the screen to control how you look at the model. While you can perform many of these actions with mouse shortcuts, this bar provides explicit buttons to Pan (move the model side-to-side), Zoom, and Orbit (rotate smoothly). You also use the display setting icons located here to change the visual style of your model (such as wireframe vs. shaded) and to turn the background grid on or off.

The Timeline

You use this strip across the bottom-left of the screen to manage the parametric history of your design. Every time you create a sketch or apply a feature (like a cut or a chamfer), Fusion 360 places a chronological icon here. You use the Timeline to literally go back in time: you can double-click any icon to change its original dimensions, or you can drag the vertical marker backward to insert new features at an earlier stage in the design process.

The Marking Menu and Context Menu

To speed up your workflow without constantly moving your mouse to the top Toolbar, you use the Marking Menu. You access this menu by simply right-clicking anywhere in the empty canvas.

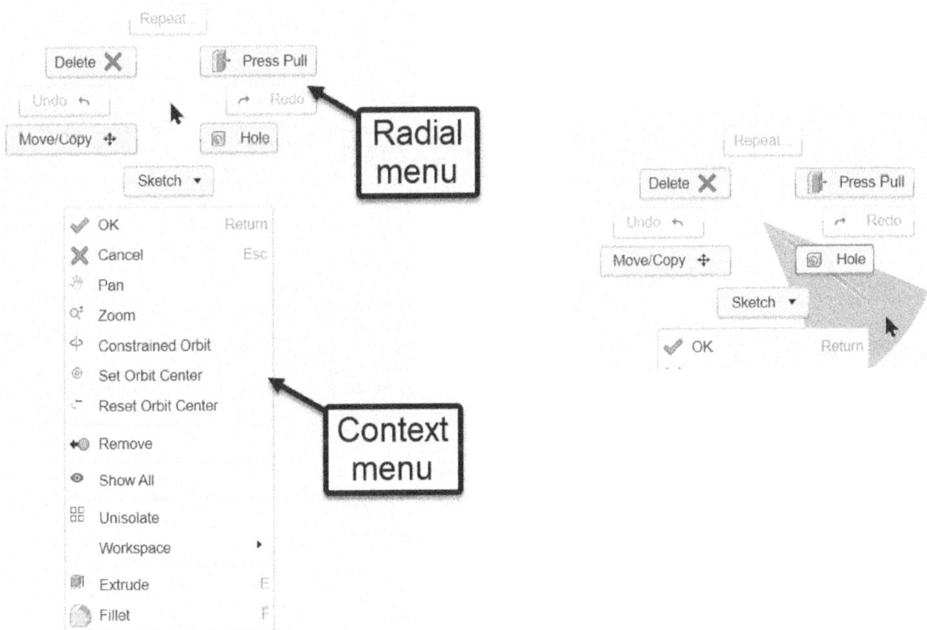

The Radial Marking Menu

You see a circular arrangement of tools at the top. This section provides immediate access to frequently used commands like Press Pull, Hole, Delete, and Undo. As you gain experience, you can activate these tools using quick "gestures" by holding right-click and swiping your mouse in the direction of the tool without even looking at the menu.

The Context Menu

You see a vertical list of commands directly below the radial menu. This list is "context-sensitive," meaning the options change based on what you have selected. If you right-click a face, it shows modeling tools; if you right-click empty space, it shows general navigation options.

Sketching

Every 3D model in Fusion 360 begins as a flat, two-dimensional drawing known as a sketch. Before you can use any solid modeling tools like Extrude or Revolve, you must define the foundational outline of your part on a flat plane.

In this chapter, you will learn the core principles of parametric sketching. You will create three specific 2D profiles: a hooked latch, an angled bracket, and a mechanical linkage arm. As you work through these exercises, you will focus on three primary skills:

Drawing Geometry: You will use tools like Line, Circle, and Arc to construct the basic wireframe shape of your design.

Applying Constraints: You will apply geometric rules to your lines. You will use constraints to force lines to remain perfectly horizontal, ensure two circles share the exact same center point, or make an arc sit perfectly tangent to a straight edge.

Adding Dimensions: You will apply specific measurements to your geometry. Instead of trying to draw a line exactly 120 millimeters long by hand, you will draw a rough shape and then use the **Dimension** tool to explicitly type in the required length, angles, and radii.

The Goal of a Fully Constrained Sketch

Your primary objective when sketching in Fusion 360 is to create a fully constrained profile. When you first draw a line, it appears blue, meaning it is free to move or change size if you click and drag it. As you add dimensions and geometric constraints, the line will turn black. A black line is fully defined; its length and position in space are mathematically locked.

You must ensure your sketches turn completely black before you move on to 3D modeling. A fully constrained sketch guarantees that your part will remain accurate and will update predictably if you need to change a dimension later in the design process.

Let's begin by opening a new design file and creating your first sketch plane.

TUTORIAL 1

In this tutorial, you create the sketch, as shown in the figure next.

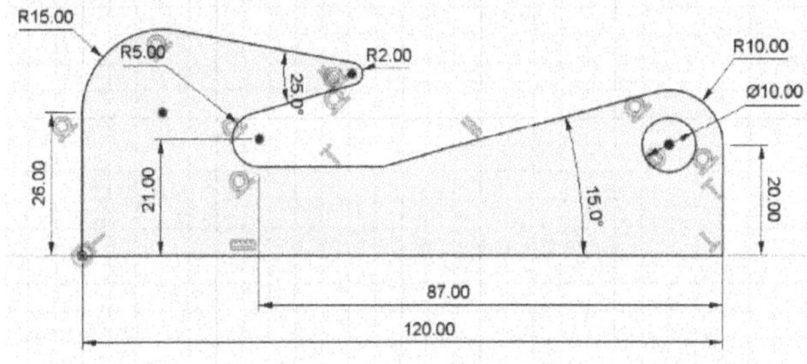

Starting a Part Desgin

1. Launch **Autodesk Fusion 360** from the desktop shortcut or from the Start menu. Wait for the workspace to load.
2. On the What do you want to design? dialog, select the **Part Design** tile on the left side.
3. On the right side of the dialog box, under **Unit System**, verify or **select millimeter (mm), gram (g)** from the drop-down menu.
4. Click **Create New** at the bottom right corner of the dialog box to open a new design file.

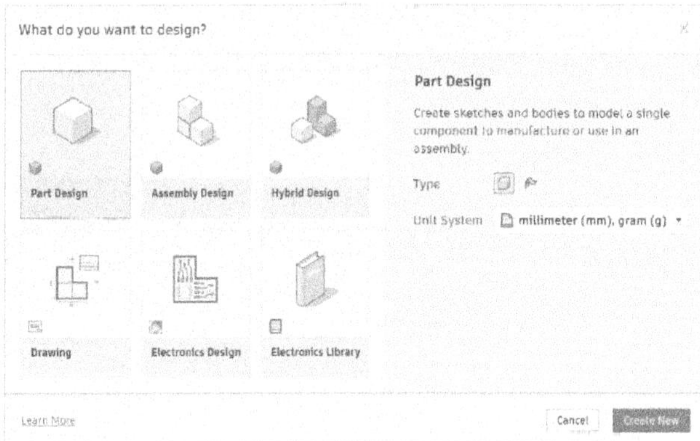

Creating the Sketch

1. On the toolbar, click **Solid > Create > Create Sketch**, then select the XZ plane to start the sketch.

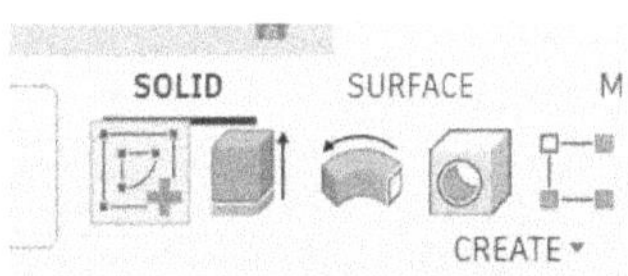

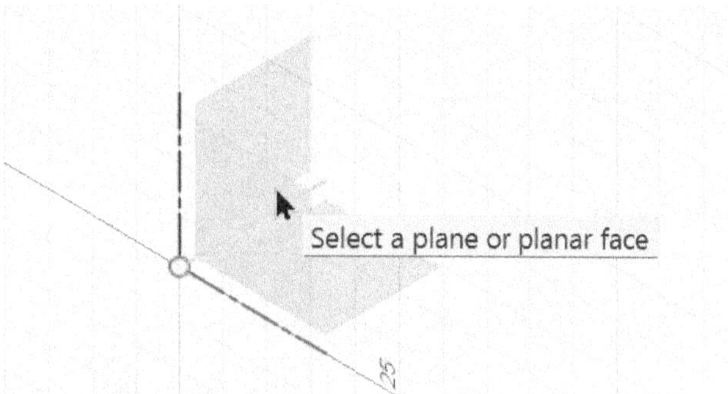

2. On the CommandManager, click **Sketch > Line** 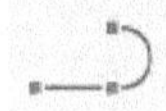.
3. Click on the origin point to define the start point of the line.
4. Move the pointer horizontally toward the right and click.

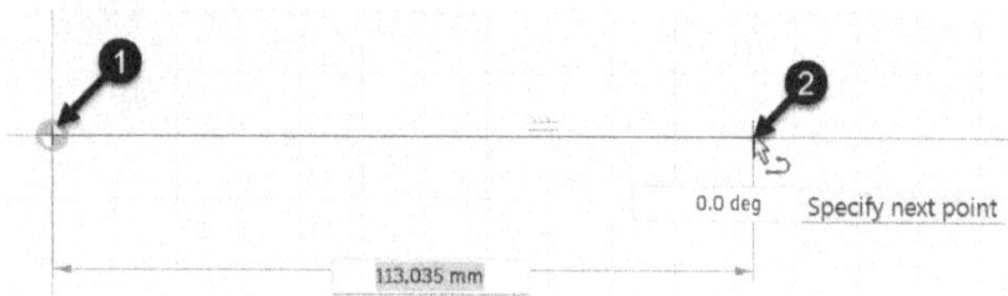

5. Move the pointer upward and click when a dotted line appears.

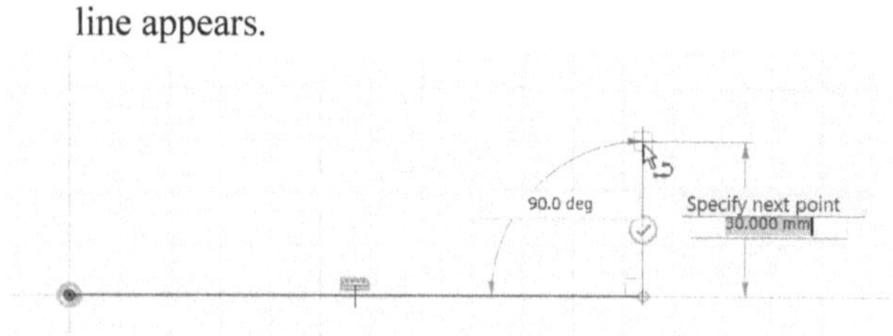

6. Move the pointer diagonally toward bottom right corner, as shown. Next, click to create an inclined line.

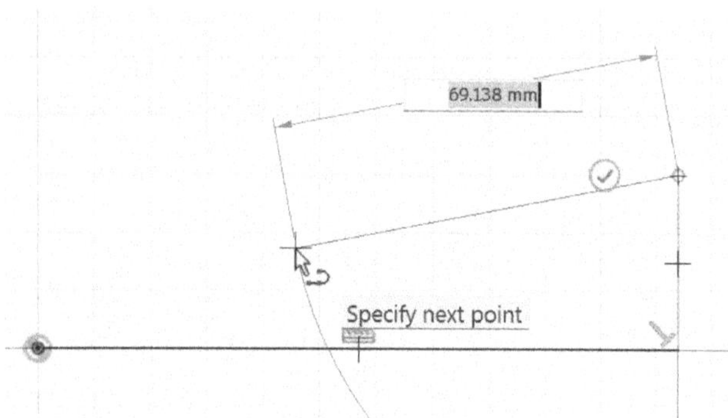

7. Likewise, create other lines, as shown.

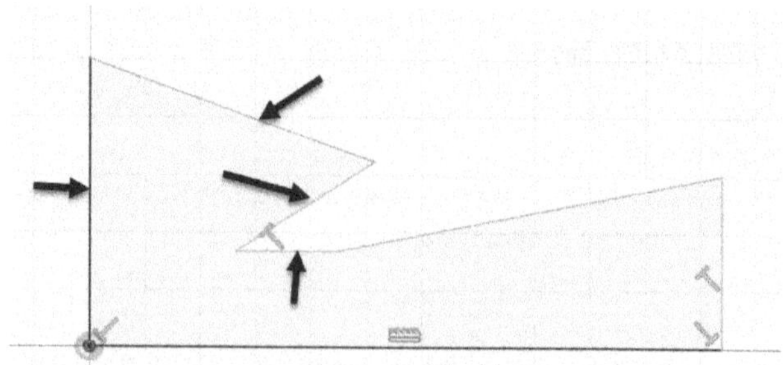

8. On the **Sketch** toolbar, click **Create > Sketch Dimension** 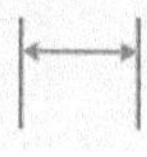 to start dimensioning the sketch.
9. To add a horizontal dimension, click the horizontal line.
10. Move your mouse cursor straight down away from the line.
11. Click once to place the dimension text on the screen.
12. In the input box that appears, type 120 for the horizontal length and press Enter.

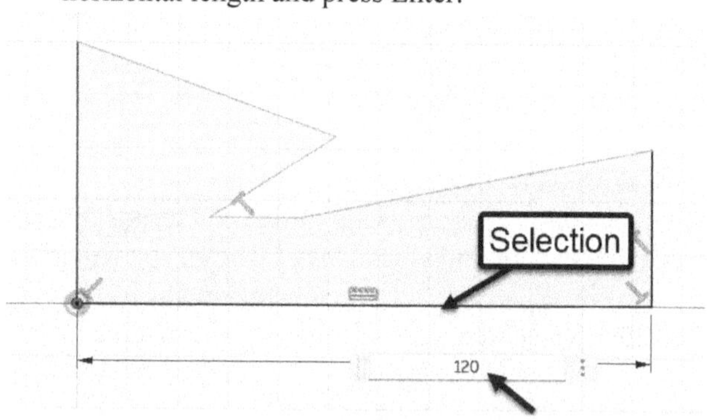

13. To add an angular dimension, ensure the **Sketch Dimension** tool is still active.
14. Click the first inclined line, and then click the horizontal line.
15. Move your mouse cursor between the two lines to preview the angle, then click to place the dimension text.
16. In the input box, type 15 and press Enter.

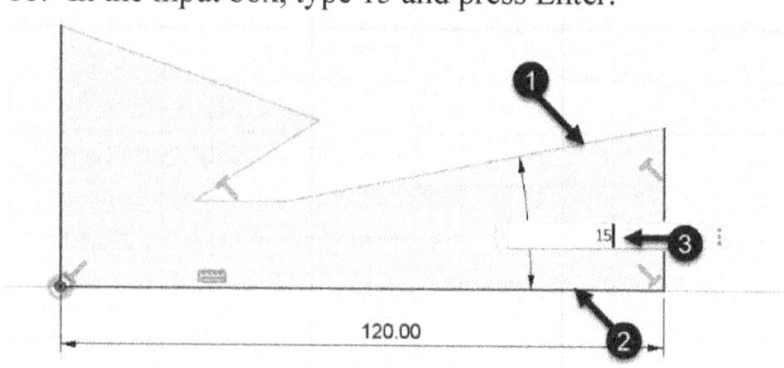

17. Likewise, apply the angular dimension between the two inclined lines, as shown.

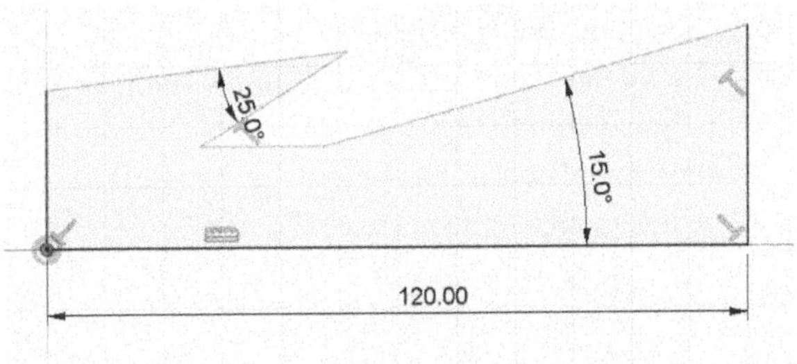

18. On the **Sketch** toolbar, click **Modify > Fillet.**
19. Click on the corner, as shown.

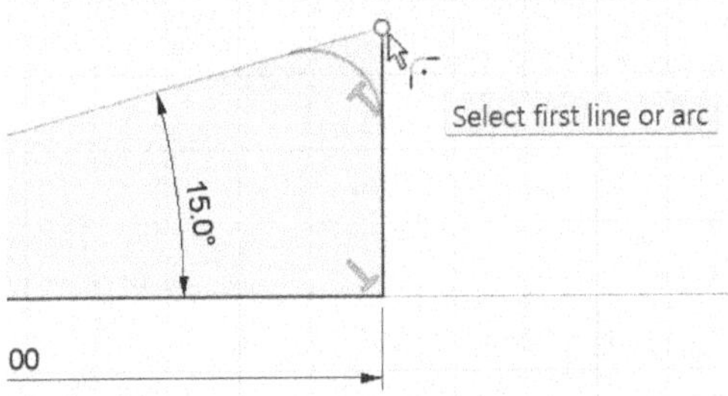

20. Type **10** in the radius input box and press Enter.
21. On the **Sketch** toolbar, click **Modify > Fillet.**
22. Click top-left corner, as shown.

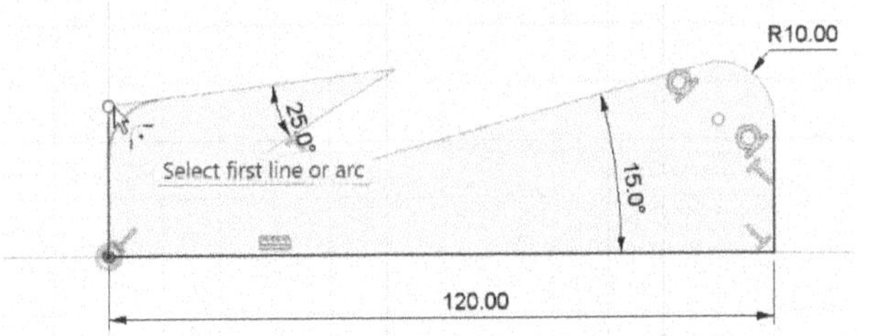

23. Type 15 in the radius input box and press Enter.
24. Likewise, create two more fillets, as shown.

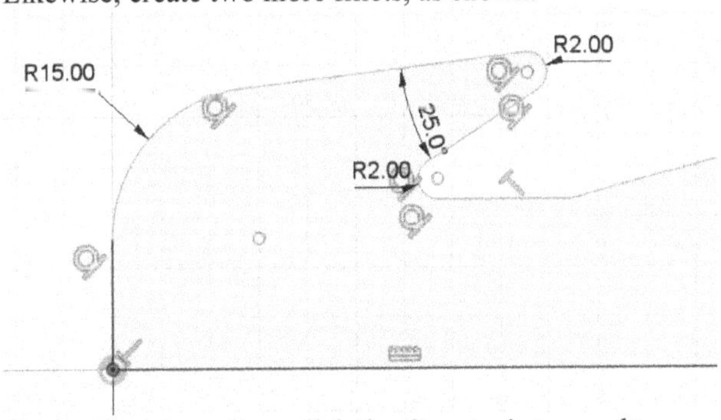

25. On the **Sketch** toolbar, click the **Constraints** panel > **Parallel** icon.
26. Select the two inclined lines, as shown.

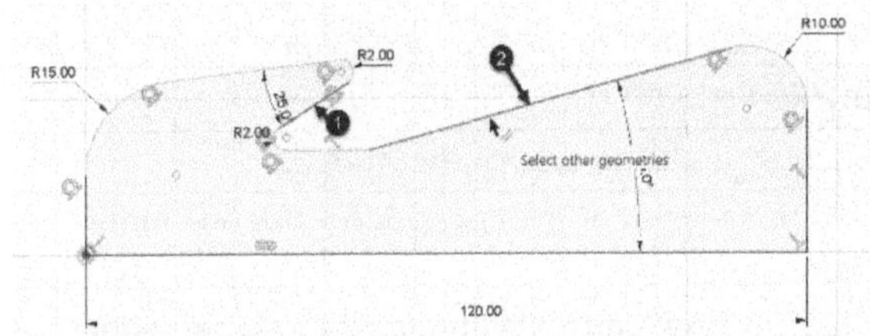

27. On the **Sketch** toolbar, click **Create > Center Diameter Circle**. Select the center point of the fillet, as shown. Move the pointer outward and click to create the circle.

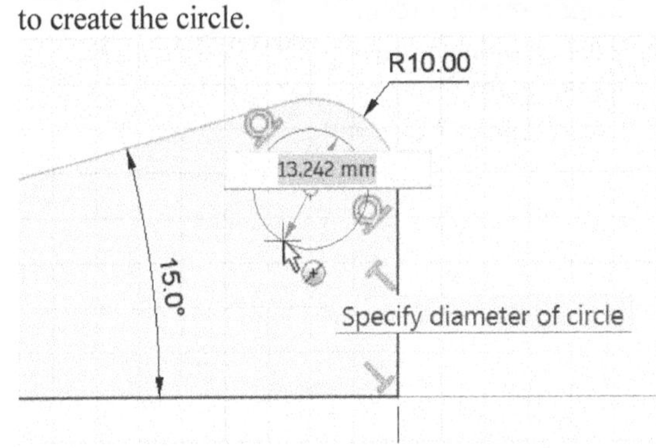

28. On the **Sketch** toolbar, click **Create > Sketch Dimension** and add dimensions to the sketch, as shown.

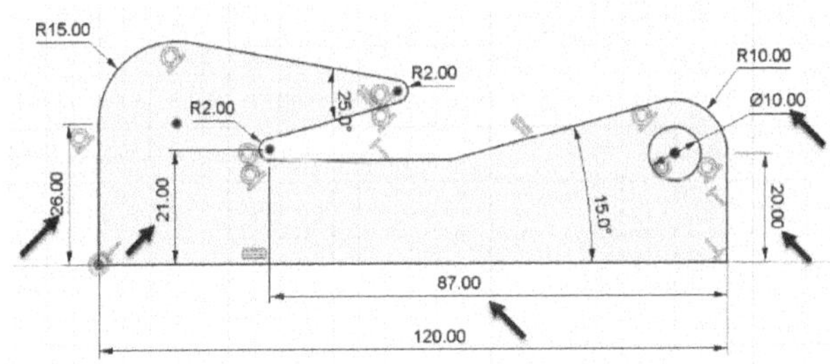

29. Double click on the radius dimension of the arc, as shown. Next, type **5** in the input box and press Enter.

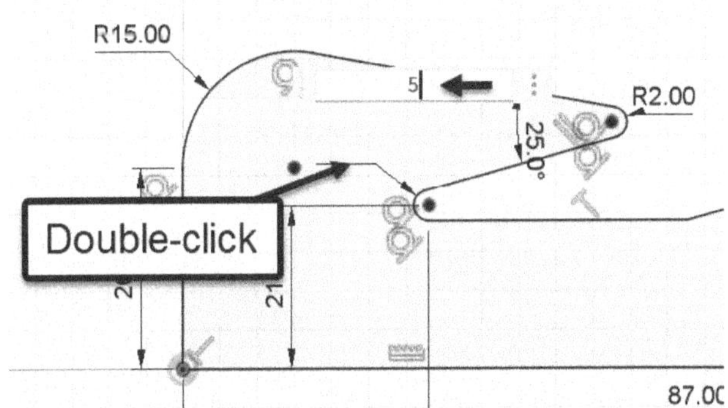

All lines should now appear black, indicating the sketch is fully constrained.

30. Click **Finish Sketch** on the right side of the toolbar to exit the sketch.

Saving the Part

1. Click **Save** on the **Application bar**.
2. On the **Save** window, type-in **C2_tutorial1** in the **Name** box.
3. Click the down arrow button next to the **Location** box.
4. Click the **New Project** button located at the bottom.
5. Type **Autodesk Fusion 360 Workbook For Beginners** and press ENTER.
6. Select **Autodesk Fusion 360 Workbook For Beginners** from the **Project** list.
7. Click **Save** to save the file.
8. Click the **Close** icon on the **File** tab.

TUTORIAL 2

In this tutorial, you create the sketch shown in the figure next.

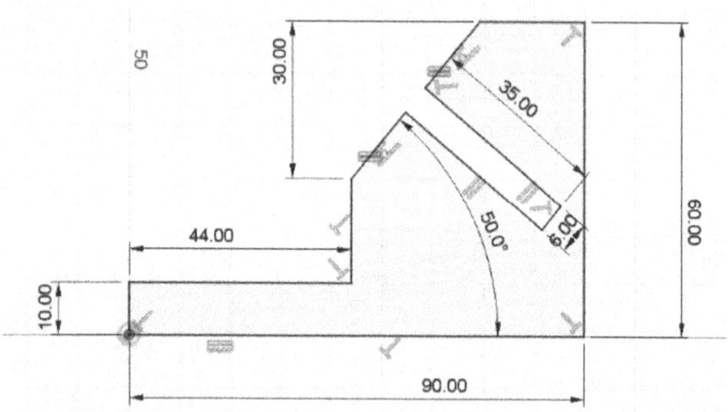

1. On the Toolbar, click the **Solid** tab, then click **Create Sketch**.

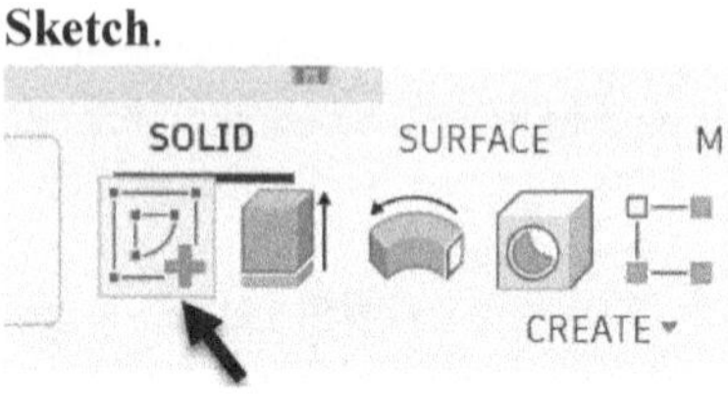

2. In the graphics window, select the YZ Plane.

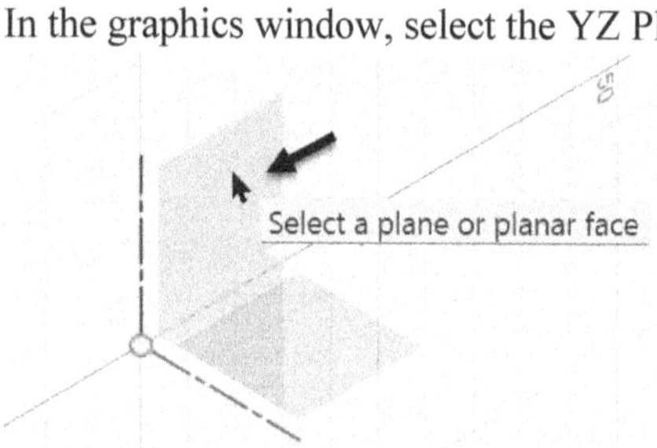

3. The sketch environment opens and the sketch grid becomes visible on the selected plane.
4. On the Toolbar, under the **Sketch** tab, click **Line** to activate the **Line** tool.
5. Select the sketch origin.
6. Move the cursor horizontally to the right, keeping it aligned with the red horizontal axis until the horizontal constraint symbol appears near the line.
7. Click to create the horizontal line.

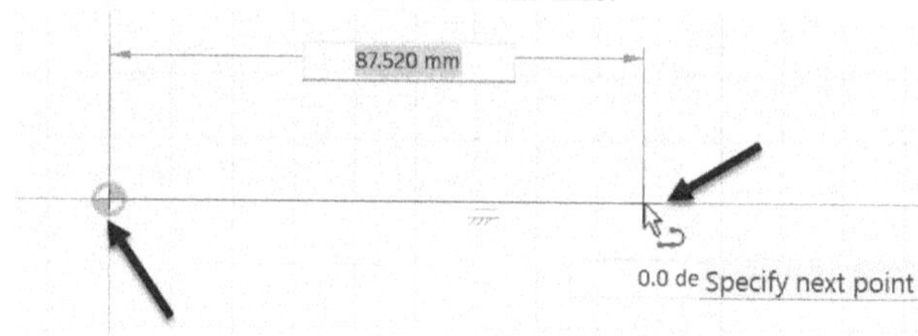

8. Move the pointer vertically upward; a small perpendicular constraint symbol appears at the corner between the horizontal and vertical lines. This indicates that Fusion 360 will keep the new line exactly perpendicular to the previous one. Next, click to create the vertical line.

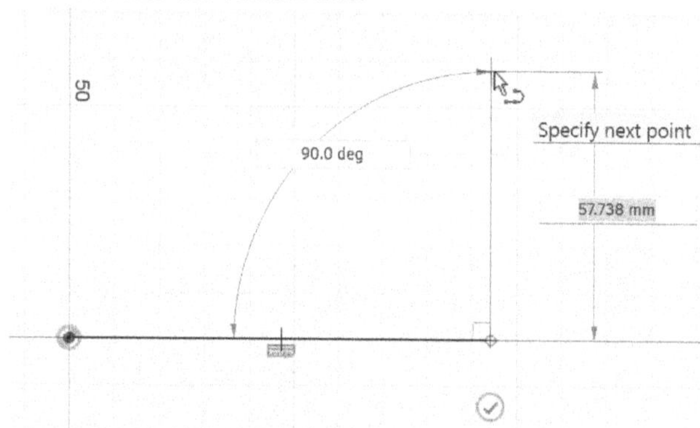

9. Move the pointer horizontally toward left; a small perpendicular constraint symbol appears between the new horizontal line and the previous vertical line. Next, click.

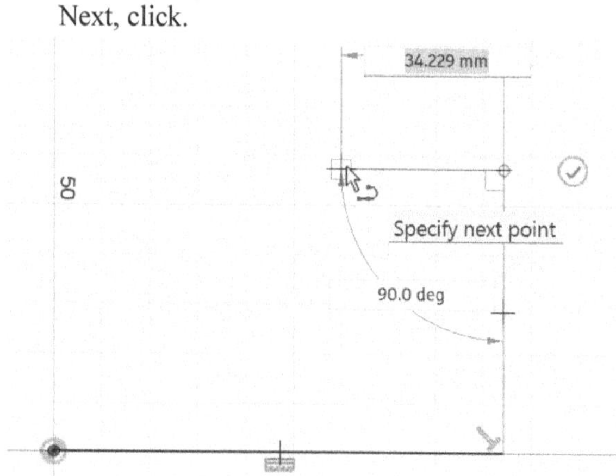

10. Move the cursor down and to the left to create a sloping segment and click.

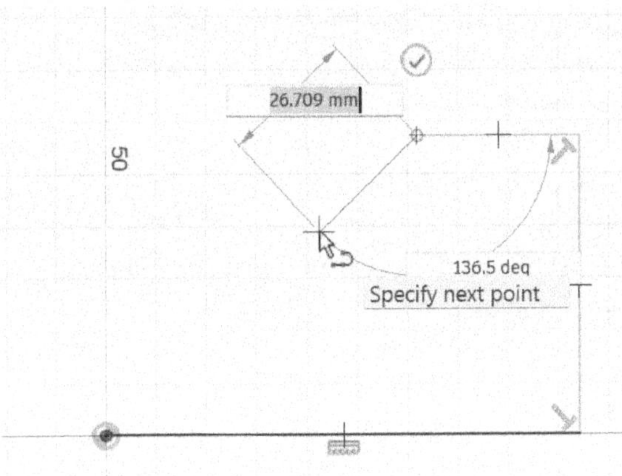

11. Move the pointer downward and click.

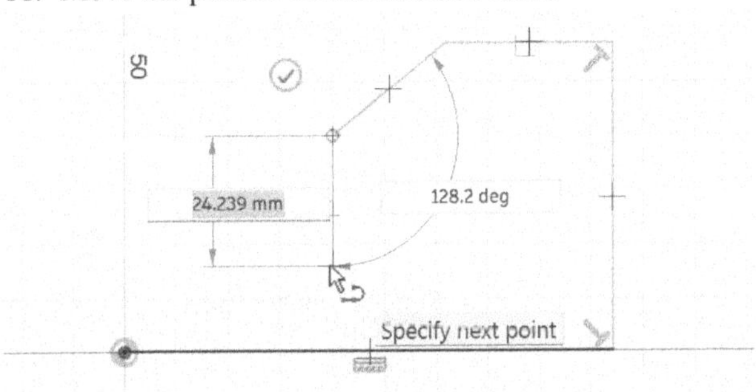

12. From the endpoint of the previous vertical line, move the cursor horizontally to the left to draw the inner step. Keep the line straight so the horizontal constraint symbol appears, and click to place the endpoint.
13. Finally, move the cursor straight down to connect back to where you started. Click exactly on the sketch origin point to close the shape.
14. Notice that the inside of the sketch turns light blue. This color change indicates that you have successfully created a fully closed profile, which is required to turn the sketch into a 3D solid.
15. Press Esc on your keyboard to exit the **Line** tool.

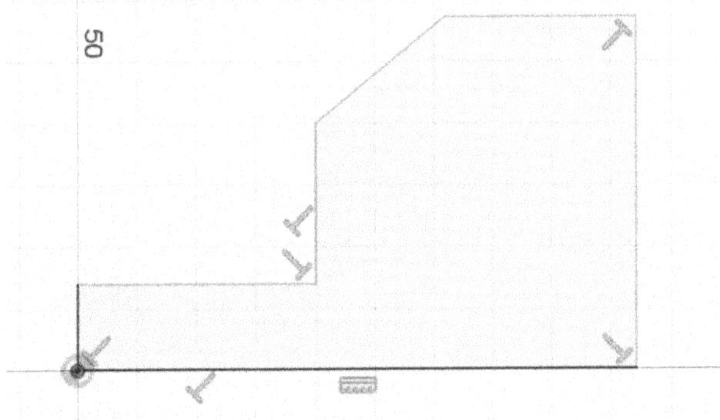

16. Click **Create > Sketch Dimension**, or press D on the keyboard.
17. First, set the overall width: click the bottom horizontal line, place the dimension below it, enter 90, and press Enter.
18. Next, set the overall height: click the rightmost vertical line, place the dimension to the right, enter 60, and press Enter.
19. Define the inner step's width: click the top horizontal line of the lower section, place the dimension above it, enter 44, and press Enter.
20. Define the small vertical step on the left: click the leftmost vertical line, place the dimension to the left, enter 10, and press Enter.
21. Set the height of the inner vertical wall: click the middle vertical line, place the dimension to the left, enter 30, and press Enter.
22. Finally, add the angle: click the sloping line, then click the bottom horizontal line. Move the cursor between them to preview the angle, click to place it, enter 50, and press Enter.

The sketch lines should now turn black (depending on your display settings), indicating the profile is fully defined. Press Esc to exit the **Sketch Dimension** tool.

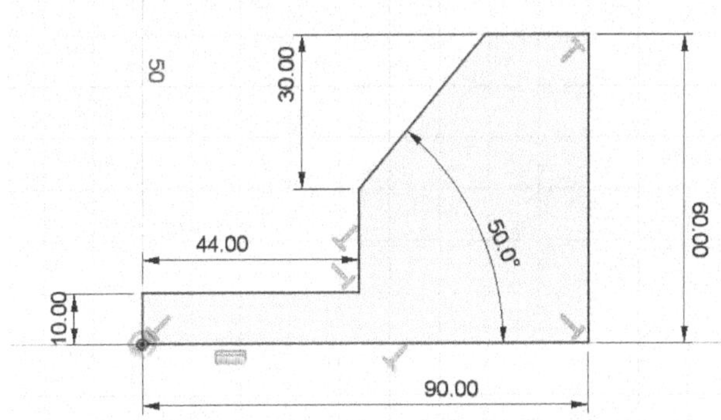

23. On the **Sketch** toolbar, click the **Create** drop-down menu, hover over **Rectangle**, and select **3 Point Rectangle**.

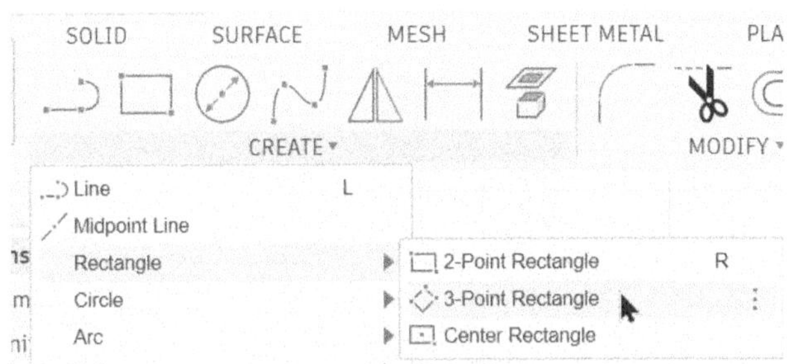

24. Hover your cursor over the upper portion of the inclined line until an X symbol appears on the line, then click once to set the first corner of the rectangle

(Point 1).

25. Move your cursor down along the inclined line. Keep the cursor on the line so the X symbol remains visible, and click again to set the second corner (Point 2). This locks the top edge of your rectangle to the exact angle of the slope.
26. Now, move the cursor inward (perpendicular to the inclined line) to define the depth of the rectangle. Click once more to place the third corner (Point 3) and complete the rectangle.

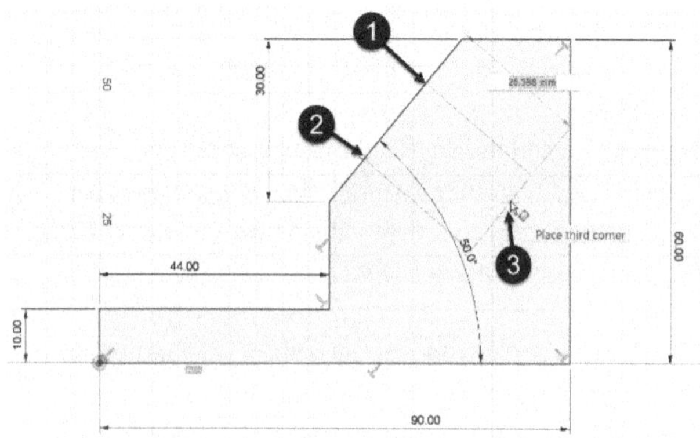

27. On the **Sketch** toolbar, click **Modify > Trim**, or press **T** on your keyboard. In Fusion 360, the **Trim** tool automatically acts like a power trim.

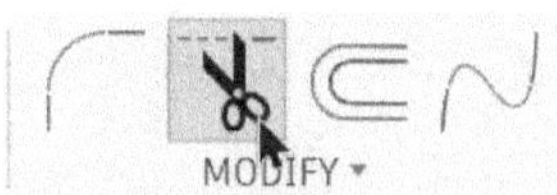

28. Press and hold the left mouse button, then drag the pointer across the inclined line segment of the rectangle, as shown. Alternatively, you can simply click directly on the segment you want to delete.

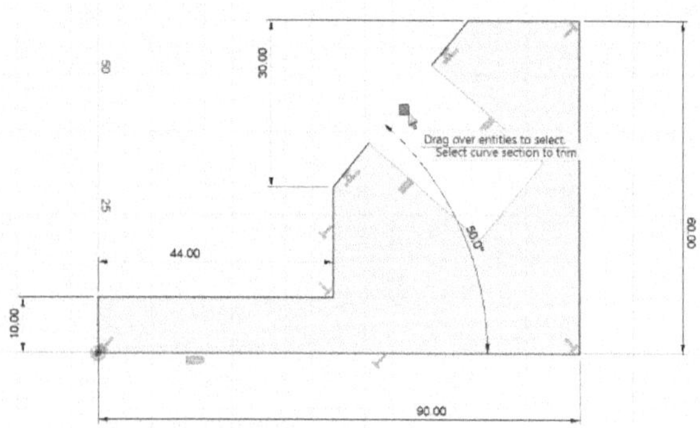

__Note:__ If you see a warning message stating "Constraints and/or dimensions were removed during operation," this is normal. It simply means that deleting the line segment also removed a dimension or constaint attached to it.

29. Press **D** on your keyboard to activate the **Sketch Dimension** tool.
30. To set the length of the newly created slot, click on the top inclined line of the slot.
31. Move the cursor away from the line at a perpendicular angle. You will notice the dimension snaps parallel to the line. Click to place the dimension, enter **35**, and press **Enter**.
32. To set the width of the slot, click the short perpendicular line at the bottom right end of the slot.
33. Move the cursor away from the line to preview the dimension. Click to place it, enter **6**, and press **Enter**.

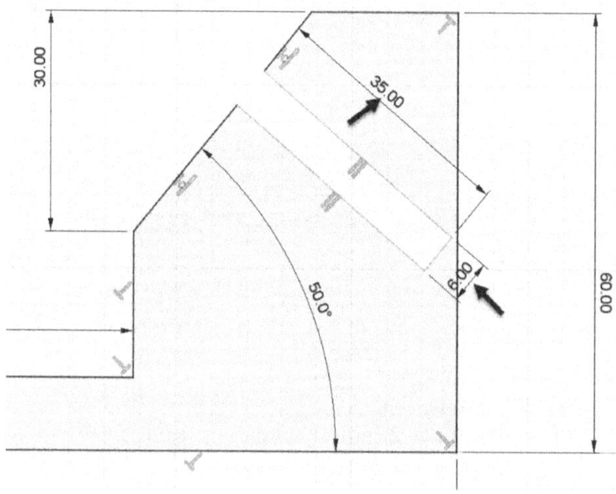

34. On the **Sketch** toolbar, click **Perpendicular** in the **Constraints** panel, then select the first pair of lines shown in the figure to make them perpendicular.

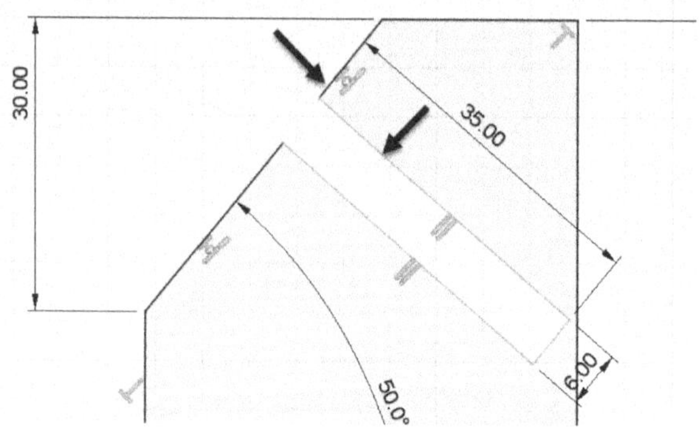

35. Select the second pair of lines so this corner is also constrained to 90 degrees.

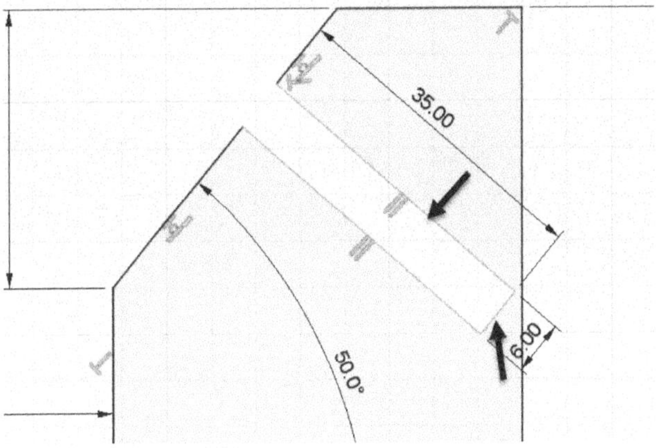

36. Click **Equal** on the **Constraints** panel in the **Sketch** toolbar.
37. Select the two short inclined lines indicated by the arrows, as shown. Both segments are set to exactly the same length.

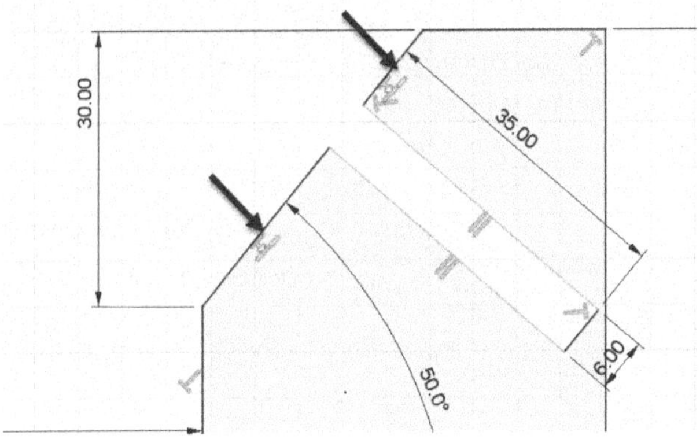

38. Click **Finish Sketch** on the **Sketch** toolbar to exit the sketch environment.

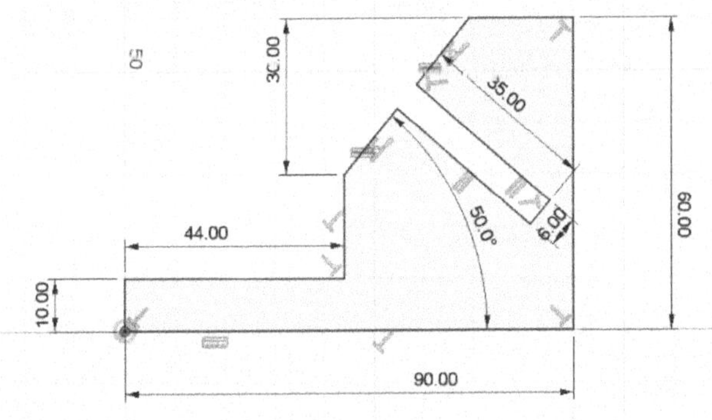

Saving the Part file

1. Click **Save** on the **Application bar**.
2. On the **Save** window, type-in **C2_tutorial2** in the **Name** box.
3. Click **Save** to save the file.
4. Click the **Close** icon on the **File** tab.

TUTORIAL 3

In this tutorial, you create the sketch, as shown in the figure next.

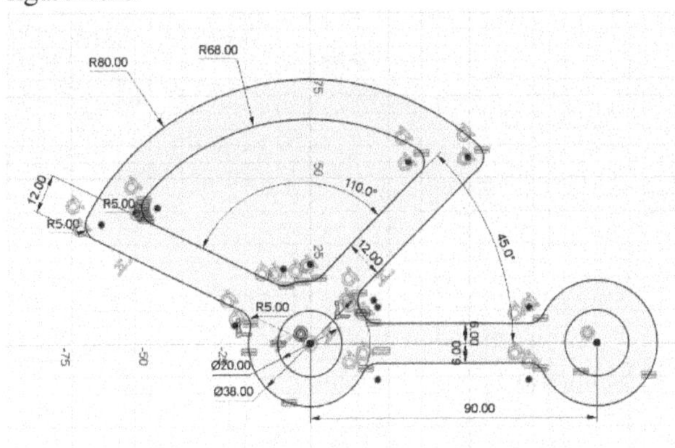

1. On the Toolbar, click the Solid tab, then click **Create Sketch**.

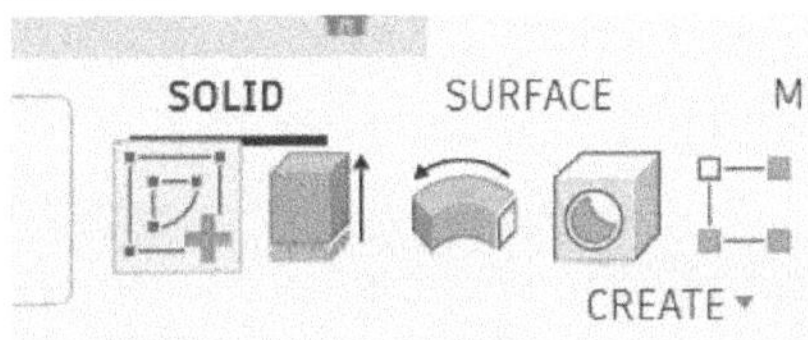

2. In the graphics window, select the YZ Plane.
3. On the **Sketch** toolbar, click **Create > Arc > Center Point Arc**.

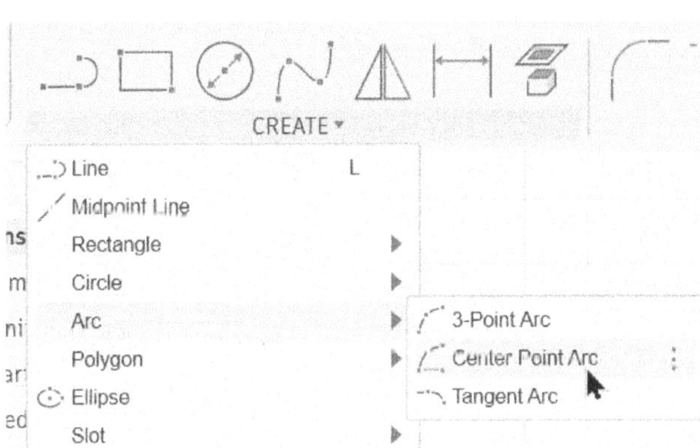

4. Click directly on the sketch origin point (Point 1). This anchors the center of your arc precisely at the origin.
5. Move your cursor diagonally up and to the right. Notice a radius line appears. Click once (Point 2) to establish the starting position and the radius of your arc.

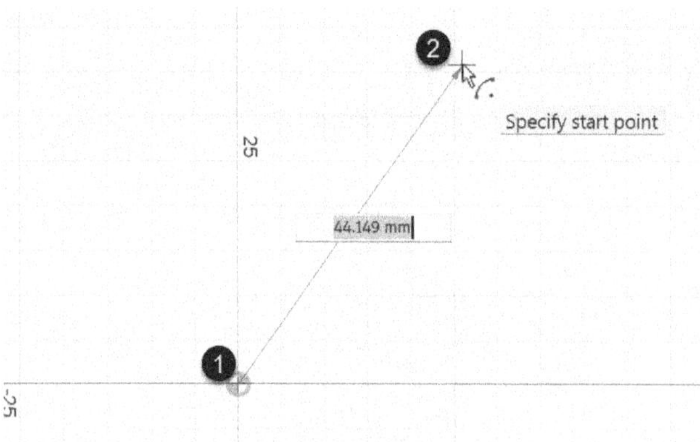

6. Now, drag your cursor in a counterclockwise direction (up and to the left). You will see the arc being drawn along the path of your cursor, along with an angle preview. Click once more (Point 3) to set the end point and finish creating the arc.

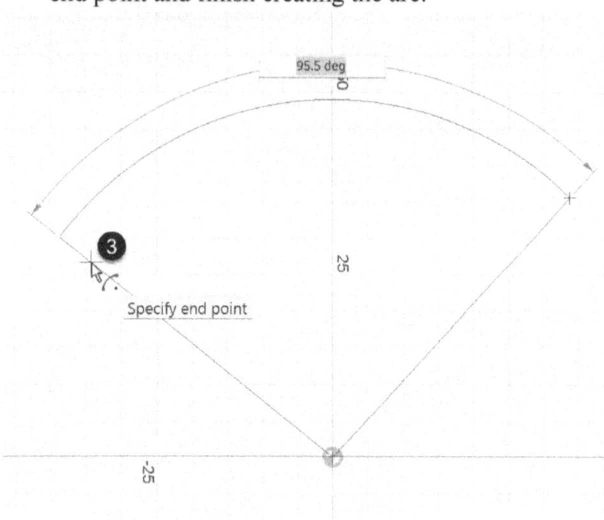

7. Click **Line** on the **Create** panel.
8. Select the endpoint of the arc, as shown.
9. Move the pointer toward right and select the sketch origin.

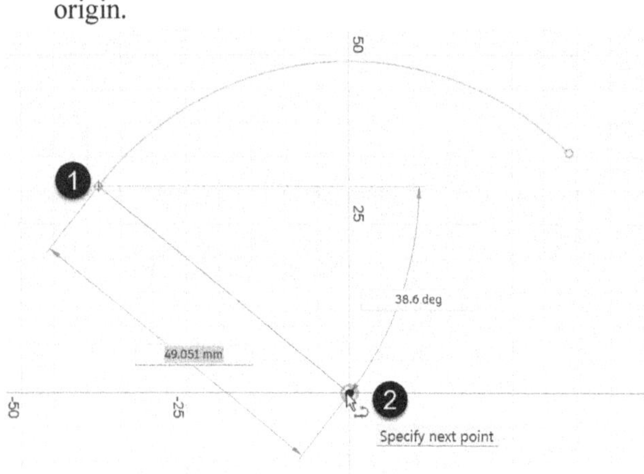

10. Move the pointer toward right endpoint of the arc.

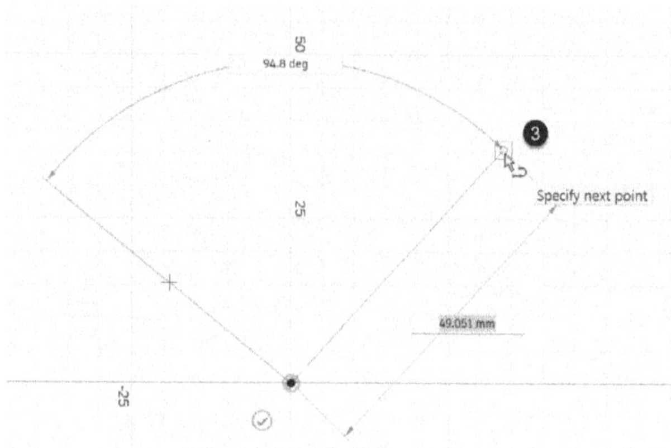

11. On the **Sketch** toolbar, click **Modify > Offset**, or press the **O** key.
12. In the **Offset** dialog box that appears on the right, ensure that the **Chain Selection** option is checked (it usually is by default). This allows Fusion 360 to automatically select all connected lines.
13. Click any line on the sketch profile. Notice that all connected lines highlight and a preview of the offset boundary appears.
14. Use the manipulator arrow to drag the offset boundary inward, or simply type -12 in the dialog box (or in the dimension input field near the cursor) to specify the inward direction and distance.

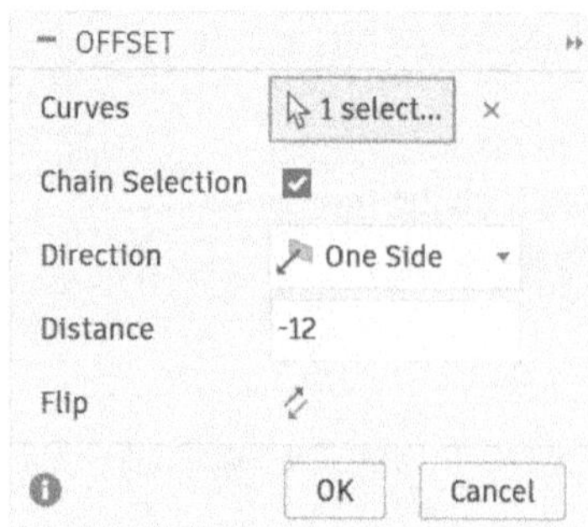

15. Press Enter or click **OK** in the dialog box to create the offset.

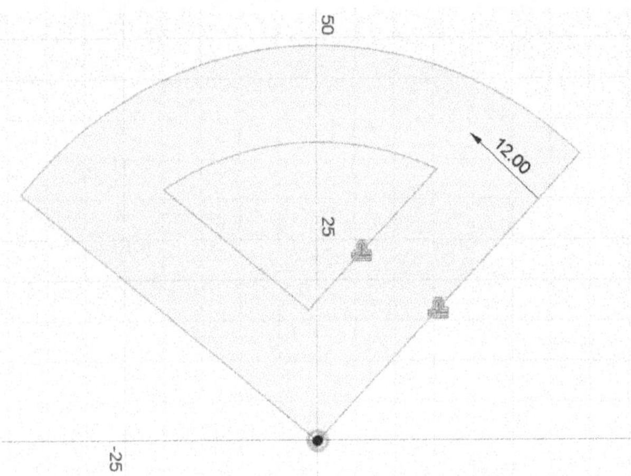

16. On the **Sketch** toolbar, click **Create > Circle > Center Diameter Circle**, or press C on your keyboard to activate the tool.
17. Click exactly on the sketch origin to set the center point of the circle. Move the cursor outward to preview the size, then click a second time to complete the circle.
18. To create a second concentric circle, make sure the **Center Diameter Circle** tool is still active. Click the sketch origin again to place the center point, move the cursor outward past the first circle, and click to complete the shape.

This sequence ensures both circles share the exact same center point at the origin, naturally making them concentric.

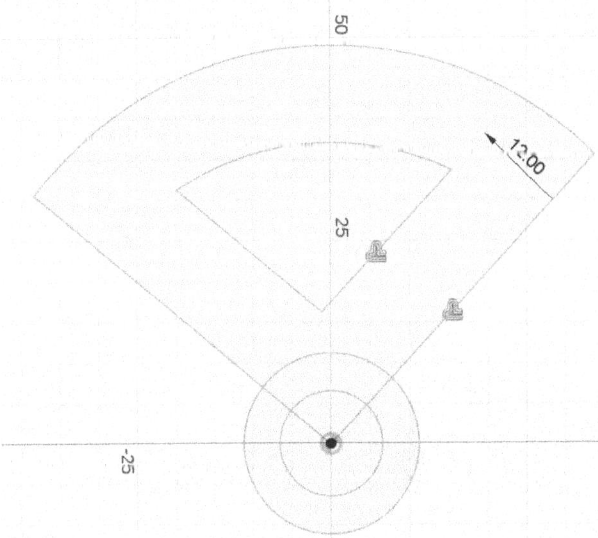

19. On the **Sketch** toolbar, click **Create > Line** (or press L) to activate the **Line** tool.
20. Before drawing the line, look at the **Sketch Palette** dialog box on the right side of the screen.
21. In the **Options** section, click the **Construction** icon (it looks like a dashed line) next to Linetype, or press X on your keyboard.

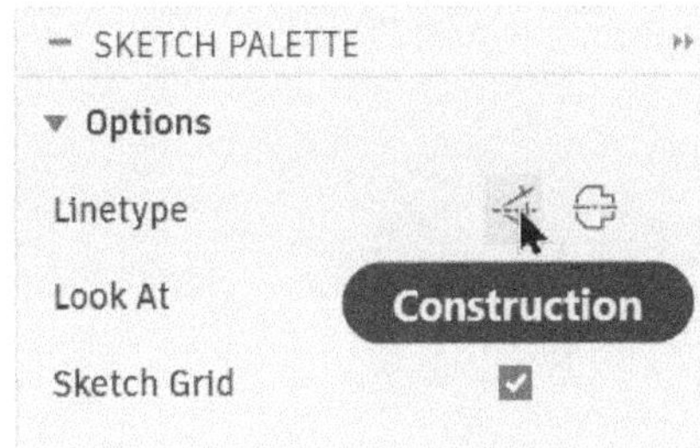

This changes the line you are about to draw into a construction line. Construction lines are used as reference geometry for dimensions and constraints, but they do not form part of the actual 3D profile when you extrude the sketch.

22. Click once to start the line, then move the pointer horizontally to the right until the horizontal constraint symbol appears, and click again to complete the line. Press Esc to exit the **Line** tool.
23. On the **Sketch** toolbar, click **Create > Circle > Center Diameter Circle** (or press C).
24. Before drawing the circle, check the **Sketch Palette** on the right side of your screen. Look for the **Linetype** options and make sure the **Construction** icon is turned off. It should look like a standard gray button, not highlighted in blue. If it is currently highlighted, click the icon once or simply press the X key on your keyboard to disable it.

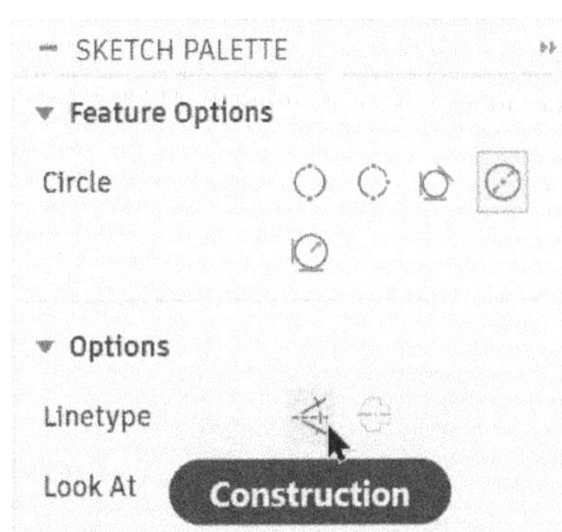

Switching this off ensures your circle will be drawn with solid lines rather than dashed reference lines.

25. Click on the right endpoint of the line you just created to set the center of the circle. Move the

pointer outward to size the circle and click to place it.

26. With the **Center Diameter Circle** tool still active, click the exact same endpoint again. Move the pointer outward to a different size and click to create a second, concentric circle. Press Esc.

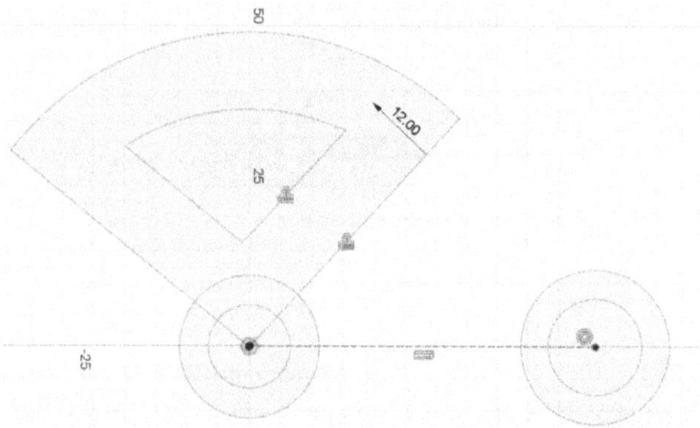

27. On the **Sketch** toolbar, click **Modify > Offset**, or press **O** on your keyboard.
28. Click on the newly created horizontal line. The Offset dialog box will appear.
29. From the **Direction** drop-down menu, select **Symmetric**. This option automatically creates offset lines on both sides of your original line.

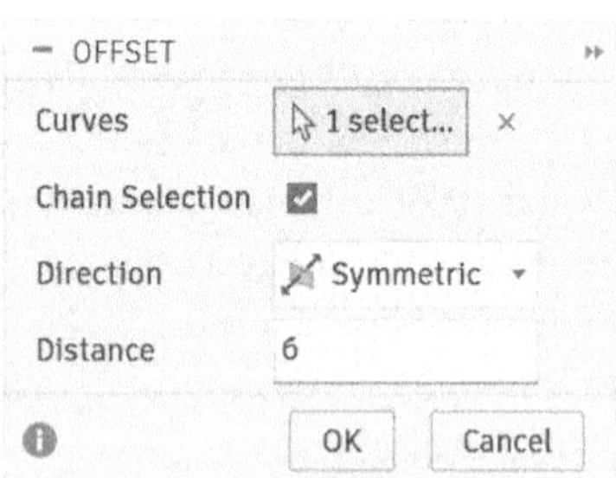

30. In the **Distance** field, type **6** and click **OK**.

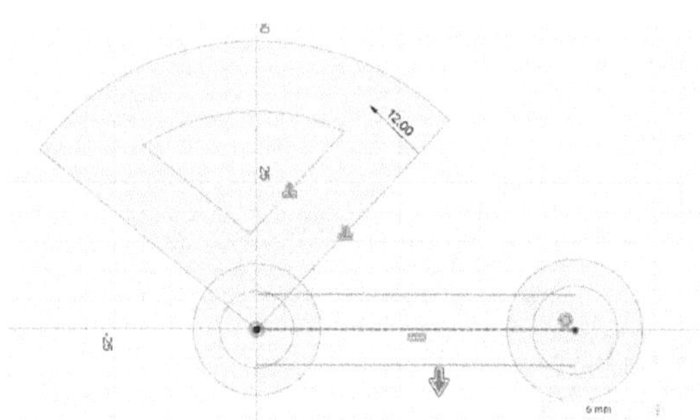

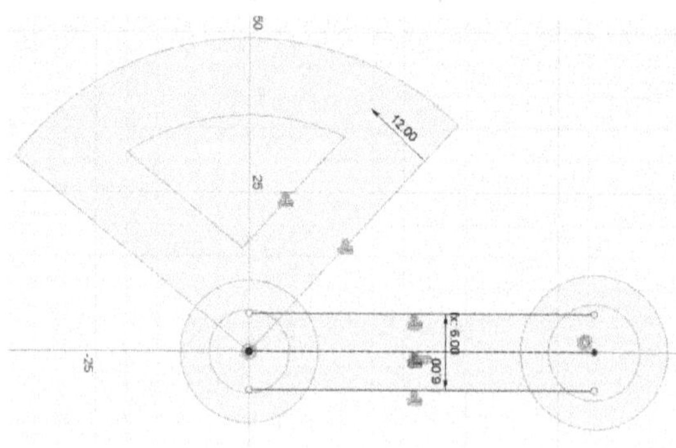

31. Press **D** on your keyboard to activate the **Sketch Dimension** tool.
32. Click the outer circle on the left, drag your cursor out, and click to place the dimension. Type **38** for the diameter and press Enter.
33. Click the inner circle on the left, place the dimension, type **20**, and press Enter.
34. To set the distance between the two main circular features, select the horizontal construction line. Drag the dimension down, type **90**, and press Enter.
35. Click the large outer arc at the top left, drag outward, type 80 for the radius, and press Enter.
36. To set the angle of the slot, click the upper angled line of the slot, then click the horizontal center dashed line. Place the angle dimension, type **110**, and press Enter.
37. Finally, to set the starting angle of the entire swept shape, click the right-side straight edge of the swept shape, then click the horizontal center dashed line. Place the dimension, type **45**, and press Enter.

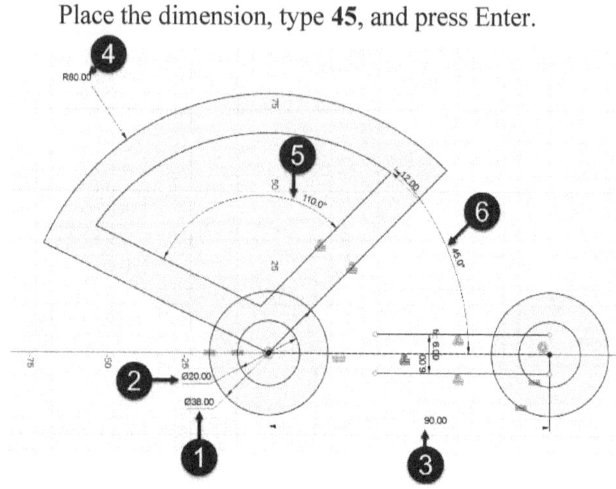

38. Click the **Equal** icon on the **Constraints** panel.
39. Select the two inner circles.
40. Select the two outer circles to make them equal in length.
41. On the **Sketch** toolbar, click the **Modify** panel and

select **Extend**.

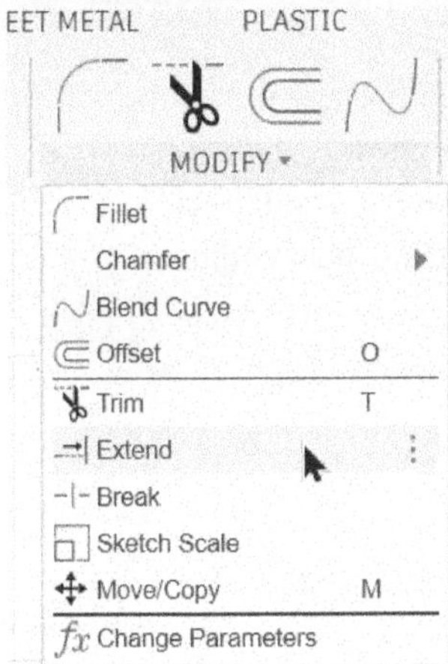

42. Hover your cursor over the lower blue offset line. A red preview line will appear, showing you how the line will extend to meet the boundary of the larger circle.

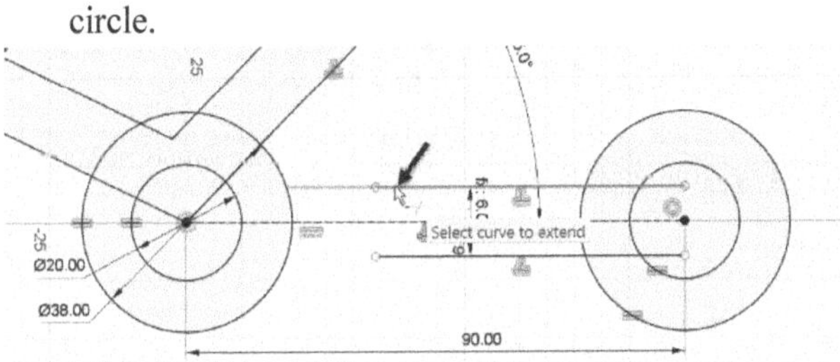

43. Click the line to confirm the extension. The line will snap to the outer circle.
44. Next, hover your cursor over the upper blue offset line. Again, you will see a red preview showing the line extending to the large circle.
45. Click the line to confirm the extension. Both lines now connect directly to the circular profile.

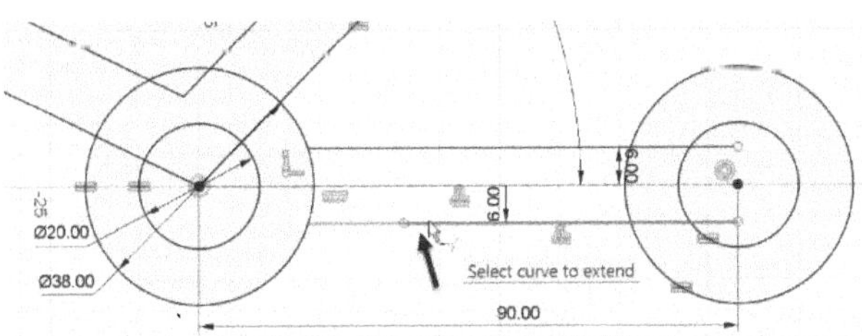

46. On the **Sketch** toolbar, click **Modify > Trim**, or press **T** on your keyboard.
47. Click on the entities to trim, as shown.

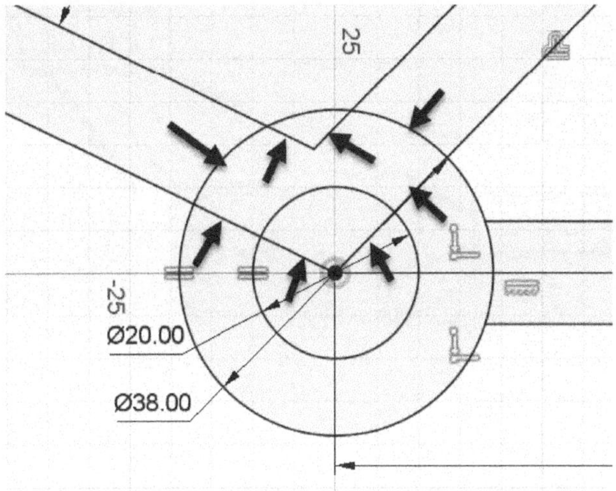

48. Click on the entities to trim, as shown.

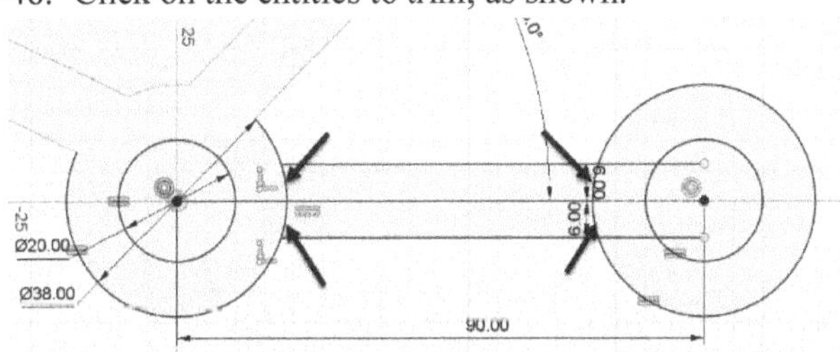

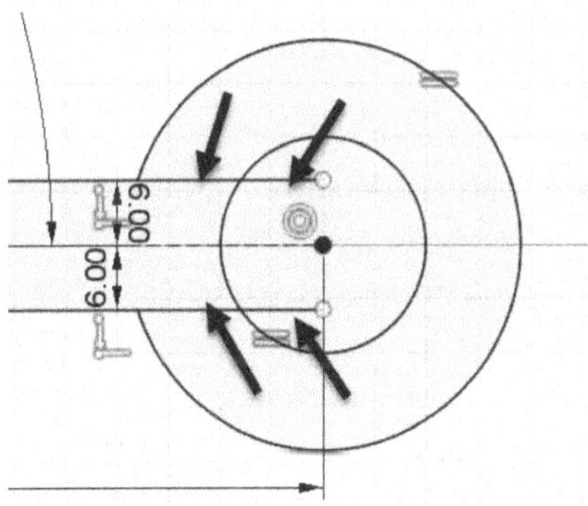

49. Click the **Equal** icon on the **Constraints** panel.
50. Select the two small arcs to make them equal, as shown.
51. Select the large arc and anyone of the small arc to make them equal.

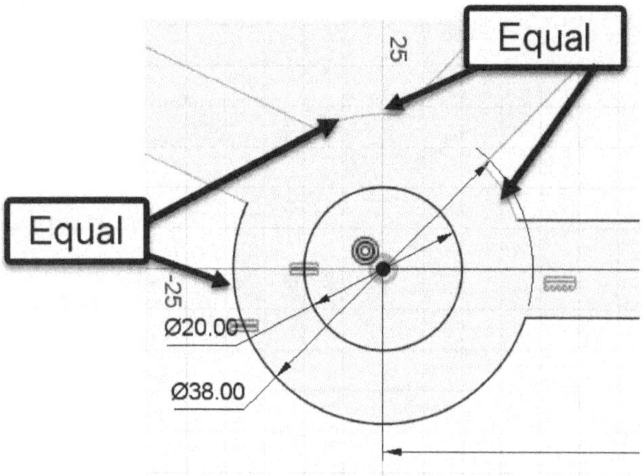

52. Add the radial dimension to the arc, as shown.

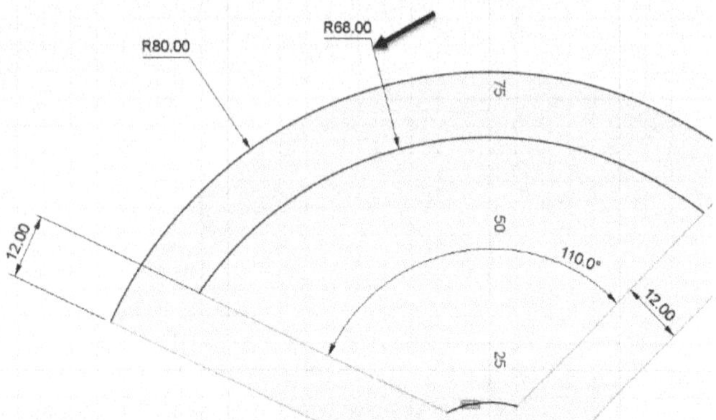

53. On the **Sketch** toolbar, click **Create > Line** (or press L) to activate the **Line** tool.
54. On the **Sketch Palette** dialog box, click the **Construction** icon next to **Linetype**, or press X on your keyboard.
55. Select the lower endpoint of the outer inclined line and the centerpoint of the circle.
56. Select the center point of the circle and the lower endpoint of the right inclined line, as shown.

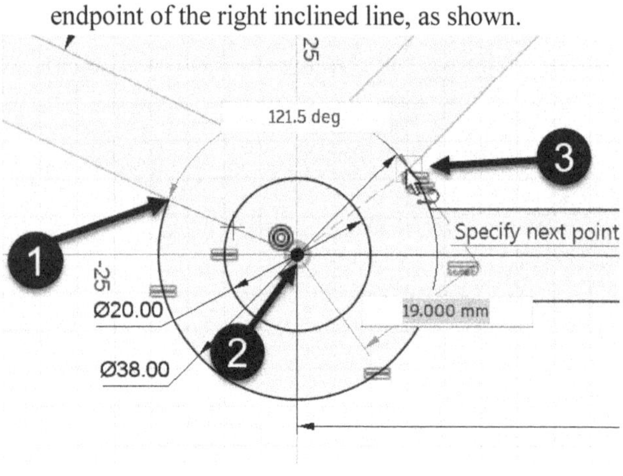

57. Go to the **Sketch** toolbar and click **Collinear** in the **Constraints** panel.
58. Select the left inclined line and the left construction line to make them collinear.
59. Select the right inclined line and the right construction line to make them collinear.

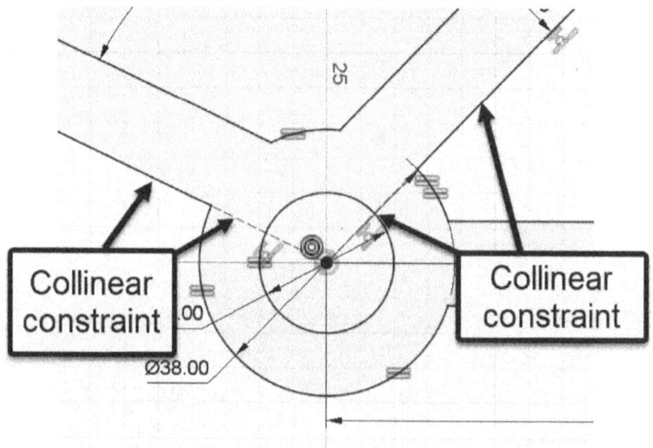

60. On the **Sketch** toolbar, click **Modify > Fillet**. This tool rounds off sharp corners.
61. Click on the first corner point of your sketch.

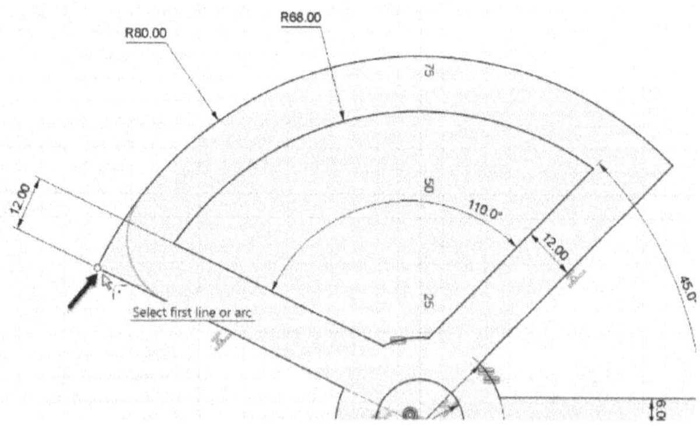

62. A small dialog box will appear on screen. Type 5 into the input box to set the fillet radius to 5mm.

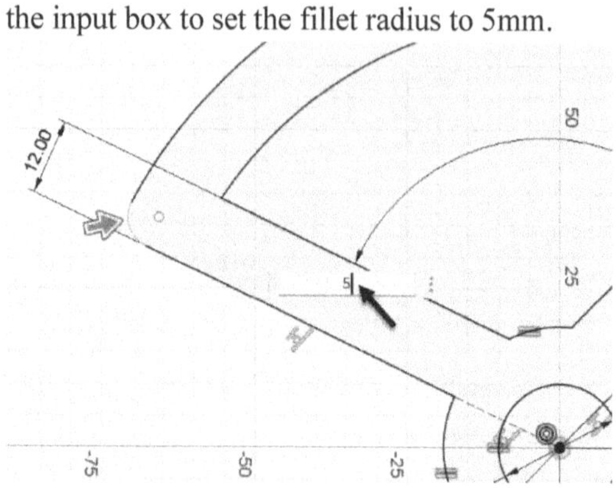

63. Activate the **Fillet** tool and select the corners of the sketch, as shown.
64. Type **5** in the **Radius** box and press ENTER.

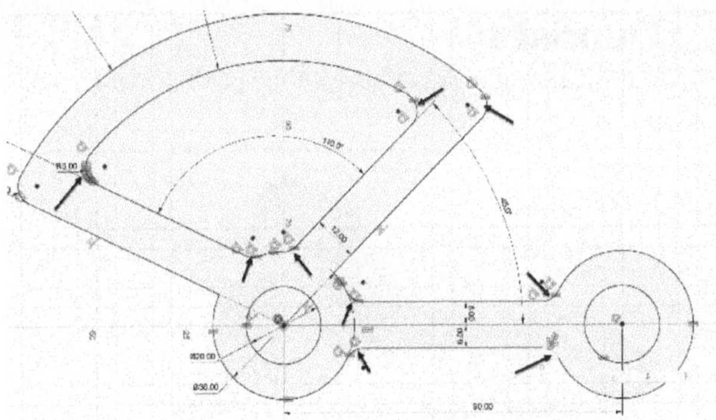

65. Activate the **Fillet** tool and select the entities forming corners, as shown.
66. Type 5 in the Radius box and press ENTER.

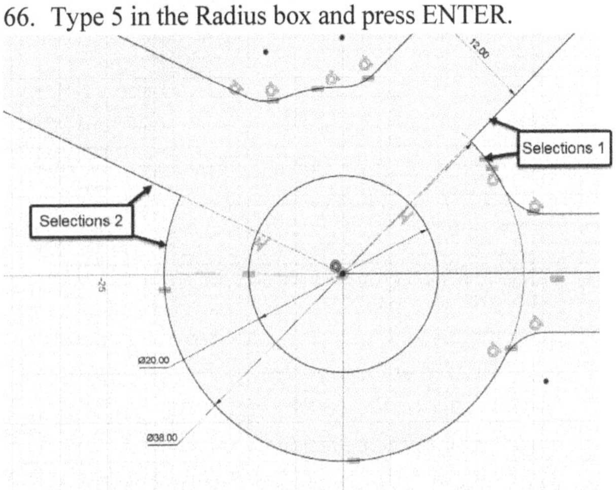

67. Click **Finish Sketch**.
68. Click **Save** on the **Application bar**.
69. On the **Save** window, type-in **C2_tutorial2** in the **Name** box.
70. Click **Save** to save the file.
71. Click the **Close** icon on the **File** tab.

3D Part Modeling

With your fully constrained 2D sketches complete, you are ready to transition from drawing flat profiles to generating physical 3D mass. In Fusion 360, this process is known as Part Modeling.

In this chapter, you will use the Solid tab to execute a series of practical exercises. You will build nine distinct mechanical parts, ranging from a basic hex bit to a complex structural hinge bracket. Through these tutorials, you will learn how to sequence modeling commands to build geometry efficiently.

You will focus on applying two main categories of tools:

Feature Creation Tools

You will use tools like Extrude, Revolve, and Sweep to push or pull your 2D sketches into 3D space. You will learn how to create symmetrical objects like a chess pawn using Revolve, and how to drive a profile along a curved path to create an exhaust manifold using Sweep.

Feature Modification Tools

Once you have a base 3D body, you will use modification tools to refine it without needing new sketches. You will apply Fillets to round off sharp edges, Chamfers to create angled corners on your hex bit, and the Shell command to hollow out a solid block into a thin-walled tray. Finally, you will apply the Thread tool to cut realistic, standardized screw threads into the barrel of your final hinge bracket.

The Parametric Timeline

As you model these parts, Fusion 360 will record every Extrude, Fillet, and Cut at the bottom of your screen in the Timeline. This history is the core of parametric modeling. If you realize your exhaust pipe needs a thicker diameter, you do not have to delete the model and start over. You simply double-click the original sketch in the Timeline, change the dimension, and watch the entire 3D model update automatically.

You must focus on the order of your operations. Learning which feature to apply first is just as critical as knowing how to use the tool itself. Let's begin by opening a new file and extruding our first shape.

Tutorial 1

In this tutorial, you will create the part shown in figure below.

1. On the Toolbar, click the **Solid** tab, then click **Create Sketch**.
2. In the graphics window, select the XZ Plane.
3. Go to the **Sketch** toolbar, click **Create > Slot**, and select **Center to Center Slot**.
4. Click exactly on the sketch origin to set the first center point of the slot.
5. Move your mouse diagonally down and to the right, then click to place the second center point. This defines the length and angle of the slot.
6. Move your mouse slightly outward from that line to define the slot's total width, and click once more to finish the shape.

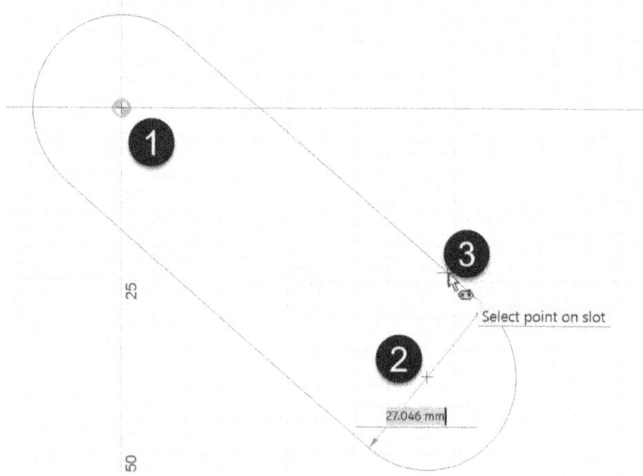

7. On the **Sketch** toolbar at the top of your screen, click the **Create** drop-down menu, hover over Arc, and choose **Center Point Arc**.
8. Click directly on the center origin point of your

sketch (the circle where the green and red lines meet) to lock the center of your arc to the middle of your workspace.

9. Move your mouse straight down from the origin. You will see a dashed blue line confirming you are perfectly vertical. Click once to set the starting point and the radius (size) of your arc.

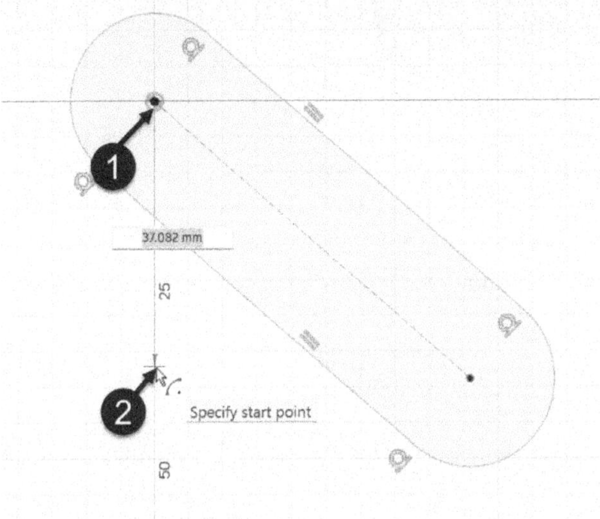

10. Move the pointer in the anti-clockwise, and then click on the slot to define the end point of the arc, as shown.

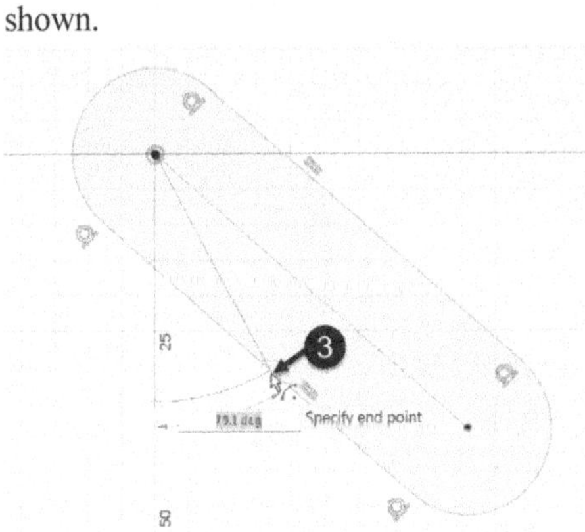

11. On the **Sketch** toolbar, click **Create > Line**, or press the **L** key on your keyboard.
12. Click exactly on the start point of the arc you drew earlier. This ensures the new line connects directly to the arc.
13. Move your mouse straight up. Look for a vertical constraint symbol (it looks like a straight line next to your cursor) to appear, which tells you the line is perfectly straight. Click again to finish drawing the line.

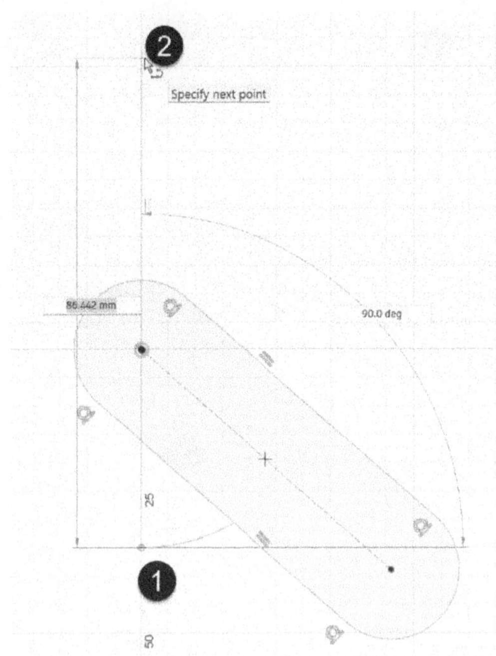

14. On the **Sketch** toolbar at the top of your screen, click the **Create** drop-down menu, hover over **Arc**, and choose **3-Point Arc**.

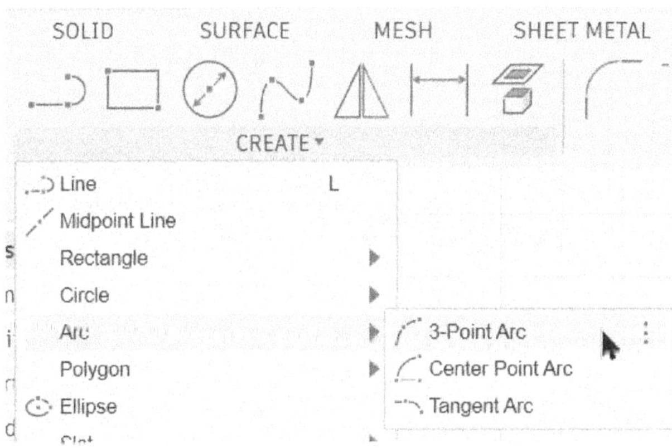

15. Click the top endpoint of the vertical line to place the first point of the arc.
16. Click on the edge of the slot you created earlier to place the second point of the arc. This defines how wide the arc will be.
17. Finally, move your mouse pointer to the left to give the arc its curve (the radius). When the shape looks right, click once more to lock the arc in place.

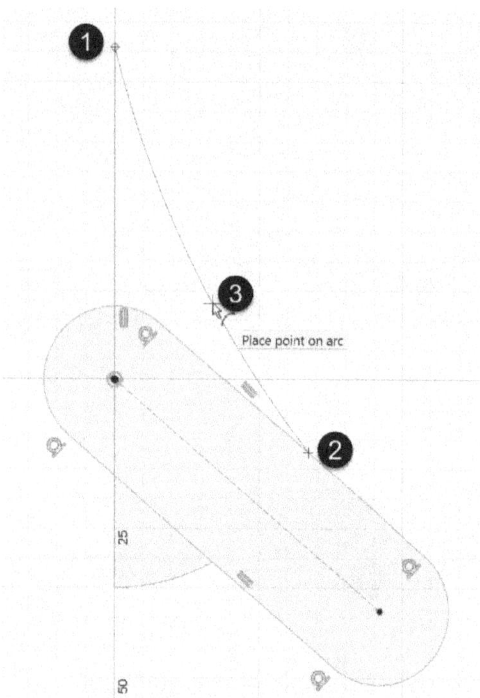

18. On the **Sketch** toolbar, click **Modify > Trim**, or press **T** on your keyboard.
19. Click on the entities to trim, as shown.

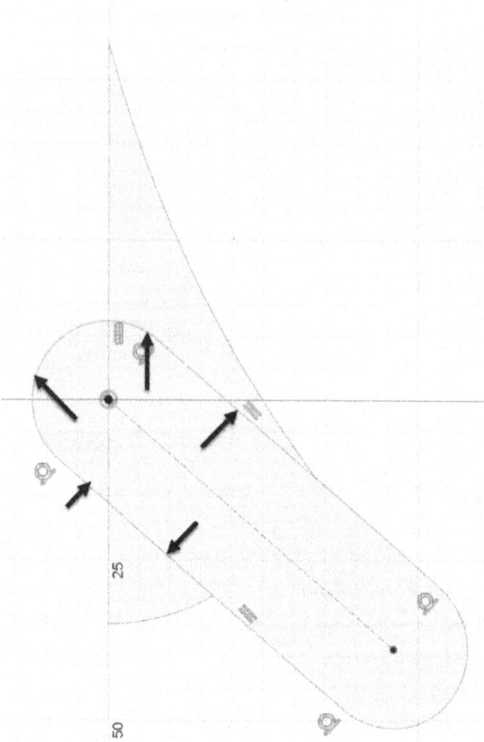

20. On the **Sketch** toolbar, click **Modify > Fillet**.
21. Select the corner point between the arc and the slot, as shown.

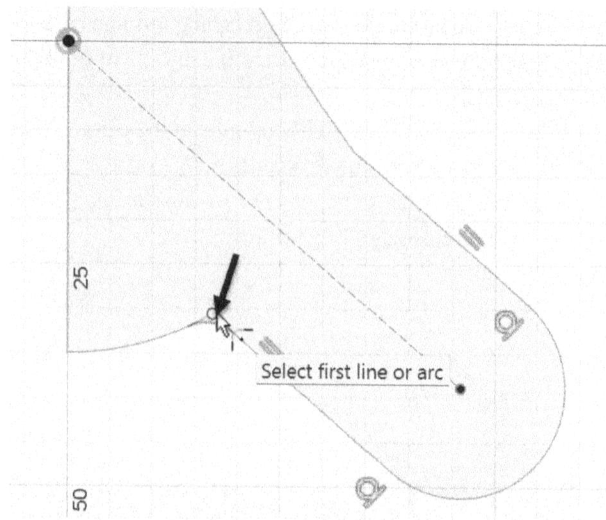

22. Type **40** in the **Radius** box and press ENTER.

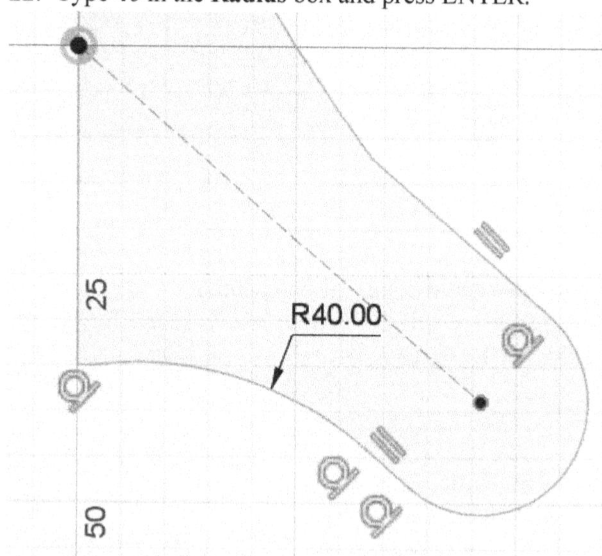

23. Click the **Tangent** icon on the **Constraints** panel of the **Sketch** tab.
24. Select the arc and the line, as shown.

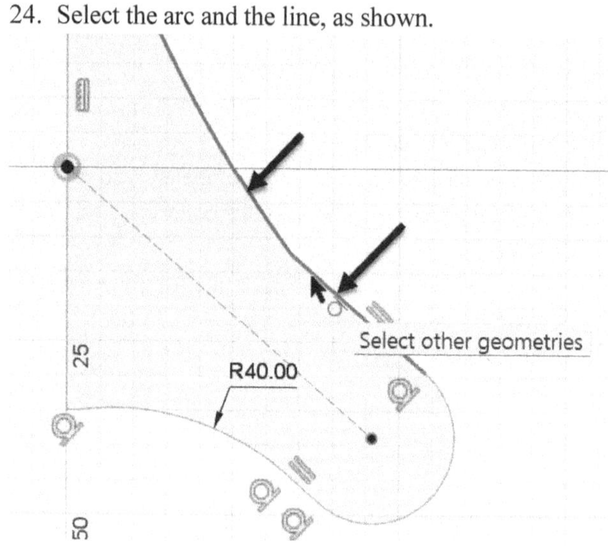

25. On the Sketch Palette, click **Options > Linetype > Construction** 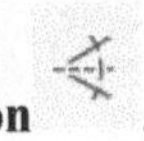 .
26. On the **Sketch** toolbar, click **Create > Line.**
27. Select the origin point of the sketch, move the pointer horizontally toward right, and click. Press Esc.

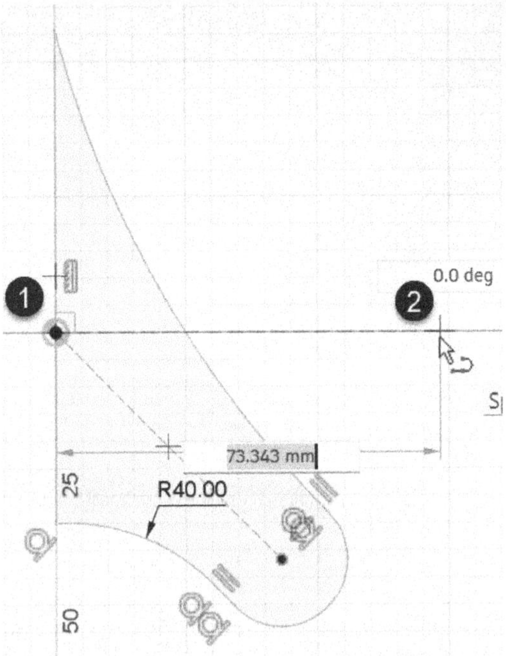

28. Add dimensions to the entities, as shown.

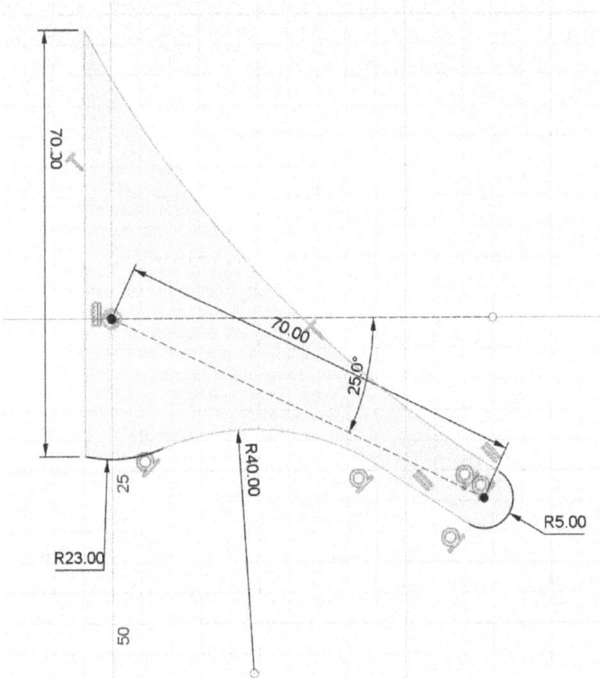

29. Select the endpoint of the line and drag toward left, as shown. The length of the line is changed.

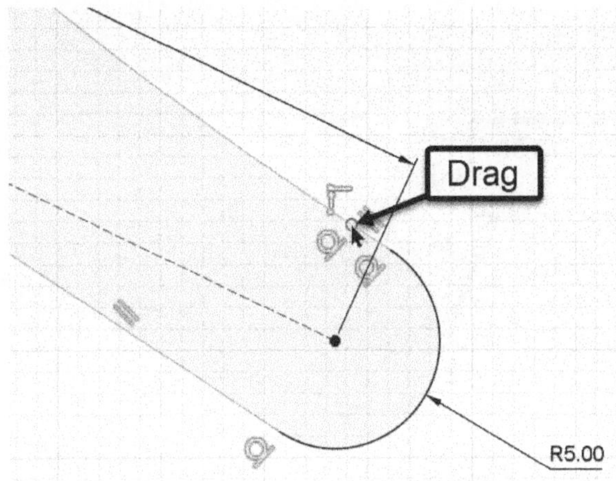

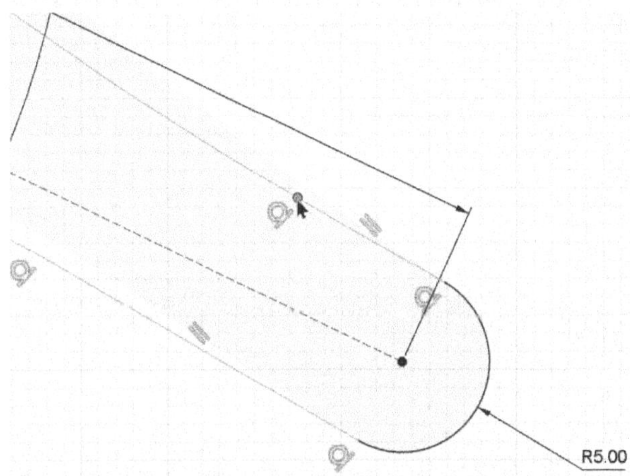

30. Click the **Parallel** icon in the **Constraints** panel of the **Sketch** tab.
31. Select the line and the centerline, as shown.

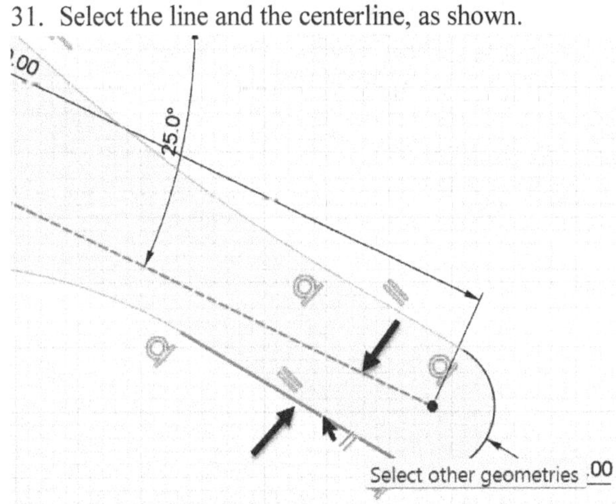

32. On the **Sketch** contextual tab of the Toolbar, click **Constraints > Coincident** 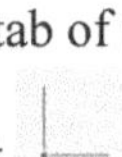 . Next, select the origin point and the vertical line.

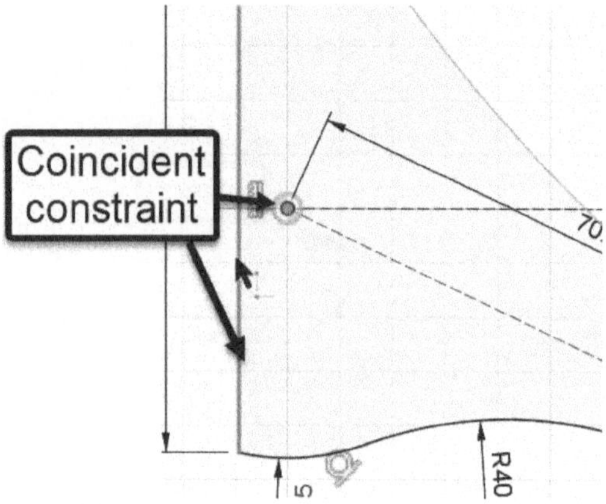

33. Add remaining dimensions, as shown.

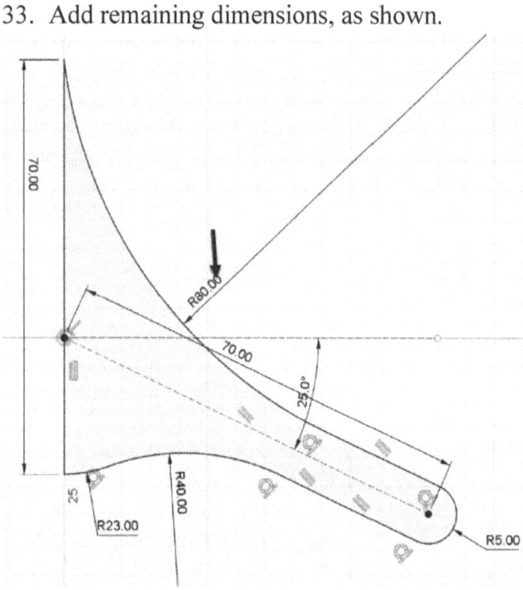

34. Click **Finish Sketch.**
35. On the **Solid** tab of the toolbar, click **Extrude**, or simply press **E** on your keyboard.
36. Click inside the sketch profile so it highlights in blue.
37. In the **Extrude** dialog box that appears on the right, look for the **Distance** box. Type **15** and press Enter to pull your flat sketch into a **15** mm thick 3D solid object.

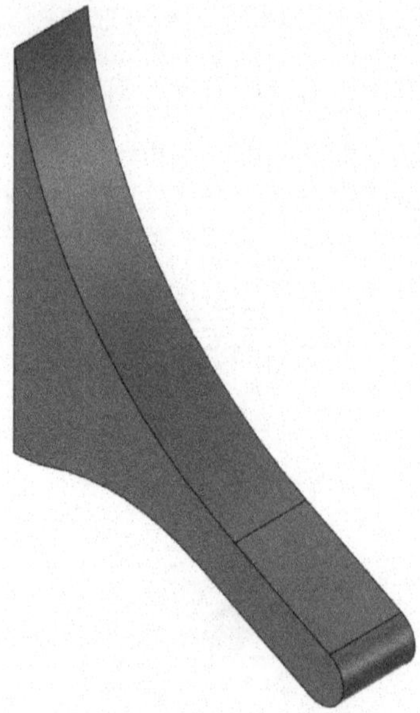

38. On the **Solid** tab of the toolbar, click the **Create** drop-down menu and select **Mirror** .
39. In the **Mirror** dialog box, make sure the **Object Type** is set to **Bodies.**
40. Click on the 3D solid body in the canvas so it highlights in blue.
41. Next, click the **Select** button next to **Mirror Plane** in the dialog box.
42. To choose your mirror plane, you can e`ither click the flat left face of the object itself, or expand the Origin folder in the browser on the left and select the YZ plane.

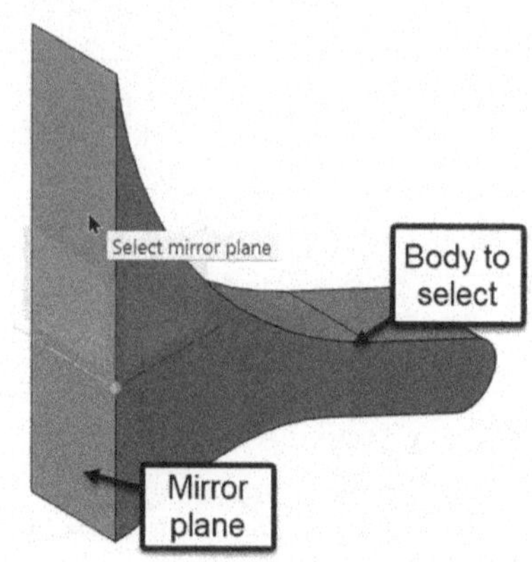

43. Ensure the **Operation** is set to **Join**, then click **OK** to merge the original body with its mirrored copy into one solid piece.

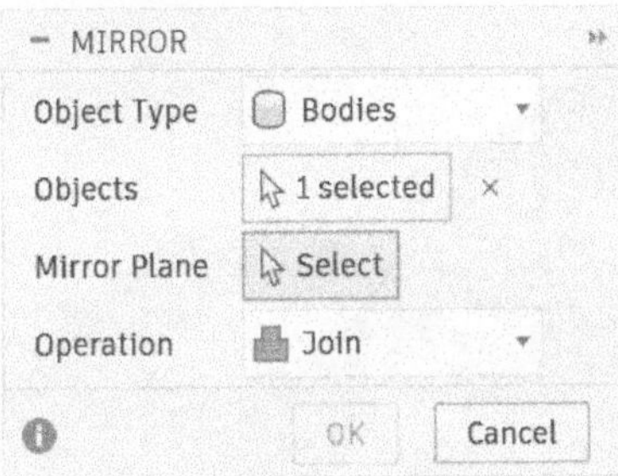

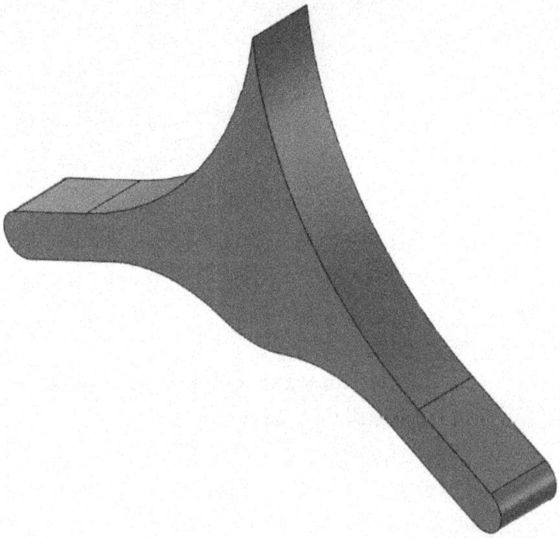

44. On the Toolbar, click the **Solid** tab > **Modify** panel > **Fillet**.
45. Select the top edge of the solid model, as shown.

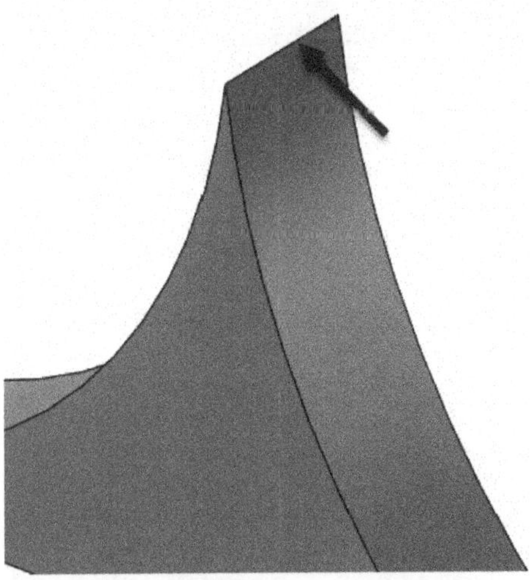

46. On the **Fillet** dialog, select **Type > Constant Radius**.
47. Type 4 in the **Radius** box.

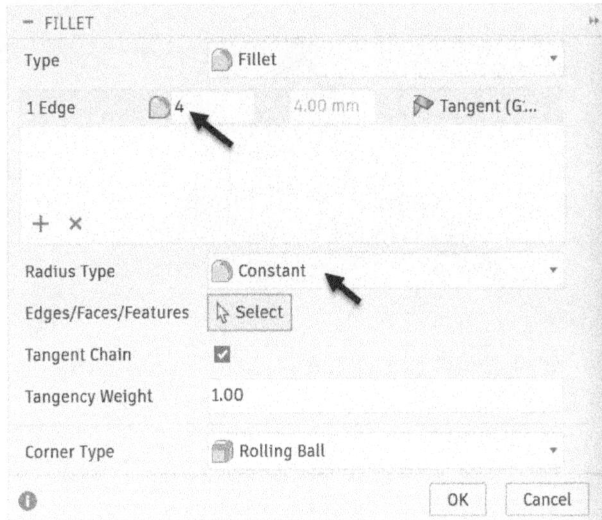

48. Click **OK** to add the fillet.

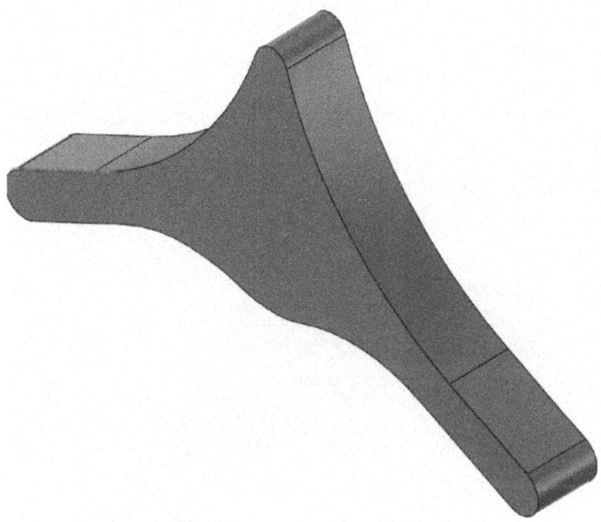

49. On the Solid tab of the toolbar, click **Create > Create Sketch**.
50. Click directly on the front flat face of your 3D model. The screen will shift so you are looking straight at that face.
51. On the **Sketch** toolbar, click the **Create** drop-down menu and select **Center Diameter Circle**, or press C on your keyboard.
52. Click exactly on the sketch origin point to set the center of the circle.
53. Move your mouse pointer away from the origin to expand the circle, then click once to set its rough size.
54. Press D on your keyboard to activate the **Sketch Dimension** tool. Click on the circle, place the dimension, type in 23, and press Enter.

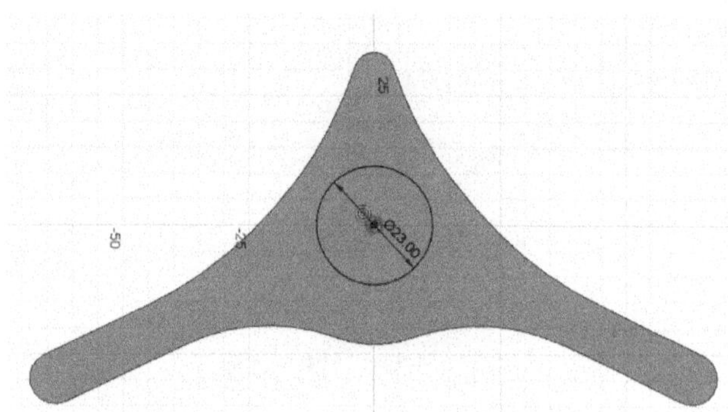

55. Click **Finish Sketch** (the green checkmark on the right side of the toolbar) to leave the sketch environment.
56. Press **E** on your keyboard to activate the **Extrude** tool. Click inside the circle you just drew.
57. In the **Extrude** dialog box, look for the **Operation** setting and change it to **Cut**.
58. Select **Extent Type > All**.
59. Click the **Flip** icon if the arrow on the extrude preview is pointing away from the geometry.
60. Click **OK**.

Tutorial 2

In this tutorial, you will create the part shown in figure below.

Starting a Part Design

1. Launch **Autodesk Fusion 360** from the desktop shortcut or from the Start menu. Wait for the workspace to load.
2. On the **What do you want to design?** dialog, select the **Part Design** tile on the left side.
3. On the right side of the dialog box, under **Unit System**, verify or **select millimeter (mm), gram (g)** from the drop-down menu.
4. Click **Create New** at the bottom right corner of the dialog box to open a new design file.

Creating the Sketch

1. On the toolbar, click **Solid > Create > Create Sketch**, then select the XY plane to start the sketch.

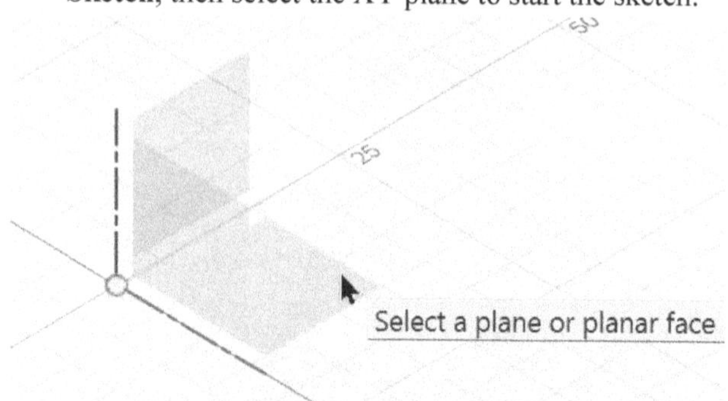

2. Press **C** to activate the **Center Diameter Circle** tool. Click exactly on the sketch origin point to set the center, drag outward, and click to draw the first inner circle.
3. With the circle tool still active, click the origin point again, drag further outward, and click to draw the larger outer circle.

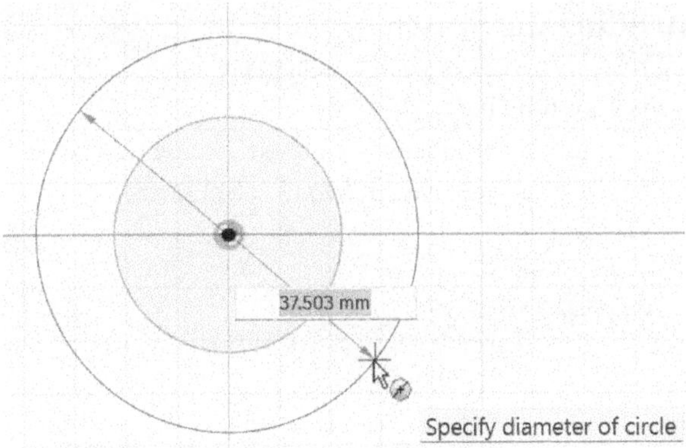

4. Move your cursor to the right, along the horizontal axis. Click to place the center of a new, smaller circle. Drag outward and click to draw it.
5. Click that same center point again, drag outward, and click to draw the outer circle for the right side.

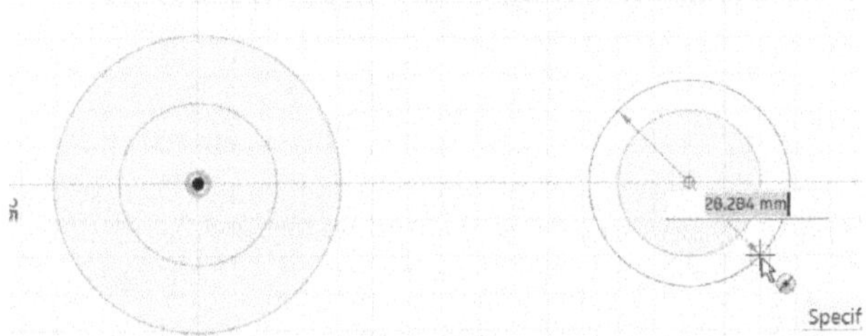

6. Press **L** to activate the **Line** tool.
7. Draw a line connecting the top of the large left circle to the top of the small right circle.

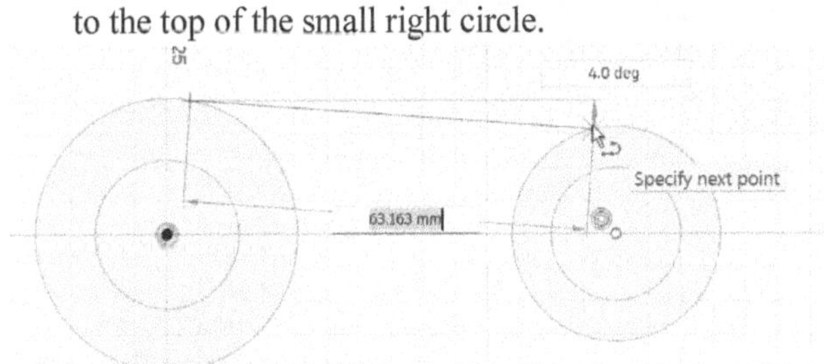

8. Draw another line connecting the bottom of the large left circle to the bottom of the small right circle.

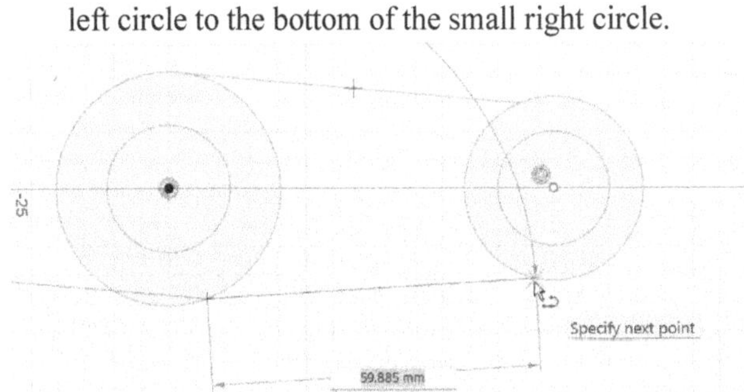

9. On the **Sketch** toolbar, click the **Tangent**  icon on the **Constraints** panel. Click the top line, then click the large left circle. Repeat this process to make both the top and bottom lines tangent to the outer circles on both the left and right sides.

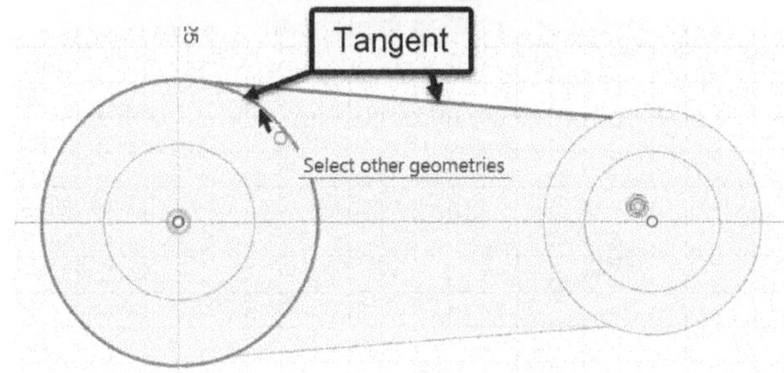

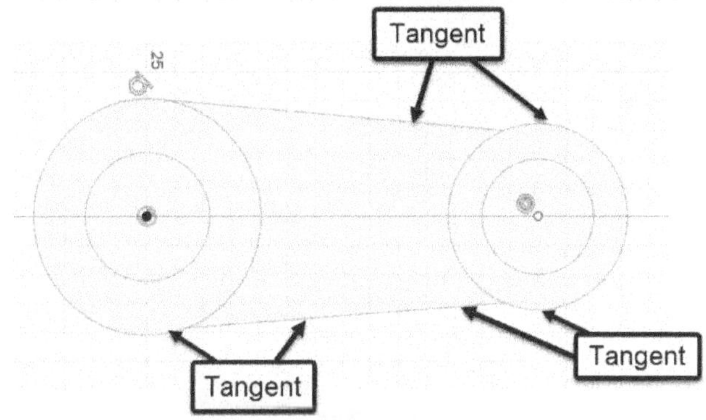

10. Press **T** to activate the **Trim** tool. Click the inner halves of the two outer circles to remove them, leaving only the rounded outer profile.

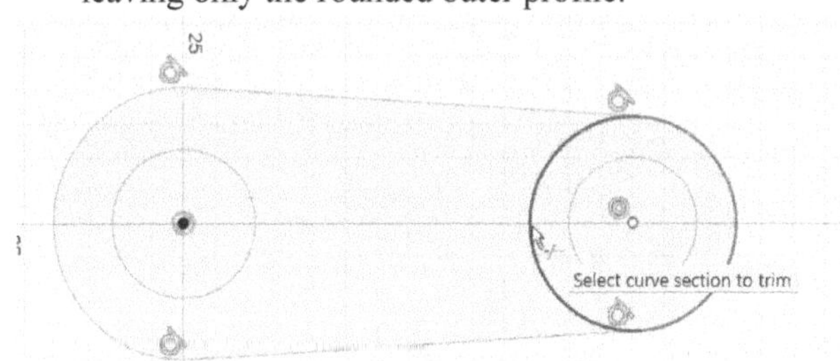

11. Press **D** to activate the **Sketch Dimension** tool.
12. Click the center point of the left circle, then the center point of the right circle. Drag downward, click, type **120**, and press **Enter**.

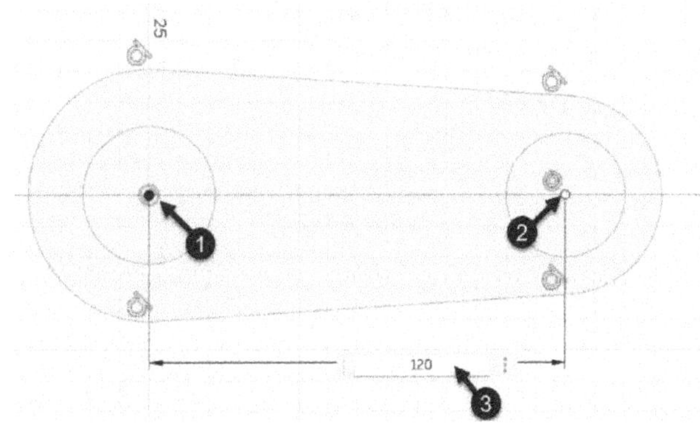

13. Click the outer arc on the left. Drag outward, click, type **25** (for the radius), and press **Enter**.
14. Click the inner circle on the left. Next, select the outer circle of the left. Drag the cursor, click, type **8.00** for the offset dimension, and press **Enter**.

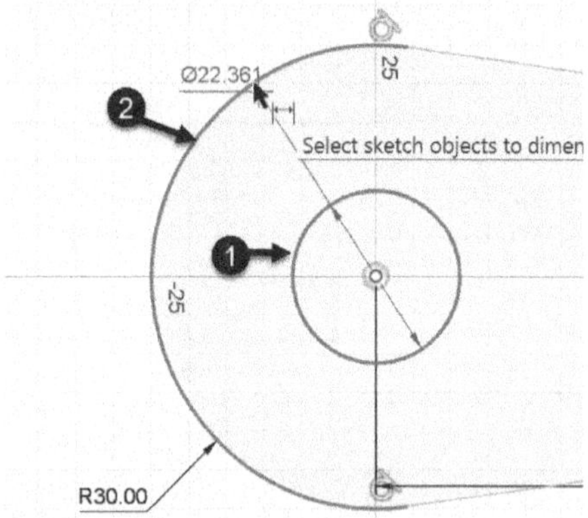

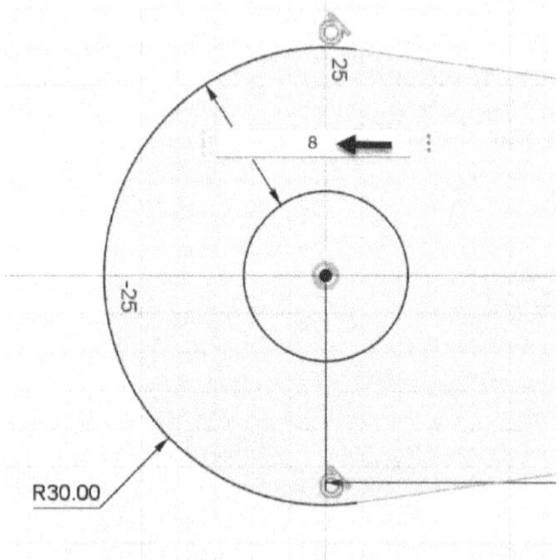

15. Click the inner circle on the right. Drag outward, click, type **15** (for the diameter), and press **Enter**.
16. Finally, click the outer arc on the right. Drag outward, click, type **15.00** (for the radius), and press **Enter**.
17. Click the **Horizontal/Vertical** icon on the **Constraints** panel, and then select the two centerpoints.

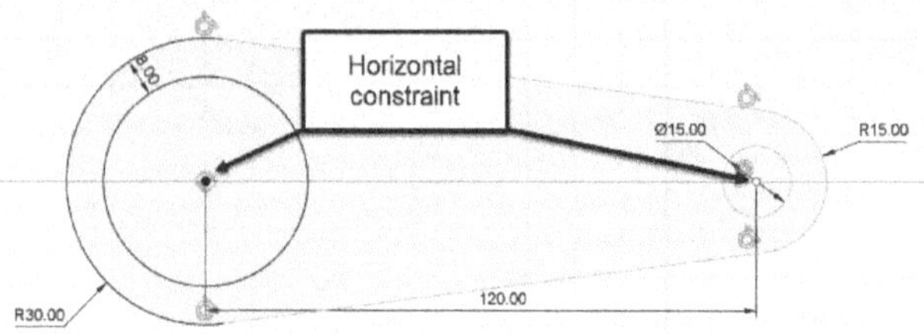

18. Click **Finish Sketch** on the **Sketch Palette**.

Extruding the Sketch

1. Press **E** on your keyboard to activate the **Extrude** tool.
2. Click inside the main body of your sketch (the large area between the two circles) to select it for extrusion.

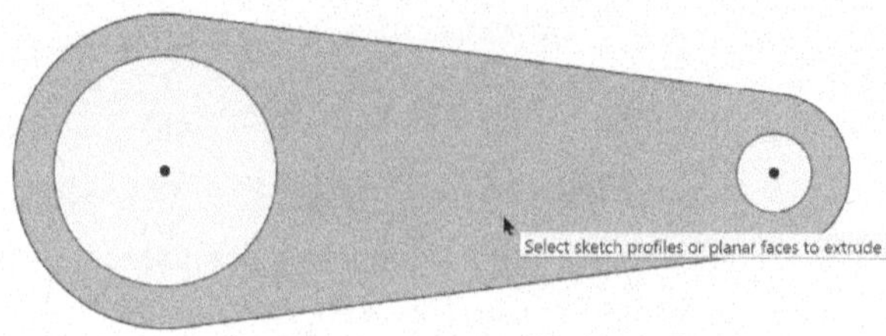

3. Look at the **Extrude** dialog box on the right side of the screen. Under the **Direction** setting, click the drop-down menu and change it to **Symmetric**. This setting ensures the 3D material grows evenly in both directions away from your sketch plane.
4. Right below that, look for the **Measurement** option. Select **Whole Length** (the icon showing the dimension arrow spanning the entire width).
5. In the **Distance** box, type **60** and press **Enter** to create a solid part that is 60 mm thick overall.

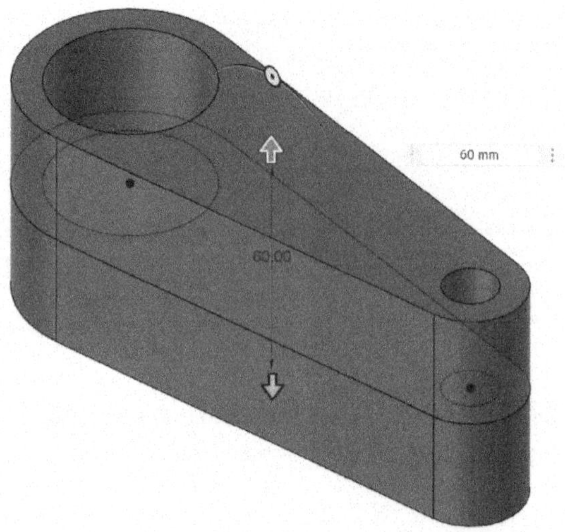

Applying a Shell Feature

Once the base extrusion is complete, the next step is to hollow out the solid body to reduce weight and material usage, while maintaining structural integrity. In Fusion 360, this is accomplished using the **Shell** tool.

1. On the **Solid** tab of the toolbar, locate the **Modify** panel and click **Shell**.

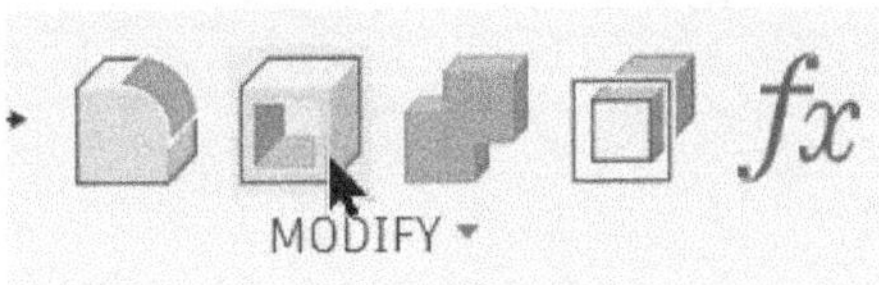

The **Shell** command requires you to select the faces you wish to remove from the solid body.

2. Click the large, top flat side face of the main connecting arm facing you. It will highlight in blue to confirm it is selected.

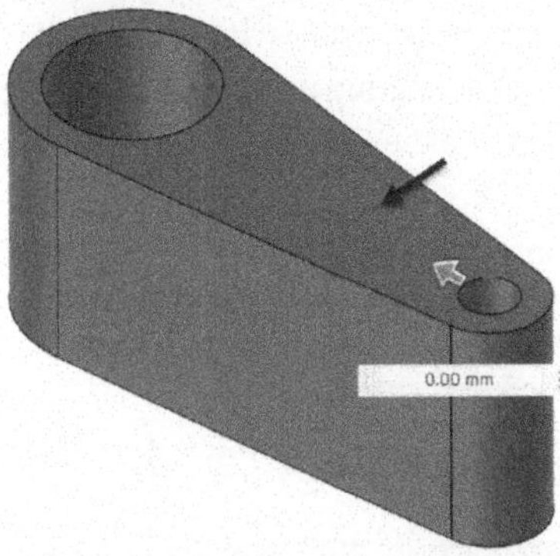

3. To select the opposite side, you must rotate the model. Move your cursor to the ViewCube located in the upper right corner of the graphics window.
4. Click bottom corner of the ViewCube; bottom side of the model is visible.

5. Select the bottom flat face of the model.

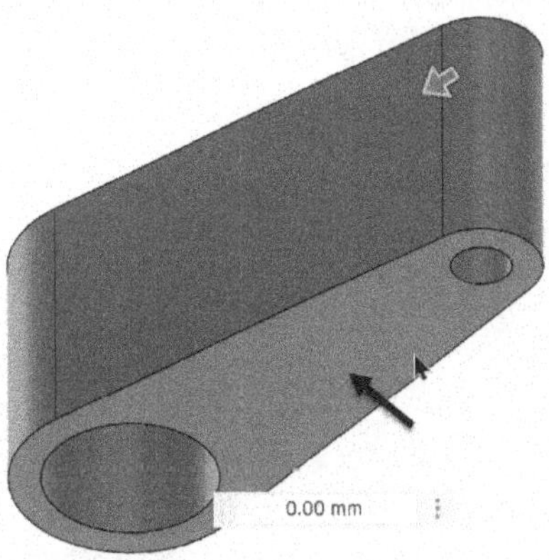

6. In the **Shell** dialog box, locate the **Inside Thickness** input field.
7. Enter a value of **8**. This defines the constant wall thickness that will remain around the inner perimeter of the hollowed section.

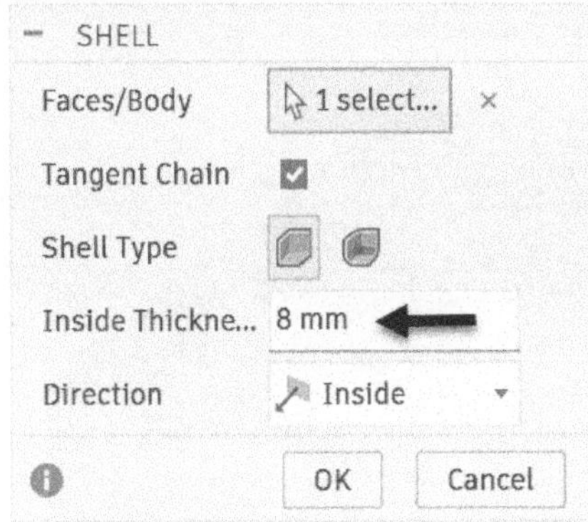

8. Click **OK** to apply the feature. The model is now a thin-walled shell.
9. Click the **Home** icon located next to the ViewCube.

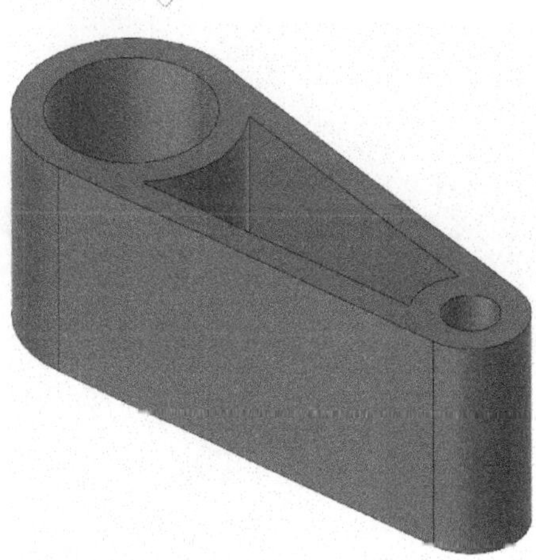

Applying Internal Fillets

After shelling the part, it is critical to round the internal sharp corners. Sharp internal corners create stress concentrations where the part is most likely to fracture under mechanical load. Adding fillets to these areas strengthens the overall structure.

1. On the **Solid** tab of the toolbar, locate the **Modify** panel and click **Fillet**, or press **F** on your keyboard.

2. In the graphics window, select the two internal vertical edges where the flat inside walls meet the circular walls of the large cylinder, as highlighted in the reference image.

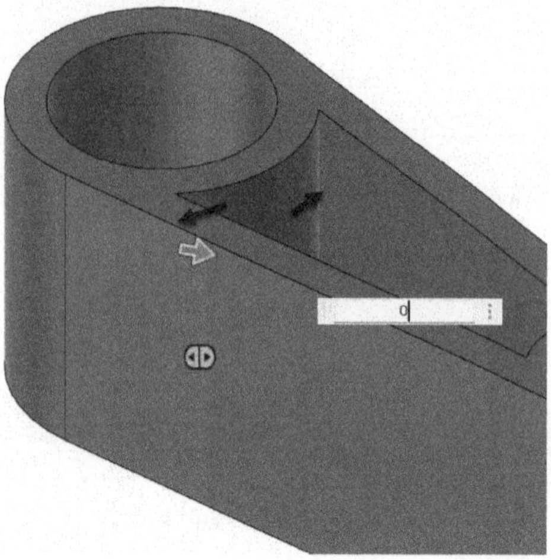

3. In the **Fillet** dialog box, locate the **Radius** input field.
4. Enter a value of **5.00 mm**.

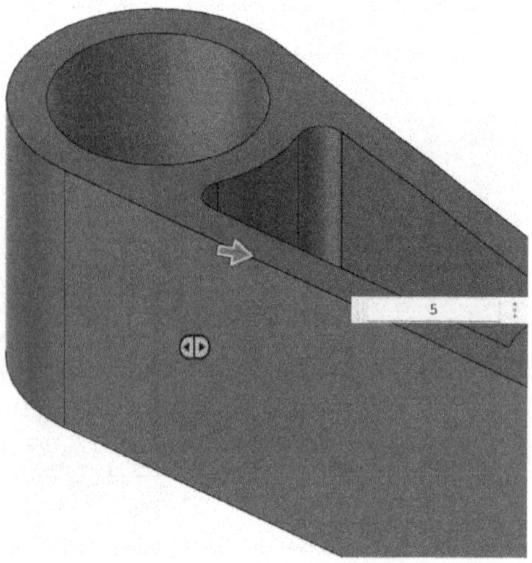

5. Click **OK** to apply the feature.
6. On the **Solid** tab of the toolbar, click **Fillet** in the **Modify** panel.
7. In the **Fillet** dialog box, click the **Type** drop-down menu and select **Full Round Fillet**. This alters the selection process, requiring you to define three distinct face groups rather than selecting specific edges.

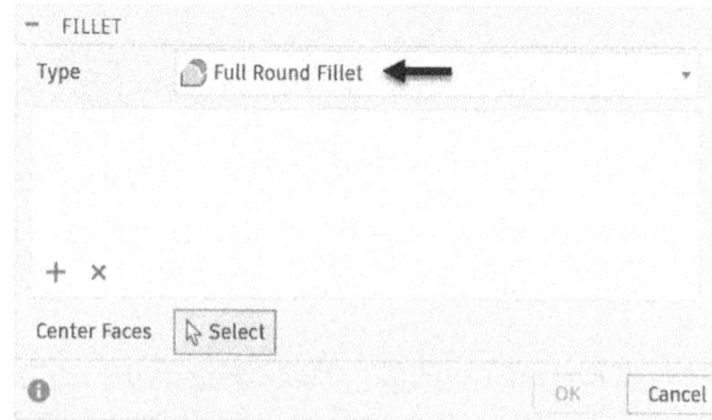

8. Locate the **Navigation bar** at the very bottom center of the Fusion 360 interface.
9. Click the **Orbit** tool icon, which looks like two circular arrows rotating around an axis. Alternatively, you can activate the **Orbit** tool at any time by pressing and holding the Shift key while simultaneously pressing and holding the **Middle Mouse Button** (the scroll wheel).

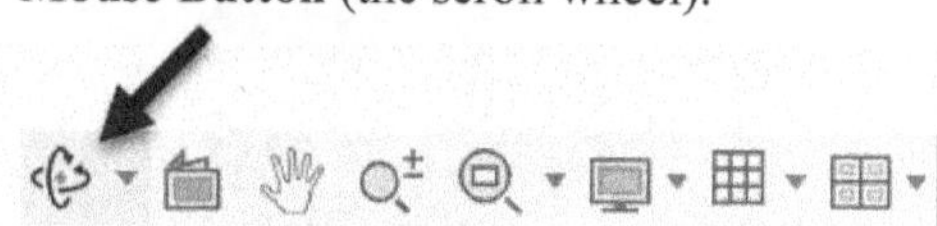

10. With the tool active, click and drag your cursor across the graphics window to freely rotate the model in 3D space until the model is oriented such that the three internal faces are displayed, as shown.

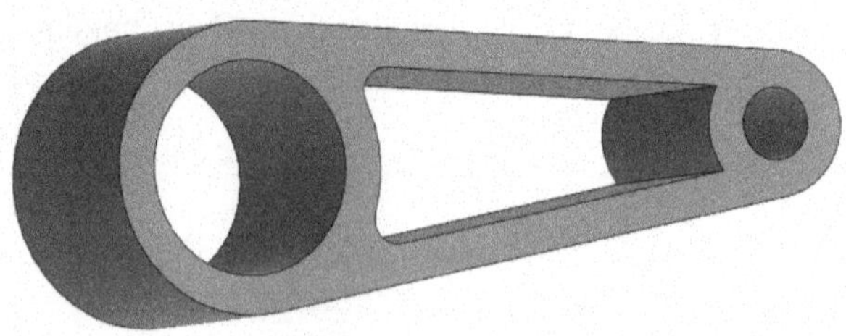

11. Right-click and select **OK**.
12. For the **Center Face** selection, click the inner vertical face connecting the upper and lower walls, near the smaller cylinder.

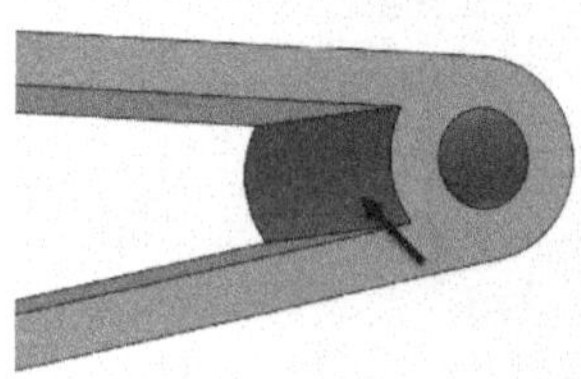

13. Fusion 360 will generate a perfectly tangent, semi-circular blend bridging the three selected faces. No radius value needs to be entered, as the software calculates it based on the distance between the side faces.

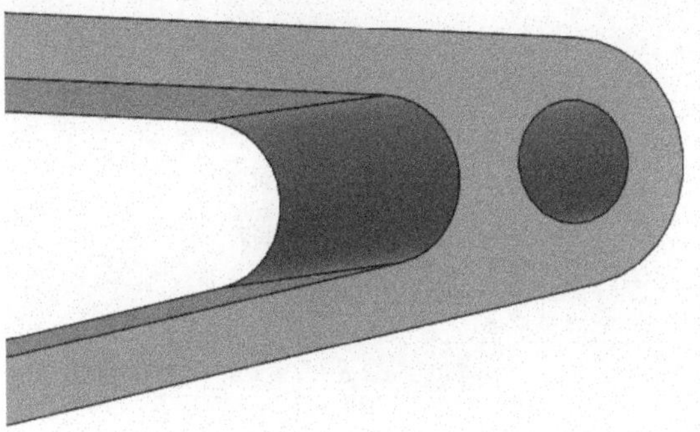

14. Click **OK** to execute the command

Creating the Slot

To create the angled slot feature, a new sketch must be created on the top face of the existing solid body.

1. On the **Solid** tab of the toolbar, click **Create > Create Sketch**.
2. Select the top, flat face of the main arm as the sketch plane.

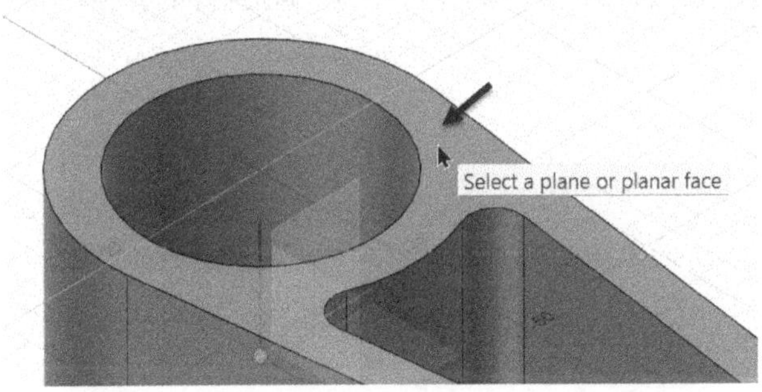

3. Press **L** to activate the **Line** tool. Press **X** to activate the construction mode.
4. Click at the bottom portion to define the start point of the line.
5. Select the sketch origin point to create the inclined line.

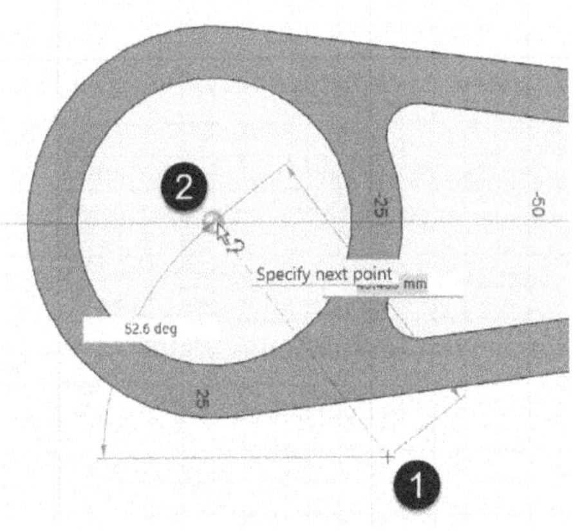

6. Draw a second line starting from the origin point, extending straight down vertically.

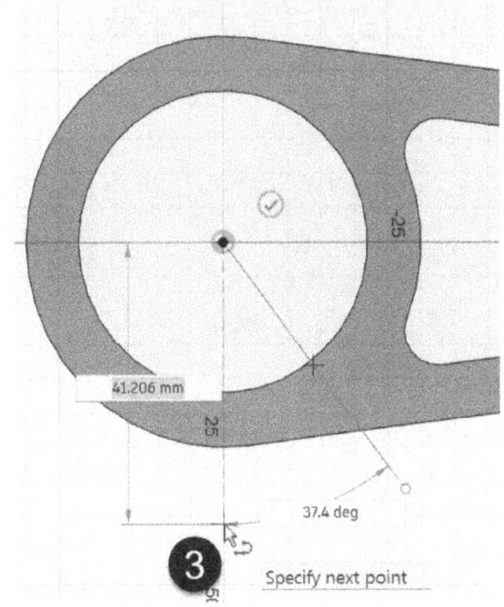

7. Press **X** to deactivate the construction mode.
8. On the **Sketch** toolbar, click the **Create** drop-down menu, hover over **Rectangle**, and select **3-Point Rectangle**.

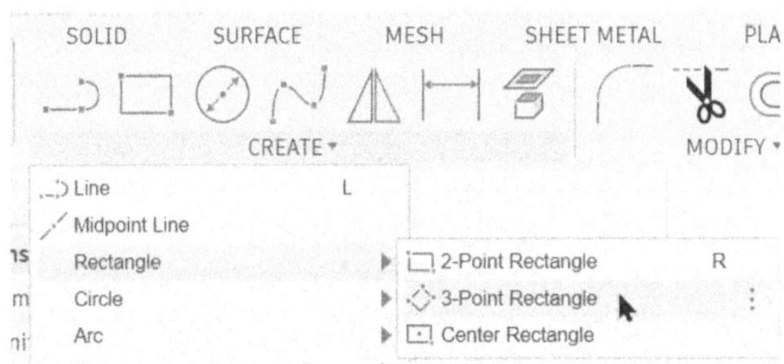

9. Click to place the first corner of the rectangle **(Point 1)**.
10. Move your cursor perpendicular to the angled line to define the width, and click to specify the second corner (**Point 2**).
11. Move your cursor further down along the same angled line and click to complete the rectangle **(Point 3).**

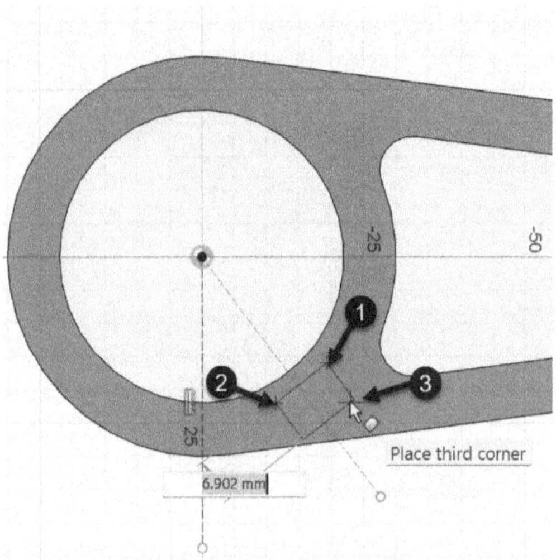

With the rough geometry in place, constraints and dimensions are applied to precisely locate and size the rectangle.

12. In the Constraints panel on the **Sketch** toolbar, click **Parallel**. Select the ledge of the rectangle, then select the angled construction line. This ensures the rectangle aligns with the construction line.

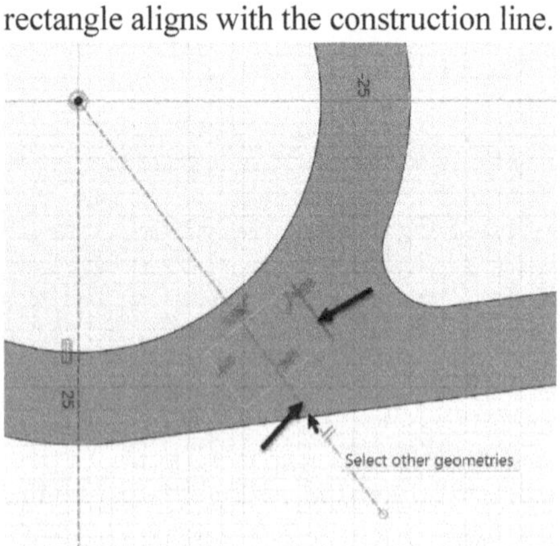

13. In the **Constraints** panel on the **Sketch** toolbar, click **Midpoint**.
14. Select the edge of the rectangle closest to the origin. Then, select the angled construction line. This snaps the center of the rectangle's width directly onto the line.

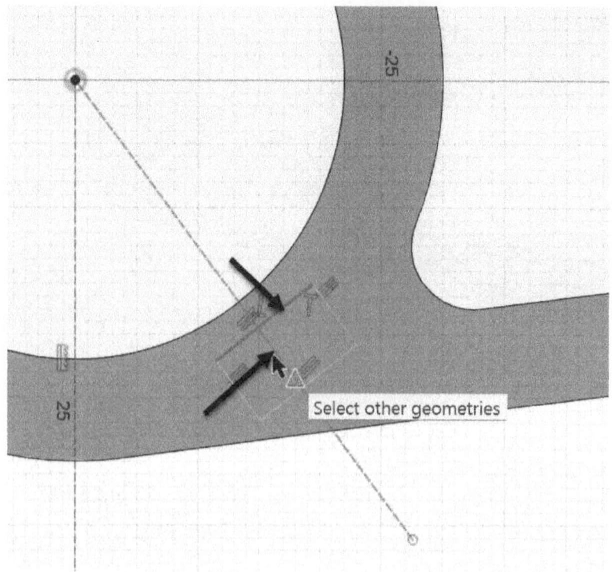

15. In the **Constraints** panel on the **Sketch** toolbar, click **Coincident** ∟.
16. Select the corner of the rectangle, as shown.

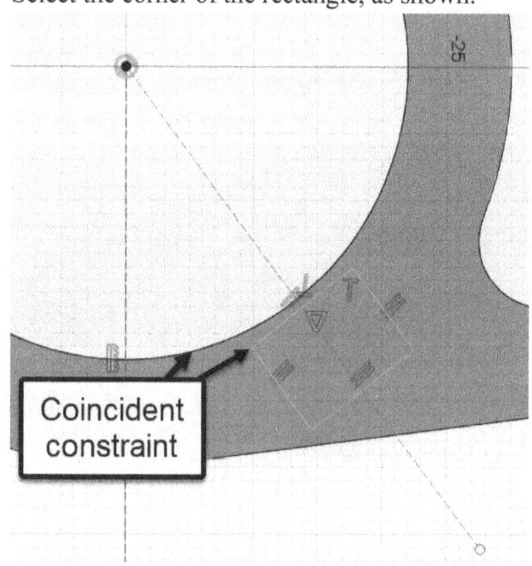

17. Press **D** to activate the **Sketch Dimension** tool.
18. Select the vertical construction line, then select the angled construction line. Place the angular dimension between them, enter **45**, and press **Enter** to set the 45-degree angle.
19. Select the two long parallel sides of the rectangle. Place the dimension, enter **4.00**, and press **Enter** to define the width.
20. Finally, select the two short parallel sides of the rectangle. Place the dimension, enter **10.00**, and press **Enter** to define the length.

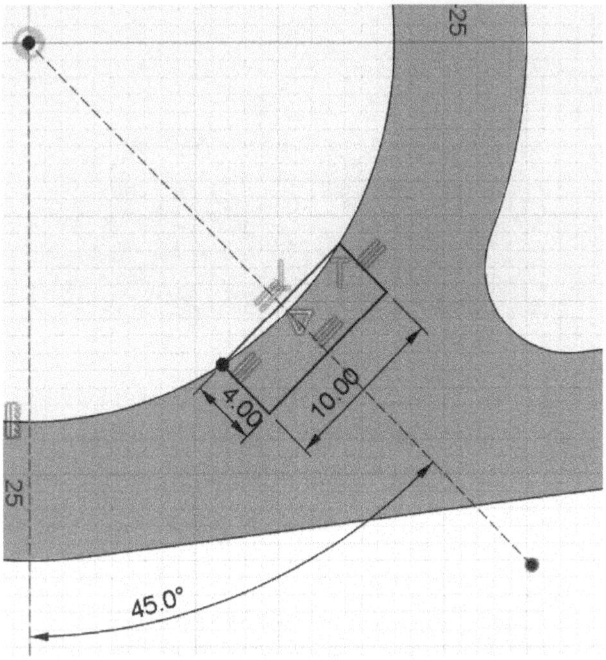

21. The sketch is now fully defined. Click **Finish Sketch** in the toolbar to proceed to the extrusion step.
22. Press **E** on your keyboard to activate the **Extrude** tool. Click in the internal area of the rectangular profile you just sketched. It should highlight to indicate it is the active contour for the operation.

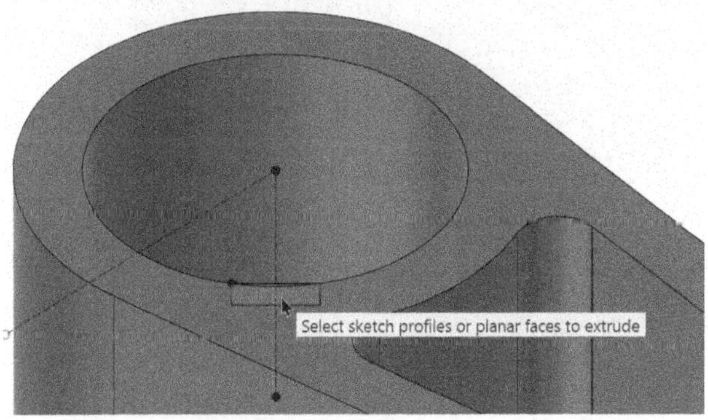

23. In the **Extrude** dialog box, look for the **Operation** setting and change it to **Cut**.
24. Select **Extent Type > All**.
25. Click the **Flip** icon if the arrow on the extrude preview is pointing away from the geometry.

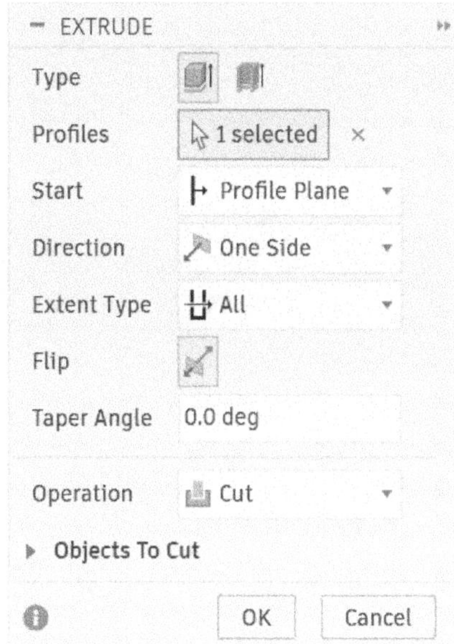

26. Click **OK**.

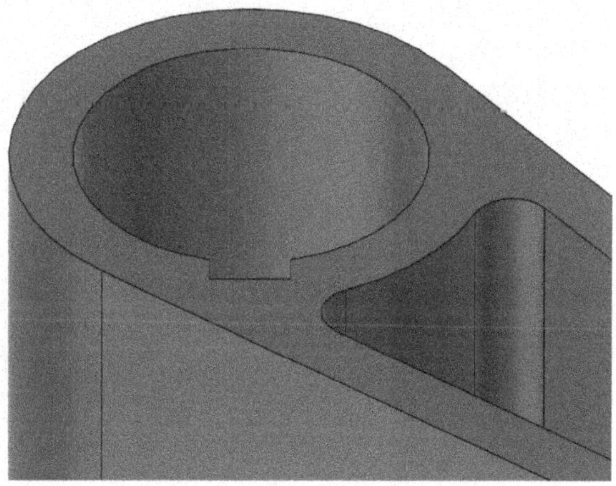

Creating the Split Channel intersection body

1. On the **Solid** tab of the toolbar, click **Create > Create Sketch**.
2. In the Browser, expand the **Origin** folder and select the XZ plane.

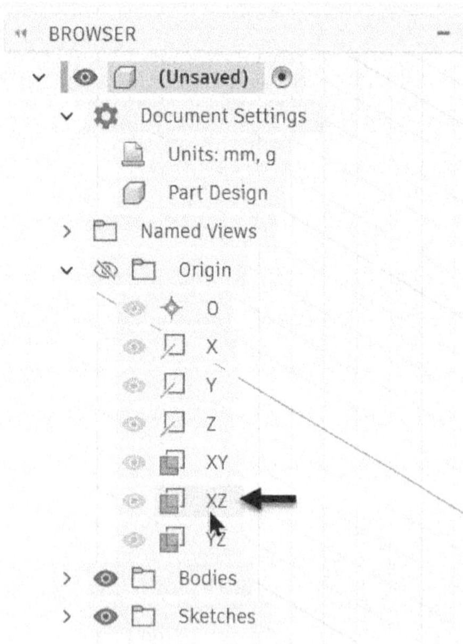

3. Press **L** to activate the **Line** tool.
4. Press **X** to activate the construction mode.
5. Draw a horizontal center line originating from the left edge and extending to the right.

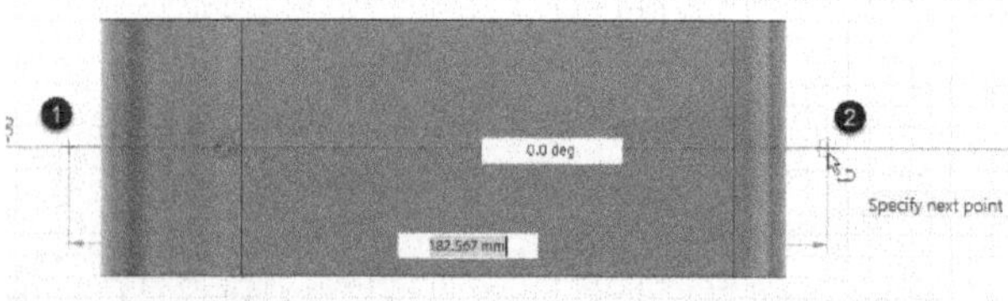

6. Press **X** to deactivate the construction mode.
7. Using the **Line** tool, sketch the upper half of the profile:
   - Draw a solid horizontal line starting from the left edge.

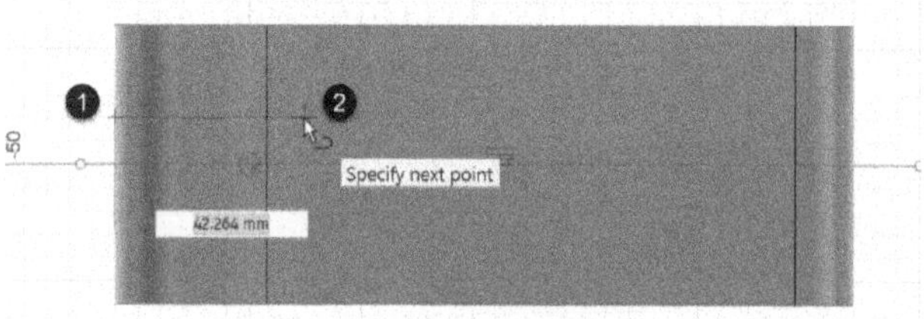

   - From the end of that line, draw an angled line pointing upward and to the right.

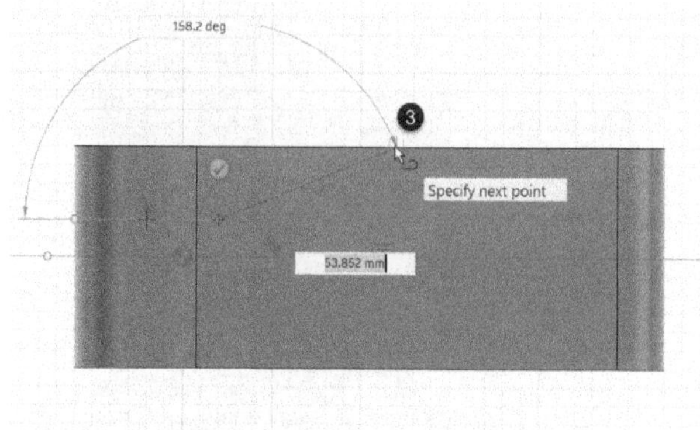

   - From the end of the angled line, draw another horizontal line to the right, stopping before the end of the part.

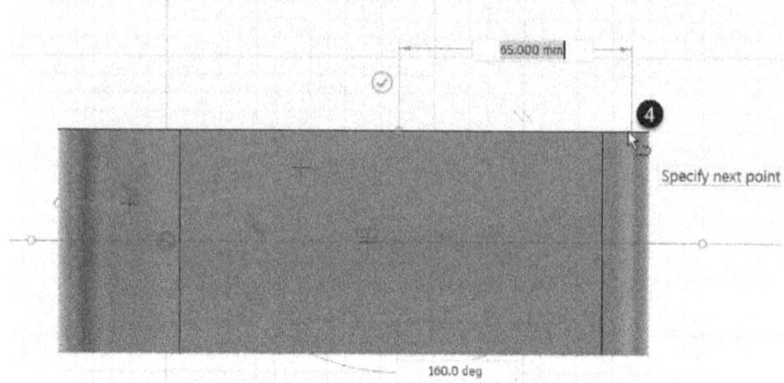

   - Draw a short vertical line downward.

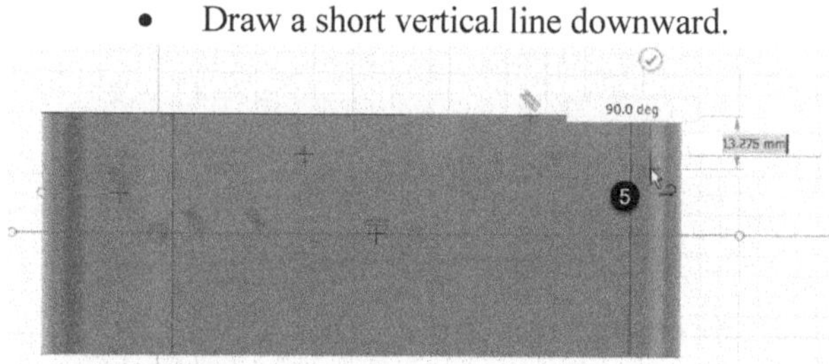

   - Draw a horizontal line back toward the left.

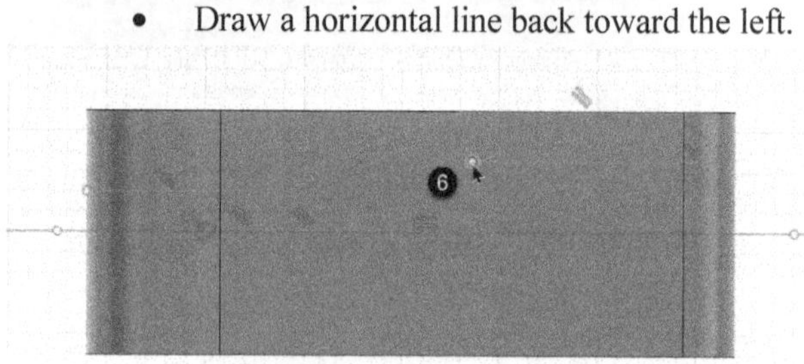

   - Draw an angled line downward and to the left, parallel to the first angled line.

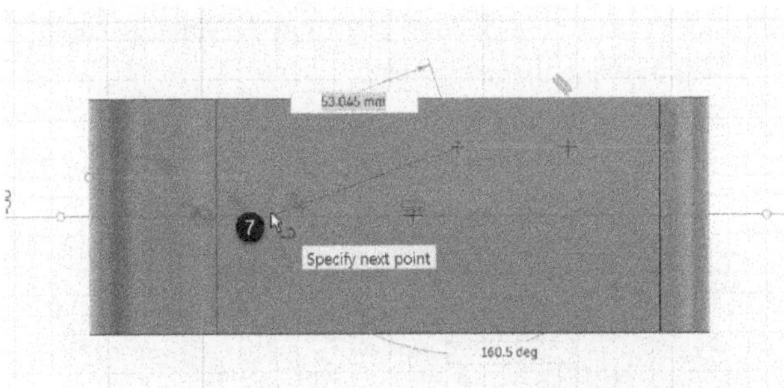

8. On the **Sketch** toolbar, click **Create > Mirror**. Select all the solid lines just drawn as the **Objects**. Select the dashed horizontal line as the **Mirror Line**.

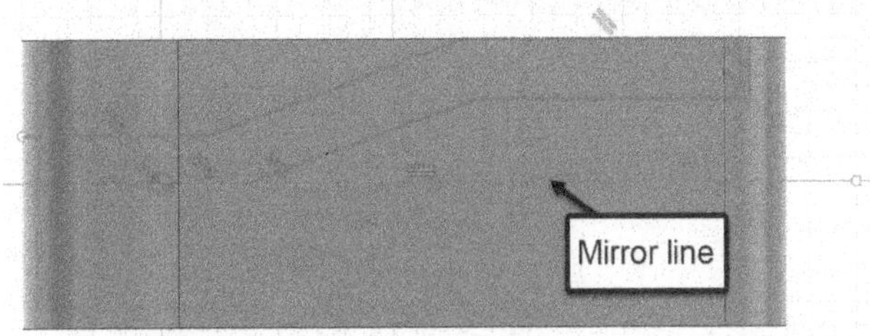

9. Click **OK** to generate the symmetrical bottom half of the channel.

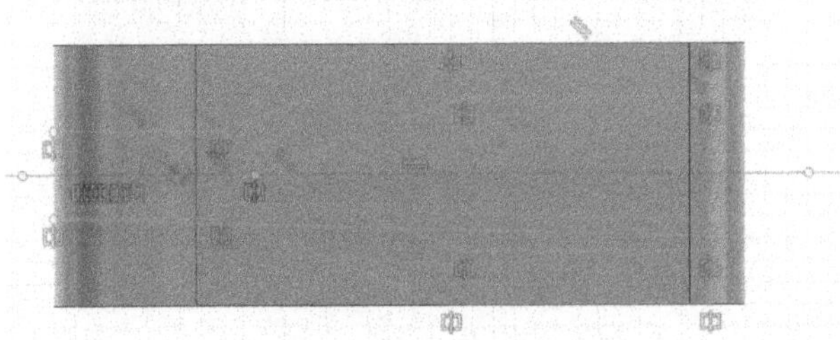

10. Press **L** to activate the **Line** tool.
11. Select the endpoints of the two left horizontal lines, as shown.

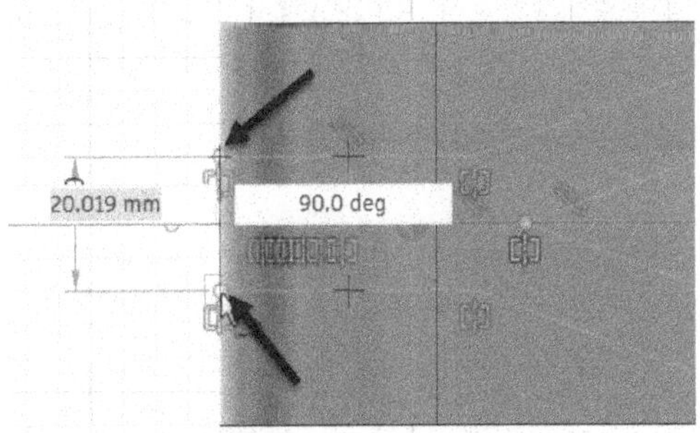

12. On the **Sketch** toolbar, select **Create > Project/Include > Intersect**. The **Intersect** dialog box will appear. You will be prompted to select objects (faces, edges, or bodies) that cross the sketch plane.

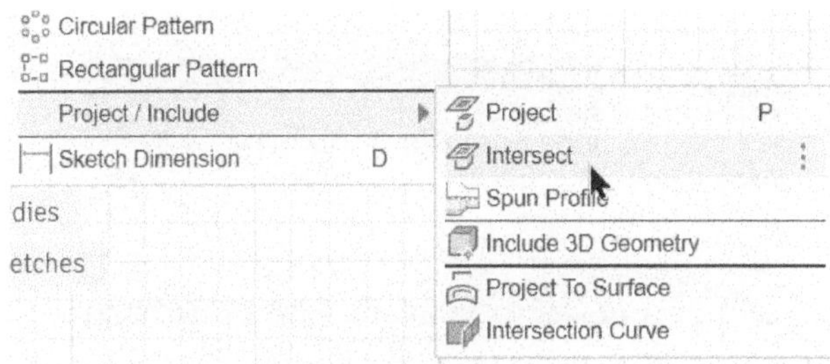

13. Hover your cursor over the right curved face of the solid body. A red preview line will appear, indicating the boundary where that face intersects the sketch plane. Click to select the face.

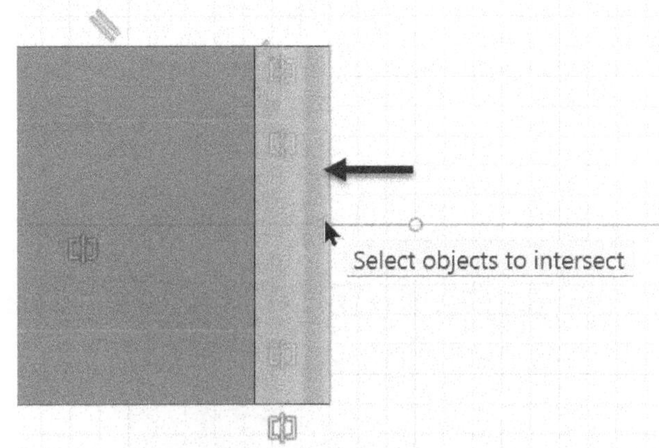

14. Repeat this process for left curved face.

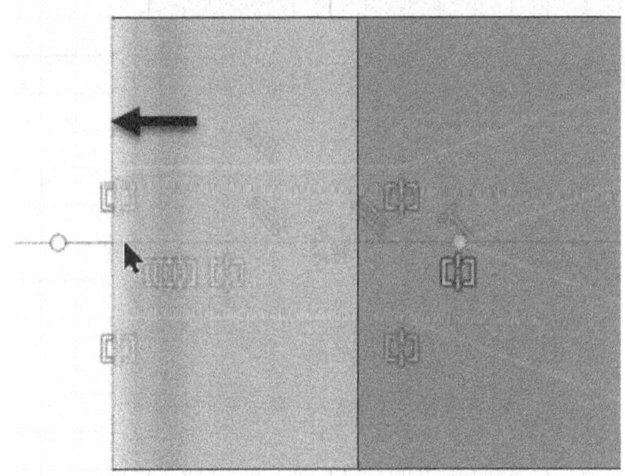

15. Once all necessary boundaries are selected and previewed in red, click **OK** in the dialog box.
16. The red preview lines will convert into purple projection lines in your sketch. These lines are parametrically linked to the solid body; if the body's dimensions change later, these lines will update automatically.

17. In the **Constraints** panel on the **Sketch** toolbar, click **Collinear**  .
18. Select the right vertical line and the select the right projected edge.

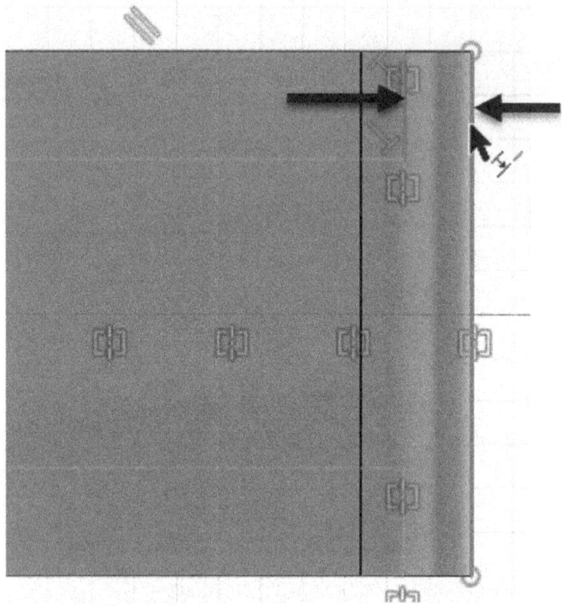

19. Select the left vertical line and select the left projected edge.

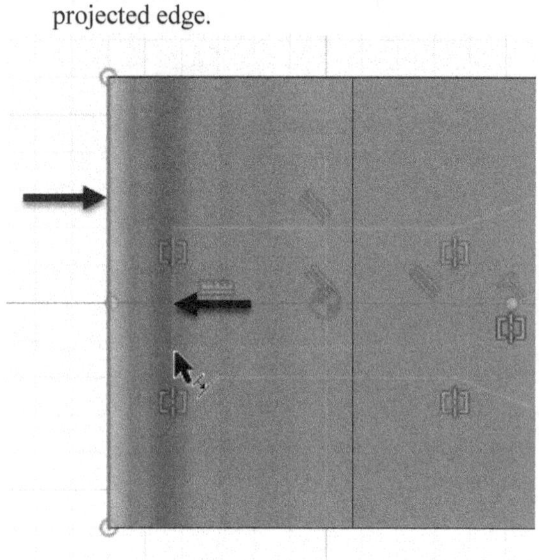

20. Select the top horizontal edge and the top horizontal line to make them collinear.
21. Select the bottom horizontal edge and the bottom horizontal line to make them collinear.

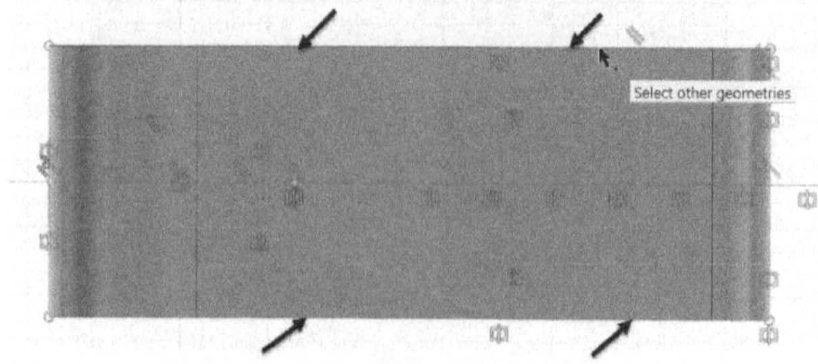

22. Press **D** to activate the **Sketch Dimension** tool.
23. Select the left vertical edge of the part and the right endpoint of the inclined line of the sketch. Drag the dimension upward, enter 110, and press Enter.

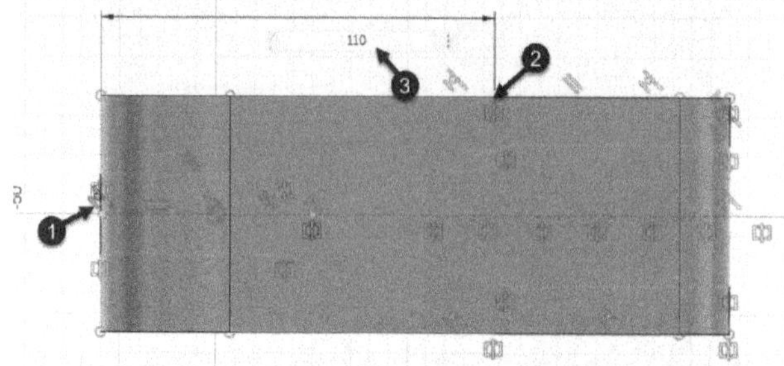

24. Select the solid horizontal line next to the construction line, as shown. Drag upward, enter 60, and press Enter.

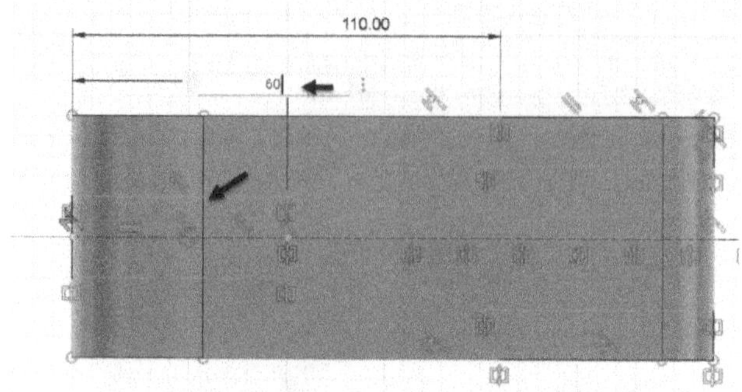

25. Select the right vertical line. Place the dimension, enter 7, and press Enter to set the channel width.

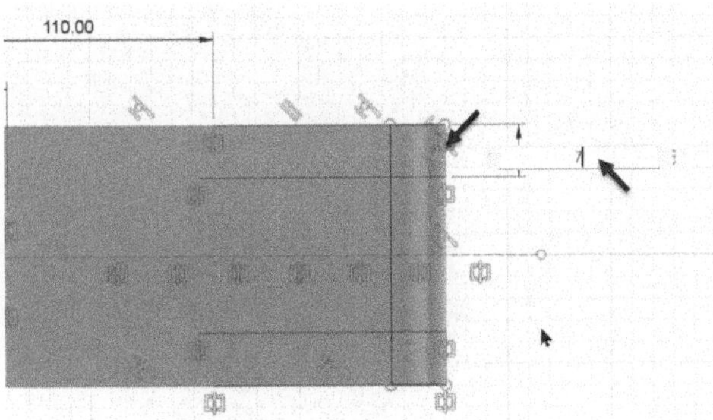

26. Select the left vertical line. Place the dimension, enter 14, and press Enter.

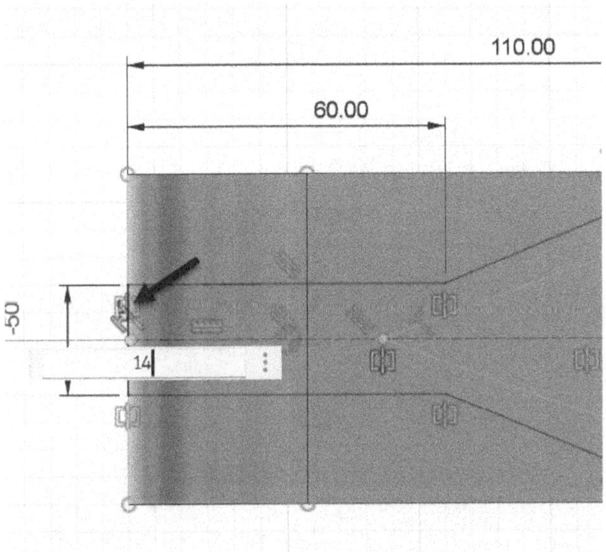

27. In the **Constraints** panel on the **Sketch** toolbar, click **Parallel**  .
28. Select the two inclined lines, as shown.

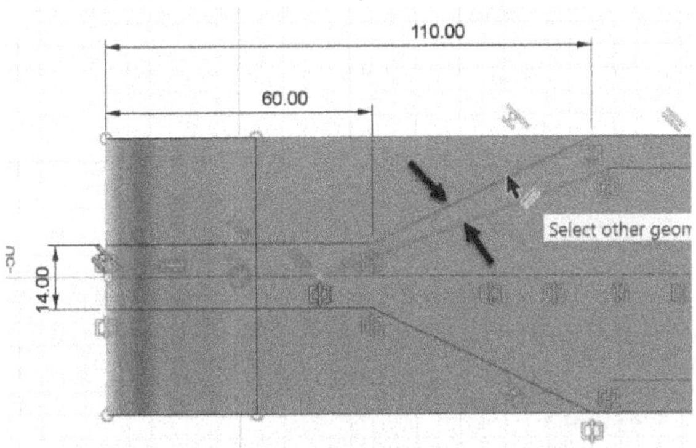

29. Press **D** to activate the **Sketch Dimension** tool.
30. Select the two parallel inclined lines. Place the dimension, type 7 and press ENTER.

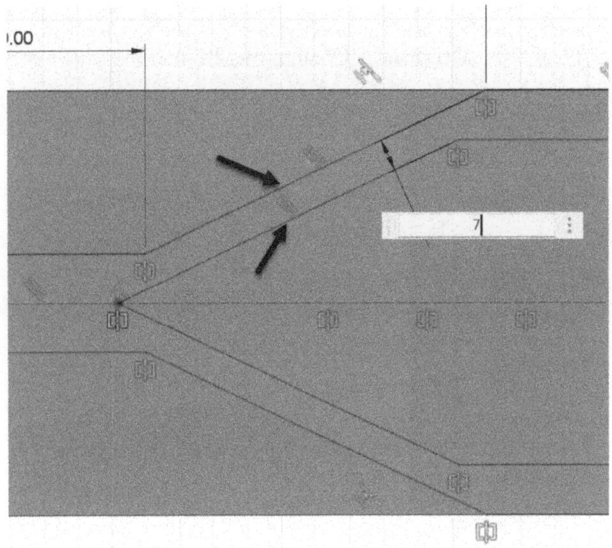

31. The sketch is fully defined. Click **Finish Sketch** in the toolbar.

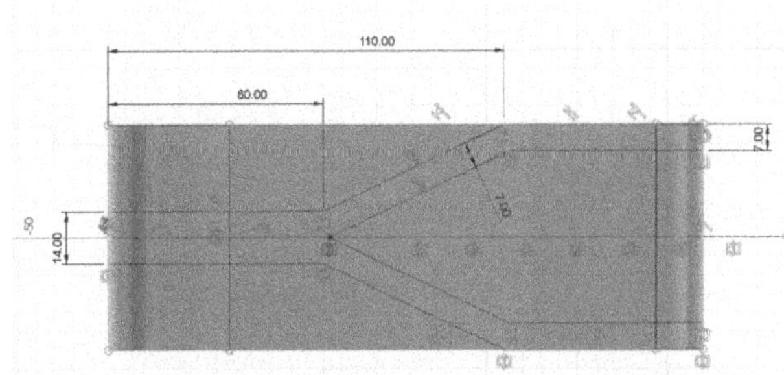

32. On the **Solid** tab of the toolbar, click **Create > Extrude** (or press **E**).
33. In the graphics area, select the internal regions of the sketched split-channel profile. The selected areas will highlight in blue, indicating they are the active profiles for the operation.

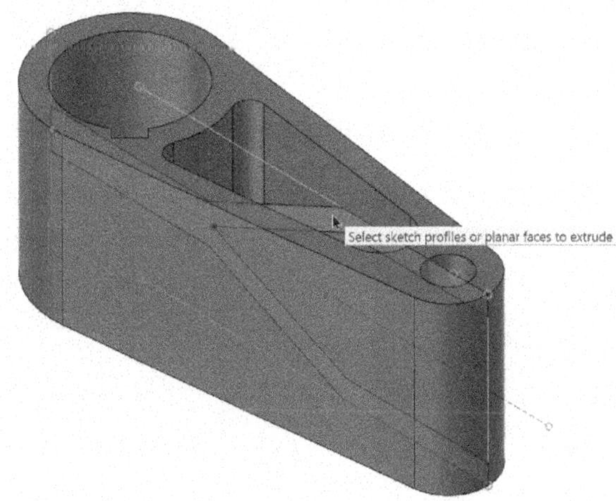

34. The **Extrude** dialog box will open. Configure the following settings:

- **Direction:** Change this from "One Side" to **Symmetric**. This ensures the extrusion projects equally in both directions away from the sketch plane, which is necessary if the sketch is located on a mid-plane of the part.
- **Extent Type:** Set this to **All**. This forces the extrusion to pass completely through the existing geometry in both directions, eliminating the need to type a specific distance.
- **Operation:** Change the default operation to **Intersect**.

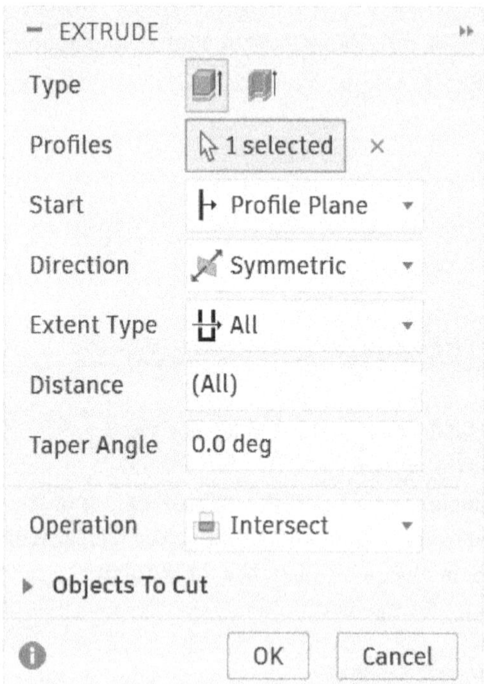

Review the preview in the graphics area. Instead of adding new material (Join) or removing material (Cut), the Intersect operation will calculate the overlapping volume between the new symmetric extrusion and the original solid body. Only the geometry common to both shapes will remain.

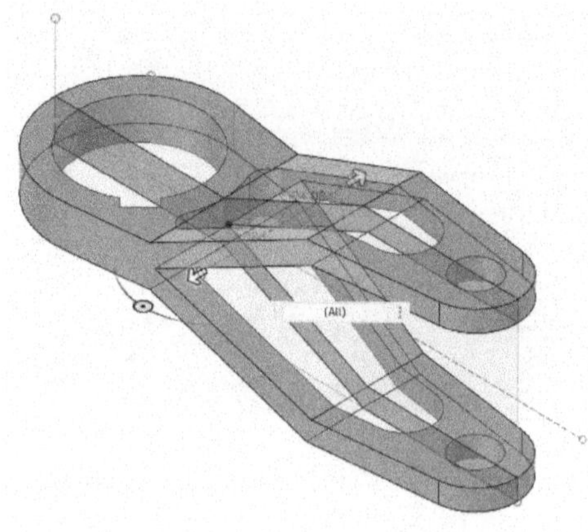

35. Click **OK** in the dialog box to execute the command. The resulting solid will be the precise intersecting volume of the two shapes.

Applying Complex Edge Fillets

Fillets are used to relieve stress and add material to sharp internal corners where different sections of a solid body converge.

1. On the **Solid** tab of the toolbar, click **Modify > Fillet** (or press **F**).
2. The **Fillet** dialog box will open. In the graphics area, navigate to the junction where the central body splits into the angled arms.
3. Carefully select the horizontal interior edges at these junctions. The selected edges will highlight, and a preview of the resulting curved face will appear in yellow.

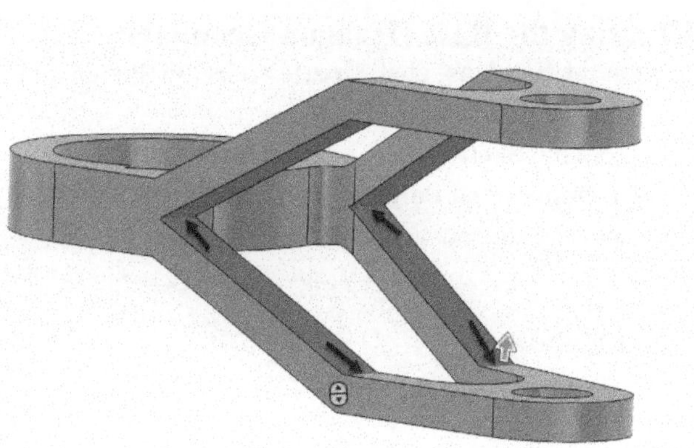

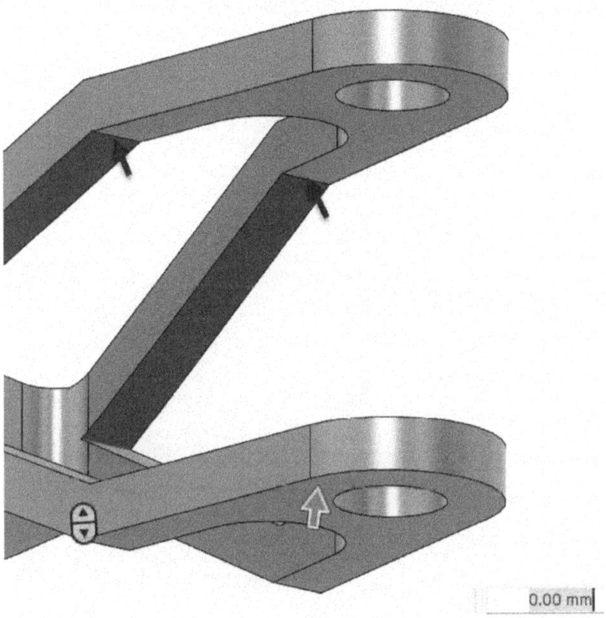

4. In the **Fillet** dialog box (or via the on-screen input box), enter a radius value of **5 mm**. Next, verify the preview correctly sweeps the material between the intersecting faces.

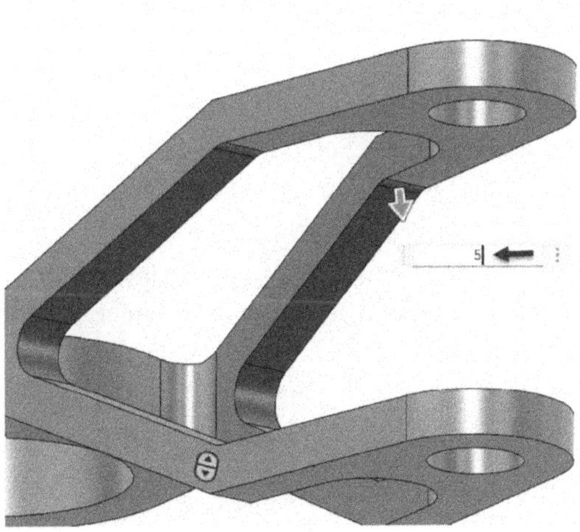

5. In the **Fillet** dialog box, click the **+ (Add new selection set)** button. This allows a different radius to be applied without leaving the command.

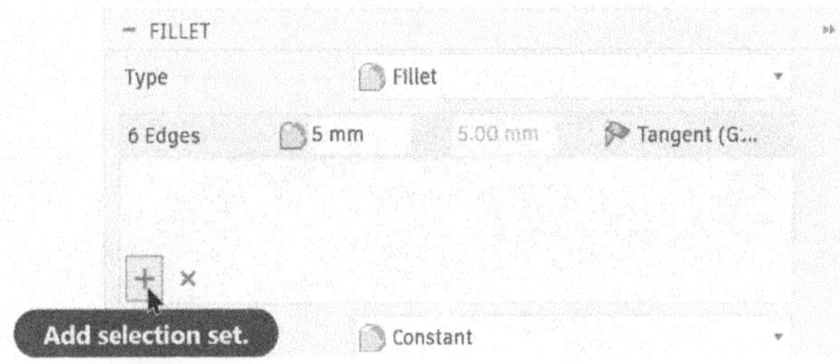

6. Select the outer horizontal edges of the model, as shown. Next, type **5** in the **Radius** box.

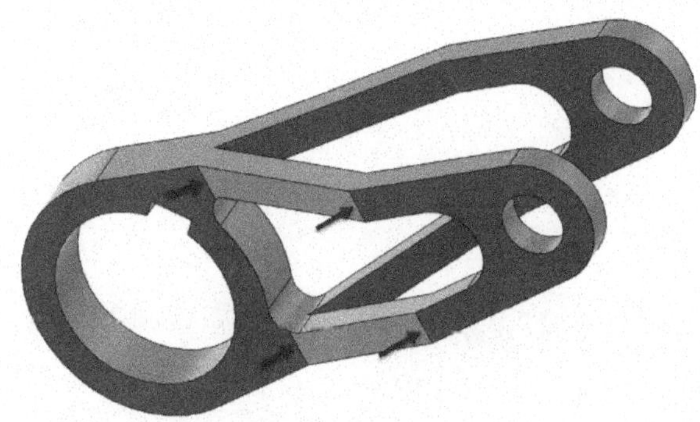

7. Click the **OK** button on the **Fillet** dialog box.
8. On the **Solid** tab of the toolbar, click **Modify > Fillet** (or press **F**).
9. Click a single segment of the top external boundary. Assuming Tangent Chain is active, the entire continuous edge loop will be selected.
10. Select the continuous external boundary edge on the

bottom side of the model in the same manner.

11. Select the sharp internal boundary edges, then specify a radius of 1 mm in the dialogue box.

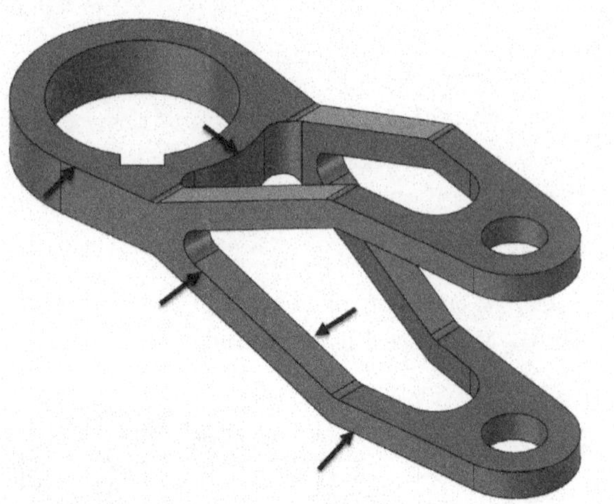

12. Click **OK** to execute the fillet operation across all selected edges.

Tutorial 3

In this tutorial, you will create the part shown in figure below.

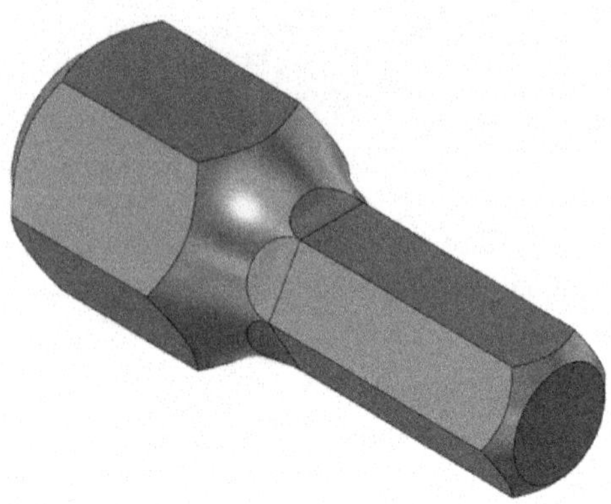

Creating the Base Hexagon Geometry

1. On the **Solid** tab, click **Create > Create Sketch** and select a YZ plane.
2. From the **Sketch** toolbar, click **Create > Polygon > Circumscribed Polygon**. This tool creates a polygon tangent to the outside of a construction circle.

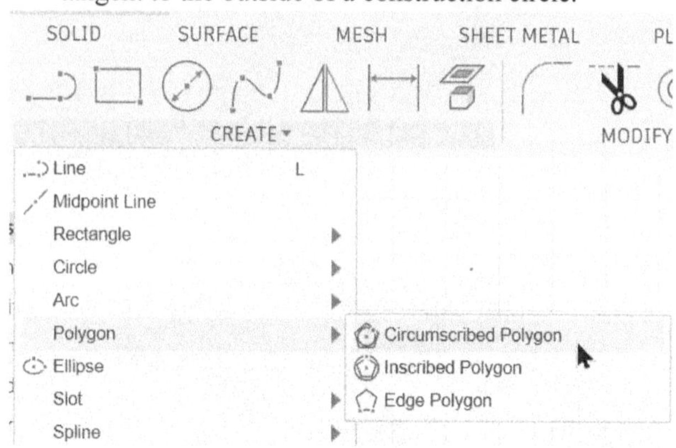

3. Click the origin point to place the center of the polygon.
4. Drag the cursor outward. In the floating dialog box, ensure the number of sides is set to **6**. Click to place the rough shape.

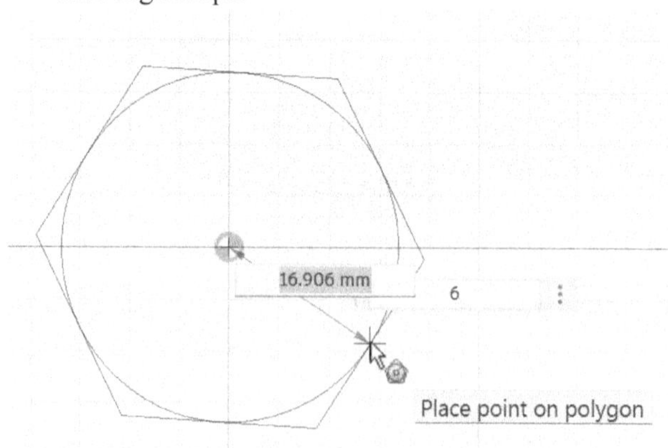

5. To orient the polygon, click the **Horizontal/Vertical**  constraint tool in the **Constraints** panel. Select the top edge of the hexagon. This locks the geometry so the top and bottom edges are perfectly horizontal.
6. Press D to activate the **Sketch Dimension** tool.
7. Select the top horizontal edge of the outer hexagon, then select the bottom horizontal edge. Drag the dimension out, enter 8, and press Enter.

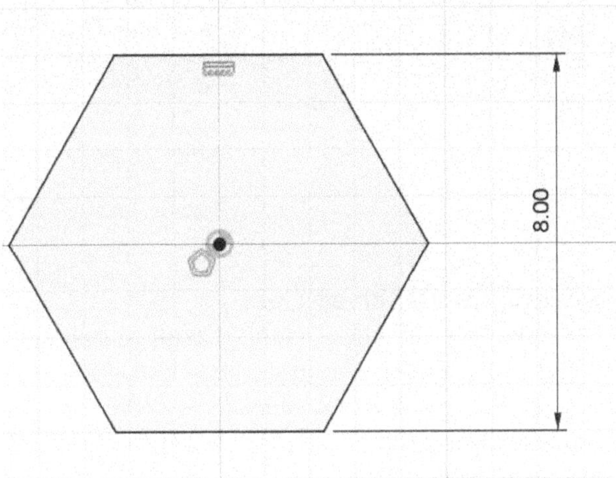

8. Click **Finish Sketch** to proceed.
9. On the **Solid** tab, click **Create > Extrude** (or press **E**).
10. In the graphics area, select the hexagon profile.
11. Drag the directional arrow or enter a distance of **10 mm** in the Extrude dialog box.
12. Ensure the Operation is set to **New Body** and click **OK**. This creates the main solid base.

Executing the Second Extrusion

1. On the **Solid** tab, click **Create > Create Sketch** and select the right face.

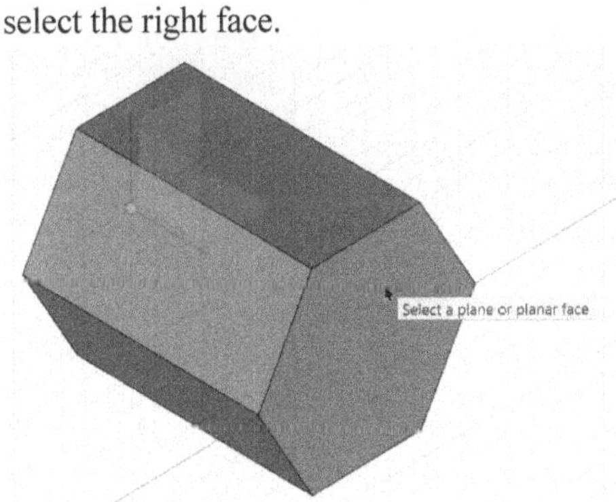

2. From the **Sketch** toolbar, click **Create > Polygon > Circumscribed Polygon**.
3. Click the origin point, drag the cursor outward, and click.

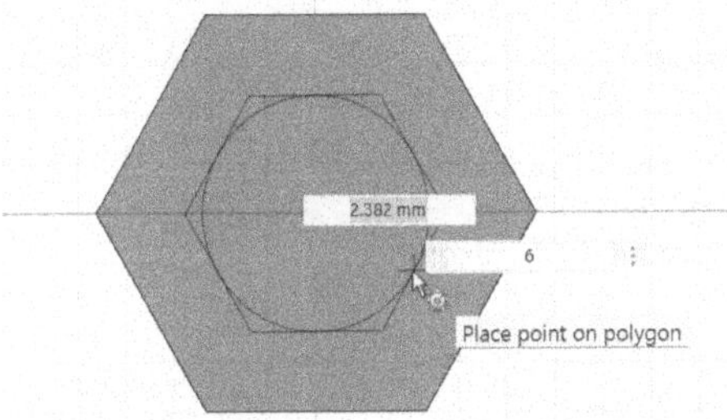

4. Apply the **Horizontal/Vertical** constraint to the top edge of the hexagon.
5. Press **D** to activate the **Sketch Dimension** tool.
6. Select the top and bottom horizontal edges of the hexagon. Place the dimension and set it to 5.

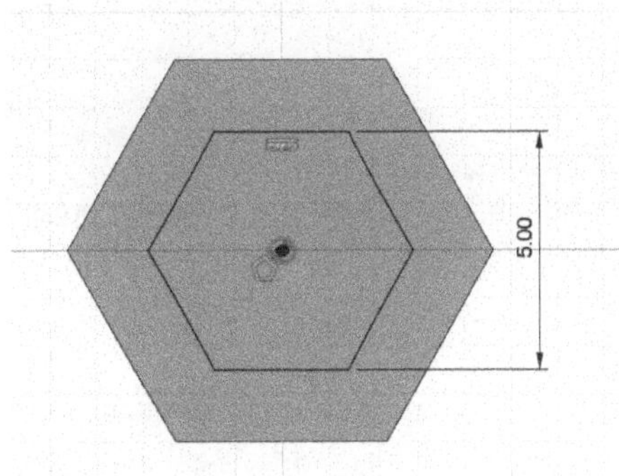

7. Click **Finish Sketch** to proceed.
8. Click **Create > Extrude** (or press **E**).
9. Click inside inner hexagonal.
10. Enter a distance of **12.00 mm**.
11. Ensure the **Operation** is set to **Join** so this new extrusion merges with the existing base.
12. Click **OK** to complete the operation.

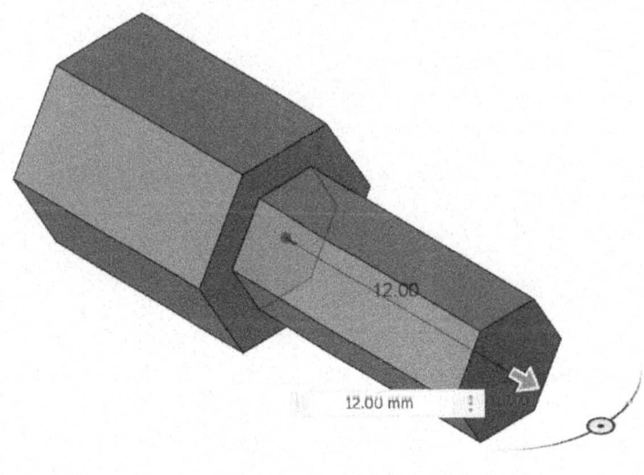

Adjusting the Visual Style

To better visualize internal or obscured geometry during editing, the display mode can be temporarily changed.

1. Navigate to the **Display Settings** menu at the bottom center of the workspace (the monitor icon).
2. Hover over **Visual Style** to expand the options.
3. Select **Wireframe** (or press Ctrl+7/Cmd+7). This removes surface shading, displaying only the structural edges of the model.

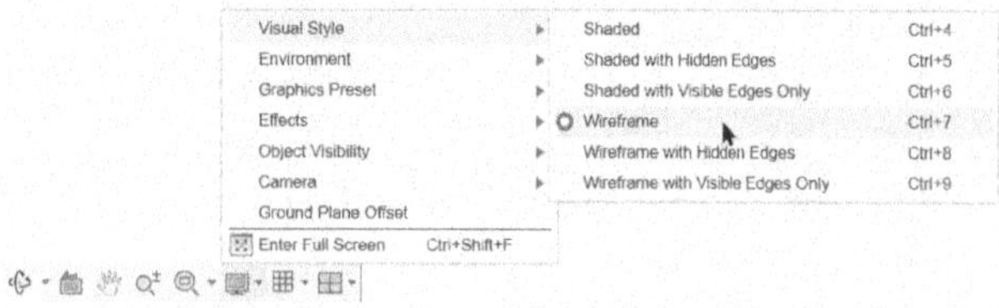

Applying Transition Fillets

1. On the **Solid** tab, click **Modify > Fillet** (or press **F**).
2. In the graphics area, navigate to the junction where the smaller hexagonal protrusion meets the larger base body.
3. Select the six individual line segments that form this complete internal boundary. Because the model is in Wireframe mode, these edges are easily selectable even if they would normally be hidden behind front-facing geometry.

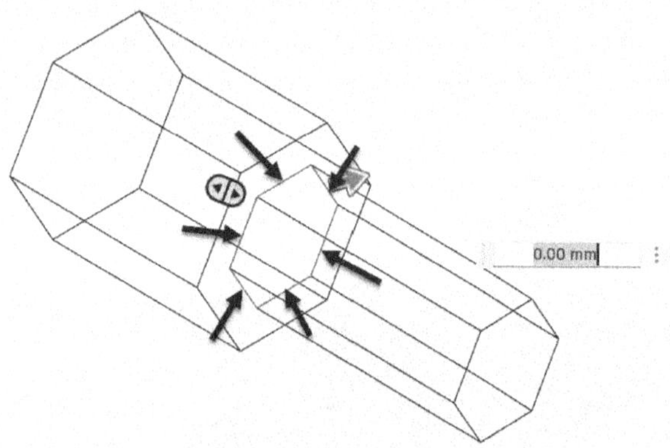

4. In the **Fillet** dialog box, or the floating input field, enter a radius value of **1.5 mm**.

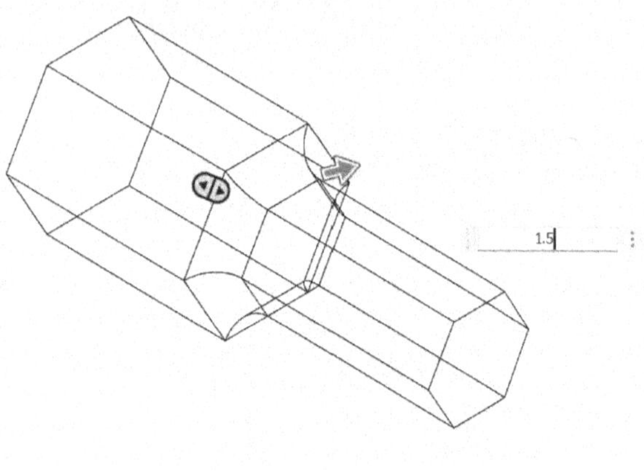

5. Verify the preview shows the fillet sweeping correctly between the intersecting faces.
6. Click **OK** to execute the command.
7. Return to the **Display Settings** menu and change the Visual Style back to **Shaded with Visible Edges Only** to resume normal modeling.

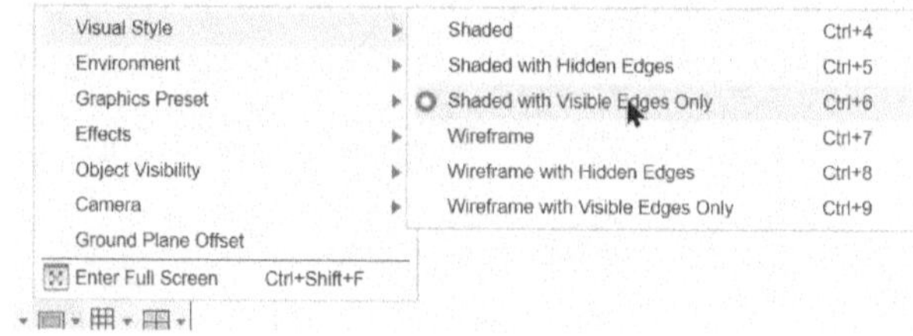

Creating the Revolved Cuts

1. On the **Solid** tab, click **Create > Create Sketch.**
2. Select the **XY** plane that bisects the existing solid body perfectly down the middle.
3. On the Toolbar, click the **Sketch** contextual tab > **Create** panel > **Project/Include > Intersect.**

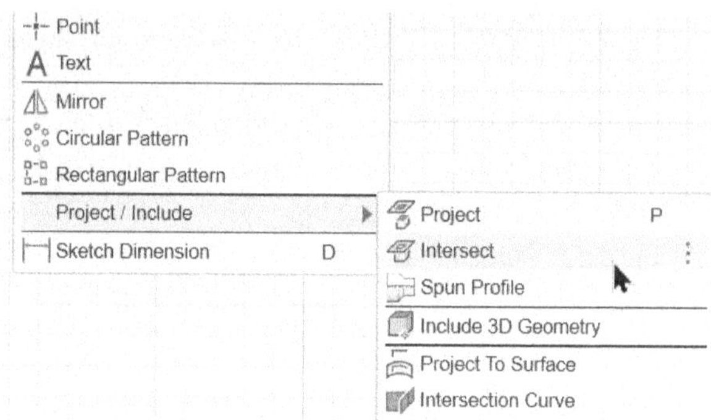

4. On the Intersect dialog, select **Selection Filter > Body**.

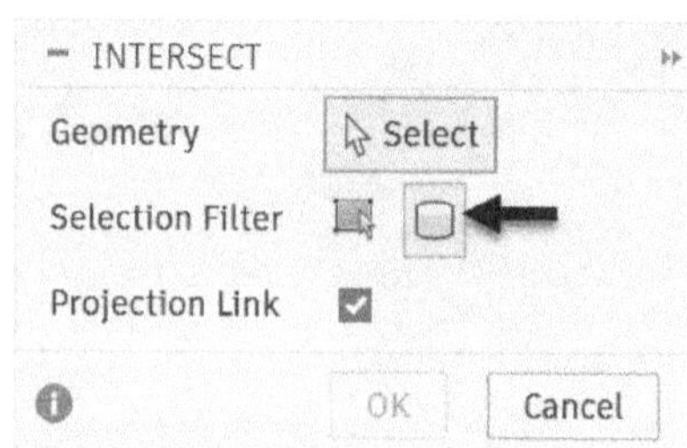

5. Click on the solid geometry and click **OK**.

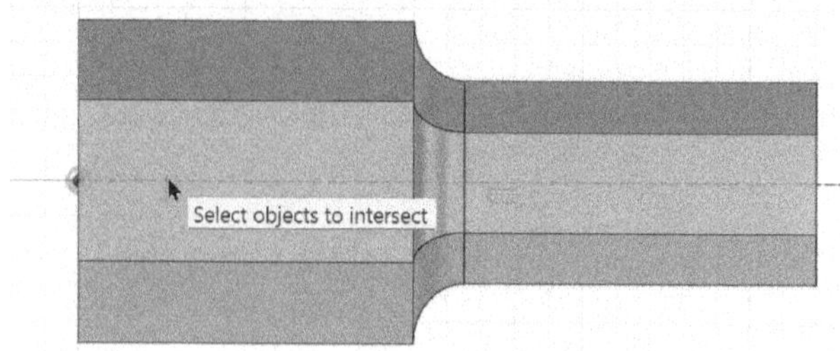

Fusion 360 automatically generates the intersection. The final output consists of purple lines and nodes positioned exactly where the solid model passes through the sketch plane. The purple color signifies that this new geometry is parametrically linked to the original 3D model, meaning it will update automatically if the source body changes.

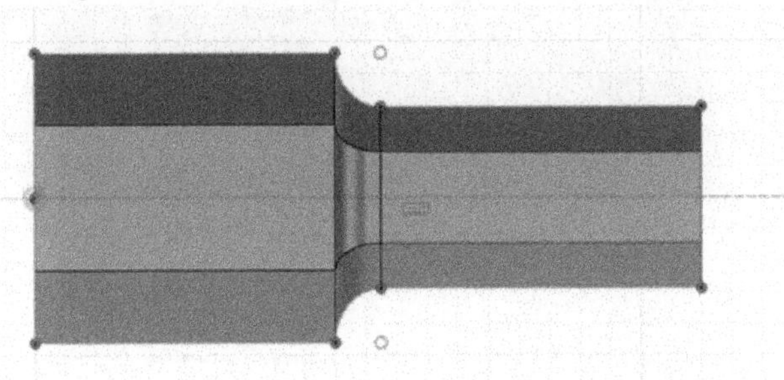

6. Look at the **Sketch Palette** on the right side of the screen and check the box for **Slice**. This temporarily sections the 3D body along the active sketch plane, providing a clear view of the internal cross-section.

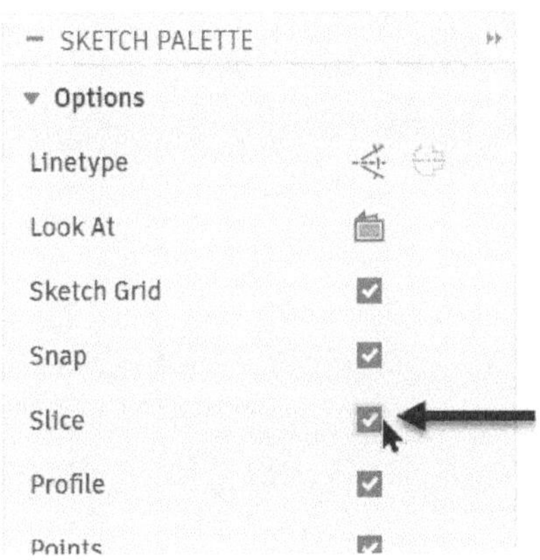

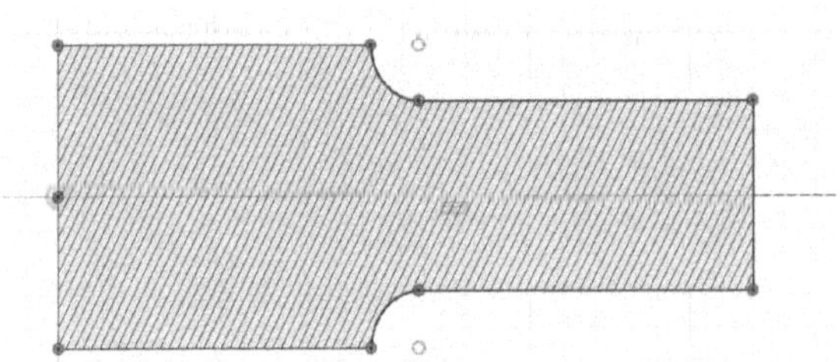

Next, you need to sketch the cutting profiles. These profiles define the material to be removed from the top edge and the internal transition area.

7. Press **L** to activate the **Line** tool. Ensure the line type is set to **Construction** (dashed) in the **Sketch Palette**.
8. Draw a horizontal construction line extending toward right from the sketch origin of the solid body.
9. Deactivate the **Construction** icon on the **Sketch Palette** to toggle the **Line** tool back to standard (solid) lines.

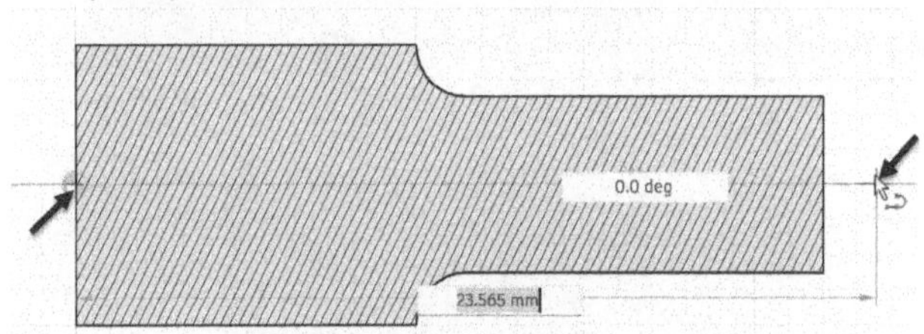

10. **Left and right Chamfer Profiles:**
    - Draw an inclined line connecting the left vertical edge and the top horizontal edge.

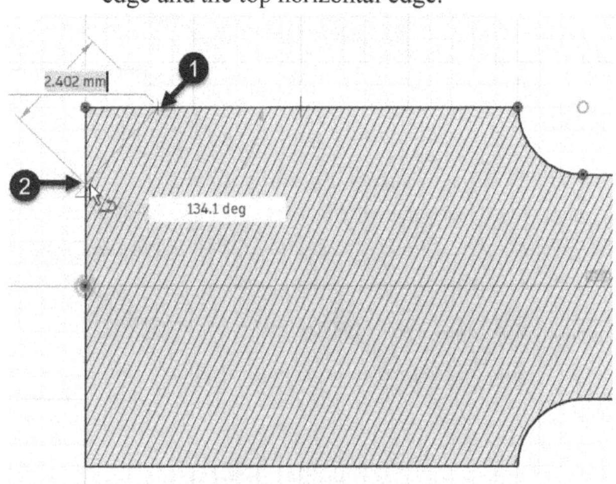

    - Draw an inclined line connecting the top horizontal edge and the right vertical edge.

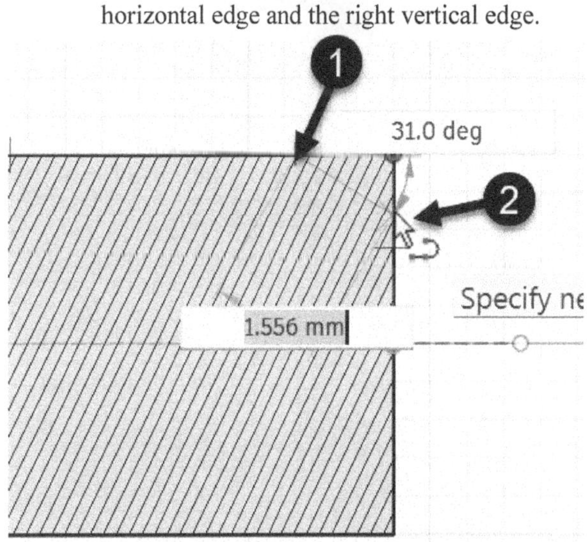

11. **Curved Relief Profile:**
    - Move to the junction where the left and right sections of the solid body meet.
    - Draw an arc (using the **3-Point Arc** tool) starting at the end point of the curved edge.

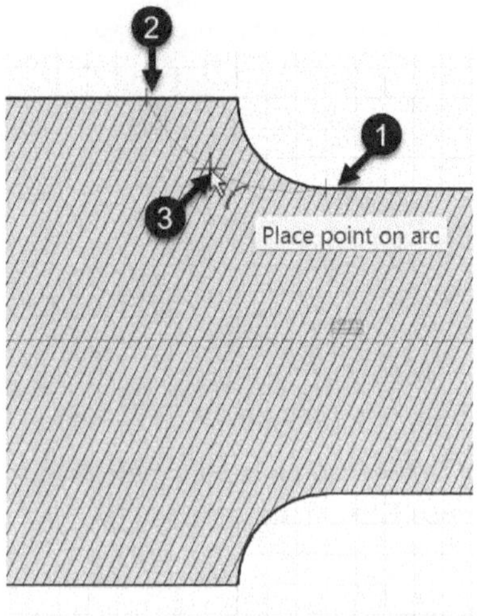

12. Press **D** for the **Sketch Dimension** tool.
13. Select the left angled line and the horizontal edge. Set the angle to **45°**.
14. Select the corner point of the model and the endpoint of the inclined line. Set its length to **1.5**.

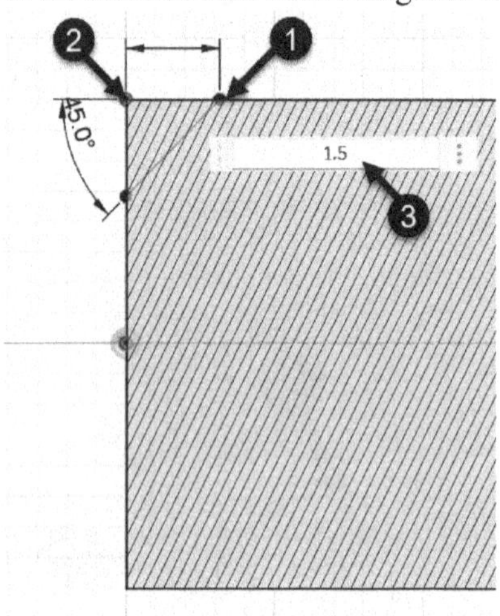

15. Select the arc. Set its radius to **R5**.

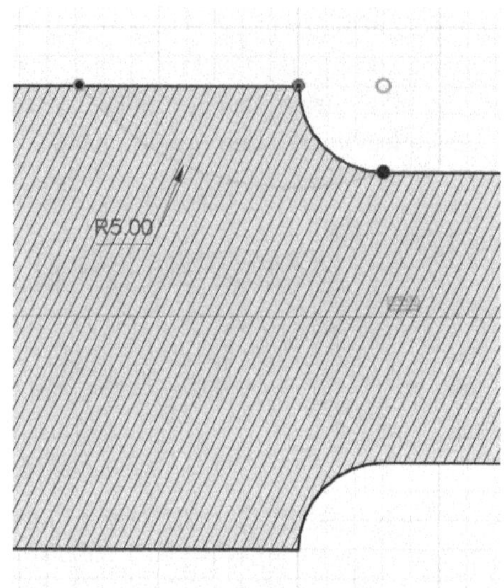

16. Select the right angled line and the horizontal edge. Set the angle to **45°**.
17. Select the corner point of the model and the endpoint of the inclined line. Set its length to **0.75.**

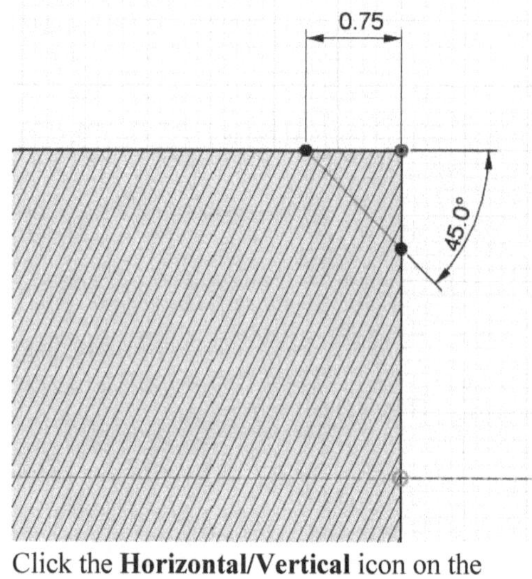

18. Click the **Horizontal/Vertical** icon on the **Constraints** panel, and then select the centerpoint of the arc and centerpoint of the circular edge, as shown.

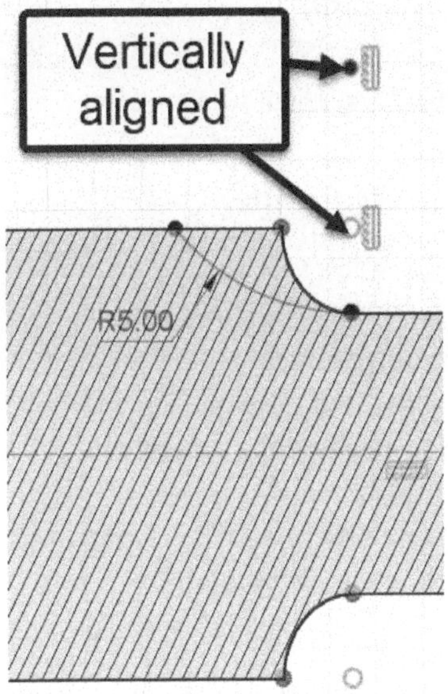

19. Ensure all lines are black, indicating the sketch is fully constrained. Click **Finish Sketch** to proceed to the revolve operation.

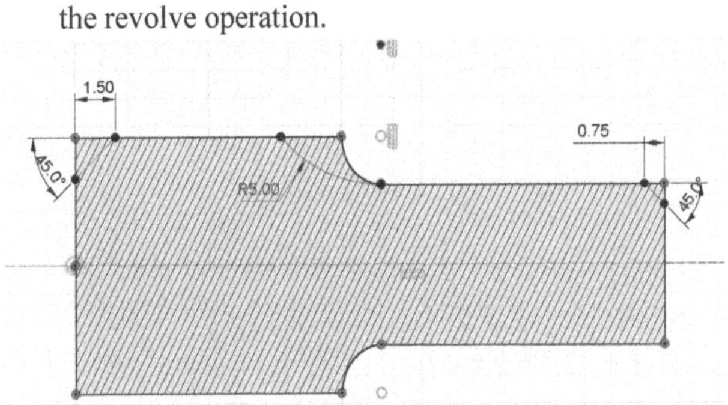

20. On the **Solid** tab, click **Create > Revolve**.

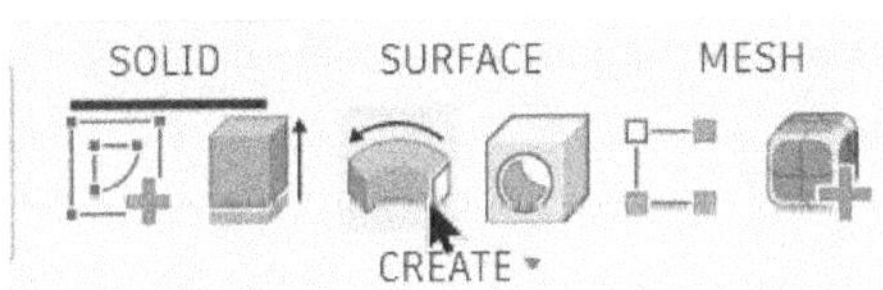

21. In the **Revolve** dialog, click the **Profile** selector, then pick the three blue sketch regions shown on the cross section.

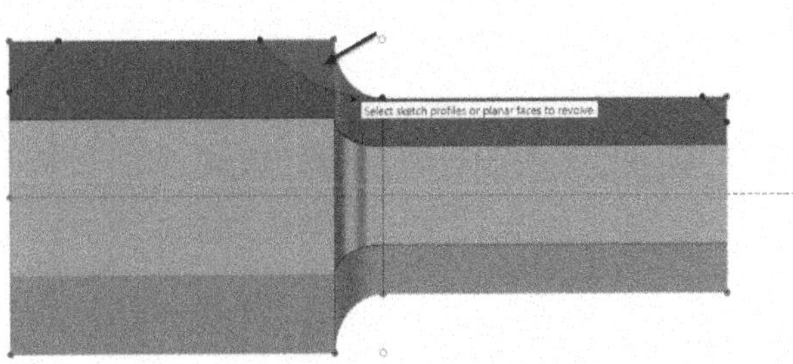

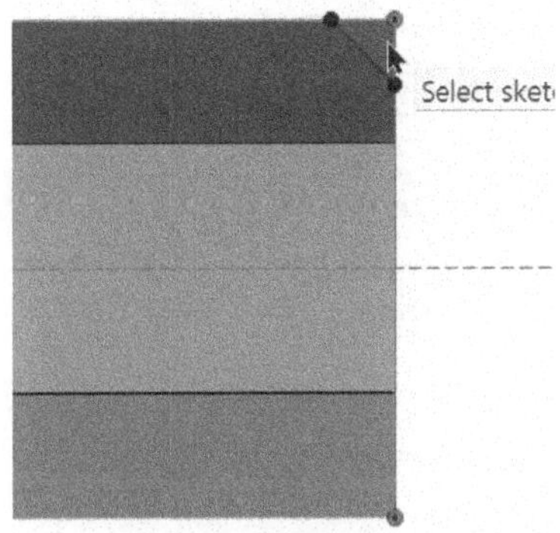

22. Click the **Axis** selector, then choose the horizontal construction line through the center of the part as the revolve axis.

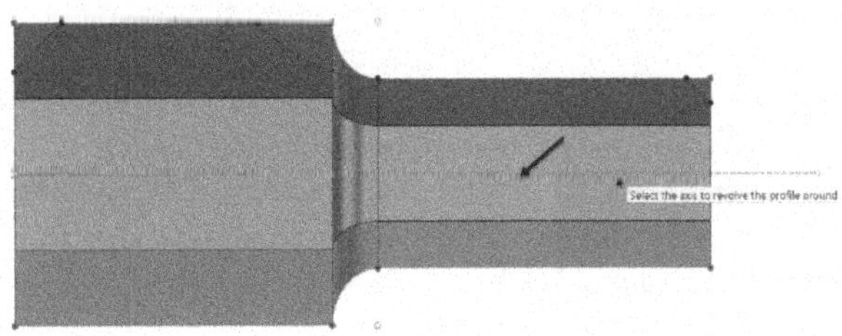

23. Set **Extent Type** to **Full** so the selected profiles revolve a complete 360 degrees around the axis.
24. Set **Operation** to **Cut** to remove material from the existing body using the revolved profiles.

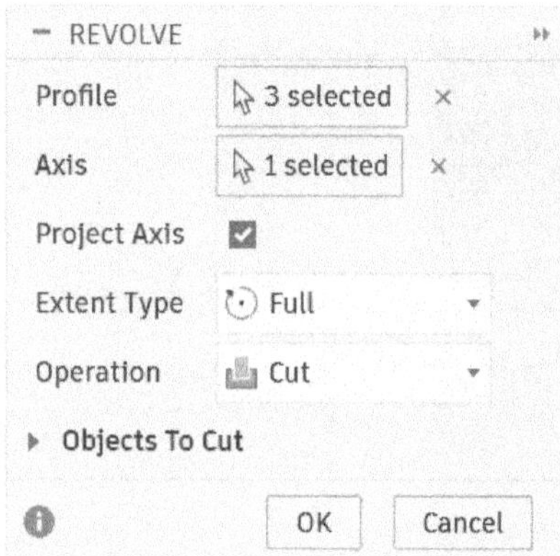

25. Confirm that the preview shows the desired removed region, then click **OK** to complete the Revolve cut.

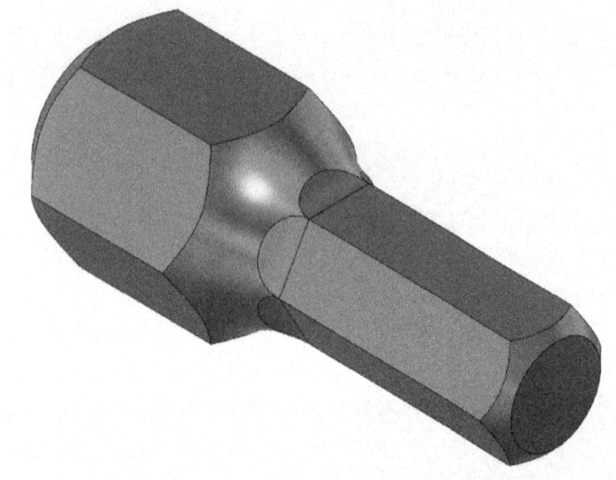

Tutorial 4

In this tutorial, you will create the part shown in figure below.

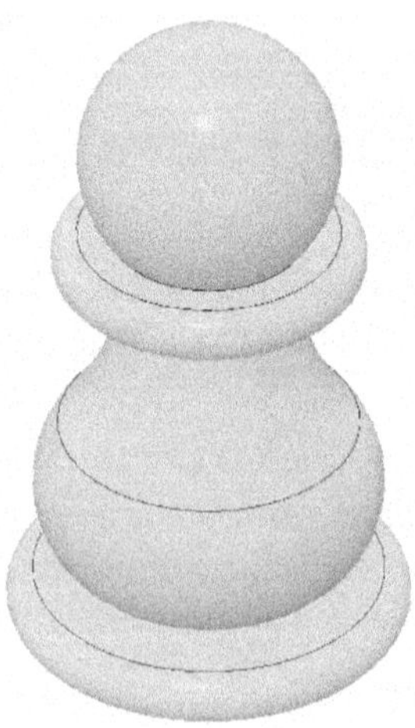

Initialize the Sketch

1. Open Fusion 360, navigate to the **Solid** tab, and select **Create > Create Sketch**. Click the Front (XZ) plane to orient the workspace.
2. Press the **L** key to activate the **Line** tool.
3. Click the origin point (0,0) and move the cursor vertically straight up. Click to place the endpoint, ensuring a Vertical constraint icon appears.

Draw the Upper Arc Profile

1. On the **Sketch** toolbar, click **Create > Arc > Center Point Arc**.
2. Click on the upper portion of the vertical line to define the center of your arc.
3. Move your cursor up and select the top endpoint of the vertical line to establish the starting position and the radius of your arc.
4. Move the pointer toward bottom right corner and click to define the endpoint of the arc.

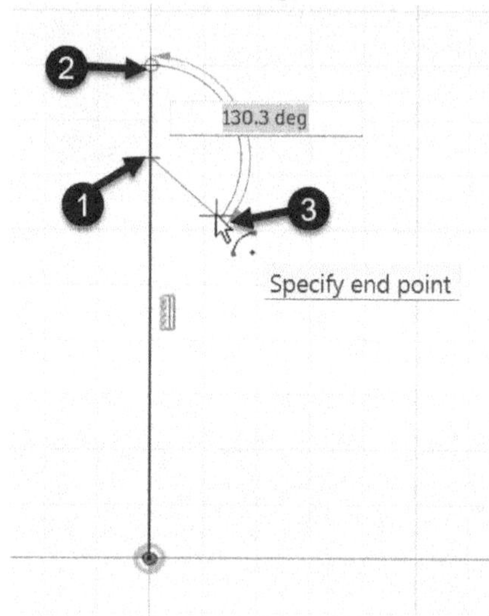

5. Press the **L** key to activate the **Line** tool.
6. Select the endpoint of the arc.
7. Move the cursor horizontally to the right and click.

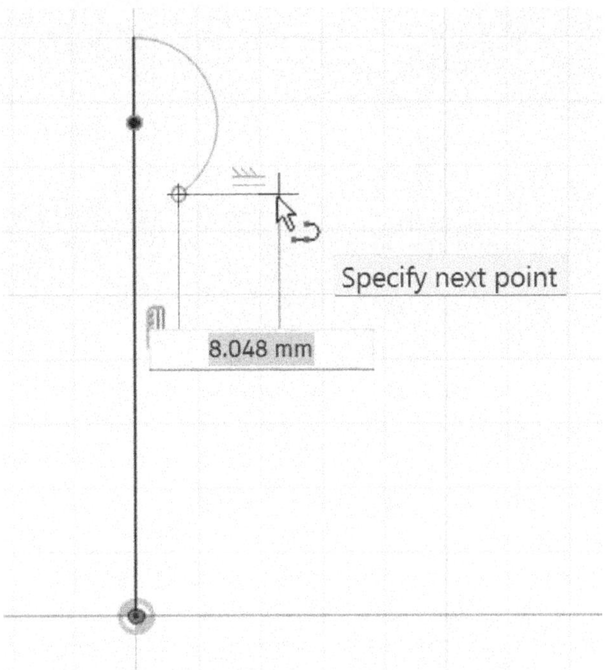

8. To transition directly into an arc, move the pointer away from the endpoint of the horizontal line. Next, move it back to the endpoint. Press and hold the left mouse button on the endpoint, then drag the cursor downward to form a tangent arc. Release the mouse button when the arc resembles the shape in the reference image.

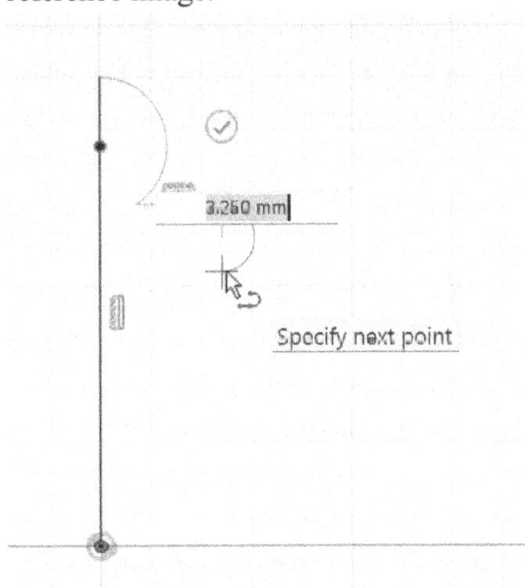

9. From the bottom endpoint of that new arc, click and drag a short horizontal line straight to the left, stopping before it intersects the vertical line.

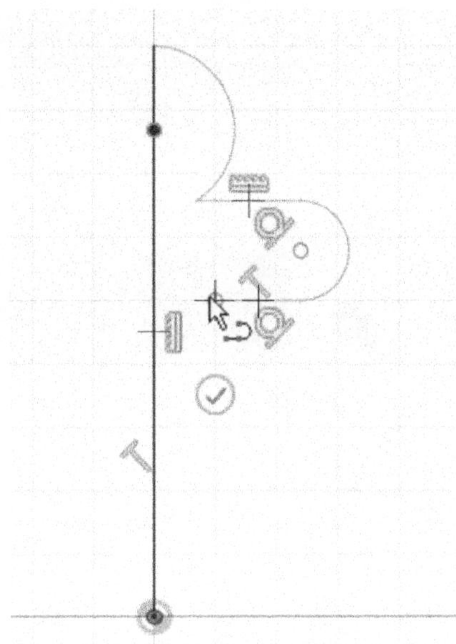

10. On the **Sketch** toolbar at the top of your screen, click the **Create** drop-down menu, hover over **Arc**, and choose **3-Point Arc**.
11. Select the endpoint of the short horizontal line, move the pointer downward and right, and then click.
12. Move the pointer toward left up to a small distance and click.

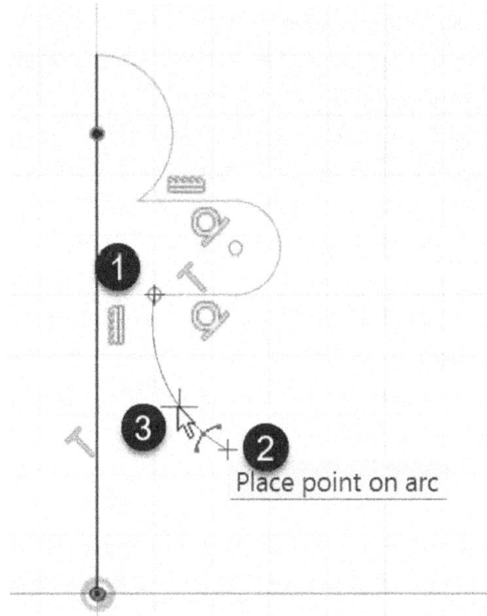

13. Select the endpoint of the arc, move the pointer downward and click. Next, move the toward right up to a small distance and click.

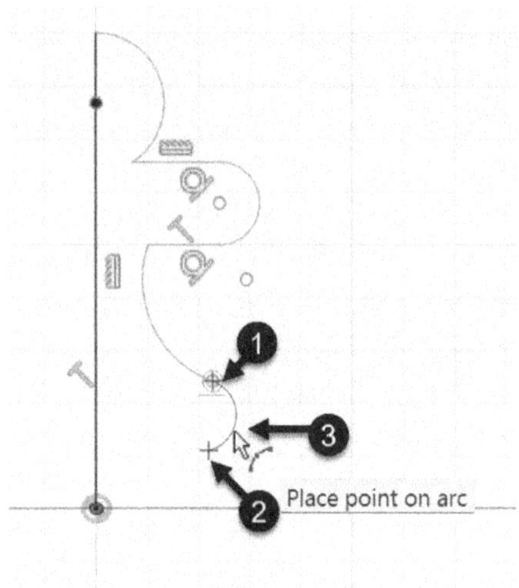

14. Press the L key to activate the **Line** tool.
15. From the endpoint of this second small arc, draw a short horizontal line straight to the right.

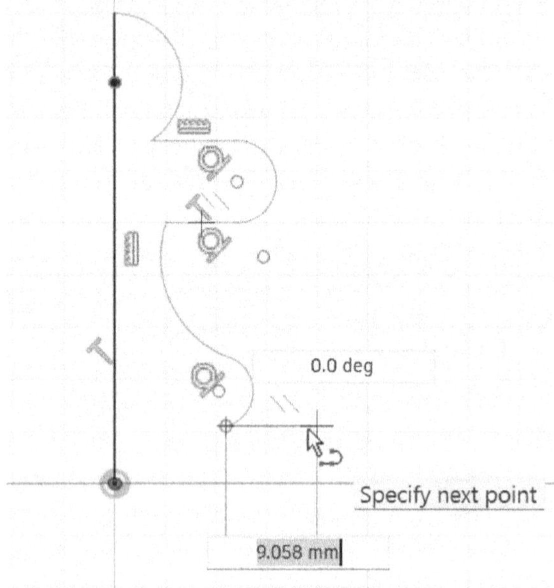

16. Use the click-and-drag method one final time to draw a 180-degree convex arc (representing the R6.00 bottom curve).

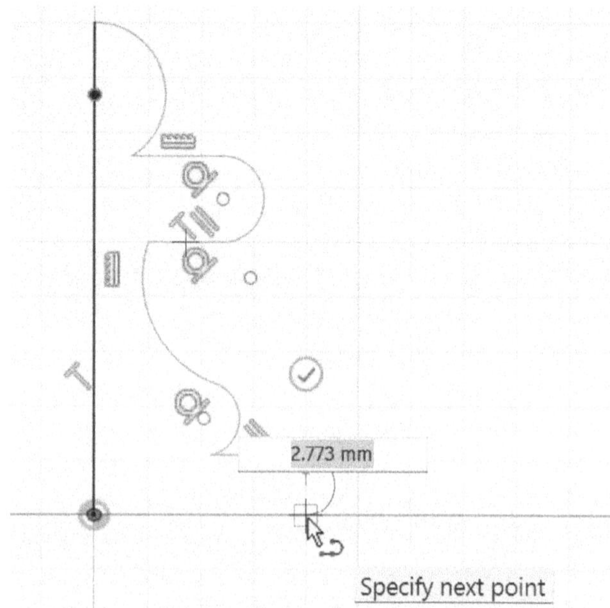

17. From the bottom of that arc, draw a horizontal line straight left until it intersects the vertical line.

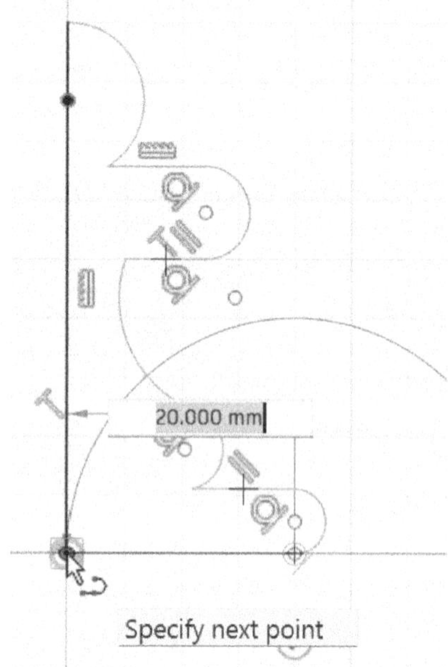

Apply Tangent Constraints

1. To ensure smooth transitions between the geometry, navigate to the toolbar and select **Constraints > Tangent**.
2. Click the large arc, then click the small lower arc to make them tangent. Repeat this process for any other line-to-arc transitions that do not already show a tangent constraint icon.

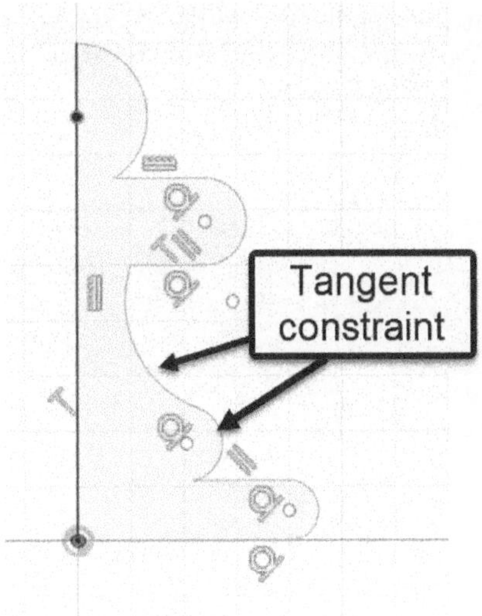

Apply Dimensions

1. Press the **D** key to activate the **Sketch Dimension** tool.
2. Select the upper convex arc and set its radius to 7.50 mm.
3. Select the two small fillet arcs and set their radii to 1.50 mm each.

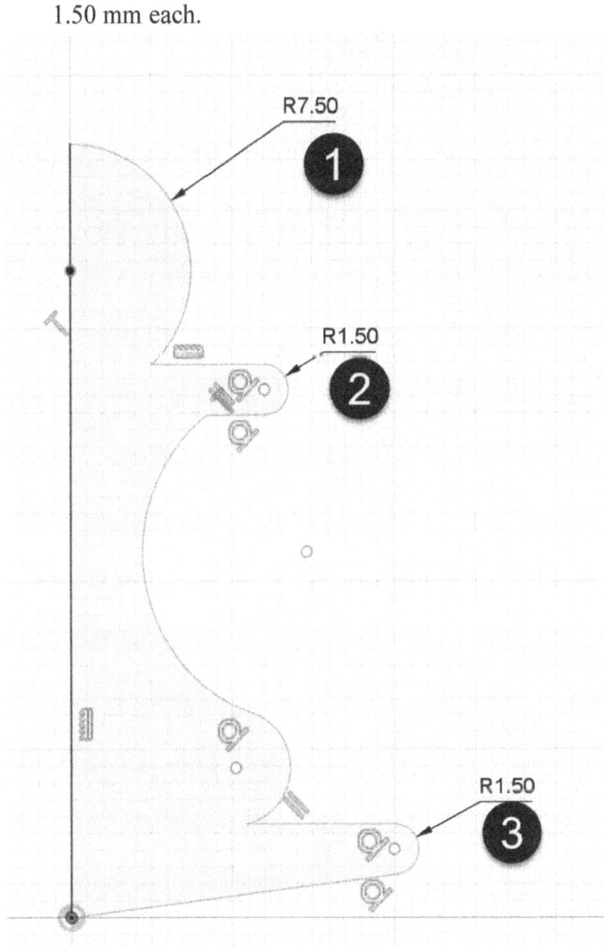

4. Create the vertical dimension between the top point and the upper horizontal line and enter 12.50 mm.
5. Select the bottom convex arc and set its radius to 6.00 mm.
6. Select the large concave arc and set its radius to 15.00 mm.

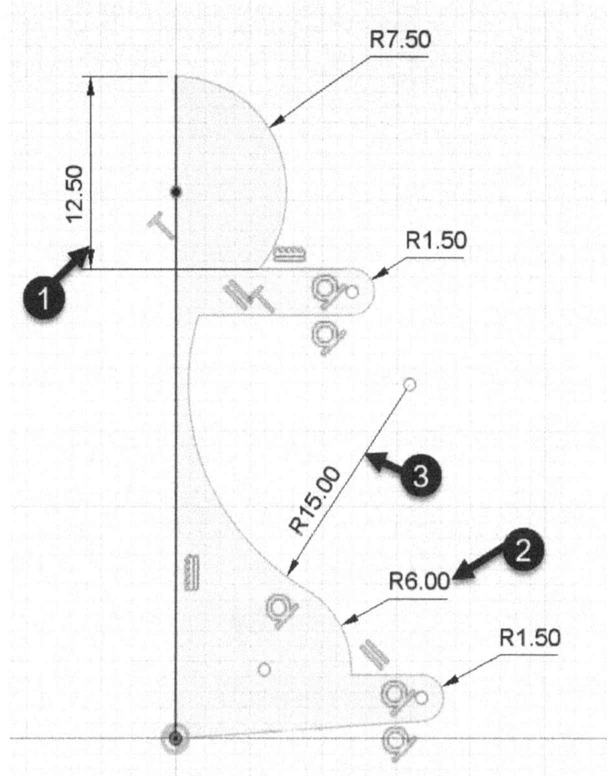

7. Click the overall vertical line and enter 38.00 mm.
8. Create a horizontal dimension between the centerpoint of the concave arc and the vertical line. The dimension value is 20.
9. Create a horizontal dimension between the centerpoint of the convex arc and the vertical line. The dimension value is 4.
10. Create a horizontal dimension between the bottom arc and the vertical line and enter 10.00 mm.
11. Create the top horizontal dimension from the vertical line the top arc center and enter 7.50 mm.

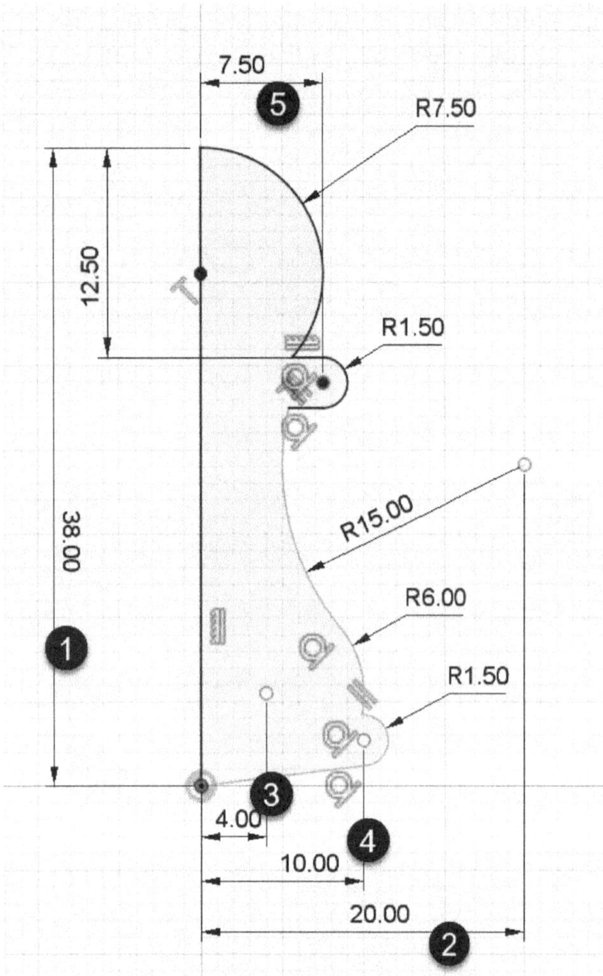

12. Click the **Horizontal/Vertical** icon on the **Constraints** panel of the **Sketch** contextual tab.
13. Select the bottom line to make it horizontal.

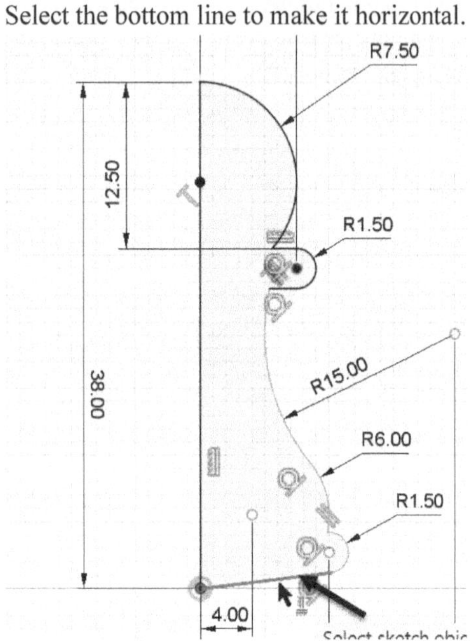

14. Create a horizontal dimension between the endpoint of the horizontan line and the verical line, as shown. The dimension value is 5.

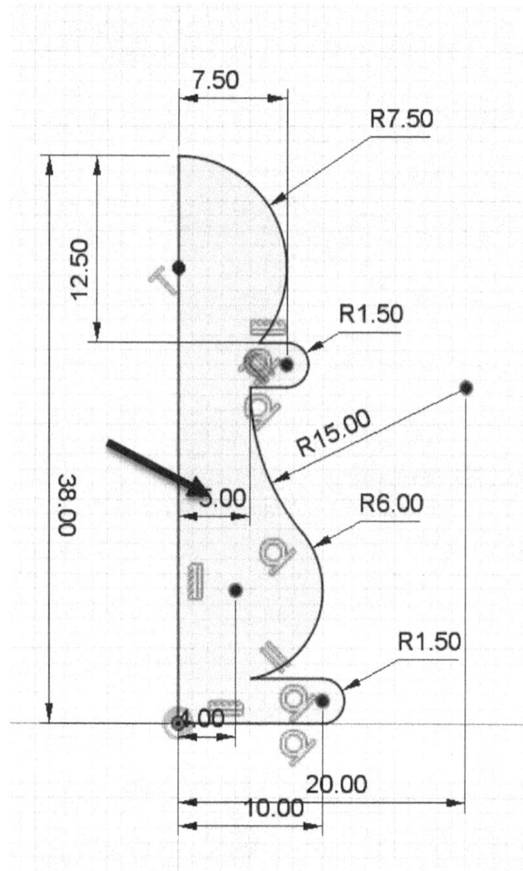

All sketch lines will turn black, confirming it is fully constrained.

15. Click **Finish Sketch**.

Creating the Revolved Feature

1. On the Toolbar, click the **Solid** tab > **Create** panel > **Revolve**.
2. Click on the region enclosed by the sketch.
3. On the **Revolve** dialog, click the **Select** button next to the **Axis** option.
4. Select the vertical line.

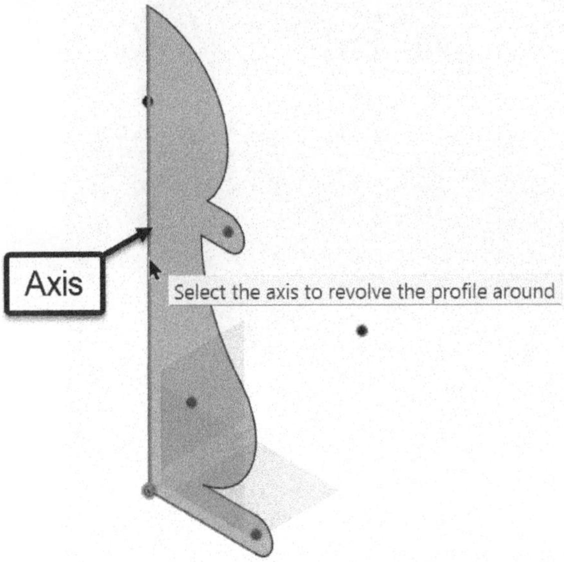

5. Set **Extent Type** to **Full** on the **Revolve** dialog.

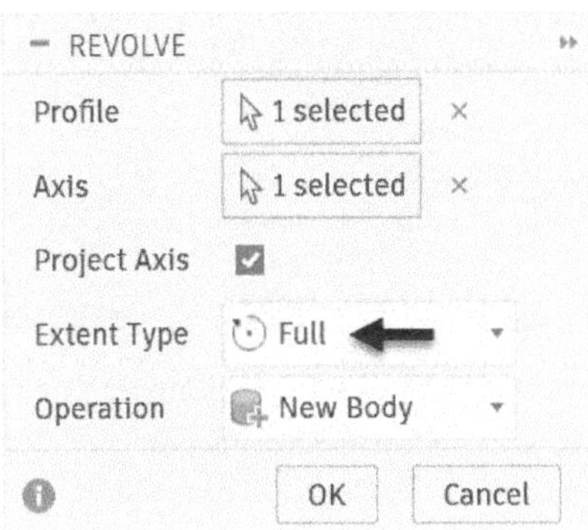

6. Click **OK** to create the revolved feature.
7. Click on the **Home** icon next to the ViewCube.

Applying a Physical Material

1. On the **Solid** toolbar, click the **Modify** drop-down menu and select **Physical Material**.

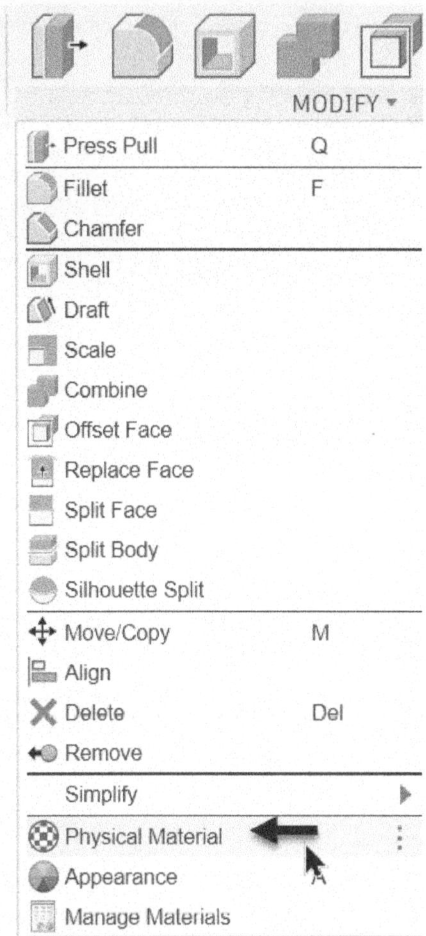

2. Scroll down to the **Library** section in the dialog box and browse the **Plastic** folder to find ABS Plastics material.
3. Click and hold the ABS Plastics material from the library, drag it into your workspace, and drop it directly onto the 3D body of your chess pawn.

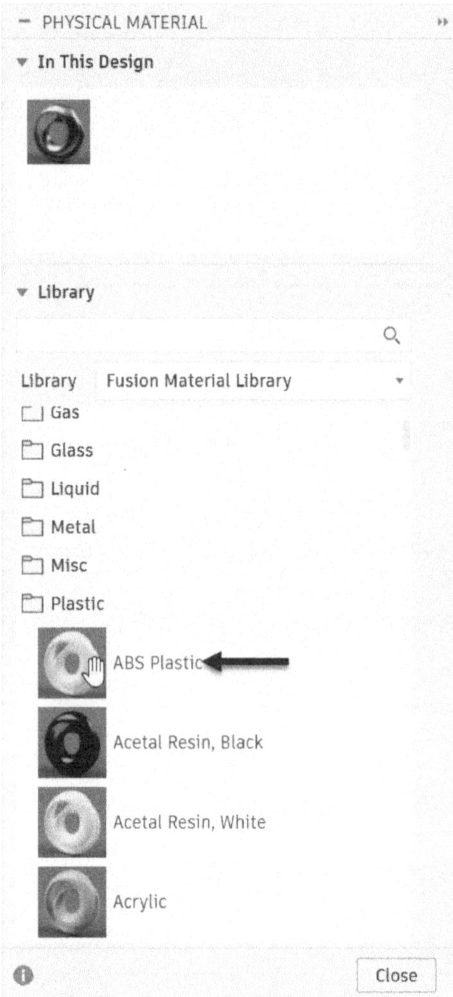

4. Click **Close** at the bottom of the dialog box to finish applying the mass and engineering properties.

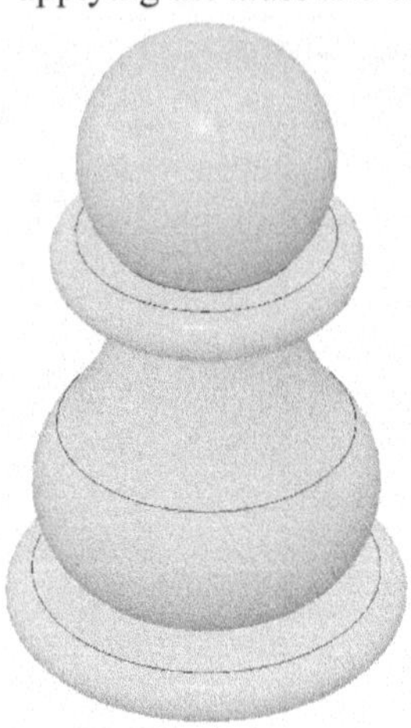

Tutorial 5

In this tutorial, you will create the part shown in figure below.

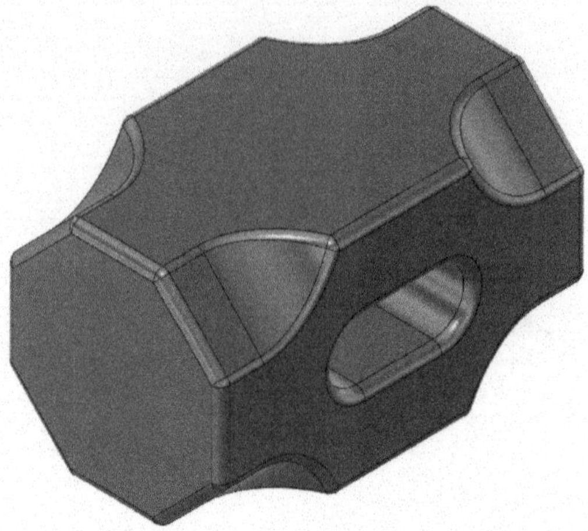

1. On the toolbar, click the **Solid** tab, then click **Create Sketch**.
2. In the graphics window, select the YZ Plane.
3. Go to the **Sketch** toolbar, click **Create**, then select **Rectangle**, then choose **Center Rectangle**.

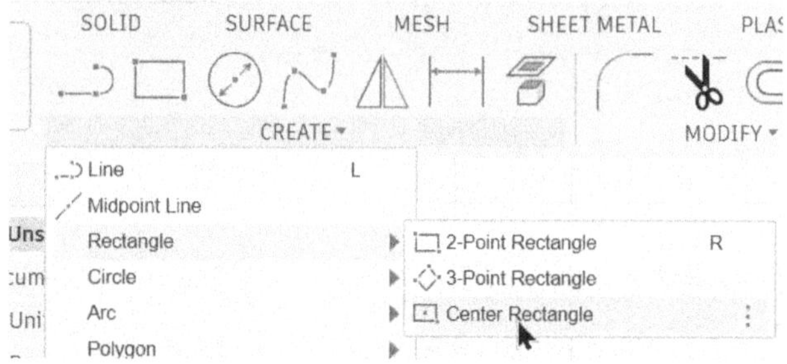

4. Click the sketch origin (0,0) to set the rectangle center point.
5. Move the cursor and click to place the rectangle.

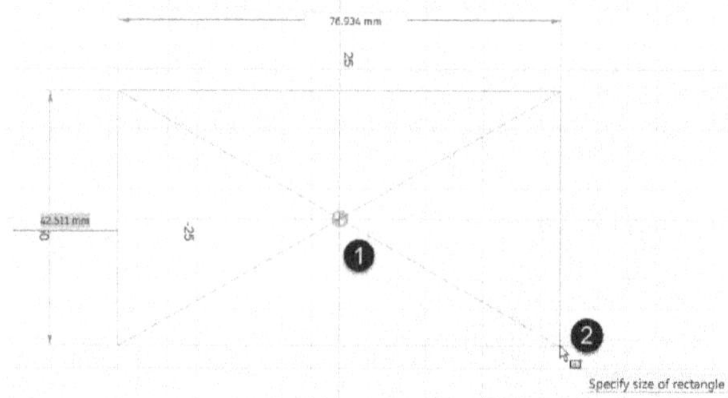

6. Press **D** to activate **Sketch Dimension**.
7. Click the horizontal edge of the rectangle, place the dimension, then enter 120.
8. Click the vertical edge of the rectangle, place the dimension, then enter 70.

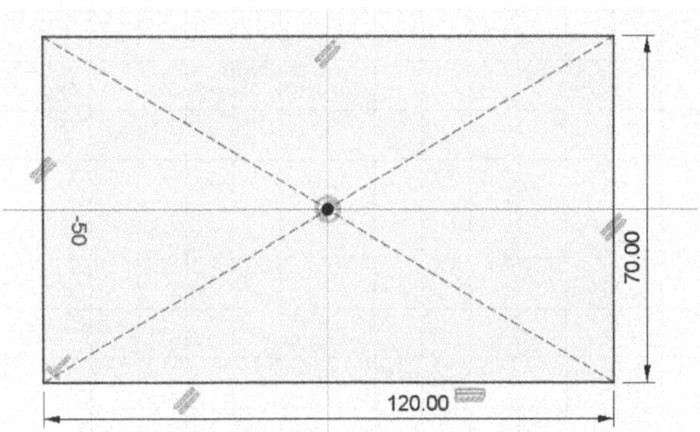

9. Go to the **Sketch** toolbar, click **Create**, select **Slot**, then choose **Center Point Slot**.

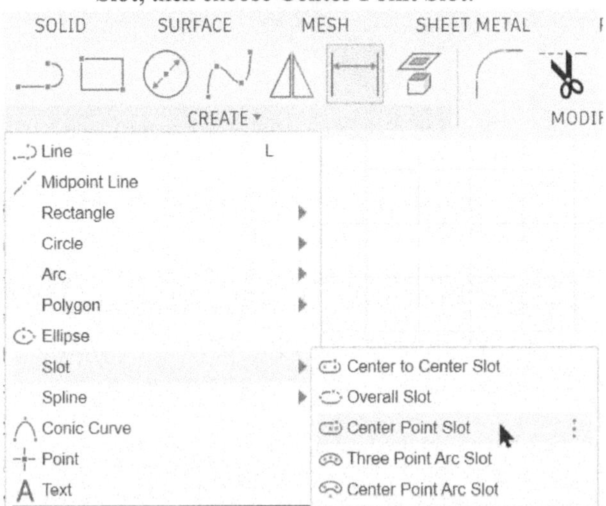

10. Click exactly on the sketch origin to set the midpoint of the slot.
11. Move the cursor horizontally and click to set the center point.
12. Move the cursor perpendicular to the centerline and click to set the slot width.

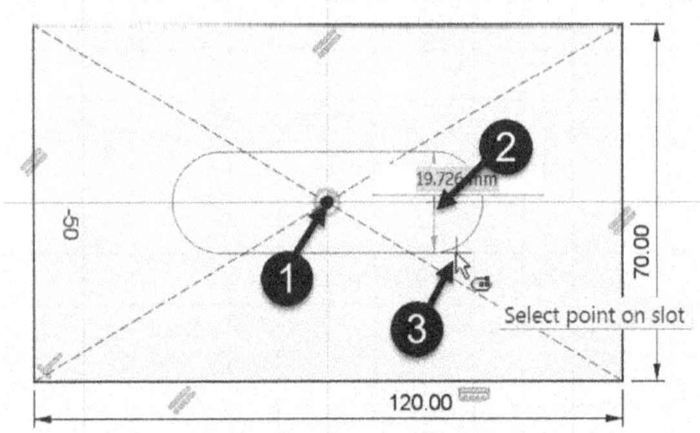

13. Press **D** to activate **Sketch Dimension**.
14. Click one of the slot arc edges and enter 10 to set the arc radius.
15. Click the two slot arc center points and enter 25 to set the center-to-center length.
16. If needed, apply constraints so the line between arc centers is horizontal, and ensure its midpoint is coincident with the origin.

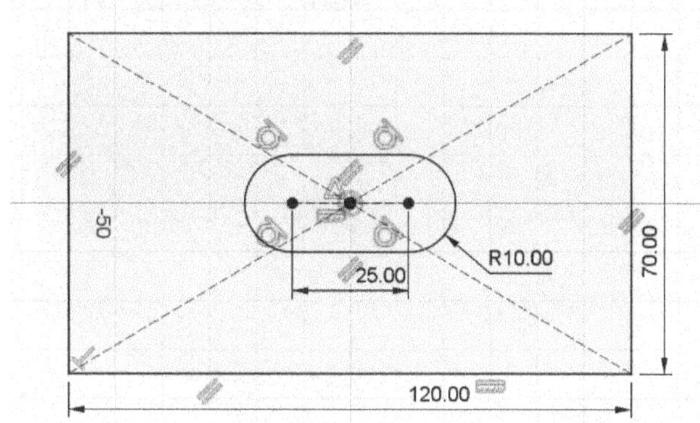

17. Click **Finish Sketch**.
18. Press **E** or click **Create** > **Extrude** on the **Solid** toolbar.
19. Click the profile region between the outer rectangle and the slot opening.

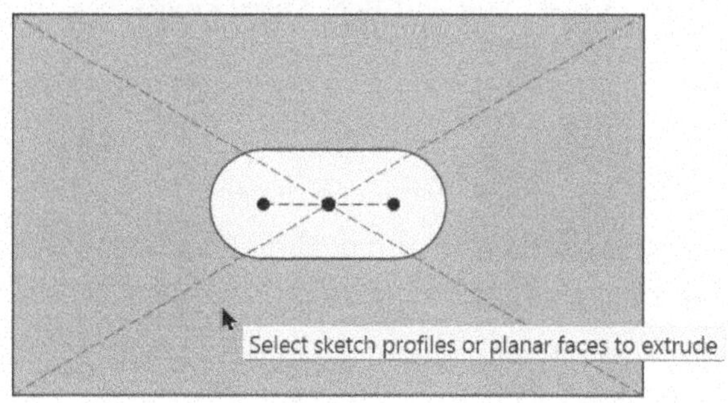

20. In the **Extrude** dialog, set **Direction** to **Symmetric**.
21. Set **Measurement** to **Whole Length**.
22. Set **Distance** to **70**.
23. Click **OK** to create the 3D body.

Creating a Plane Through Three Points

1. On the **Toolbar**, click the **Solid** tab, then open the **Construct** dropdown menu.
2. Click **Plane Through Three Points**.

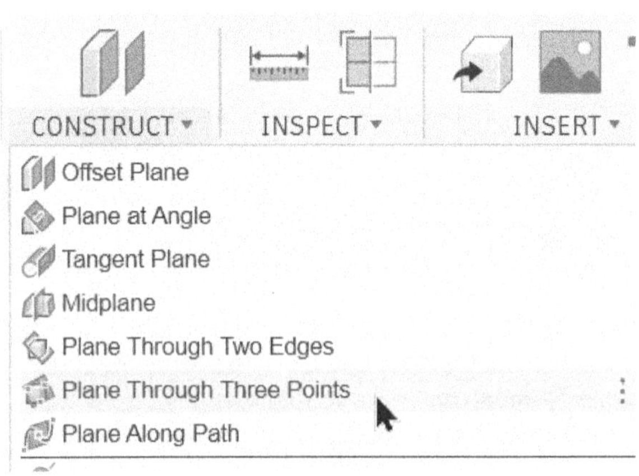

3. In the graphics window, click three distinct vertices on the existing model to define the plane orientation.

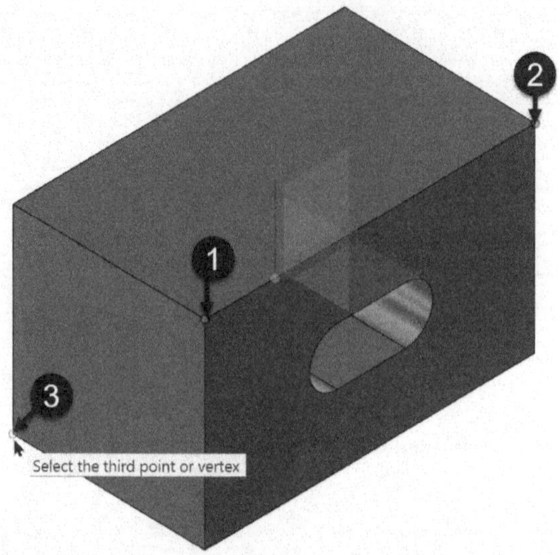

4. Click **OK** to create the new reference plane.
5. Click **Create Sketch**.
6. Select Plane1 to start the sketch and let the view align normal to the plane.
7. Check the **Slice** option on the Sketch Palette.
8. On the Toolbar, click the **Sketch** contextual tab > **Create** panel > **Project/Include** > **Project** .
9. Click on the face of the model, as shown.

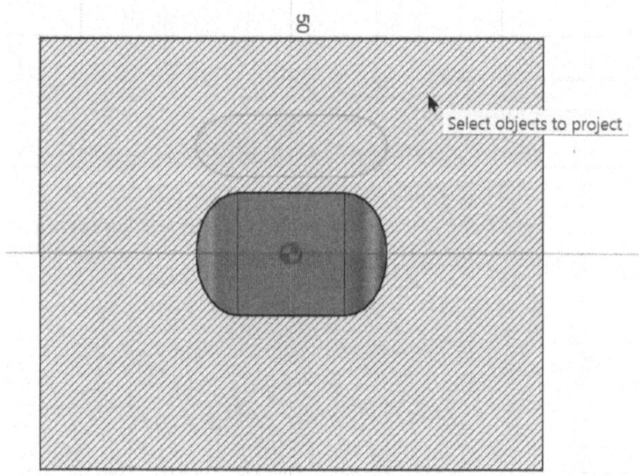

10. Click **OK** on the **Project** dialog.
11. On the **Sketch** toolbar, choose **Rectangle**, then select **2-Point Rectangle** .
12. Select the top-right corner of the model.
13. Click to place the second corner.

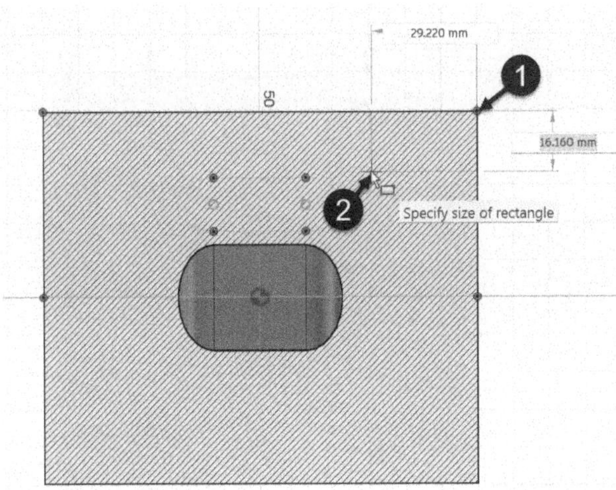

14. On the toolbar, click **Create > Arc > 3-Point Arc**.
15. Select the top-left corner of the rectangle.
16. Click at the location on he lower horizontal line of the rectangle.
17. Move the cursor and click when the Tangent constraint glyph is displayed.

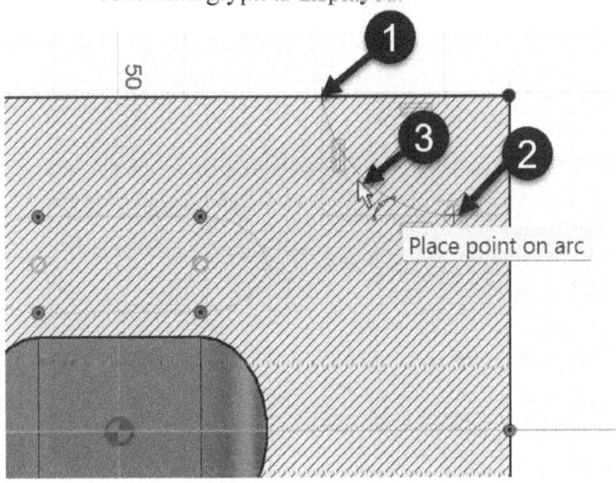

18. On the Toolbar, click the **Sketch** contextual tab > **Modify** panel > **Trim** .
19. Click on the portions of the rectangle, as shown.

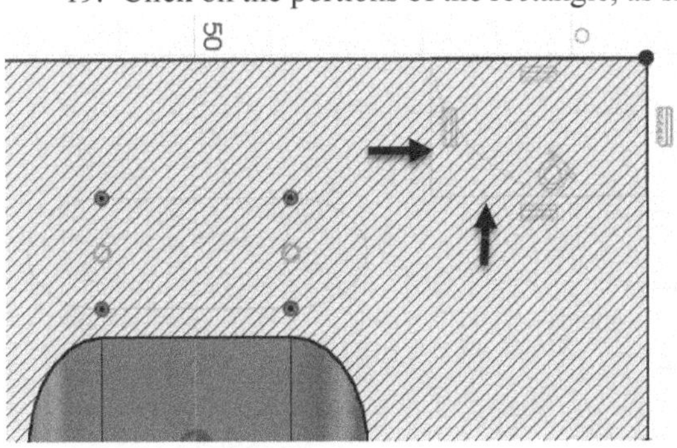

20. Click the **Sketch** tab > **Create** panel > **Mirror**  on the Toolbar; the **Mirror** dialog appears.
21. Select the lines and the arc, as shown.

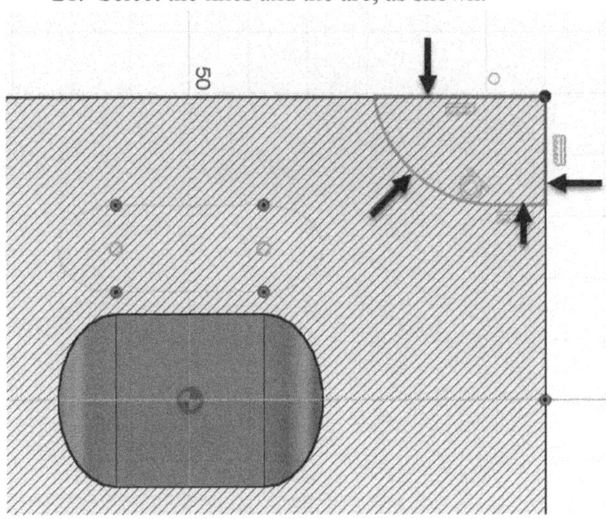

22. Click the **Select** button next to the **Mirror line** option on the **Mirror** dialog, and then select the line passing the origin.

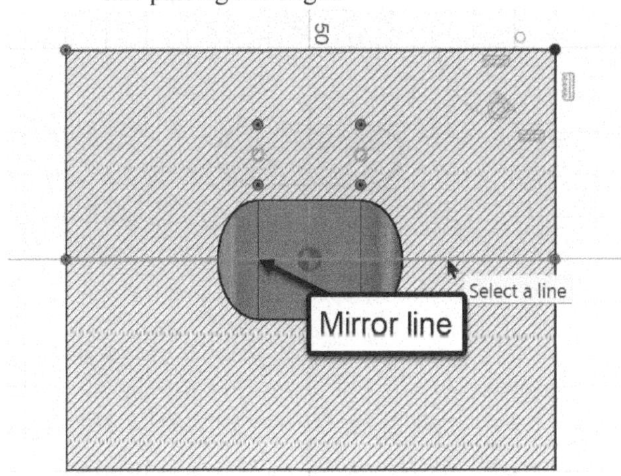

23. Click **OK**.

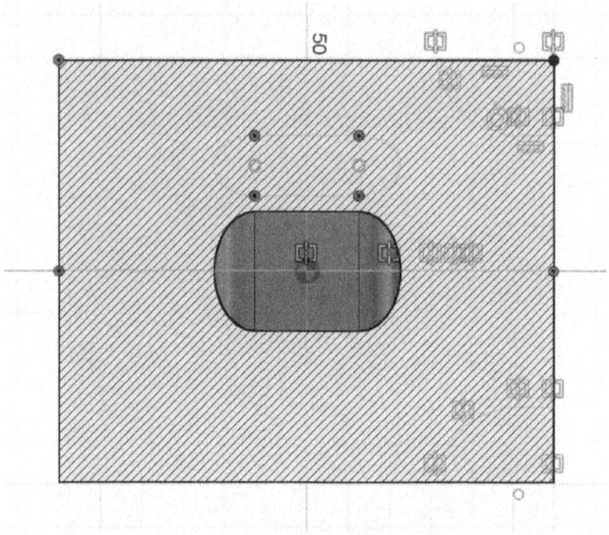

24. Create a vertical construction line from the sketch origin.

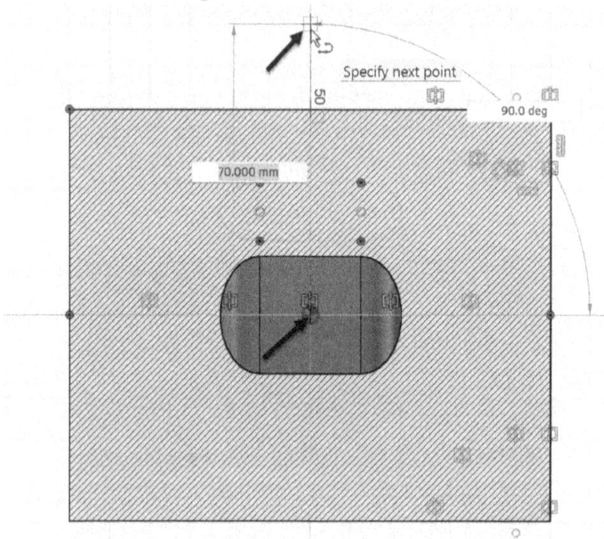

25. Click the **Sketch** tab > **Create** panel > **Mirror**  on the Toolbar; the **Mirror** dialog appears.
26. Select the lines and the arc, as shown.

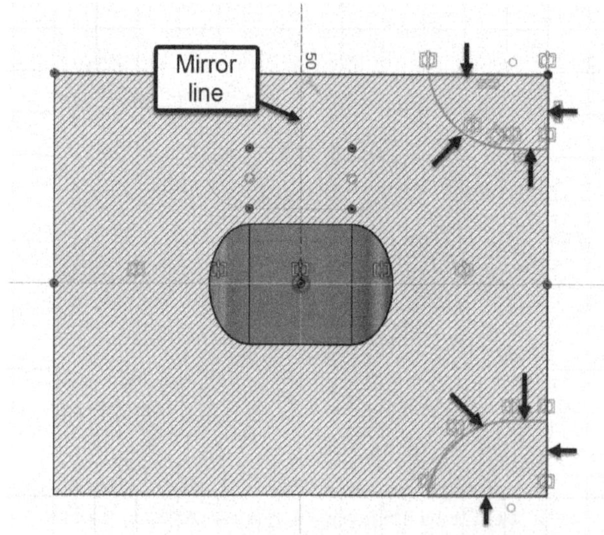

27. Click the **Select** button next to the **Mirror line** option on the **Mirror** dialog, and then select the vertical construction line passing the origin.
28. Click **OK**.

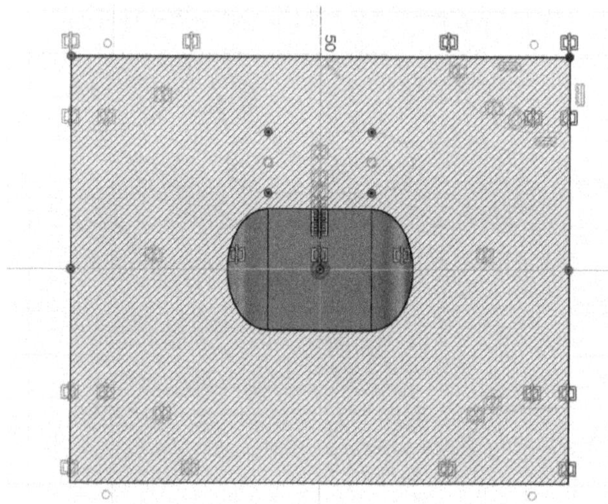

29. Press D to activate **Sketch Dimension**.
30. Add dimensions to the sketch, as shown.

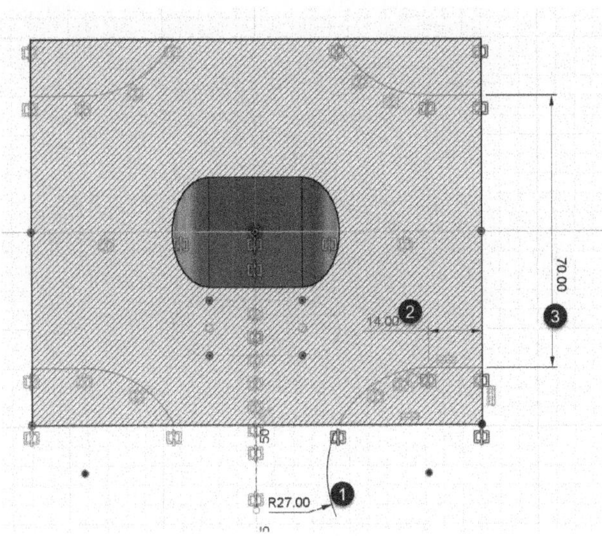

31. Check constraints and sketch status. Fully defined geometry should display as black, and you can press Shift + C to toggle constraint visibility.
32. Click **Finish Sketch**.
33. Press **E** to activate the **Extrude** command.
34. Navigate to the Browser tree on the left side of the workspace. Click the visibility icon next to the **Bodies** folder to hide the existing 3D geometry. This action ensures the solid body does not interfere with your sketch profile selection.

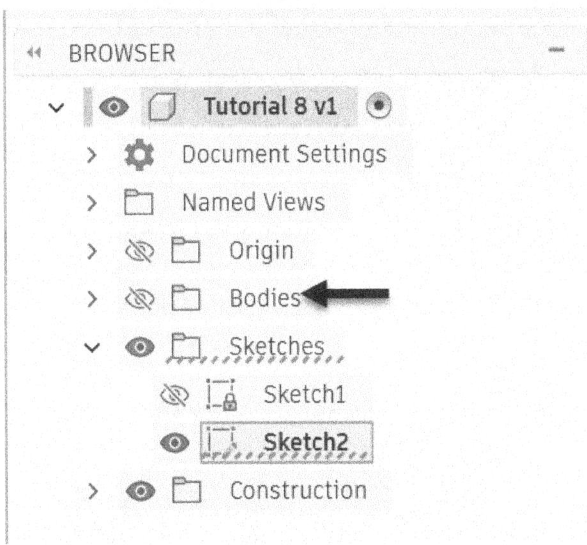

35. Select the four newly created corner profiles.

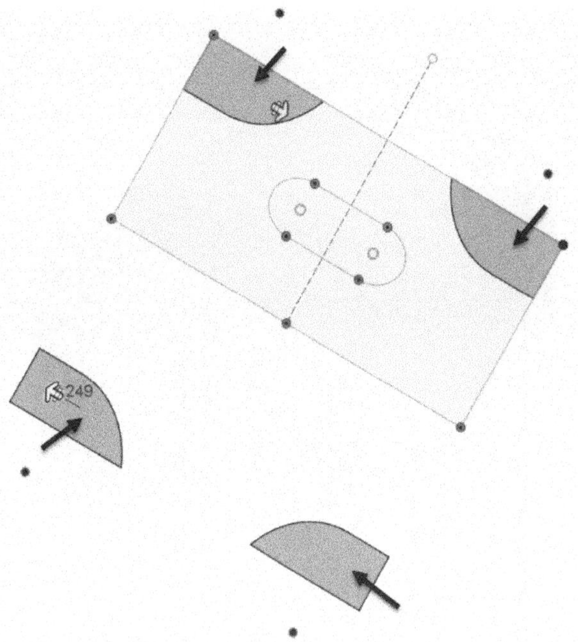

36. Click the visibility icon next to the **Bodies** folder to unhide the existing 3D geometry.

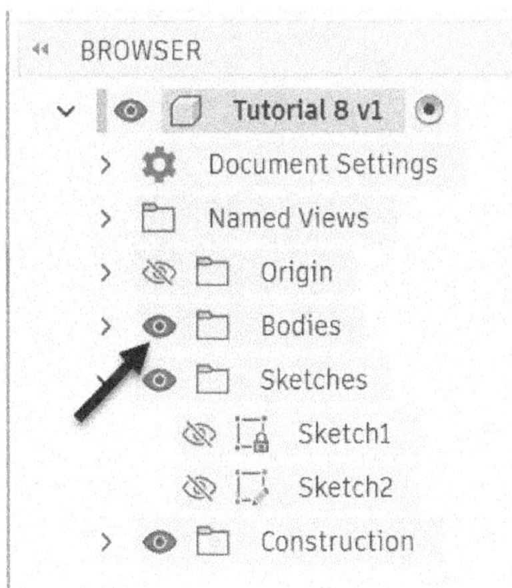

37. Under the **Extent Type** dropdown, select **All** as the termination method.
38. Select **Direction > Symmetric**.
39. Set the **Operation** to **Cut** to remove material from the main body.

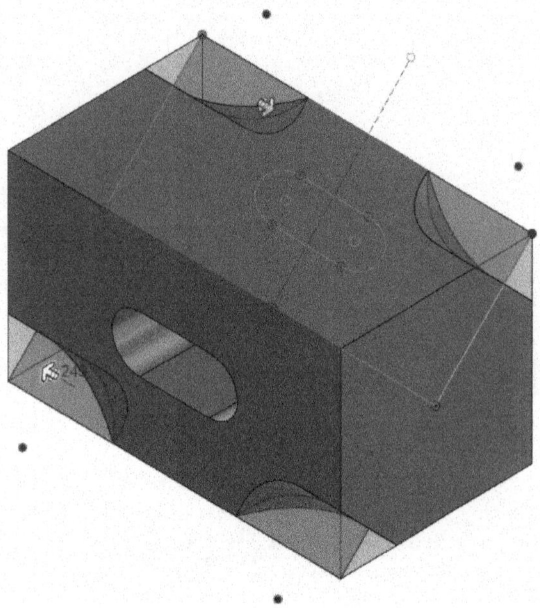

40. Click **OK** to execute the feature and complete the operation.

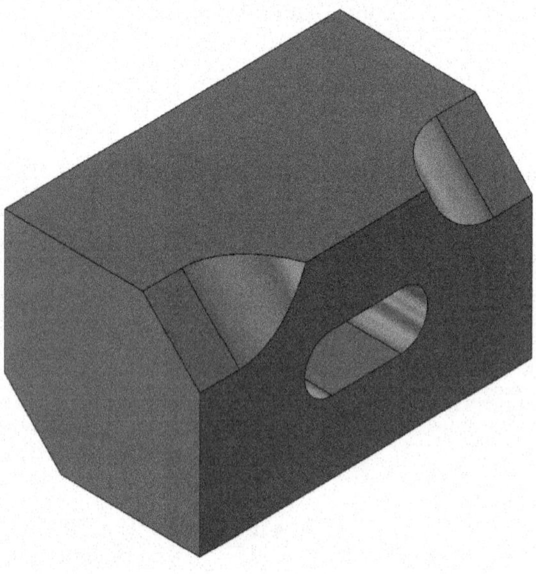

Creating the Mirror Feature

1. On the **Solid** tab of the toolbar, click the **Create** drop-down menu and select **Mirror** .
2. In the **Mirror** dialog box, make sure the **Object Type** is set to **Features**.
3. Select the extruded cut feature from the solid body.
4. Next, click the **Select** button next to **Mirror Plane** in the dialog box.
5. To choose your mirror plane, expand the Origin folder in the browser on the left and select the YZ plane.

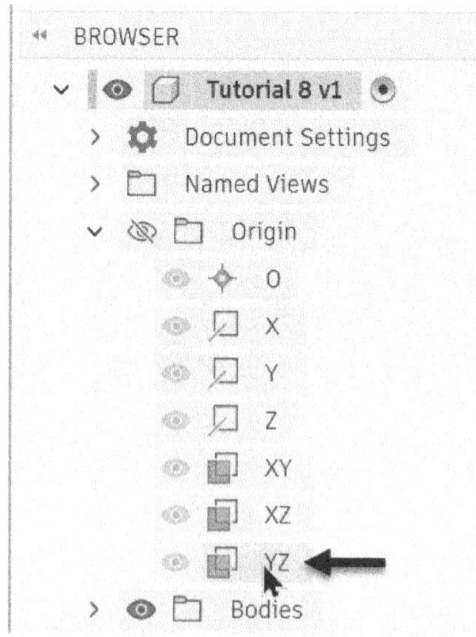

6. Click **OK** to mirror the extruded cut feature.

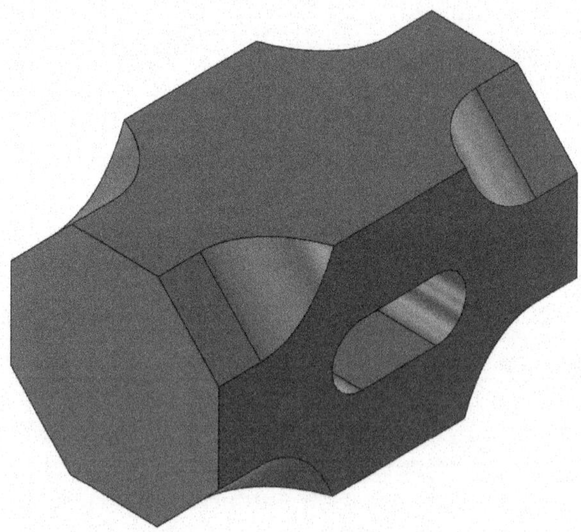

Apply Feature Fillets Using the Timeline

1. Direct your attention to the parametric timeline located at the bottom of the Fusion 360 interface. This timeline displays a sequential record of all operations.
2. Press and hold the **Ctrl** key (Windows) or **Cmd** key (Mac) and click the three features the timeline.

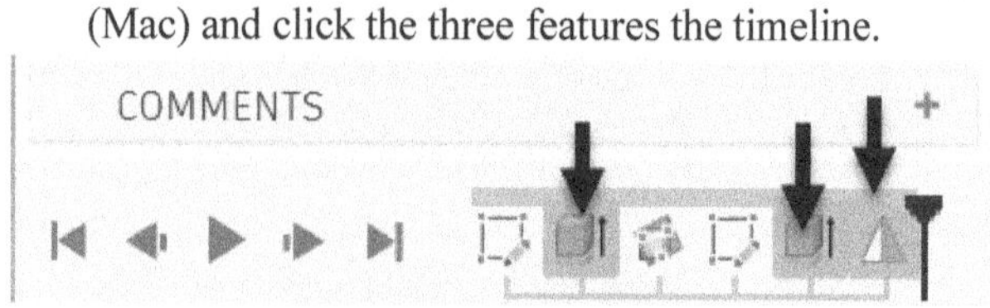

3. With the timeline features highlighted, navigate to the main Toolbar under the **Solid** tab.
4. In the **Modify** panel, select the **Fillet** tool. By

preselecting the features directly from the timeline, Fusion 360 automatically targets all the 3D solid edges generated by those specific operations. This eliminates the need to manually click each edge in the graphics window.

5. The **Fillet** dialog box will appear. Type exactly **3 mm** into the radius field.

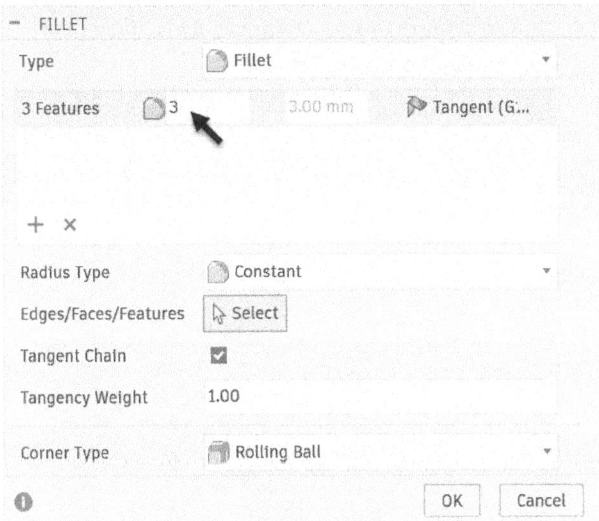

6. Click **OK** to execute the command. The system will instantly apply a uniform 3 mm round to all edges associated with your selected timeline features.

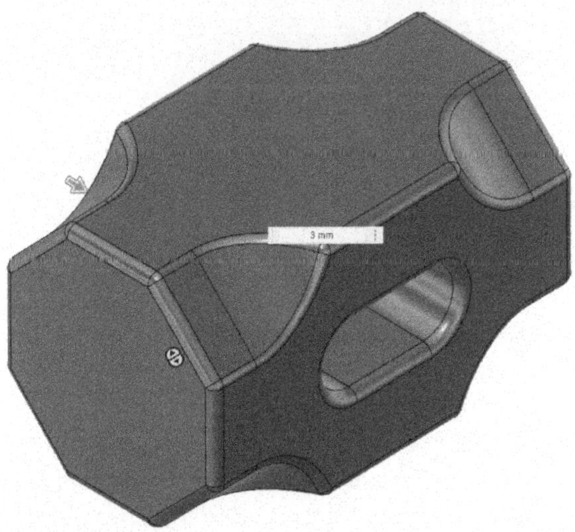

Tutorial 6

In this tutorial, you will create the part shown in figure below.

Create User Parameters

1. On the main Toolbar under the **Solid** tab, locate the **Modify** panel. Next, select **Change Parameters**.

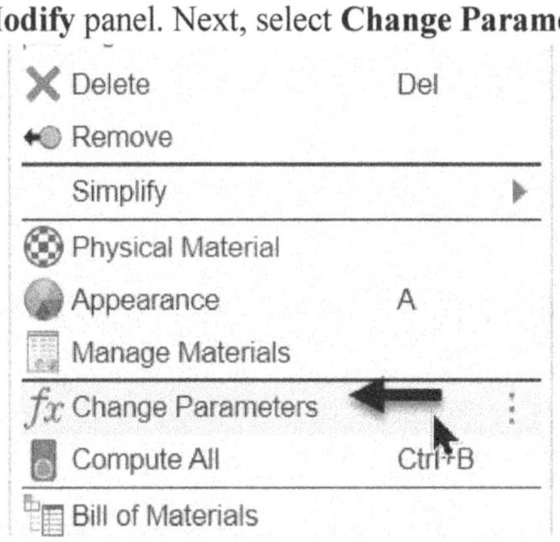

2. In the **Parameters** dialog box, click the **plus** icon to add a new parameter.

3. Click **OK** on the **Parametric Text** dialog.

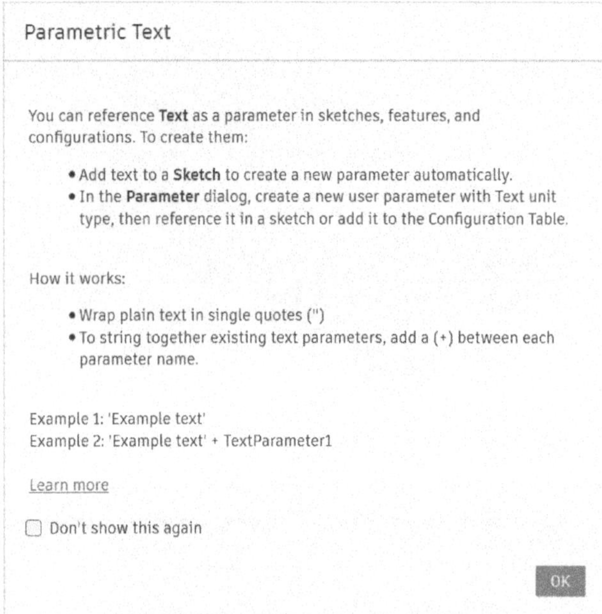

4. In the **Name** field, type **a**.
5. In the **Expression** field, type **4** mm.
6. Click **OK**.

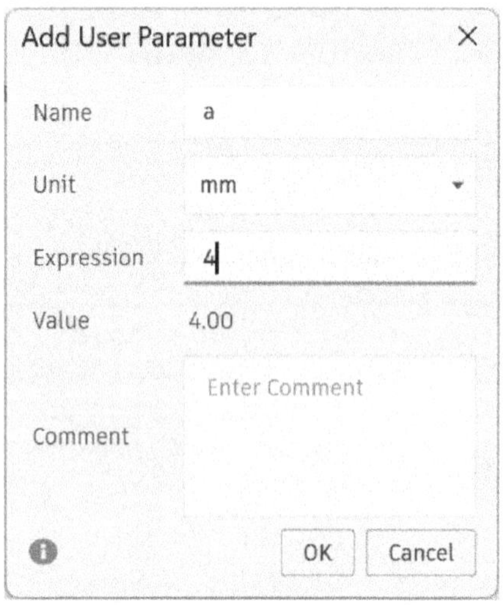

7. Likewise, create two more parameters:

- Name: b, Expression: 83 mm.
- Name: w, Expression: 11 mm.

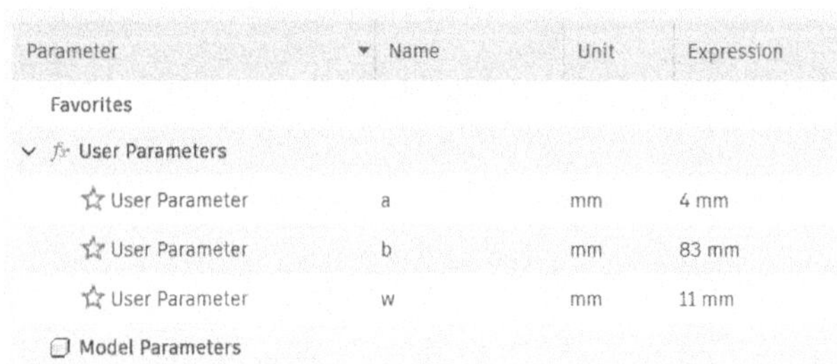

Parameter	Name	Unit	Expression
Favorites			
User Parameters			
User Parameter	a	mm	4 mm
User Parameter	b	mm	83 mm
User Parameter	w	mm	11 mm
Model Parameters			

8. Click **OK** to save and close the dialog

Create the Base Sketch

1. Click **Create Sketch** and select the Front plane in the graphics window.
2. Select the **Line** tool. Draw a vertical line downward from the origin. Select this line and press the X key to convert it into a construction line. This line will act as the central axis of revolution.

Next, you need to draw the closed geometric profile of the pot section on one side of the construction line.

3. Draw a horizontal line starting from the construction line extending outward to form the inner bottom floor.
4. Draw an angled line upward to form the main inner wall of the pot.
5. Draw a horizontal line outward for the top lip.

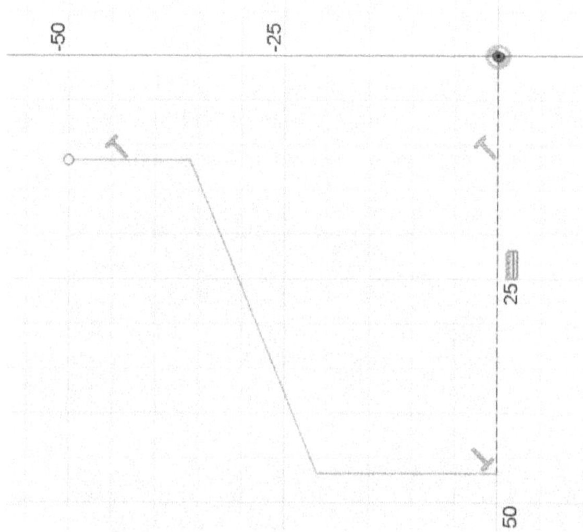

6. Navigate to the **Sketch** toolbar, open the **Modify** panel, and select **Fillet**.
7. Select the corner points of the sketch.
8. Set the radius to 6 mm. The sharp corners will now be replaced with smooth curved transitions. This is your primary path line, ready for offsetting.

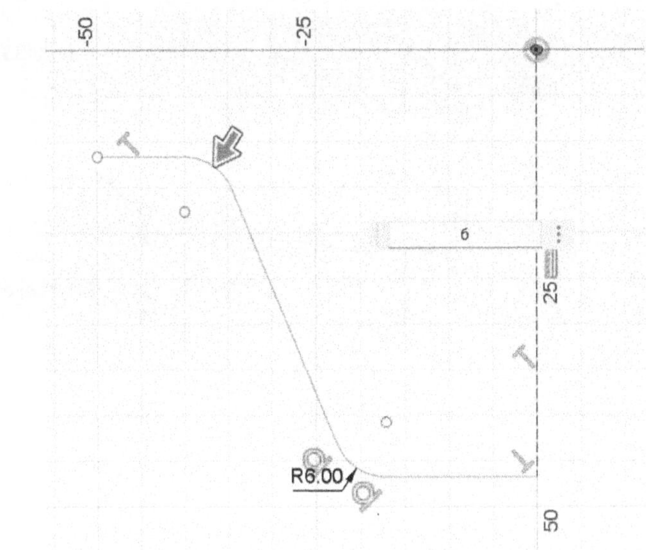

9. Press the **D** key to activate the **Sketch Dimension** tool.
10. Select the central axis and the center point of the upper fillet.
11. Right-click and select **Diameter Dimension**.

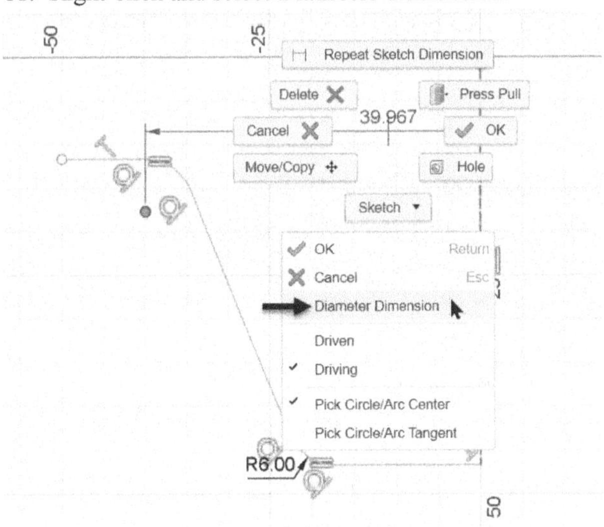

12. Place the dimension. In the dimension input field, type b and press ENTER to apply the 83 mm parameter.

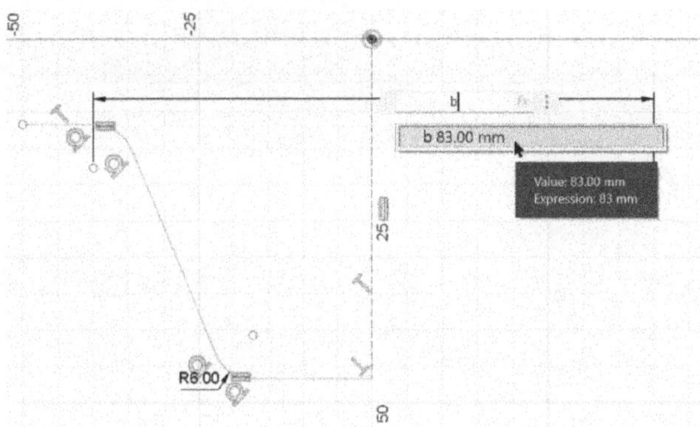

13. Navigate to the **Sketch** toolbar, open the **Create** menu, and select **Offset**.
14. Click the primary path line you just created, which includes the three lines and two fillets. Fusion 360 will highlight the entire connected chain.
15. Move the cursor to the inside of the profile and type **a** into the **Distance** field to set the offset distance. This value creates the wall thickness of the pot.
16. Click the **Flip** icon.

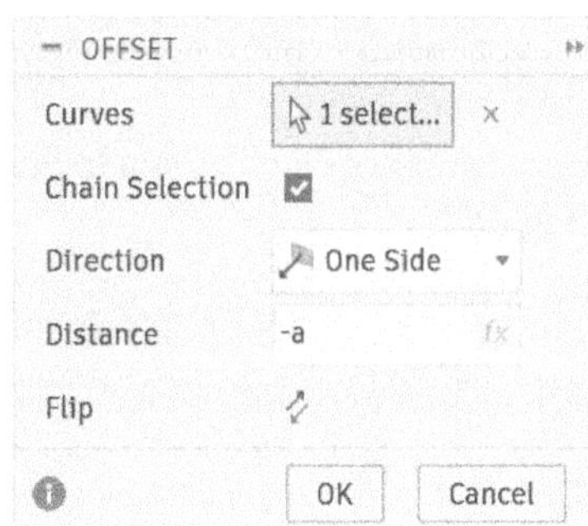

17. Click **OK**.

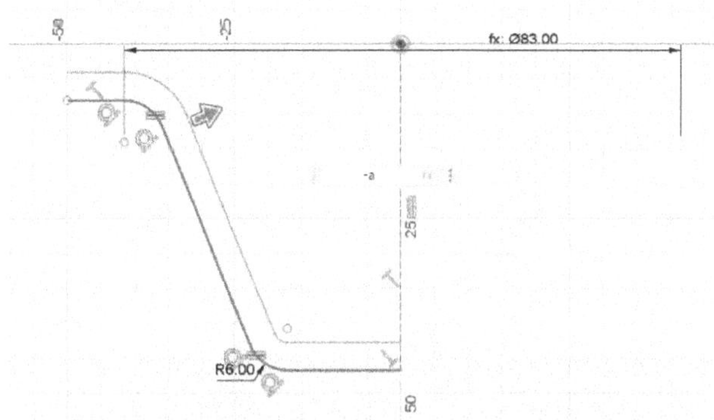

18. Connect the outer wall back to the starting point at the central axis to fully close the profile. A correctly closed profile will highlight in light blue.

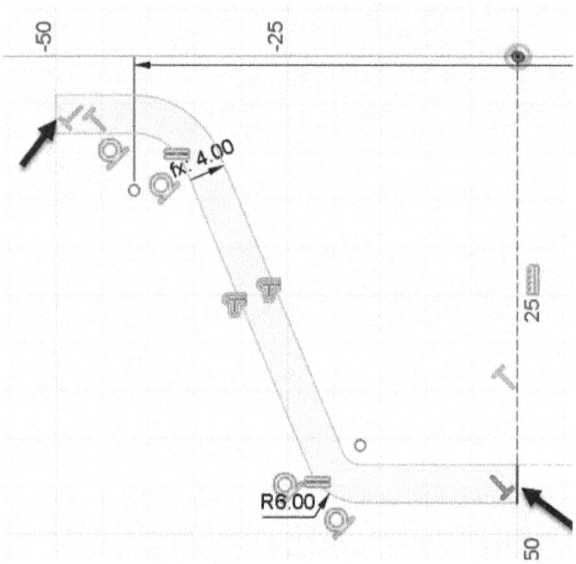

19. Press the **D** key to activate the **Sketch Dimension** tool.
20. Select the angled wall and the vertical construction line to place an angle dimension. Set this value exactly to 9 degrees.
21. Apply a vertical dimension of 63 mm to define the total height of the pot wall.
22. Apply a horizontal dimension of 1 mm to the outer edge of the top lip.

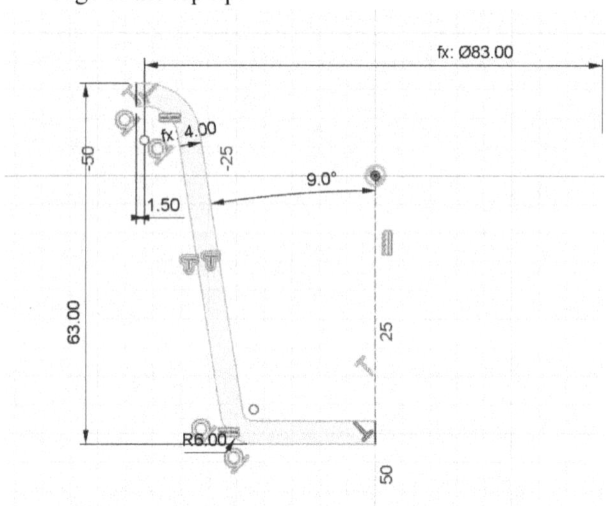

23. Click the **Horizontal/Vertical** icon on the **Constraints** panel, and then select the two points, as shown.

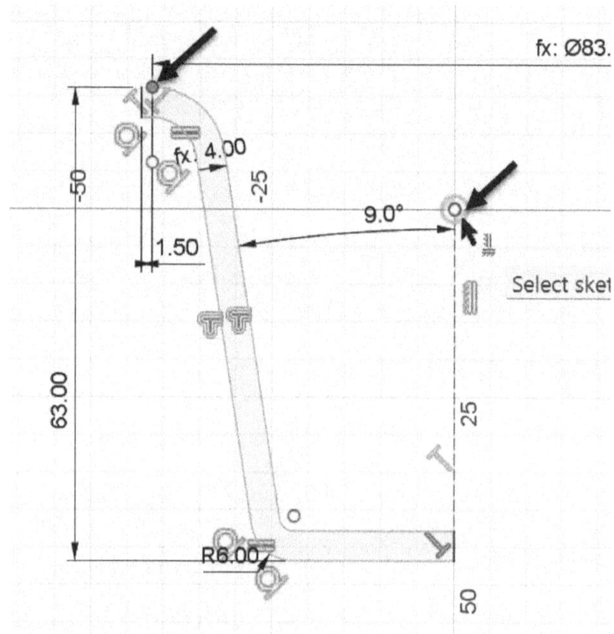

24. Ensure all lines are fully constrained and appear black. Click **Finish Sketch**.

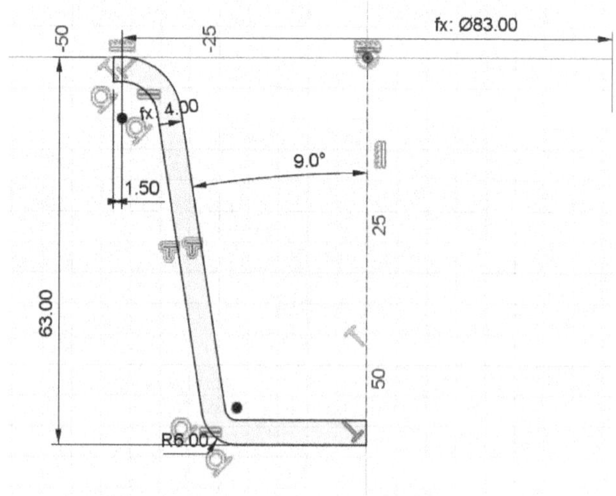

Create the Revolve Feature

1. Press the **R** key on the keyboard, or go to the **Create** panel and select **Revolve**.
2. In the **Revolve** dialog box, select the closed sketch profile you just created.
3. For the **Axis** selection, click the vertical construction line drawn in the sketch.
4. Verify that the operation type is set to **New Body** and the angle is set to 360 degrees.
5. Click **OK** to generate the 3D parametric pot model.

Apply a Rectangular Pattern

1. On the **Solid** tab, open the **Create** panel menu and select **Pattern**, then choose **Rectangular Pattern**.

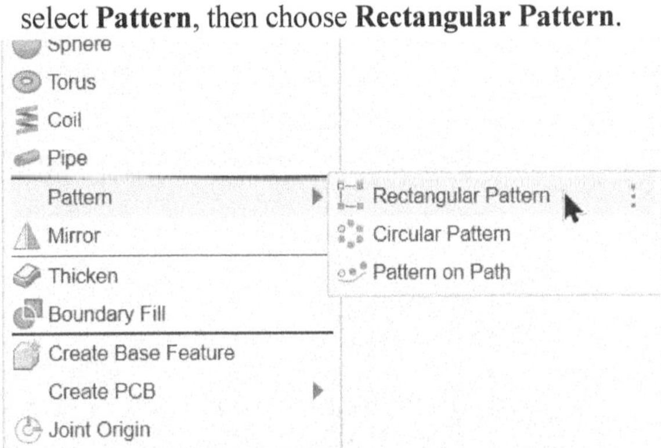

2. In the **Pattern** dialog box, set the **Pattern Type** to **Bodies**.
3. Click the revolved pot body in the graphics window to select it as the pattern source.
4. For the Axes selection, click the X axis from the **Origin** folder to define the primary direction.

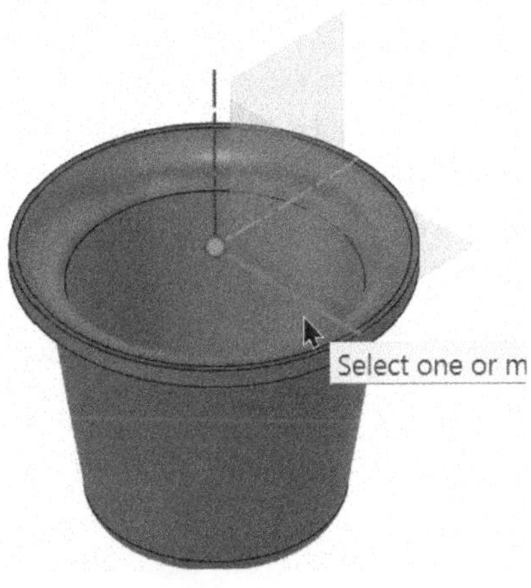

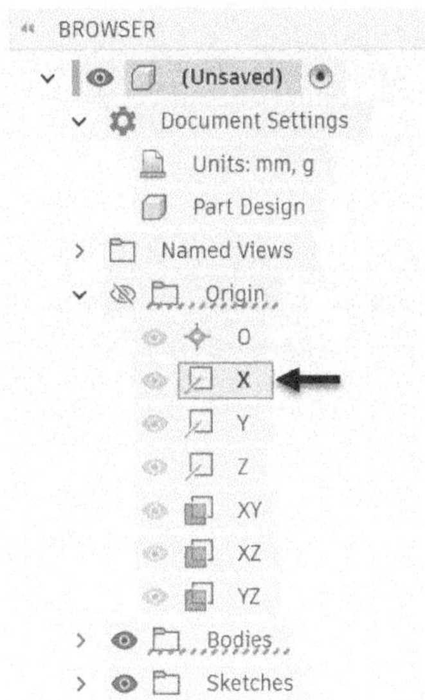

5. In the dialog box, ensure the **Distribution** dropdown is set to **Spacing**. This ensures the distance value applies between each item, matching the reference geometry.
6. Configure the first direction using the primary set of input fields:
   - In the **Quantity** field, enter **2**.
   - In the **Distance** field, type the expression b+w (which evaluates to 94 mm).
7. Configure the second direction using the secondary set of input fields located directly below the first:
   - In the **Quantity** field, enter 4.
   - In the **Distance** field, type the expression w+b (which evaluates to 94 mm).

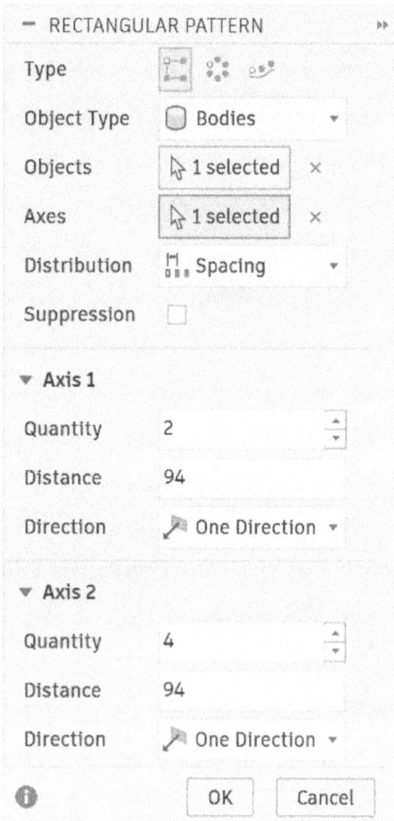

8. Confirm the graphical preview displays a grid of 8 total pot bodies (2 columns by 4 rows).

9. Click **OK** to finalize the rectangular pattern.

Creating the Top Extruded Feature

1. On the **Solid** tab, click **Create Sketch**.
2. Select the Top plane or the flat top face of the rectangular pattern result as the sketch plane.
3. Navigate to **Create > Project / Include > Project**. Select the top circular edges of all 8 pot bodies to project them into the active sketch. This will stamp 8 precise circles onto the sketch plane, each centered on a pot.

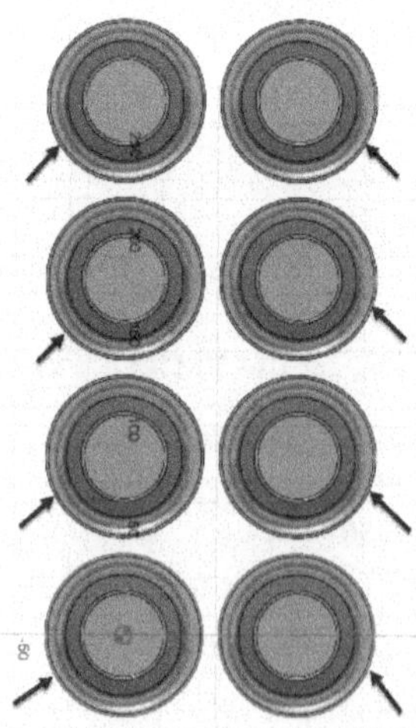

4. Click **OK**.
5. Navigate to **Create > Rectangle > Two Point Rectangle** and draw a large rectangle enclosing all 8 projected circles.

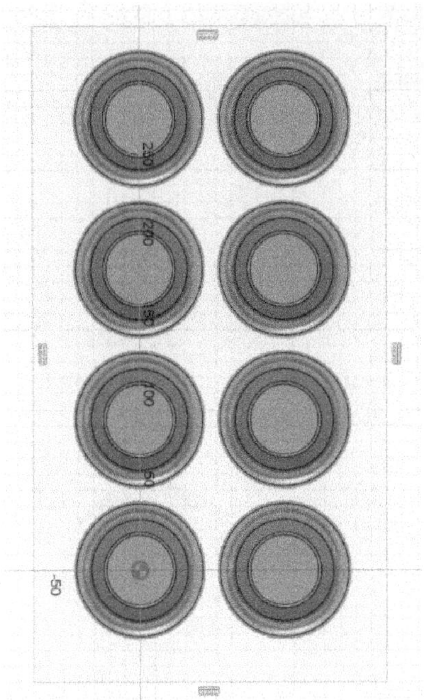

6. On the **Sketch** toolbar, click **Create > Line** (or press L) to activate the **Line** tool.
7. On the **Sketch Palette**, in the **Options** section, click the **Construction** icon (it looks like a dashed line) next to Linetype, or press X on your keyboard.
8. Create four lines connecting the porojected circular edges and the rectangle, as shown.

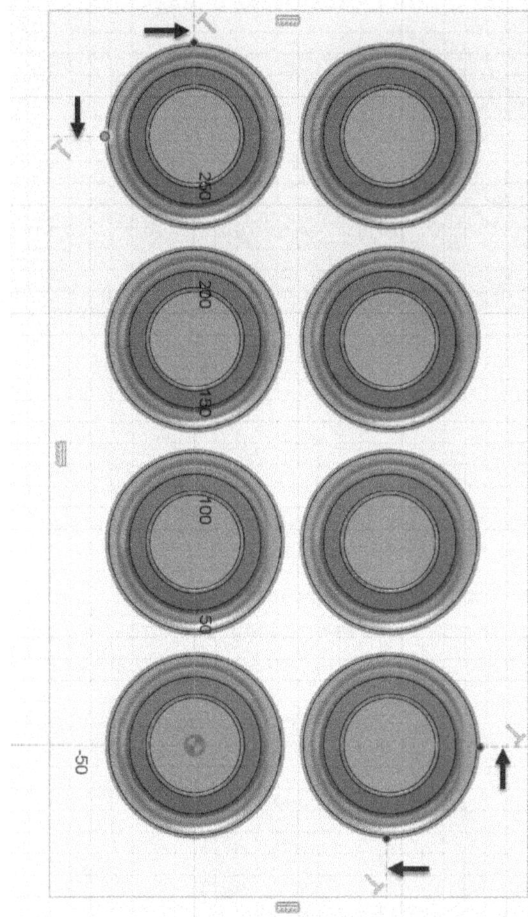

9. Select the **Sketch** toolbar and choose **Constraints > Horizontal/Vertical**.
10. Click the center point of a projected circle and endpoint of the horizontal construction line.
11. Select **Constraints > Horizontal/Vertical**.
12. Click the same center point and the endpoint of the vertical construction line.

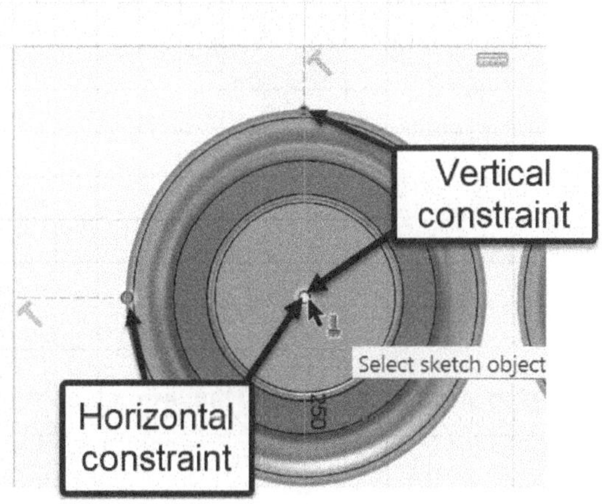

13. Repeat this Horizontal and Vertical constraint pair for bottom right circle, as shown.

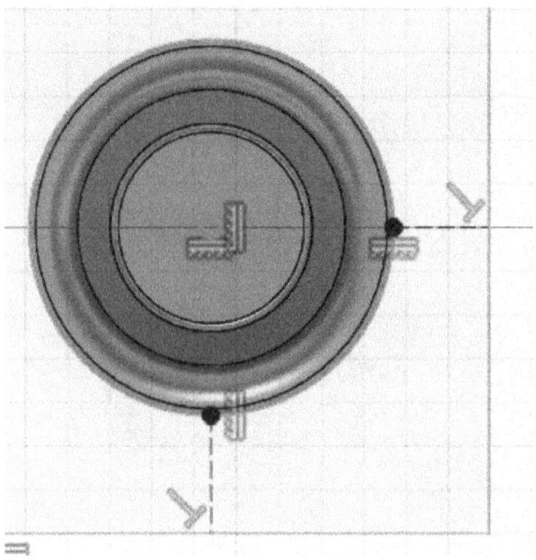

14. On the Toolbar, click the **Sketch** tab > **Constraints** panel > **Equal**.
15. Select the two horizontal construction lines.
16. Select the two vertical construction lines.
17. Select the anyone of the vertical and horizontal construction lines.

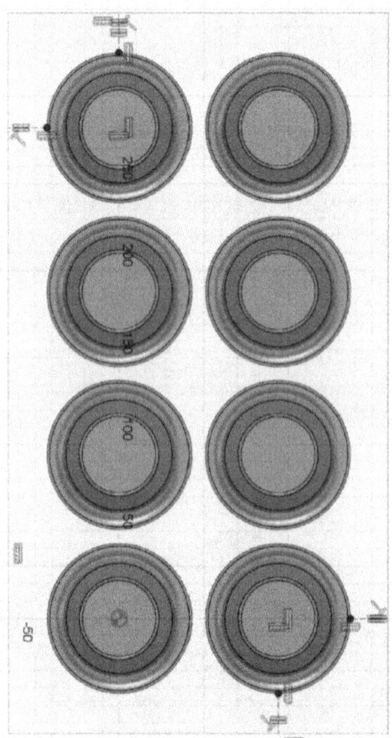

18. Press **D** to activate the **Sketch Dimension** tool.
19. Click one of the horizontal construction lines to dimension its length. In the dimension input field, type **w** and press Enter. This links the horizontal spacing between circle and rectangle to the parameter w (11 mm).

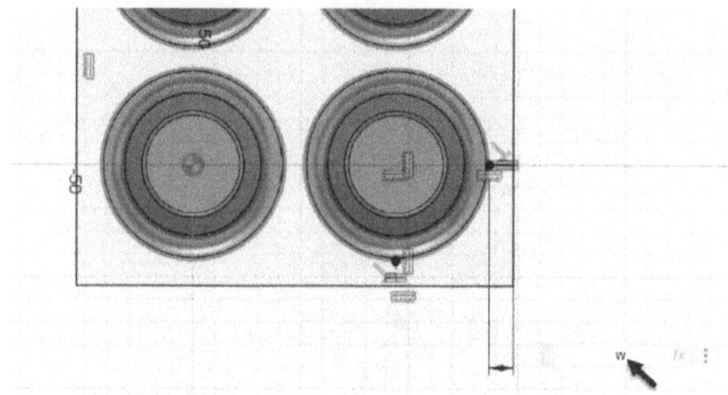

20. Navigate to **Create > Fillet** within the **Sketch** toolbar. Click each corner of the rectangle and enter a radius of 10 mm to create the rounded tray outline.

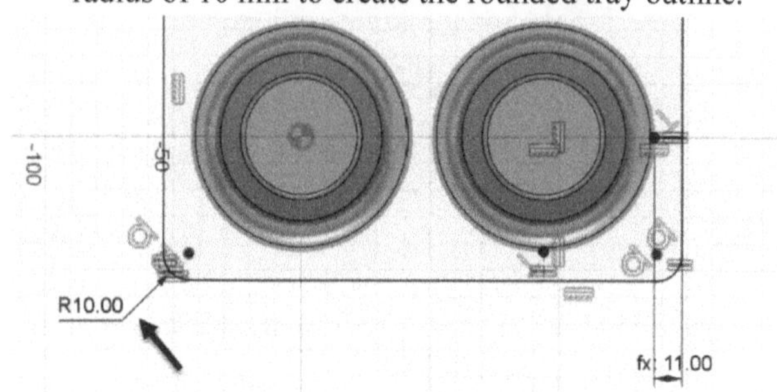

21. Verify the sketch is fully constrained and all lines display as black. Click **Finish Sketch**.
22. Press **E** on the keyboard to open the **Extrude** command.
23. In the **Extrude** dialog box, click the **Profile** selection field and select the closed tray outline in the graphics window. Fusion 360 will automatically detect the region between the rounded rectangle boundary and the 8 circular cutouts as the valid extrudable area. The circles will remain as open holes through the tray floor.
24. Set the **Start** dropdown to **Profile Plane**. This ensures the extrusion begins exactly at the sketch plane rather than at any offset position.
25. Set the **Direction** dropdown to **One Side**.
26. Click the **Flip** button in the dialog box, or drag the arrow in the graphics window downward,
27. In the **Distance** field, type **-a** and press Enter. This links the tray floor thickness to parameter a (4 mm). Make sure that the arrow points downwards to confirm that the extrusion direction points below the sketch plane. The preview must show material generating downward, not upward into the pot bodies.

If you later update **a** under **Modify > Change Parameters**, the tray thickness will update automatically.

28. Set the **Operation** dropdown to **Join** so the tray base merges with the existing revolved pot bodies into one unified solid.
29. Verify the preview in the graphics window shows a flat tray floor 4 mm thick sitting below the sketch plane, with 8 circular openings aligned to the pot tops.

30. Click **OK** to execute the extrusion and complete the tray base geometry.
31. On the **Solid** tab, open the **Modify** panel and select **Fillet**.
32. Click just one edge along the top outer perimeter of the tray base. Because **Tangent Chain** is active, Fusion 360 will automatically select the entire continuous outer boundary loop.

33. Rotate the model to view the bottom face of the tray.
34. Click one edge along the bottom outer perimeter of the extrude feature to instantly select the entire bottom outer boundary loop.

35. In the **Fillet** dialog box, set the radius to **1** mm.
36. Confirm the preview shows a smooth 1 mm round along all selected top edges.
37. Click **OK** to apply.

Tutorial 7

In this tutorial, you will create the part shown in figure below.

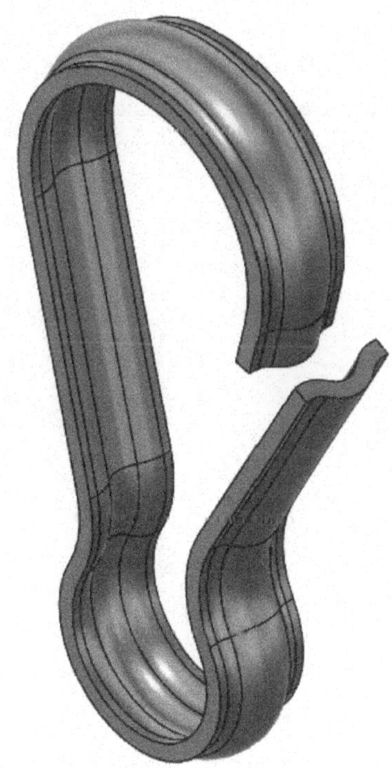

Creating the Path of the Sweep feature

1. Open Autodesk Fusion 360 and click on **Create Sketch** in the **Solid** toolbar.
2. Select the XZ Plane to begin your drawing.
3. Press the L key for the **Line** tool, click the **Construction** icon in the Sketch Palette, and draw a vertical centerline starting from the origin.
4. Draw a horizontal centerline at the origin, draw a second horizontal construction line from the top endpoint of the vertical construction line, press the **D**

key for **Sketch Dimension**, and set the vertical distance between them to 26.00.

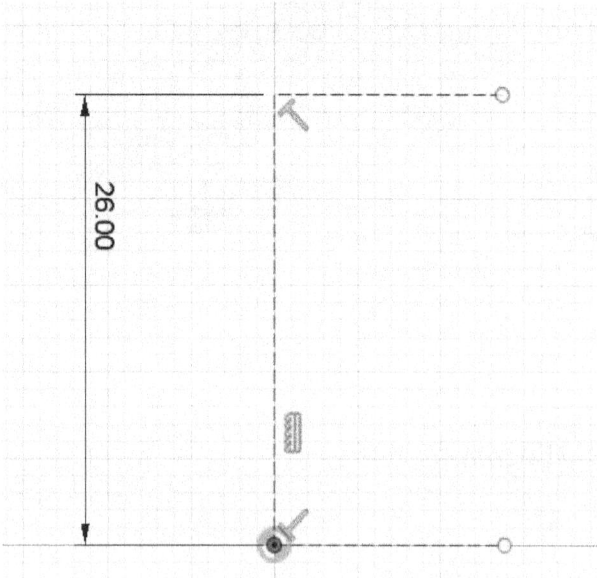

5. Disable **Construction** in the Sketch Palette, press the **C** key to activate the **Center Diameter Circle** tool, and draw a **14.00** diameter circle at the origin.
6. Press the **C** key again and draw a **20.00** diameter circle centered exactly at the intersection of the upper horizontal construction line and the vertical centerline.

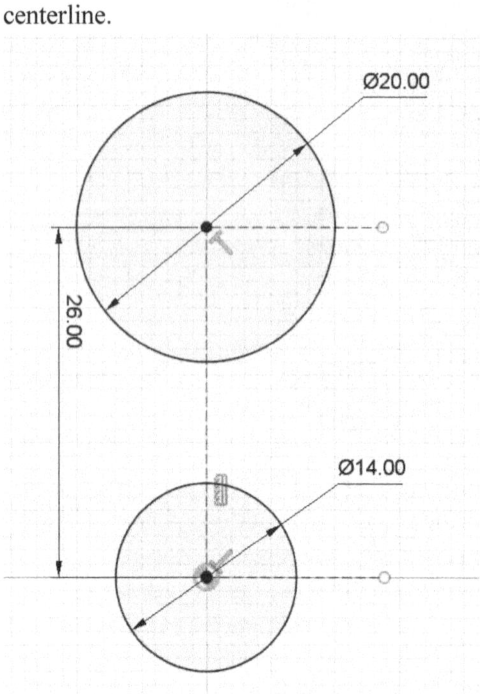

7. Press the L key to activate the **Line** tool and click exactly on the left intersection point where the top horizontal centerline meets the top Ø20.00 circle.
8. Drag your cursor downwards and to the right, clicking a point anywhere on the upper left curve of the bottom Ø14.00 circle.

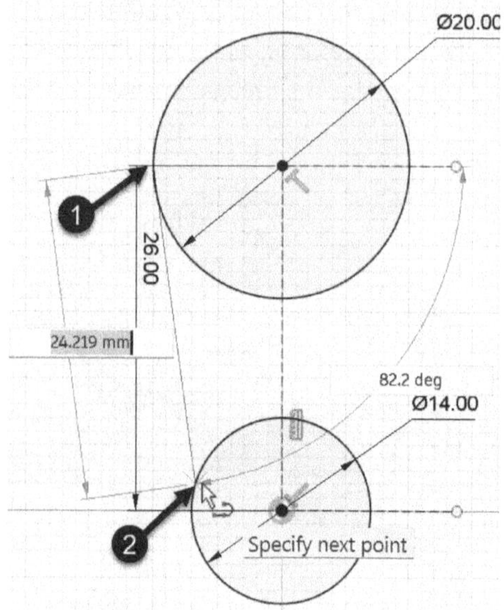

9. Press the L key to activate the Line tool again, click on the right side of the top circle.
10. Drag your cursor straight down from this point.
11. Click to place the line.

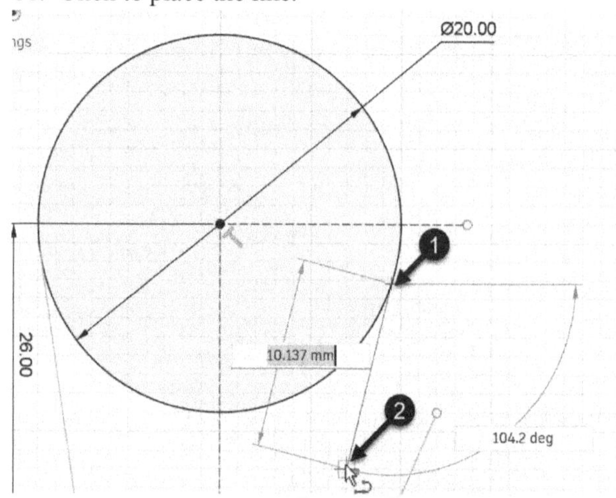

12. With the **Line** tool still active, click on the top right-side of the bottom circle.
13. Drag your cursor upward and to the right, and the click to create the line.

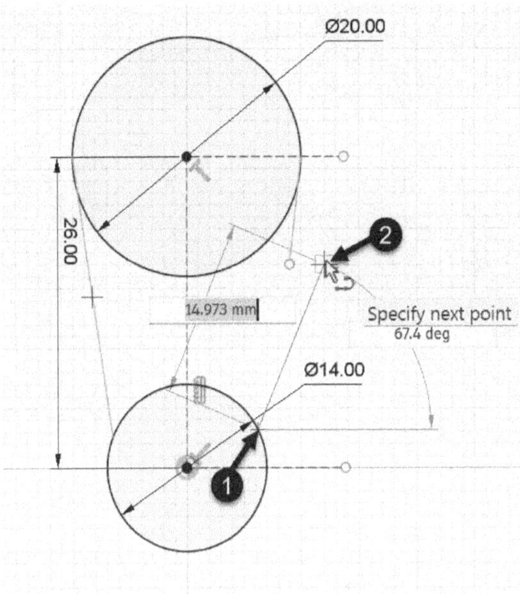

14. Add the **Tangent** constraints between the top circle and the lines connected to it.

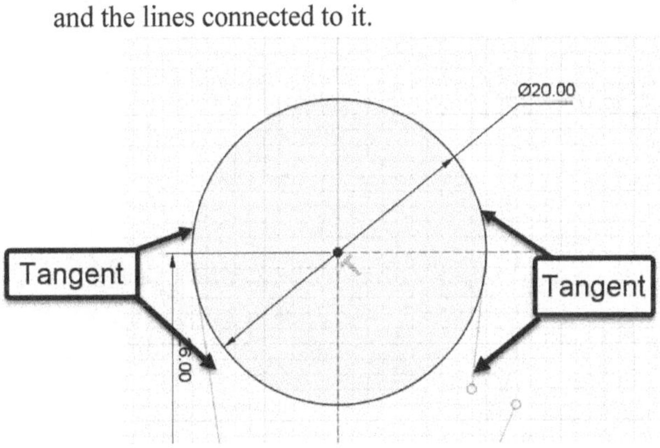

15. Press the **T** key to activate the **Trim** tool.
16. Click on the entities to trim, as shown.

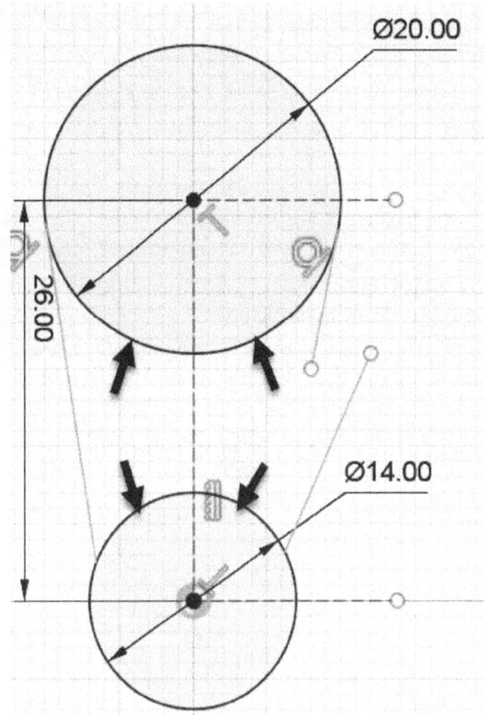

17. On the **Sketch** tab of the Toolbar, click **Modify** > **Fillet**.
18. Click on the intersection points between the lower arc and the lines, as shown.

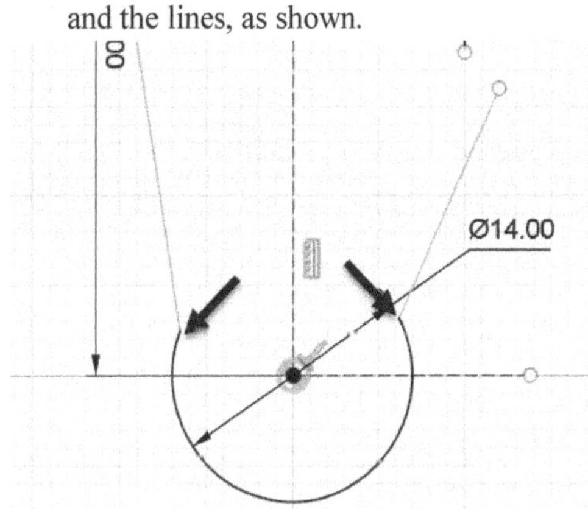

19. Type **5** in the fillet radius box and press ENTER.

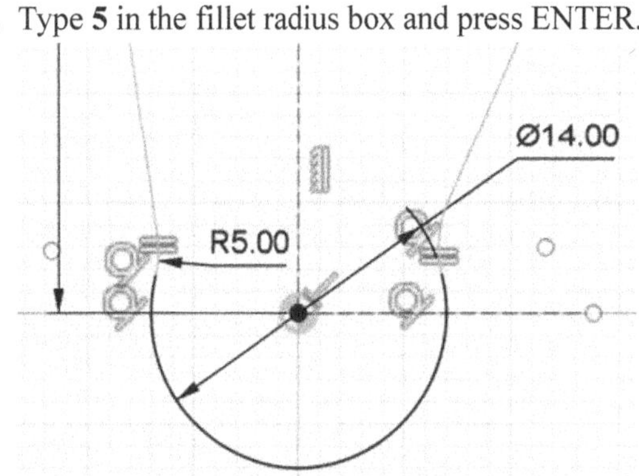

20. Press the **D** key for **Sketch Dimension**.

21. Click the left angled line, then click the vertical centerline.
22. Place the dimension, type 14, and press Enter.
23. Click the left angled line, then click the right-angled line.
24. Place the dimension, type 28, and press Enter.
25. Click the two right-angled lines.
26. Place the dimension, type 15, and press Enter.
27. Click the top horizontal construction line, then click the end point of the circle edge.
28. Drag your mouse to the right, click to place the dimension, type 5, and press Enter.

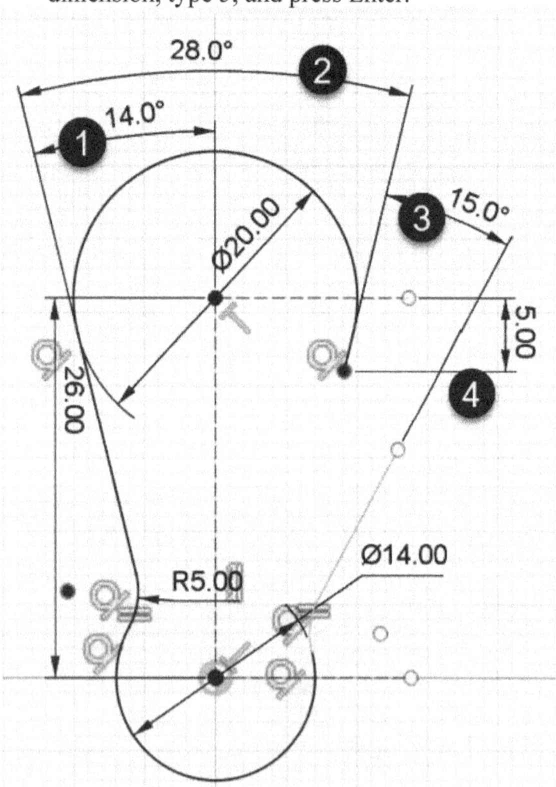

29. Select the endpoint of the right side angled line, drag your cursor, and drop the point near the tip of the other angled line as shown.

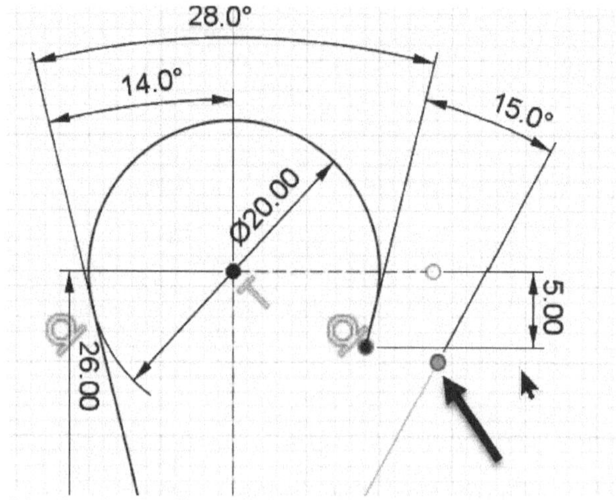

30. On the Toolbar, click **Sketch > Constraints > Horizontal/Vertical**.
31. Select the endpoints of the two angled lines.

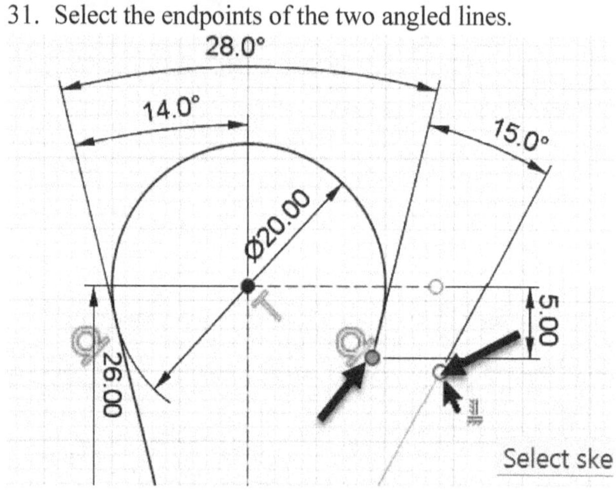

32. Select the centerpoints of the two arcs, as shown.

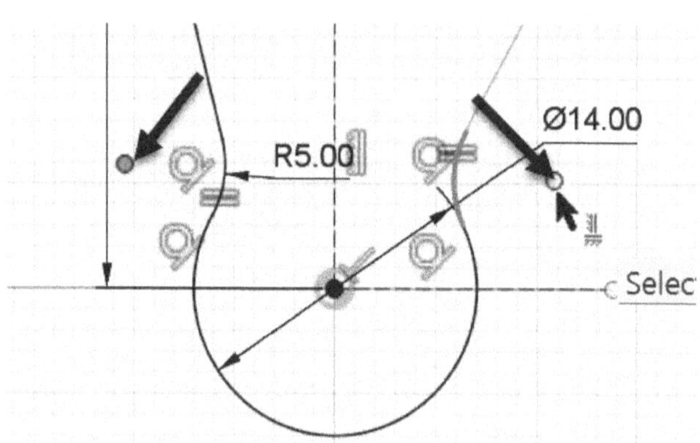

33. Click **Finish Sketch** in the top right corner to complete your profile.

Creating a Plane Along Path

1. On the **Solid** toolbar, locate the **Construct** panel menu at the top of the screen. Next, click on **Plane Along Path** from the list of options.

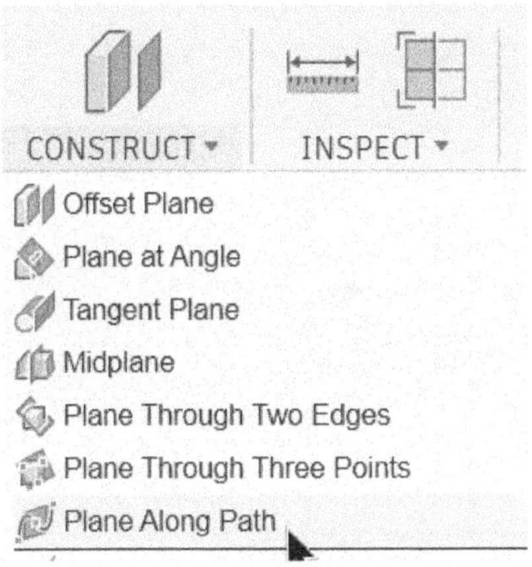

2. Select the sketch path from workspace to serve as the path.
3. In the **Plane Along Path** dialog box that appears on the right side, verify the **Extent Type** is set to **Proportional**.

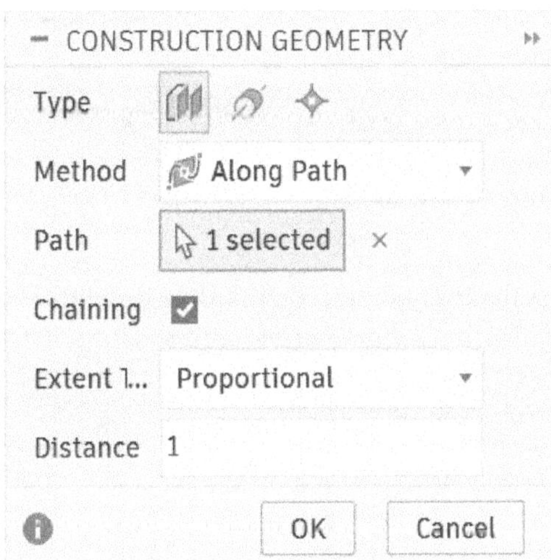

4. Drag the blue arrow to the endpoint of the sketch. You can also type a value from 0.00 to 1.00 in the Distance box to slide the plane exactly where you need it along the selected path.

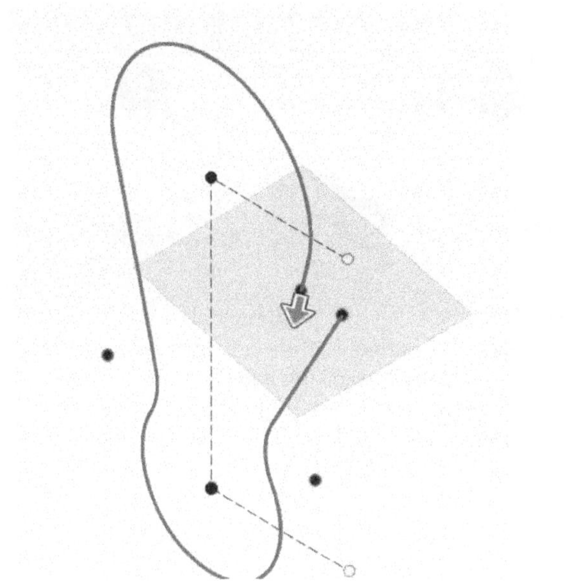

5. Click **OK** in the dialog box to generate the new construction plane.

Creating the Sweep Profile

1. Go to the **Create** panel, select **Create Sketch**, and click directly on the newly created Plane Along Path instead of a default origin plane.

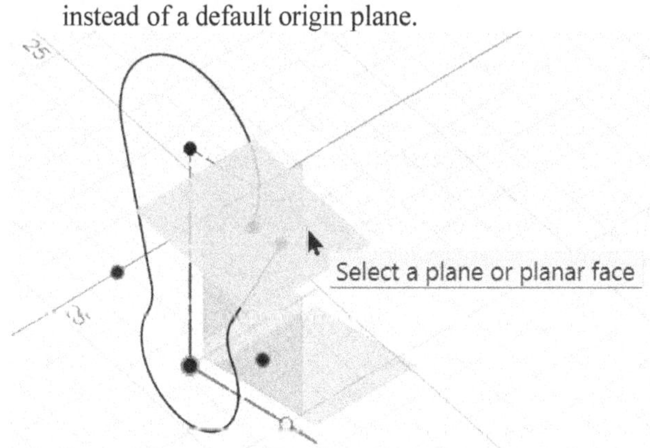

2. On the **Sketch** toolbar at the top of your screen, click the **Create** drop-down menu, hover over **Arc**, and choose **3-Point Arc**.
3. Select the sketch origin.
4. Move the pointer toward top-left direction and click to specify the endpoint of the line.
5. Move the pointer downward and click to specify the third point of the arc.

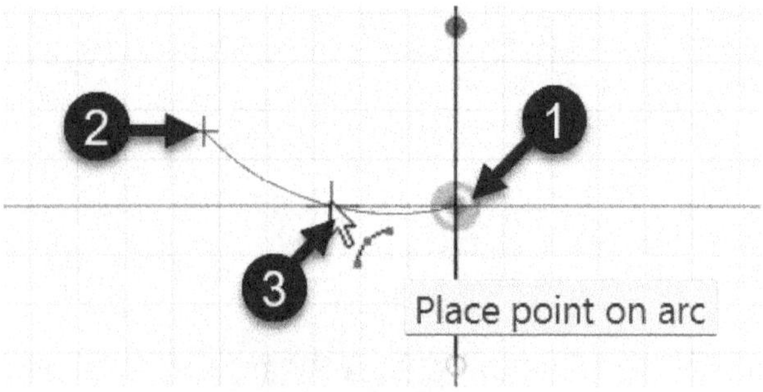

6. Press the L key for the **Line** tool.
7. Select the endpoint of the arc, move the pointer horizontally toward left and click.
8. Move the pointer vertically up and click.
9. Press ESC.

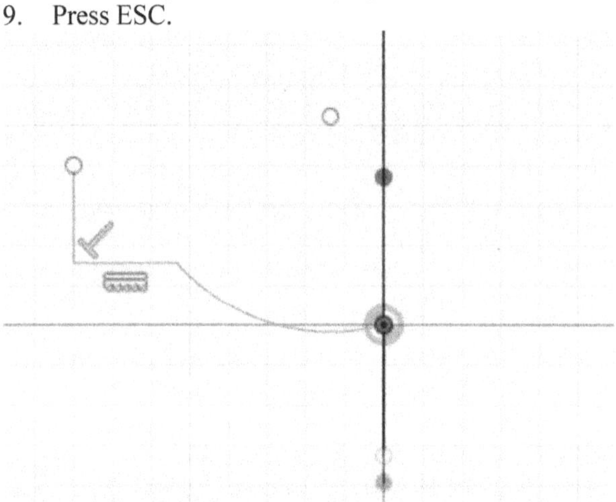

10. Press the **L** key for the **Line** tool.
11. On the **Sketch Palette**, select **Linetype > Construction**.
12. Select the sketch origin, move the vertically pointer upward and click.

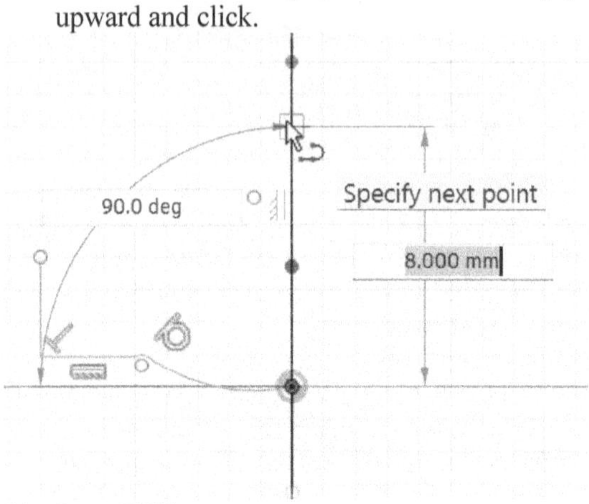

13. Press ESC.
14. Deactivate the **Construction** icon on the **Sketch Palette**.
15. On the **Sketch** toolbar, click **Modify > Fillet**.
16. Click on the corner, as shown.

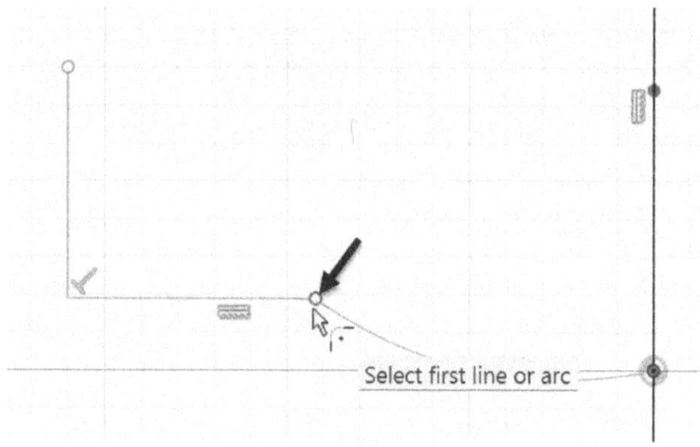

17. Type **1** and press ENTER.
18. Press the **D** key for the **Sketch Dimension** tool.
19. Add dimensions to the sketch, a shown.
20. On the Toolbar, click the **Sketch** contextual tab > **Constraints** panel > **Coincident**.
21. Select the centerpoint of the large arc and the construction line.

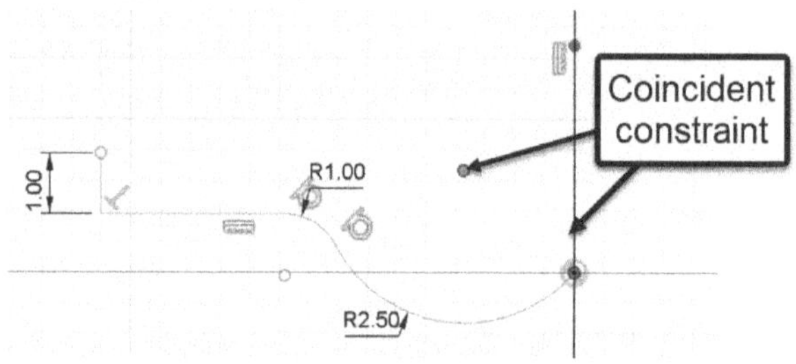

22. Press the **D** key for the **Sketch Dimension** tool.
23. Add remaining dimensions to the sketch, a shown.

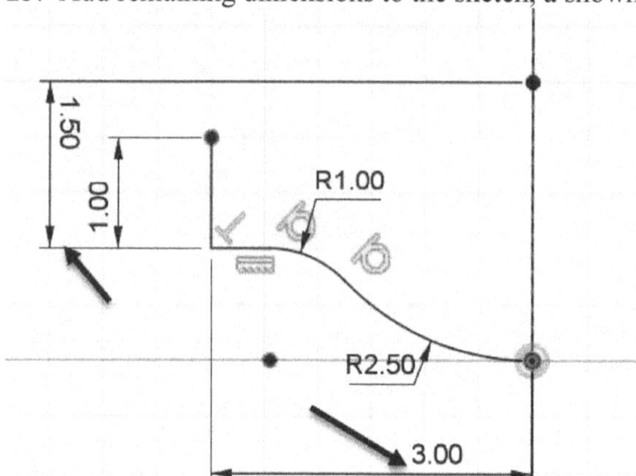

24. Go to the Solid toolbar, click the **Modify** dropdown menu, and select **Offset** (or press the O key).
25. The **Offset** dialog box will appear. Make sure the box next to **Chain Selection** is unchecked.
26. Select the two arcs and the horizontal line.
27. Type **-1** in the **Distance** box.

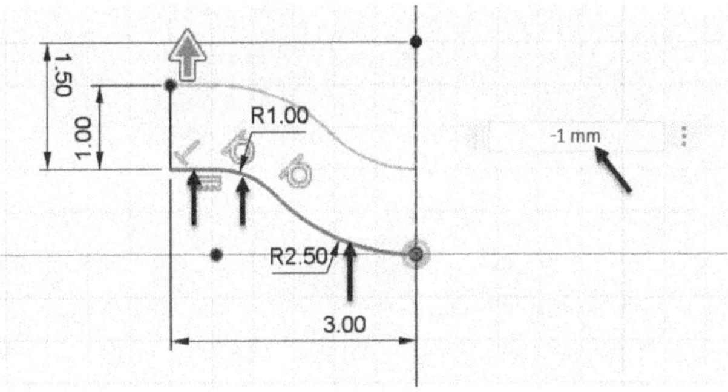

28. Click **OK** in the dialog box.
29. Navigate to the **Sketch** toolbar and locate the **Create** panel.
30. Click the word **Create** or the dropdown arrow at the bottom of that panel to expand the full list of sketch tools.
31. Look down the menu list and click **Mirror**. The icon displays two identical triangles separated by a vertical dashed line. The **Mirror** dialog box will immediately appear on the right side of your screen.
32. Inside this dialog box, the **Objects** selection arrow should be highlighted blue. If it is not, click the **Select** button next to **Objects**.
33. In your canvas, click exactly on the lines and arcs.
34. Return your cursor to the **Mirror** dialog box on the right side of the screen and click the **Select** button located exactly next to **Mirror Line**.
35. In the canvas, click the construction line. A phantom preview of the mirrored geometry will appear on the opposite side of your selected mirror line.

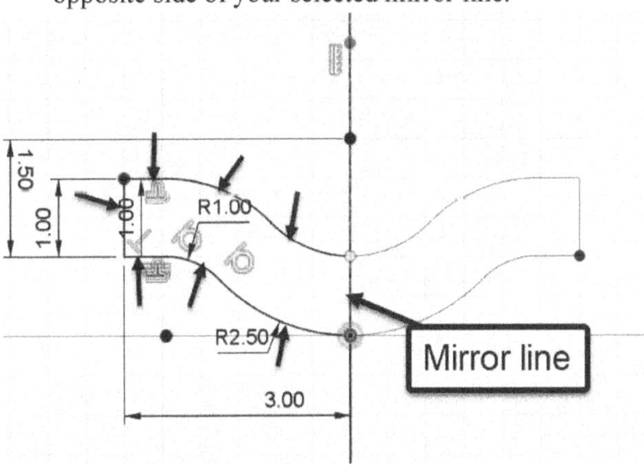

36. Click the **OK** button at the bottom right corner of the **Mirror** dialog box to generate the mirrored entities.

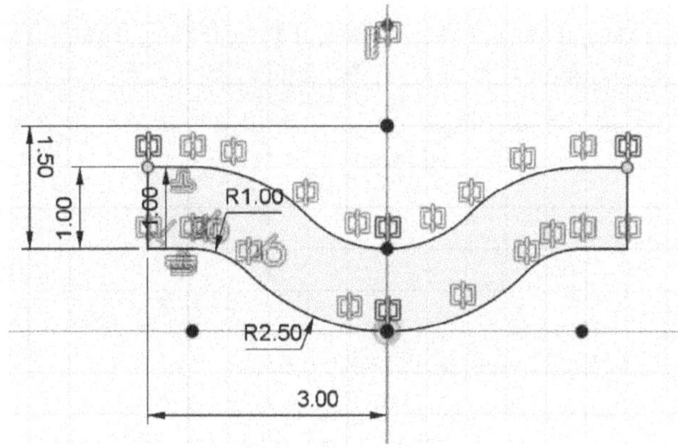

37. Click the large green **Finish Sketch** checkmark located either on the far right of the top ribbon or at the bottom of the **Sketch Palette**.

Executing the Sweep Feature

1. Go to the Toolbar at the top of the screen and ensure the **Solid** tab is active.
2. Within the Toolbar, locate the **Create** panel, click to expand it, and select **Sweep**.

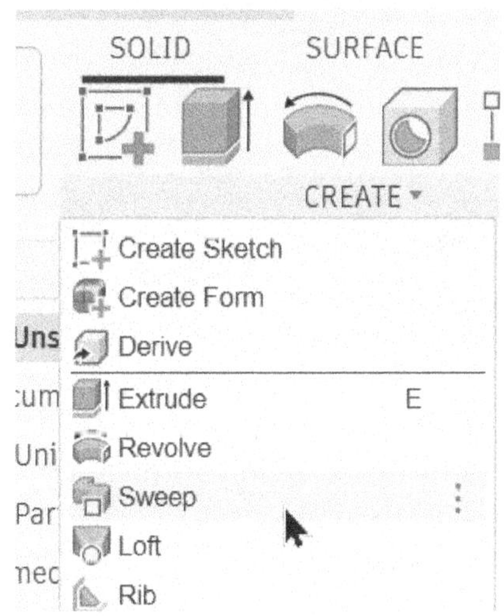

3. The **Sweep** dialog box will appear on the right side of the screen.
4. Confirm the **Type** setting at the top of the dialog box is set to **Single Path**. The Profile selection arrow should automatically be highlighted blue.
5. Click directly on the enclosed regions of your completed sketch in the main canvas to select them.

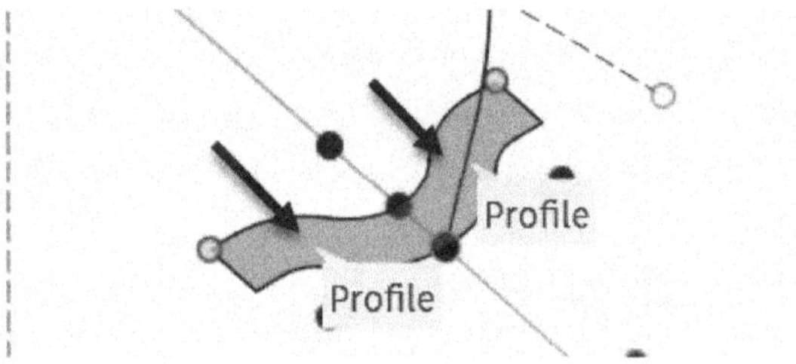

6. Return your cursor to the dialog box and click the **Select** button located next to **Path**.
7. In the canvas, click the original sketch curve or model edge that you utilized to create your Plane Along Path earlier.

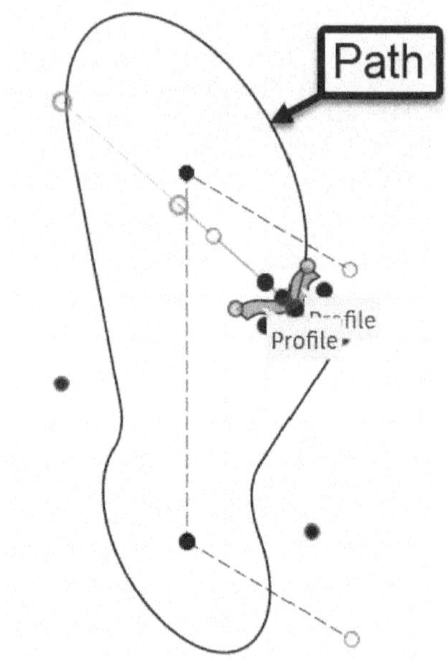

8. Look near the bottom of the dialog box to ensure the **Operation** dropdown is set to **New Body**.

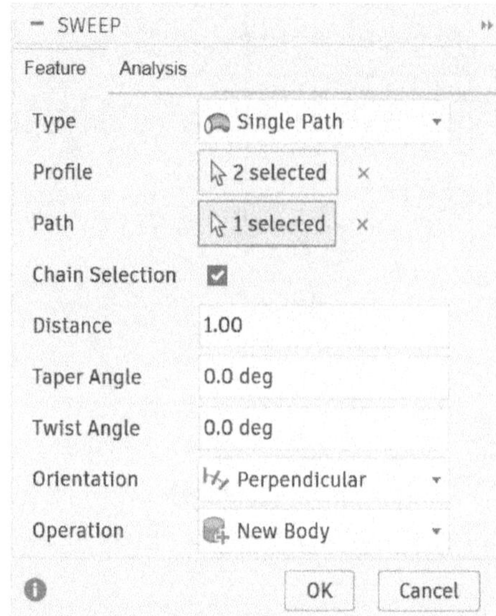

9. Click the **OK** button at the bottom right of the dialog box to finalize and generate your solid model.

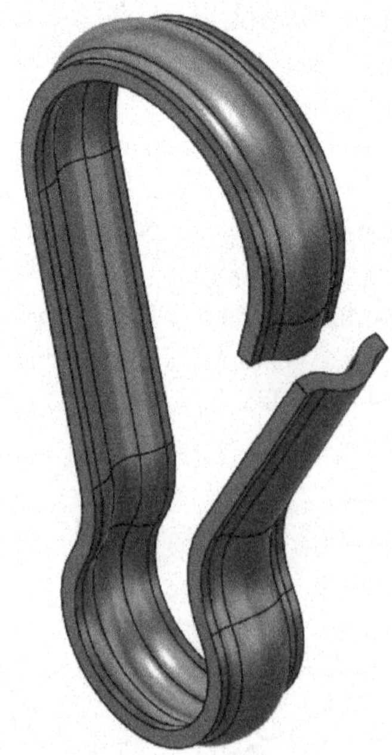

Tutorial 8

In this tutorial, you will create the part shown in figure below.

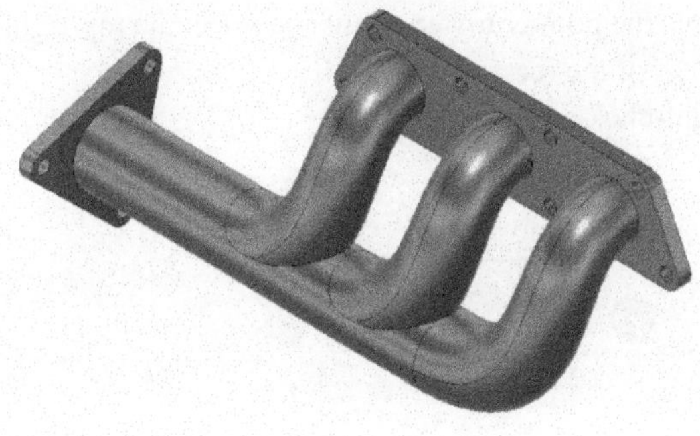

Start the first sketch

1. Open Fusion 360 and create a new design.
2. Click the **Create Sketch** icon on the **Solid** toolbar.
3. Choose a standard sketch plane, such as the XZ plane
4. Select **Create > Rectangle > 2 Point Rectangle** on the toolbar.
5. Activate the **Construction** icon on the **Sketch Palette**.
6. Select the sketch origin, move the pointer in the top-right direction and click.
7. Add dimensions to the rectangle, as shown.

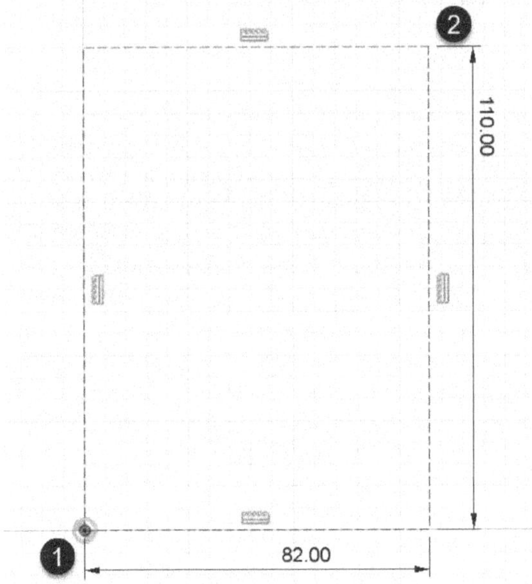

8. Deactivate the **Construction** icon on the **Sketch Palette**.
9. On the **Sketch** toolbar, click **Create** panel > **Spline** > **Control Point Spline**.

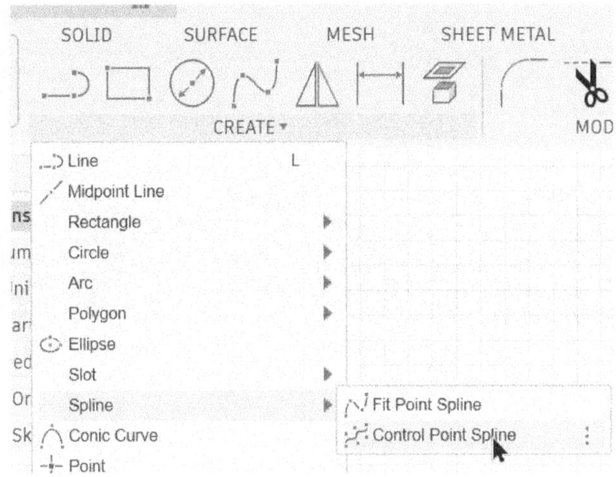

10. Select the sketch origin.
11. Move the pointer toward right and select the bottom-right corner of the rectangle.
12. Move the pointer upward and select top-right corner of the rectangle.
13. Right-click and select **OK**.

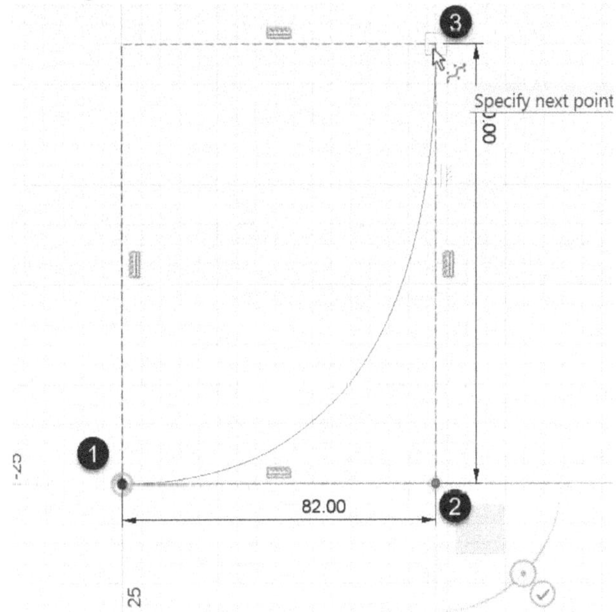

14. Click **Finish Sketch** when the profile matches the reference.

Creating the Second sketch

1. Click the **Create Sketch** icon on the **Solid** toolbar.
2. Choose a standard sketch plane, such as the YZ plane.

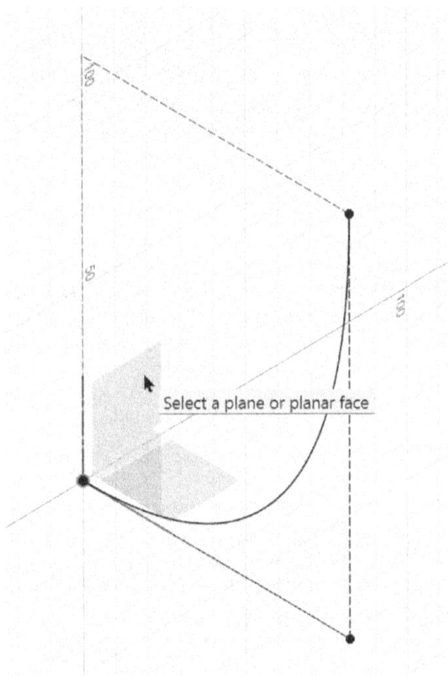

3. Select **Create > Rectangle > 2 Point Rectangle** on the toolbar.
4. Activate the **Construction** icon on the **Sketch Palette**.
5. Select the sketch origin, move the pointer in the top-right direction and click.
6. Add dimensions to the rectangle, as shown.

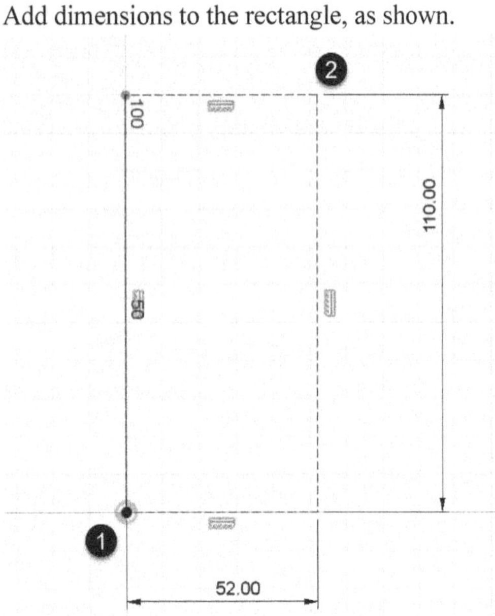

7. On the **Sketch** toolbar, click **Create** panel > **Spline** > **Control Point Spline**.
8. Select the sketch origin.
9. Move the pointer upward and select top-left corner of the rectangle.
10. Move the pointer toward right and select the top-right corner of the rectangle.
11. Right-click and select **OK**.

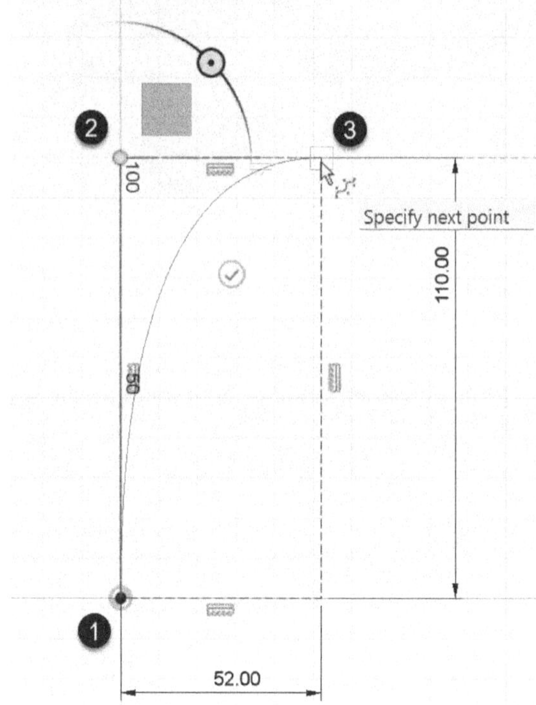

12. Click **Finish Sketch**.

Creating the Project to Surface Curve

1. Locate the workspace toolbar at the top of the screen and switch from the **Solid** tab to the **Surface** tab.
2. Select **Create**, then choose **Extrude**.

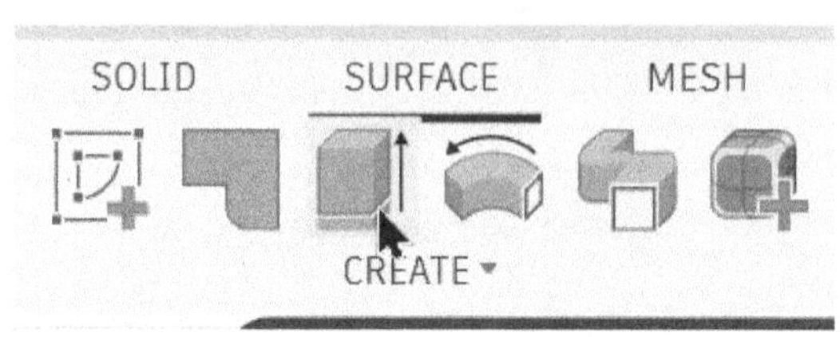

3. Select the first spline from your sketch as the profile.
4. Drag the arrow toward right to set the height of the surface body.

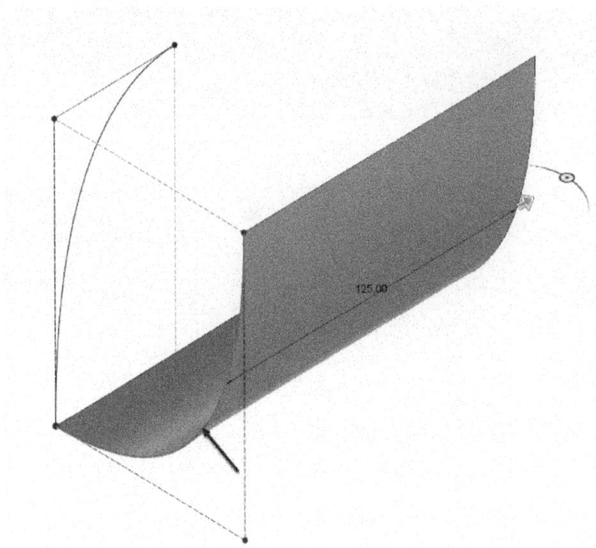

5. Select **OK** to complete the surface extrusion.
6. Click **Create Sketch** on the toolbar and click on anyone of the origin planes.
7. Locate the **Sketch Palette** dialog box on the right side of the screen. Look for the **3D Sketch** option and check the box to enable it. This ensures your sketch curves can successfully leave the 2D plane during projection.

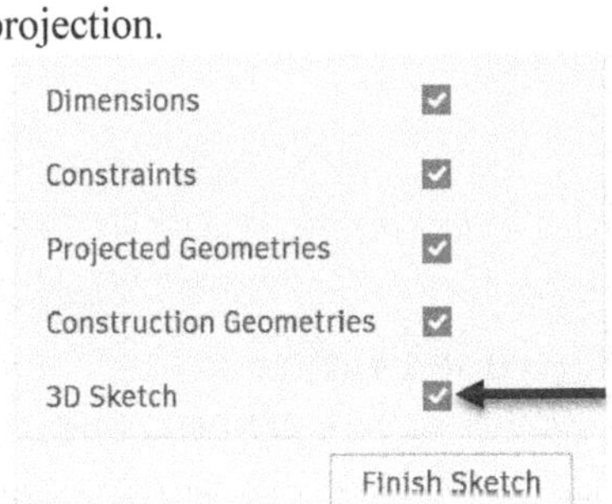

8. Click the **Home** icon next to the ViewCube.

9. On the **Sketch** toolbar, navigate to the **Create** panel menu.
10. Select **Project/Include**, then choose **Project to Surface**.

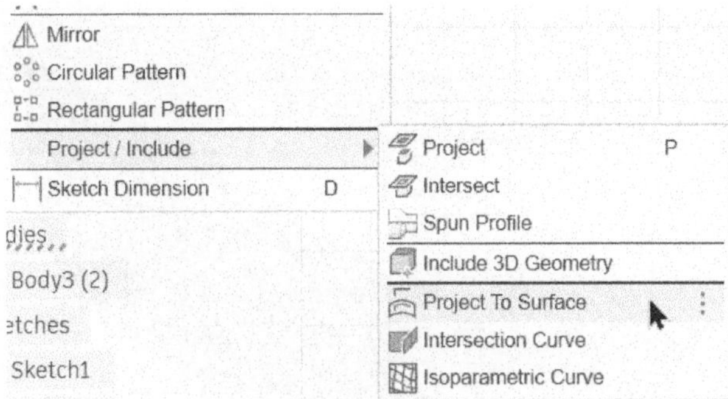

11. In the dialogue box, click the **Faces** selection and pick the face of your extruded surface.
12. Click the **Curves** selection and pick the lines of the shape you just drew.
13. Select **Project Type > Along Vector** and click the **Select** button next to the **Project Direction** option.

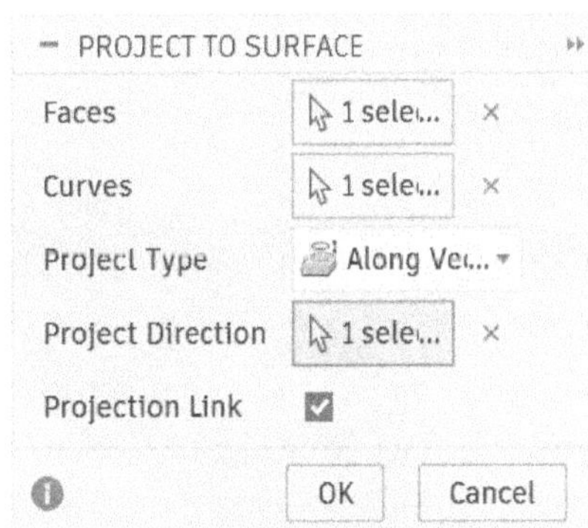

14. Select the plane on which the sketch is created. Fusion 360 uses the normal direction of the selected sketch plane to project the 2D sketch in a straight path through 3D space until it reaches the target surface. This is similar to projecting light from the sketch plane onto the curved surface, so the resulting 3D curve keeps the same shape as the original 2D sketch when viewed from that direction.

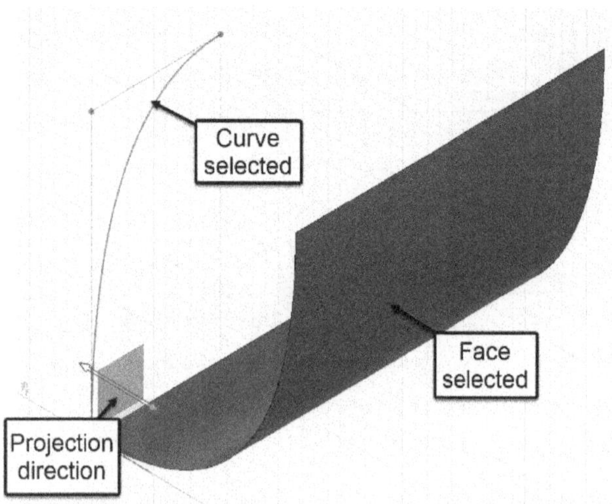

15. Click **OK** to apply the command. You will now see a purple 3D curve resting precisely on the contoured surface.

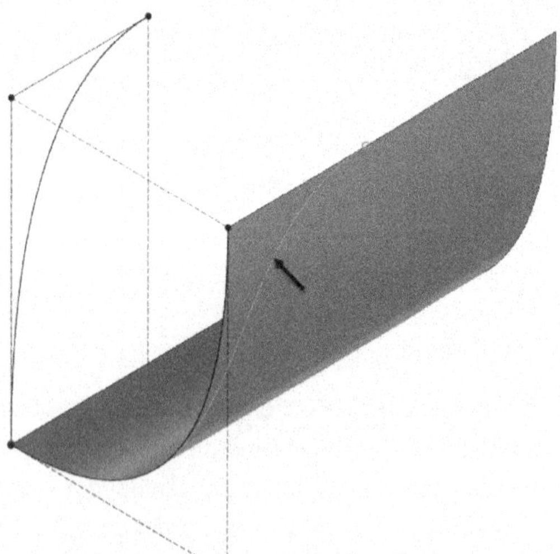

16. Select **Finish Sketch** to conclude the operation.
17. Locate the **Browser** panel on the left side of the Fusion 360 workspace.
18. Click the small arrow next to the **Bodies** folder to expand the list of all bodies in your design.
19. Click the eye icon next to the body. The icon will change to show a line through it, confirming the body is now hidden.
20. Click the small arrow next to the **Sketches** folder to expand the list of sketches.
21. Click the eye icon next to the first sketch you want to hide.
22. Click the eye icon next to the second sketch you want to hide.

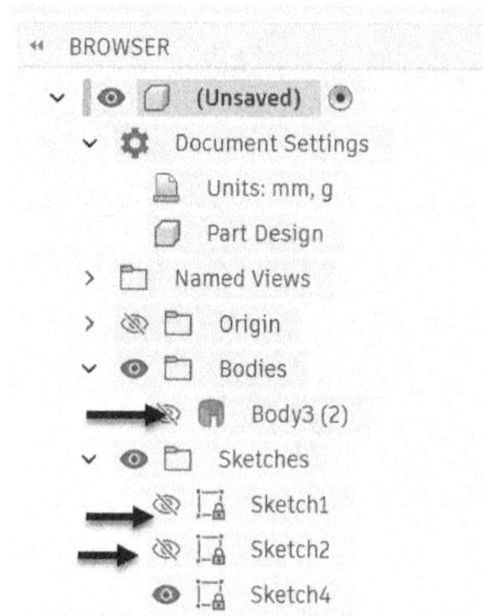

Creating the Extrude Feature

1. Click **Create Sketch** on the toolbar and click on anyone of the origin planes.
2. Click the **Home** icon next to the ViewCube.
3. Create a circle at the sketch origin and add a diameter dimension of 52 to it.

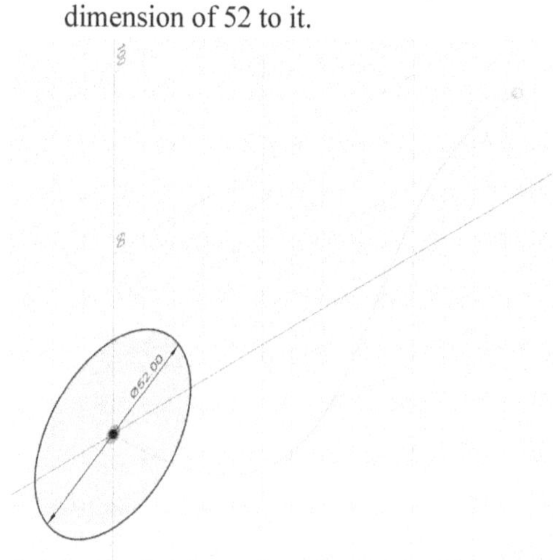

4. Click **Finish Sketch**.

5. On the **Solid** tab of the toolbar, click **Extrude**, or simply press **E** on your keyboard.
6. Click inside the circle.
7. In the **Extrude** dialog box that appears on the right, look for the **Distance** box. Type **-275** and press Enter.

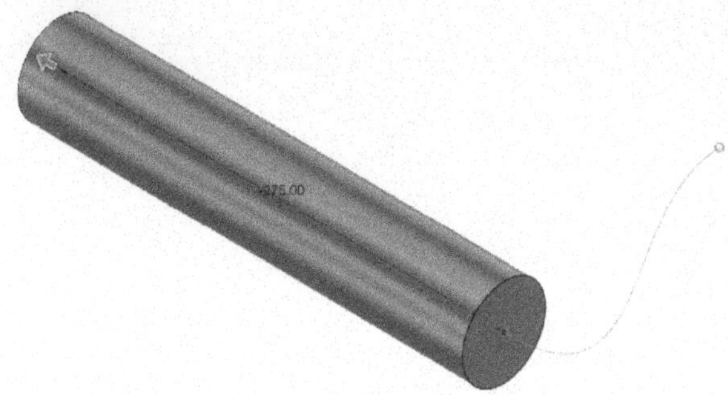

Creating the Loft feature

1. On the **Solid** toolbar, locate the **Construct** panel menu at the top of the screen. Next, click on **Plane Along Path** from the list of options.
2. Select the curve from workspace to serve as the path.
3. In the **Plane Along Path** dialog box that appears on the right side, verify the **Extent Type** is set to **Proportional**.
4. Type **0** in the **Distance** box.

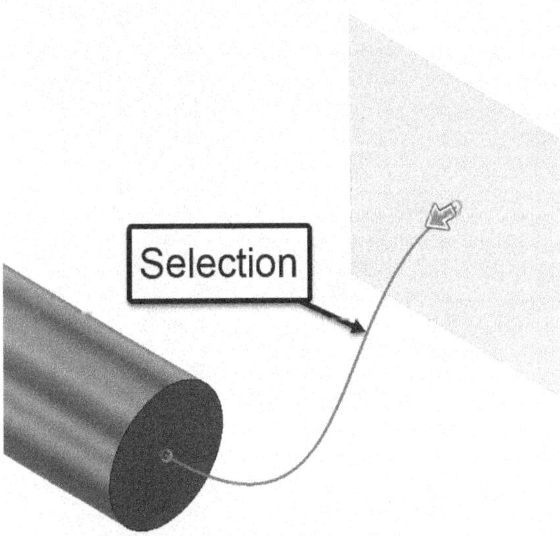

5. Click **Create Sketch** on the toolbar and click on plane normal to the curve.
6. Draw a circle at the sketch origin and add a diameter dimension of 41.

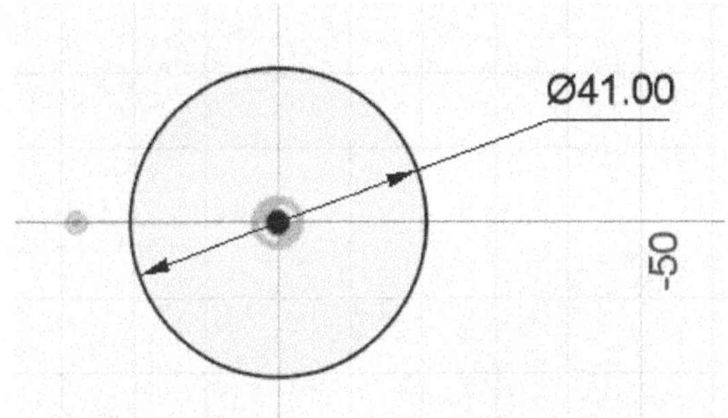

7. Click **Finish Sketch**.
8. Navigate to the top ribbon and ensure you are in the **Solid** workspace.
9. Open the **Create** panel menu.
10. Select the **Loft** command from the list. The **Loft** dialogue box will appear on the right side of the screen.

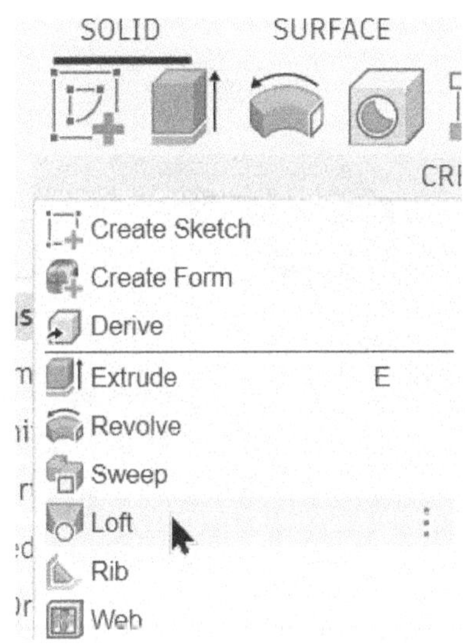

11. In the **Loft** dialogue box, ensure the **Profiles** selection box is active (highlighted in blue).
12. Click on the floating circular sketch. This will be registered as **Profile 1**.
13. Click on the circular end face of the existing solid cylinder. This will be registered as **Profile 2**.

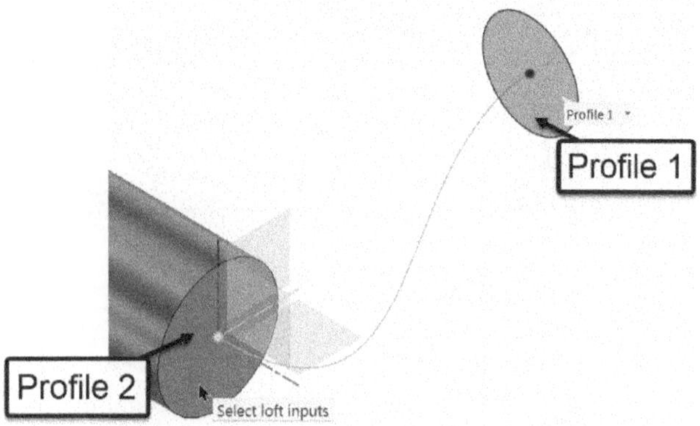

14. At this point, Fusion 360 will generate a straight, direct preview connecting the two profiles. Do not click OK yet.

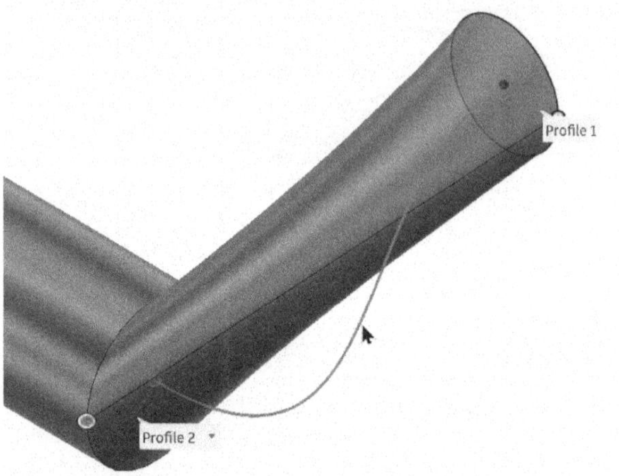

15. In the **Loft** dialogue box, select **Guide type** > **Centerline**.
16. Click the **Centerline** selection button
17. Click on the 3D curved connecting the two profiles. The preview will immediately update, forcing the lofted body to curve and follow the exact path of the selected centerline.
18. Check the **Operation** setting at the bottom of the Loft dialogue box. If you want the new loft to merge seamlessly with the original cylinder, ensure it is set to **Join**.

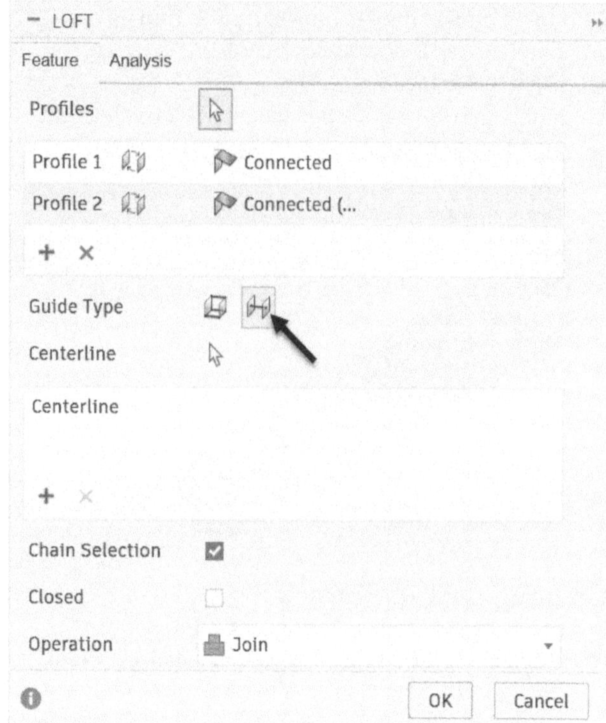

19. Verify that the preview looks correct and smoothly follows the curved rail.

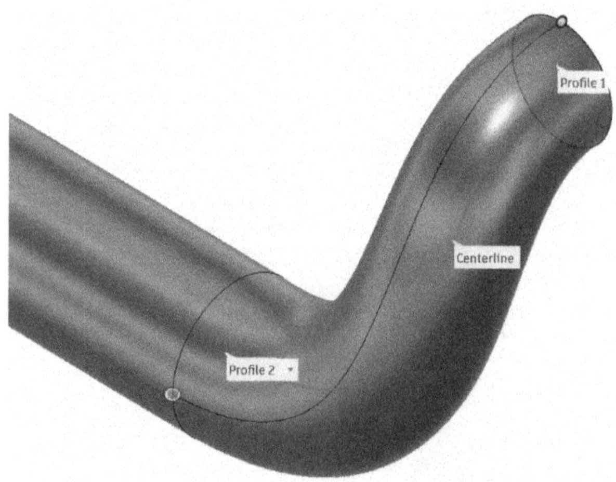

20. Click **OK** to complete the operation and generate the final solid body.

Creating the Rectangular Pattern

To duplicate the loft feature along the straight pipe, use the **Rectangular Pattern** command set to "**Features**" object type, select the original loft feature from your timeline, and define the straight axis and spacing parameters to generate multiple identical instances.

1. Navigate to the toolbar and ensure you are in the **Solid** workspace.
2. Open the **Create** dropdown menu.
3. Locate the **Pattern** submenu and select **Rectangular Pattern**. The **Rectangular Pattern** dialogue box will appear on the right side of the screen.

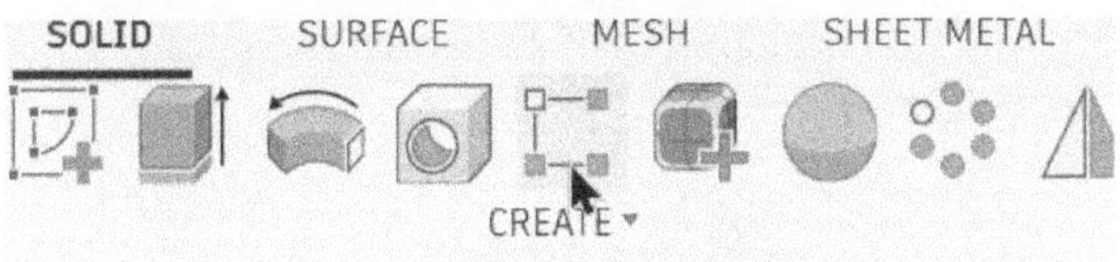

4. In the dialogue box, locate the **Object Type** dropdown and set it to **Features**.
5. Click the **Objects** selection button.
6. Select the loft feature from the model geometry. Once selected, the feature will highlight in blue.

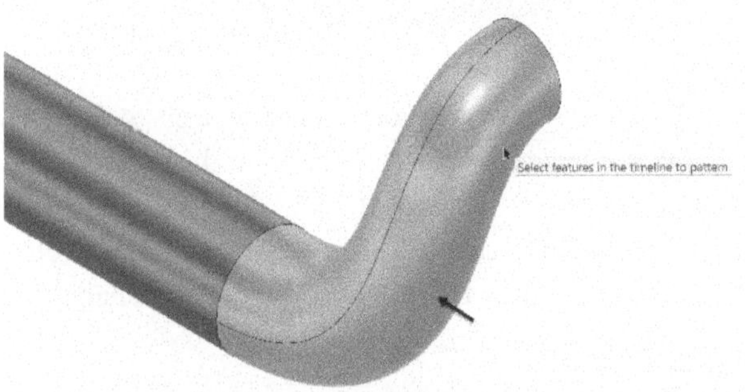

7. In the dialogue box, click the **Axes** selection button.
8. Select the X-axis from the graphics window. A set of directional arrows will appear on your model, indicating the intended path.

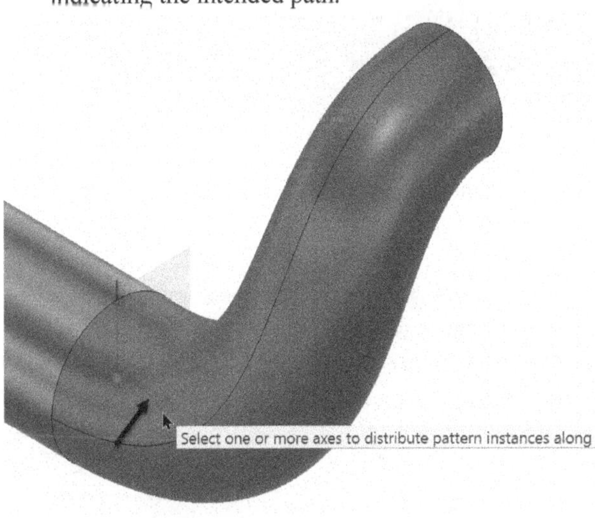

9. Set the **Distribution** type to **Spacing**. This specifies the exact distance between each individual instance, rather than the overall total length.
10. In the **Axis 1** section, set the **Quantity** to **3** to match the desired number of instances shown in the reference image.
11. Set the **Distance** to **-85 mm**. The negative value determines the direction of the offset along the selected axis.
12. Ensure the **Direction** setting is left at **One Direction**.

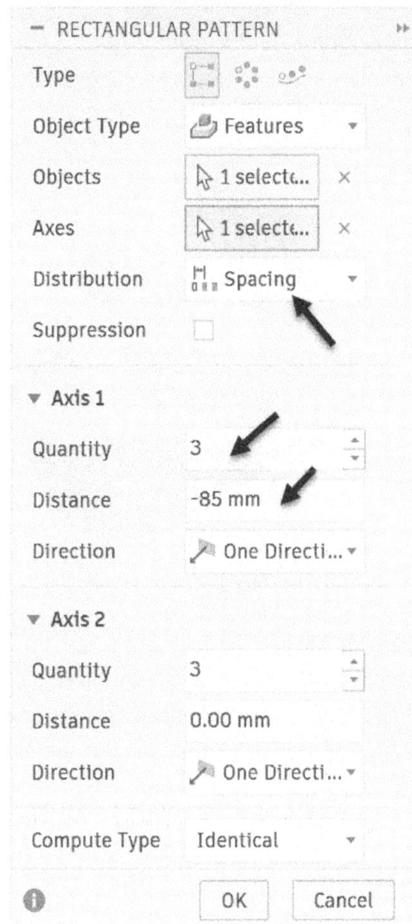

13. Review the preview in the workspace. You should see translucent representations of the two new curved sections spaced evenly along the straight pipe.
14. Verify that the **Compute Type** at the bottom of the dialogue box is set to **Identical**. This ensures the duplicated features match the exact shape of the original.

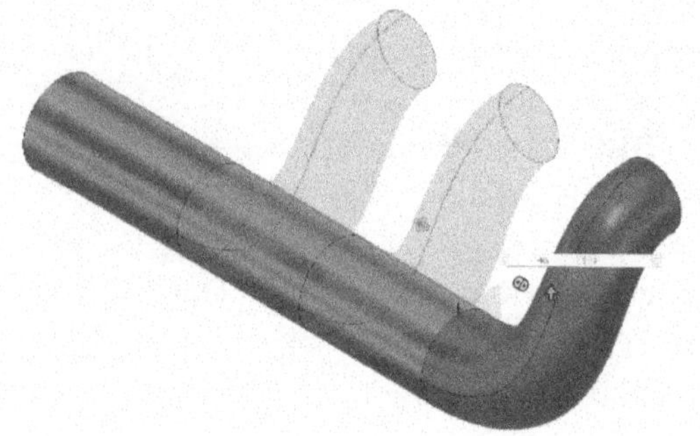

15. Click **OK** to execute the command and generate the final solid geometry.

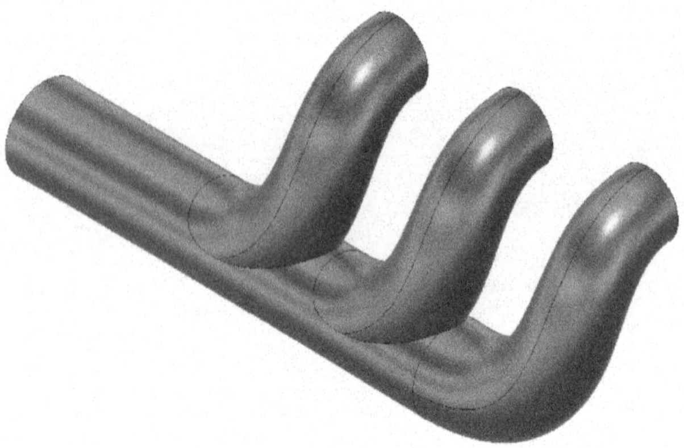

Shelling and Section Analysis

To hollow out the solid pipe model, use the **Shell** command and select the four end faces (the three curved branches and the main pipe end) to remove them, then apply a 2 mm inside thickness. Finally, use the **Section Analysis** tool on a central plane to cut the model in half visually and verify the wall thickness rounded edges.

1. Ensure you are in the **Solid** toolbar at the top of the interface.
2. Locate the **Modify** panel and select the **Shell** command. The **Shell** dialogue box will appear on the screen.

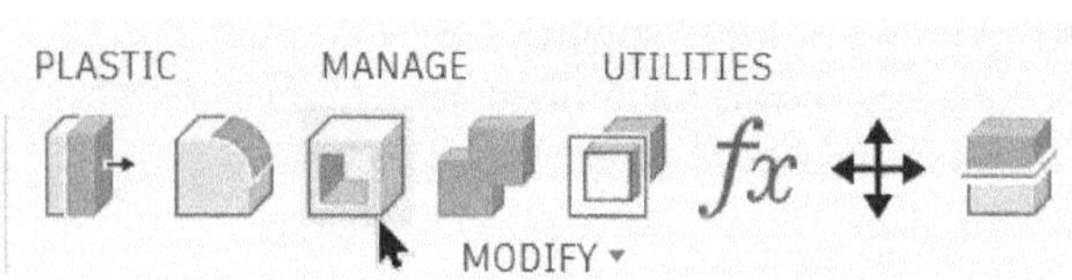

3. In the workspace, use the **Orbit** tool and navigate to the three upward-curving branches of the pipe model.

4. Click on the flat, circular top faces of the first branch to select it.
5. Click on the top faces of the second and third branches.

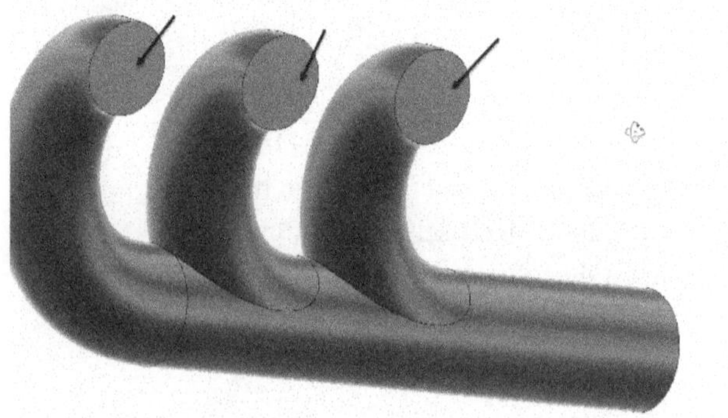

6. Use the **Orbit** tool or your mouse controls to rotate the camera and view the open end of the main straight pipe.
7. Click on the circular end face of the main pipe. You should now have four faces selected in the Shell dialogue box.

8. In the **Shell** dialogue box, set the **Shell Type** to **Rounded Shell**. It automatically applies smooth, rounded fillets to the new offset corners that are created during the shelling process, rather than leaving them as sharp edge.
9. Enter **2** in the **Inside Thickness** field.
10. Set the **Direction** to **Inside**.

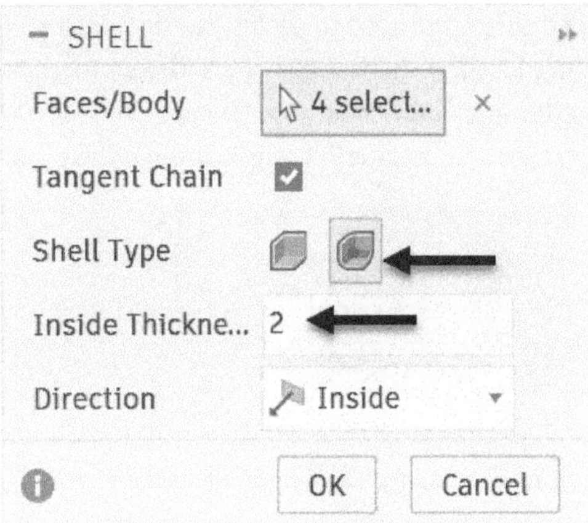

11. Click **OK** to execute the command. The solid body will now be hollowed out, leaving only a 2 mm wall thickness connecting all the branches.

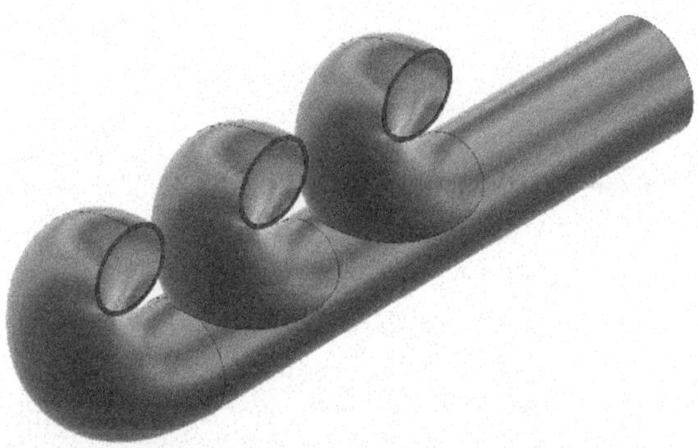

Next, use the **Section Analysis** tool to visually cut through the model and verify that the **Rounded Shell** option successfully created smooth, curved edges on the internal corners, rather than sharp angles.

12. Navigate to the **Utilities** tab of the toolbar and locate the **Inspect** panel. Next, select **Section Analysis**.
13. In the **Section Analysis** dialogue box, clickthe **Cut Plane** selection button.
14. Select the XZ plane that perfectly bisects the pipe model.

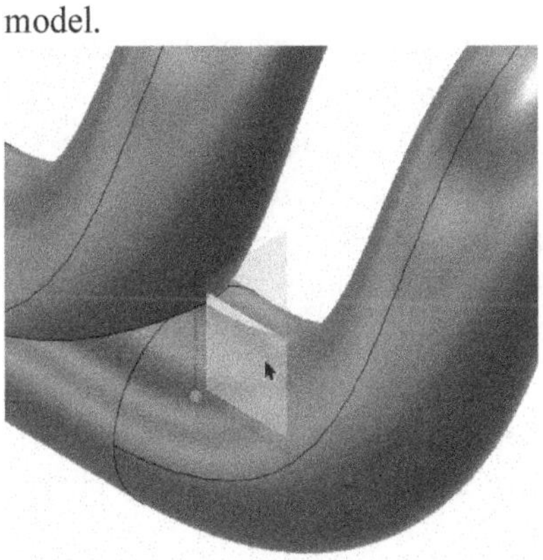

15. Ensure the **Distance** is set to **0.00 mm** and the **Angle** settings align the cut directly down the center of the pipes.

The model will appear sliced in half, revealing the internal hollow structure. You can look directly at the interior walls of your part. If the **Rounded Shell** option worked correctly, you will clearly see continuous, smooth arcs transitioning between the inner walls and the floor of the hollowed space.

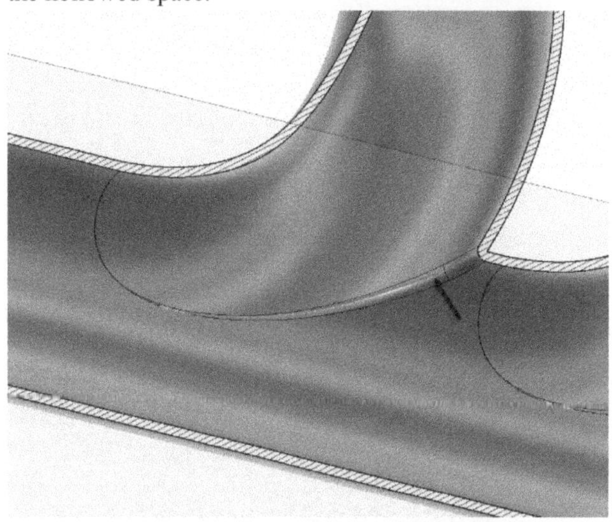

16. Click **Cancel** on the **Section Analysis** dialog.

Creating Flange on the Single pipe end

To recreate the flange, create a sketch on the end face of the pipe and draw a 3-sided circumscribed polygon. Then, use the **Fillet** tool to round the polygon corners, apply the **Project** command to bring the inner and outer circular edges of the pipe into the sketch, and finally add mounting holes at the three rounded corners.

1. Use the **Orbit** tool and rotate the mode such that the end of the hollow pipe body is visible.

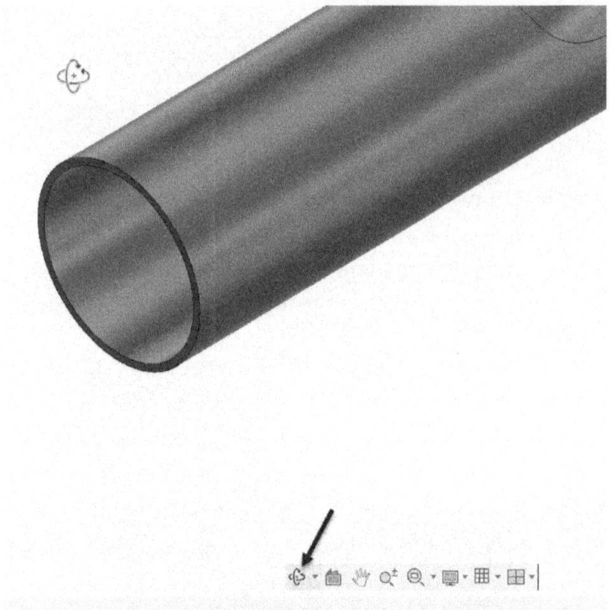

2. Select **Create Sketch** from the **Solid** toolbar.
3. Click the flat, circular end face of the hollow pipe to set it as your active sketch plane.

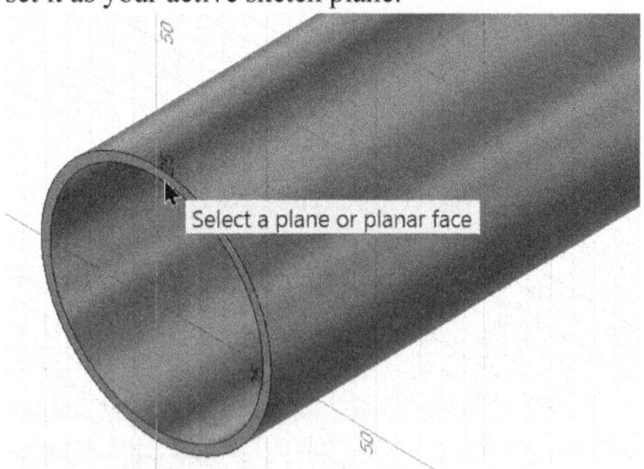

4. Navigate to **Create > Polygon > Circumscribed Polygon**.

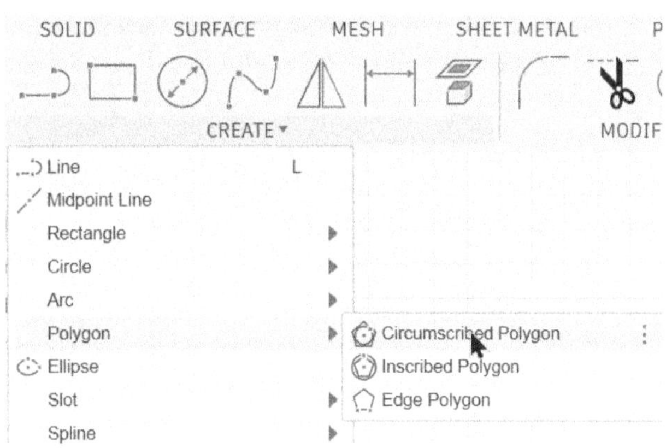

5. Click the center origin point of the pipe to place the center of the polygon.
6. Move your cursor outward to define the size. Before clicking to place the shape, press the **Tab** key to switch to the sides input box, type **3**.
7. Click to create an equilateral triangle around the pipe.

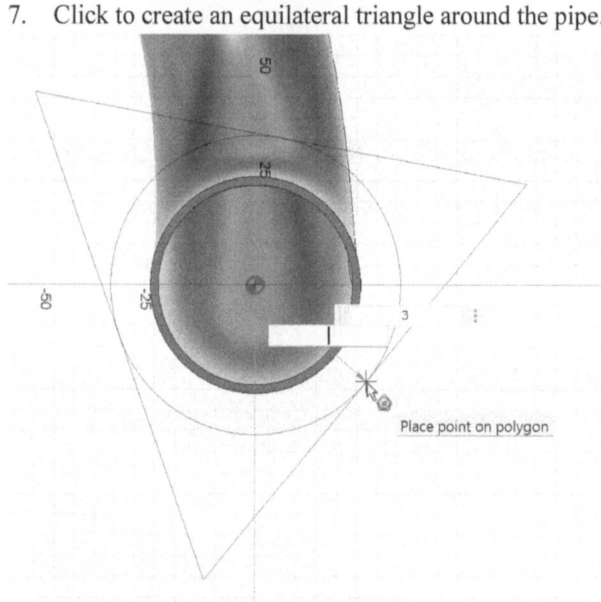

8. Select **Fillet** from the **Modify** panel.
9. Select all the corners of the triangle. Type **10** for the radius and press Enter. The sketch will place a dimension labeled R10.00. The small icons with equal signs (=) visible near the corners in the image confirm that an **Equal** constraint is applied to them.
10. Press **C** for **Circle**, select the center origin point, and draw a circle outward.
11. Select the drawn circle line and press X on your keyboard (or click the "**Construction**" icon in the Sketch Palette). This changes the line to a dashed construction line, meaning it will guide the shape but will not be extruded into a 3D solid.
12. On the **Sketch** toolbar, click **Constraints > Coincident**.
13. Select anyone of the centerpoints of the fillet and the construction circle.
14. Likewise, make the centerpoints of the other two fillet coincident with the construction circle.
15. Press **D** for **Sketch Dimension.**
16. Click the left angled line of the triangle. Drag your cursor directly downward and click to place the dimension parallel to the line.
17. Type 88.50 and press Enter. This determines the exact length of the flat sides before filleting
18. Press **L** for **Line** and draw a vertical line straight up from the center origin. Press **X** to make it a dashed construction line.

19. Press **D** for **Sketch Dimension**.
20. Click the top angled line of the triangle, then click the vertical construction line you just drew.
21. Drag your cursor between them to place the angular dimension. Type 106.0 and press Enter. This locks the entire shape's rotation angle.

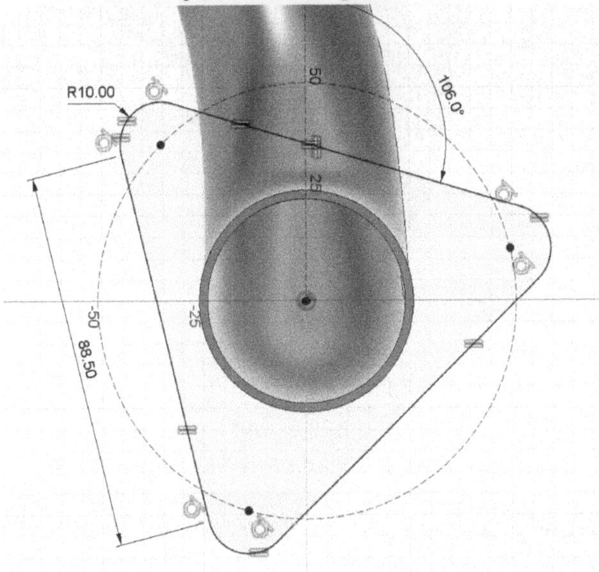

22. Press the letter **P** on your keyboard or go to **Create > Project/Include > Project**.

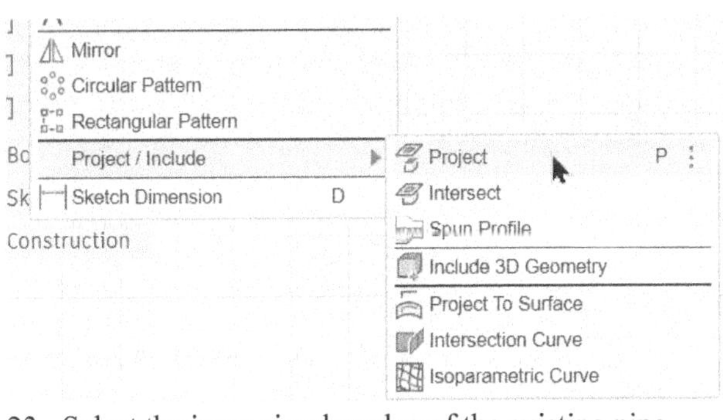

23. Select the inner circular edge of the existing pipe body.

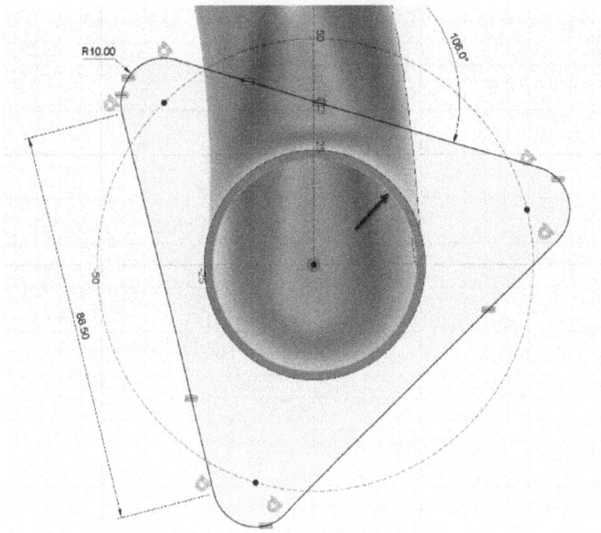

24. Click **OK**. This generates a purple edge in your sketch, linking the physical pipe dimensions directly to your flange profile. This ensures that if the pipe diameter changes later, the flange hole will automatically update.
25. Press the letter **C** on your keyboard to activate the **Center Diameter Circle** tool.
26. Hover your cursor near one of the newly created R10.00 rounded corners until a small crosshair appears, indicating the center point of that arc. Click the center point.
27. Drag outward and type **10.00** to create a 10 mm diameter hole.
28. Repeat this process for the other two rounded corners. Alternatively, you can draw the remaining two circles and use the **Equal** constraint to lock their diameters to the first 10 mm circle.

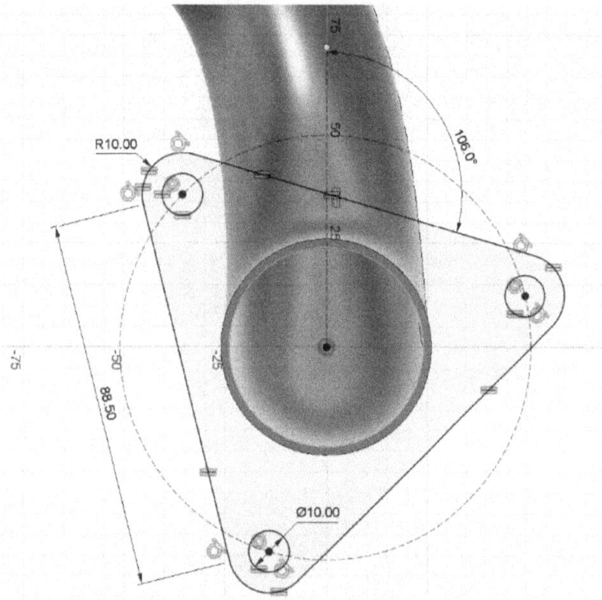

29. Verify your dimensions match the provided image, then click **Finish Sketch**.
30. Navigate to the **Solid** toolbar.
31. Go to **Create > Extrude**, or press the letter **E** on your keyboard to launch the tool quickly. The Extrude dialogue box will appear on the right side of your screen.
32. In the **Extrude** dialogue box, verify that the **Profiles** selection box is active (highlighted in blue).
33. Move your cursor over the flat triangle shape you just sketched.
34. Click the main body of the triangle. Ensure you do not select the three 10 mm corner holes or the large central pipe hole. If selected correctly, the area representing the solid flange material will turn dark blue, leaving the holes empty.
35. Likewise, click in the region between the projected circular edge and the outer circular edge. An arrow will appear pointing perpendicularly away from your sketch. You can click and drag this arrow, but for exact measurements, use the dialogue box.
36. In the **Distance** field, type **10**
37. Locate the **Operation** dropdown menu at the bottom of the Extrude dialogue box.
38. Set the operation to **Join**. This ensures the new 10 mm thick flange physically merges with the existing metal pipe to become one single, continuous solid body.
39. Click **OK** to complete the operation.

Creating the Manifold Flange

To design the manifold flange, create a sketch on the open faces of the pipe branches, draw a large trapezoid, round the corners with a 10 mm fillet, project the inner and outer circular edges of all three pipes into the sketch, align the flange symmetrically using a vertical construction line and the Midpoint constraint, and apply the final driving dimensions.

1. Select **Create Sketch** from the **Solid** toolbar.
2. Click on the flat, circular top face of one of the three curved pipe branches to define the sketch plane. Because the three branches were patterned or modeled evenly, this plane will intersect all three ends.

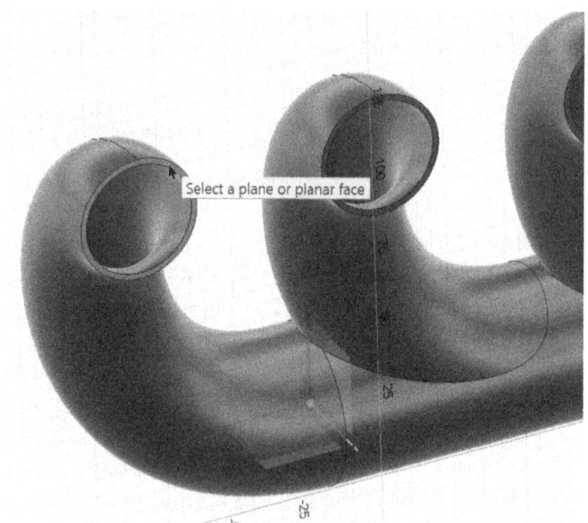

3. Press **L** for the **Line** tool. Draw a horizontal top line, a horizontal bottom line, and two angled sides connecting them to form a large trapezoid that spans across all three pipes.
4. Apply a **Horizontal** constraint to the top and bottom lines if they are not already constrained.

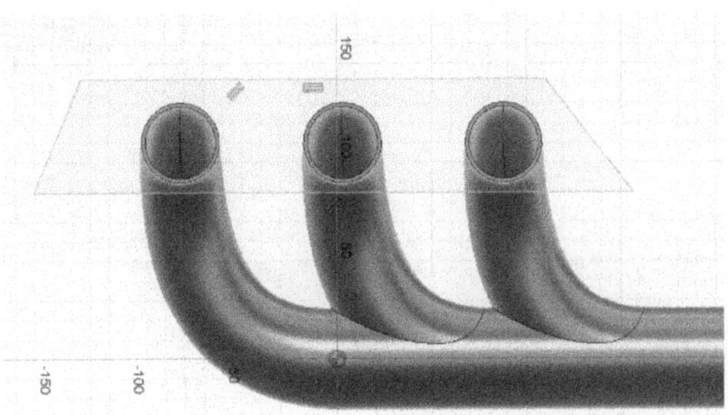

5. Select the **Fillet** tool from the **Modify** panel.
6. Click the four corners of the sketch, enter **10** for the radius, and press Enter.

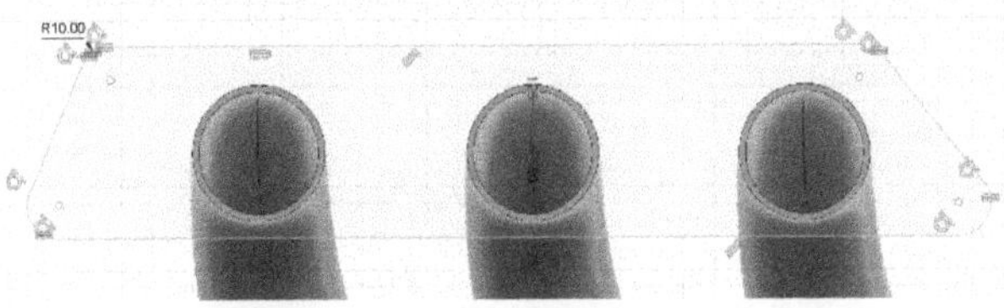

To keep the flange perfectly centered, you need a vertical construction line.

7. Press **L** for the **Line** tool and **X** to activate **Construction** mode.
8. Draw a straight vertical line.

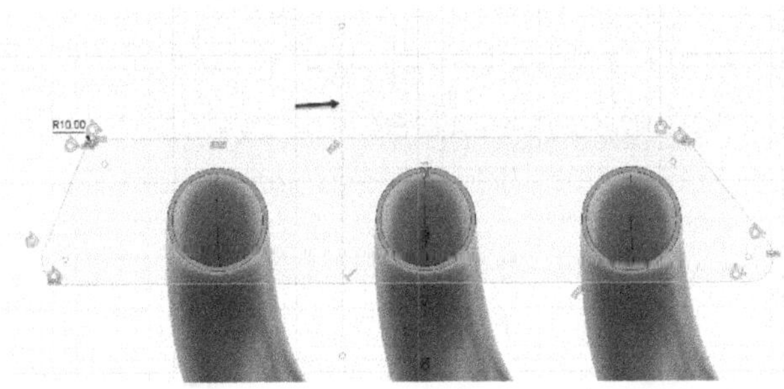

9. On the toolbar, click **Constraints** panel > **Midpoint**.
10. Select the newly created vertical construction line and the bottom horizontal line of the sketch.

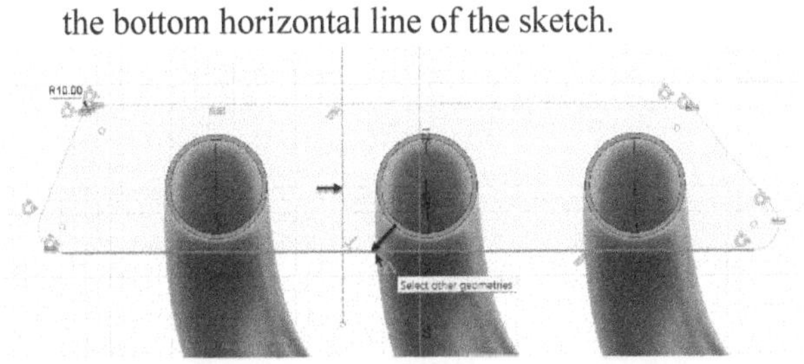

11. Press the letter **P** on your keyboard or go to **Create > Project/Include > Project**.
12. Select the inner circular edges of the three pipe branches.

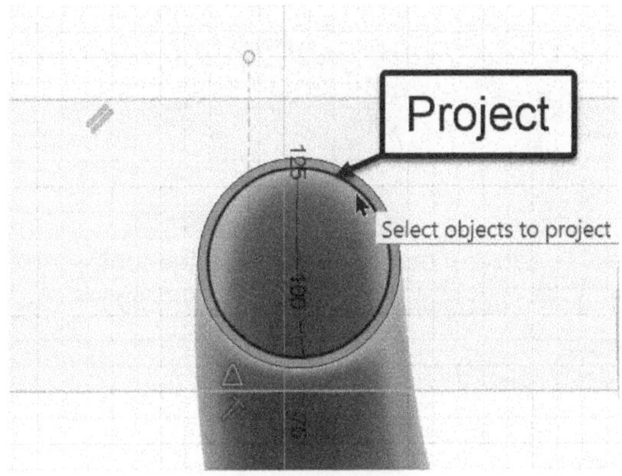

13. Click **OK**. The circular edges will appear as purple lines in your sketch, linking the flange directly to the existing 3D pipe geometry.
14. Select the **Coincident** constraint, click the newly drawn vertical construction line, and then click the center point of circular edge of the middle pipe. This anchors the entire flange centrally over the middle branch.

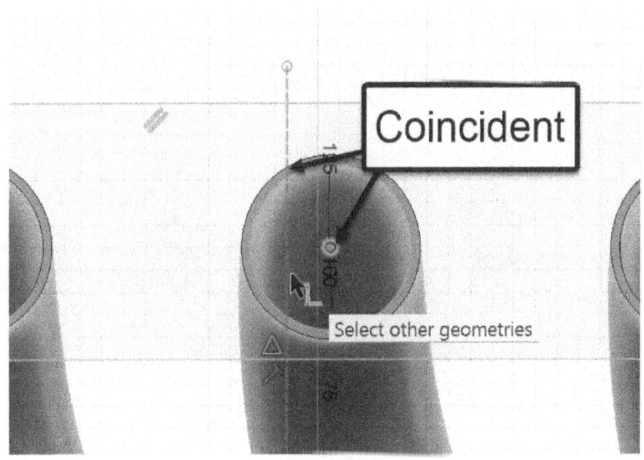

15. On the toolbar, click **Constraints** panel > **Symmetry**.

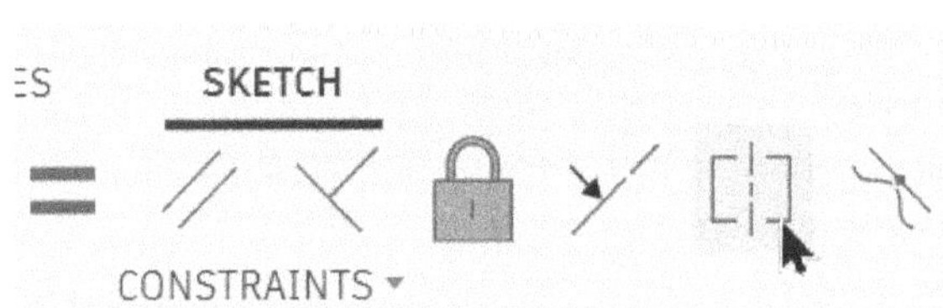

16. Select the two angled lines.
17. Select the vertical construction line to define the symmetry line. This ensures that the left and right sides of the trapezoid remain identical.

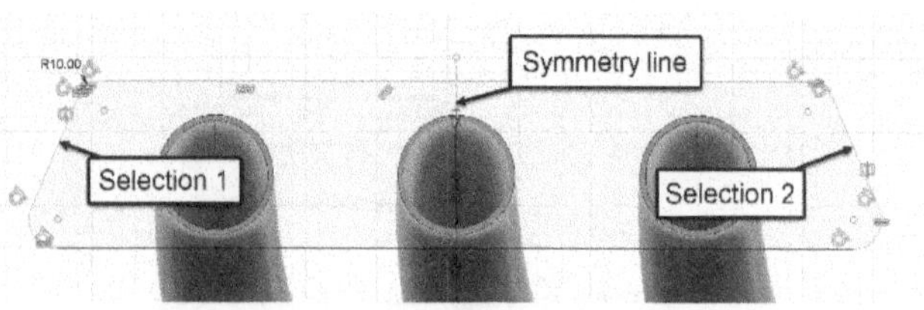

18. Press **D** to activate the **Sketch Dimension** tool.
19. Click the top horizontal line and enter **210.00** for the top width.
20. Select the vertical construction line and the centerpoint of the bottom right fillet. Next, enter **127.50**.
21. Click the top horizontal line and then the bottom horizontal line, drag the cursor to the side, and enter **66.00** for the overall height.
22. Click the center point of the middle pipe hole, then click the bottom horizontal line of the flange, drag out, and enter **33.00**. This dictates how far the flange extends below the pipe centers.

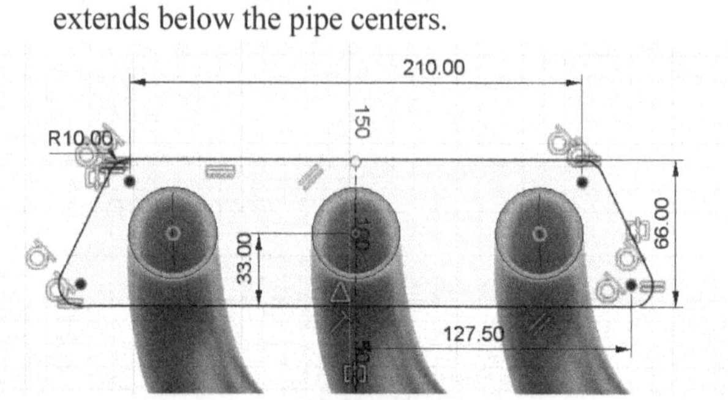

23. Verify that all lines have turned black (fully constrained) and click **Finish Sketch**.
24. Rotate the model slightly, if needed, so the flange sketch is easy to select from the front side of the manifold.
25. Go to the **Solid** tab and select **Create > Extrude**.
26. In the canvas, click the flange sketch region that lies between the outer boundary and the three circular pipe openings. Make sure the three circular openings are not filled in blue, because they must remain open after extrusion.

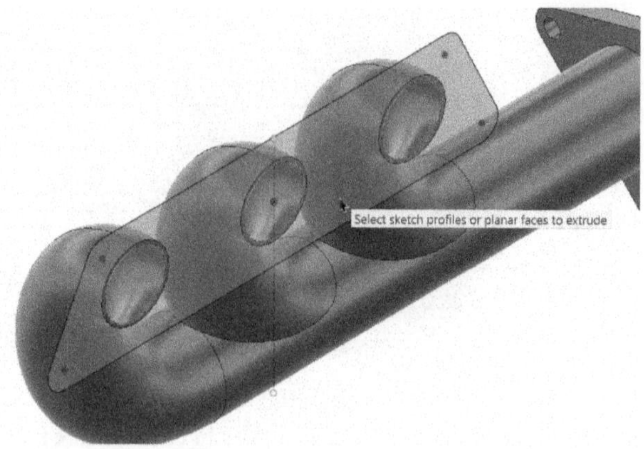

27. Ensure the selection includes the space between the projected inner circle and the outer circular edge. Click directly on these specific areas to select them if necessary.

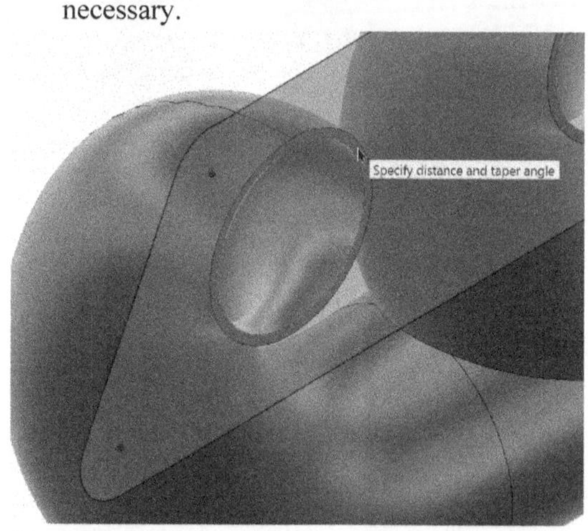

28. In the Extrude dialog, use **One Side** as the extent type.
29. Enter the flange thickness value of 10 in the **Distance** box, such as **10 mm**. If the preview grows in the wrong direction, click the direction arrow to reverse it so the flange extends outward from the pipe ends.
30. Set the operation to **Join**.
31. Check the preview carefully and confirm that the three port holes remain open through the flange before clicking **OK**.

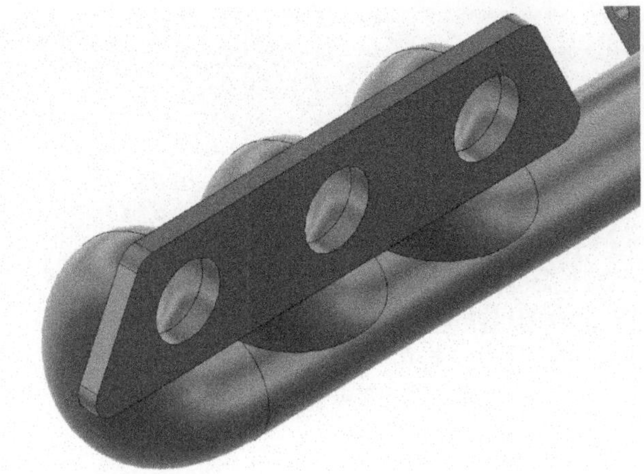

Adding Mounting Holes to the Flange

To create the mounting holes, first start a new sketch on the outer face of the flange and place four sketch points at the exact center of the rounded corners. Next, exit the sketch and use the solid **Hole** command, set the placement type to **From Sketch**, select the four points, and configure the hole diameter and depth to cut entirely through the plate.

1. Ensure you are in the **Solid** toolbar.
2. Select **Create Sketch**.
3. Click on the large, flat front face of the newly extruded manifold flange to set it as your active sketch plane.

4. Press the letter **P** on your keyboard or go to **Create > Project/Include > Project**.
5. Select the fillet edges of the extruded feature.
6. Click **OK**.

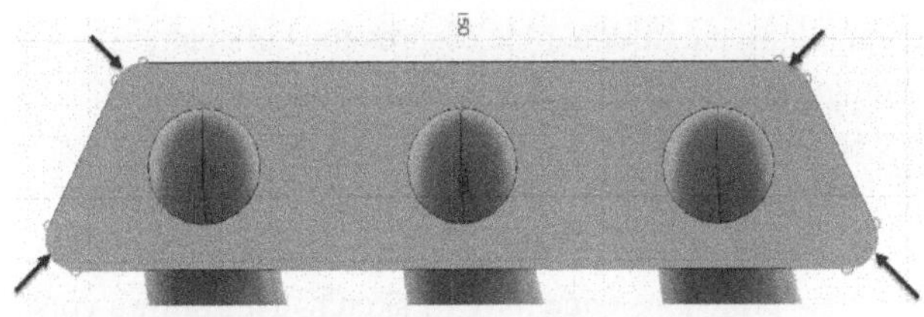

7. Navigate to the top ribbon and select **Create > Point** from the dropdown menu.

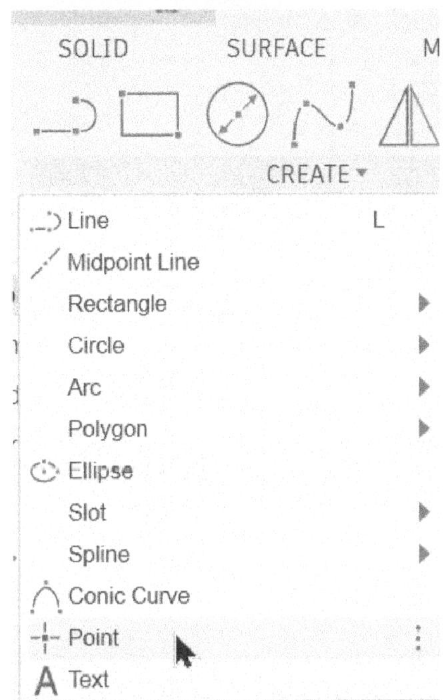

8. Hover your cursor near the top-left rounded corner of the flange until a small crosshair appears, indicating the exact center point of that arc. Click to place a point. The point will appear as a small black dot.
9. Repeat this process for the bottom-left, top-right, and bottom-right corners. You should now have four points located precisely at the center of the four fillets.

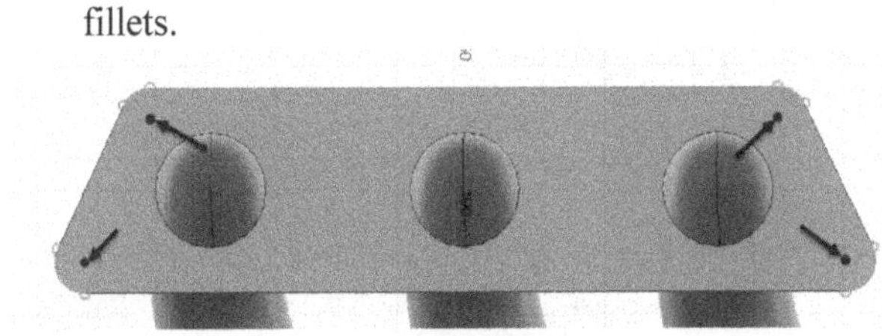

To position the four central holes, draw a construction rectangle starting from the center point of the middle pipe. Add sketch points to the four corners of the rectangle and apply dimensions for the required spacing. Linking the rectangle to the middle pipe ensures the hole pattern remains symmetrical and centered on the flange.

10. Press **P** for the **Project** tool.
11. Select the circular opening of the middle pipe to project its edge into the sketch. This allows you to find and snap to the exact center point of the middle hole. Click **OK**.

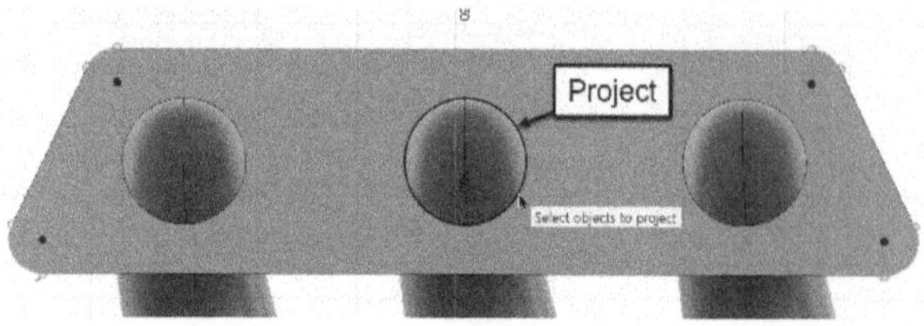

12. Go to **Create > Rectangle > Center Rectangle**.

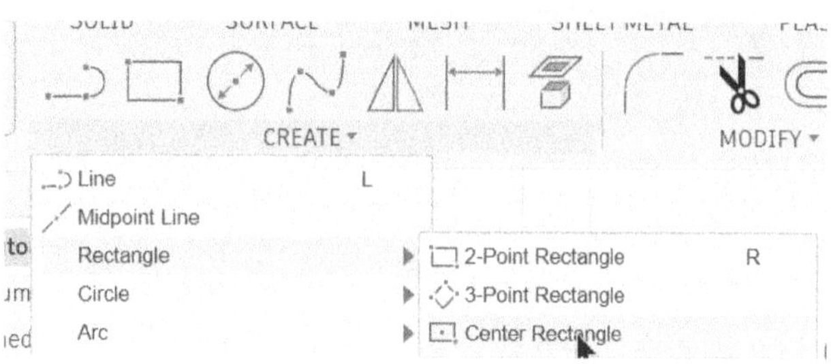

13. Click **Linetype > Construction** on the Sketch Palette.
14. Click the center point of the newly projected middle pipe opening to place the rectangle's origin.
15. Drag the cursor outward and click to place the rectangle.

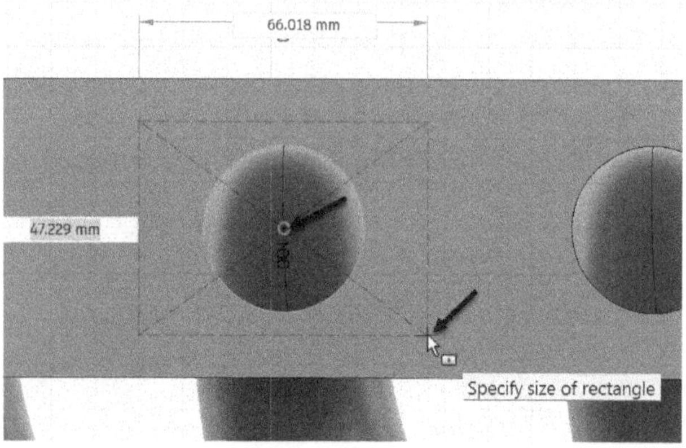

16. To ensure the rectangle follows the angle of the outer flange corners, select the **Horizontal/Vertical** constraint tool.
17. Click the top-right corner of the rectangle.
18. Click on the center point of the top right curved edge to align them horizontally.

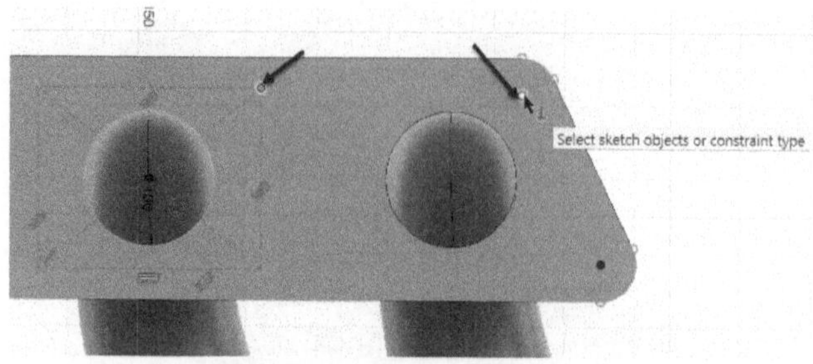

19. Press **D** for the **Sketch Dimension** tool.
20. Click the top horizontal line of the construction rectangle, drag upward, and enter **70.00**. This sets the width.
21. Go to **Create > Point** on the toolbar.
22. Click on the four outer corners of the dashed construction rectangle to place four sketch points.
23. Click **Finish Sketch** to exit the sketch environment.
24. In the **Solid** toolbar, locate the **Create** panel and click the **Hole** command. Alternatively, press the letter **H** on your keyboard.

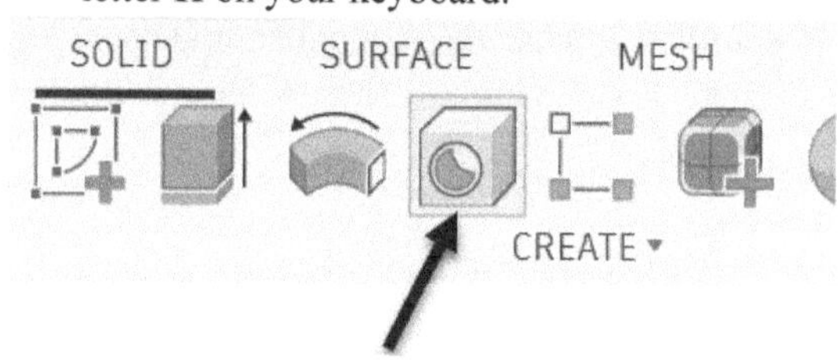

The **Hole** dialogue box will appear on the right side of the screen.

25. In the **Hole** dialogue box, look at the **Placement** setting. Change it to **From Sketch** (the icon showing multiple dots).

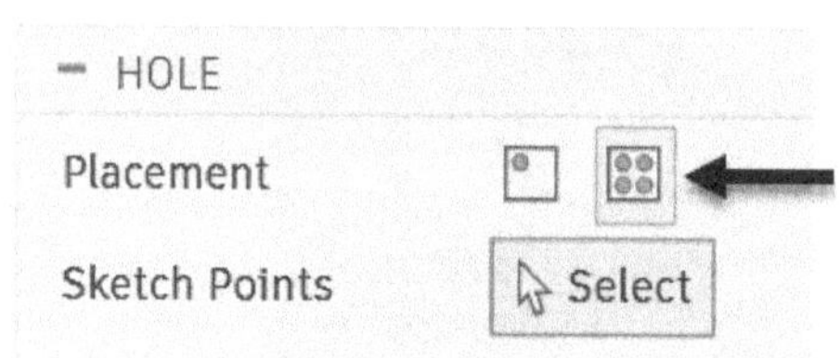

26. Click directly on the eight sketch points you just created. The dialogue box should update to show "8 selected".

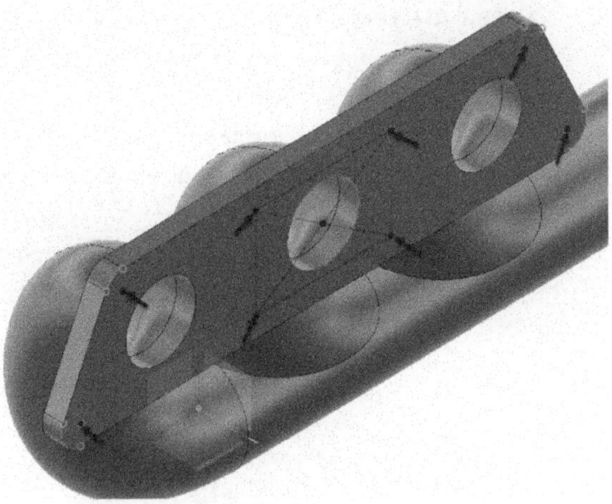

27. Under the **Shape Settings**, change the **Extents** dropdown to **All**. This ensures the holes cut completely through the flange regardless of its thickness.
28. Set the **Hole Type** to **Simple** (the left-most icon).
29. At the bottom of the dialogue box, locate the diameter input field and enter **10.00 mm**.

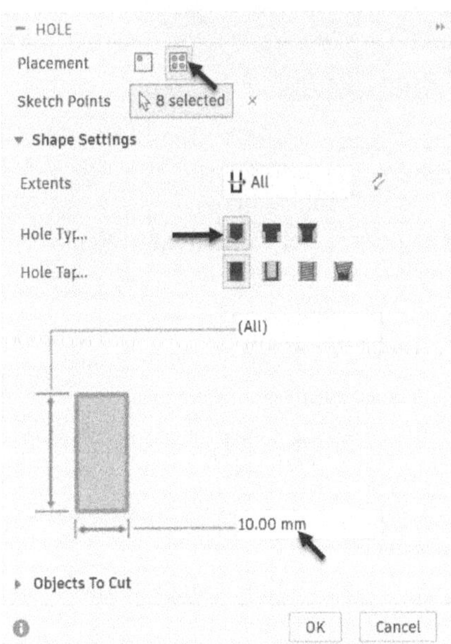

30. Click **OK** to execute the command. The software will generate four identical 10 mm holes through the corners of the flange.

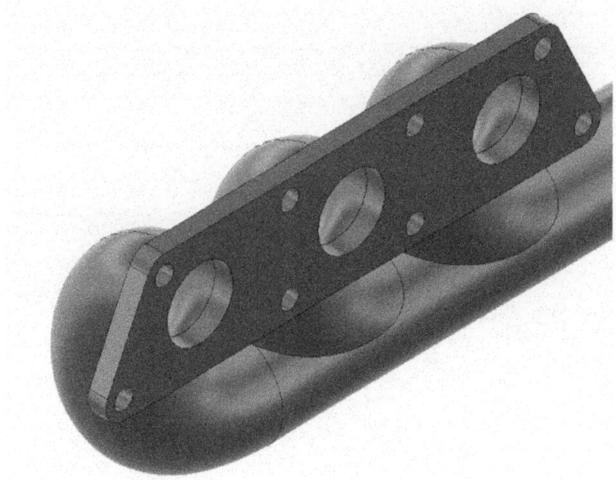

Tutorial 9

In this tutorial, you will create the part shown in figure below.

Start the first sketch

1. Open Fusion 360 and create a new design.
2. Select **Create Sketch** from the Solid workspace and choose the Top plane (XY).
3. Press **C** for the Circle tool. Click the center origin and draw an inner circle with a diameter of **57.00 mm**.
4. Click the center origin again and draw an outer circle with a diameter of **124.00 mm**.

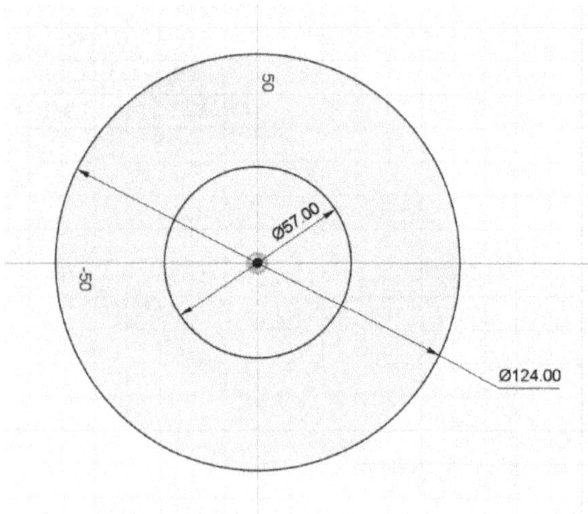

5. Click **Finish Sketch**.
6. Press **E** to activate the **Extrude** tool.
7. Select the shaded area between the two circles. Enter an extrusion distance of **12.00 mm** to generate the solid ring body. Click **OK**.

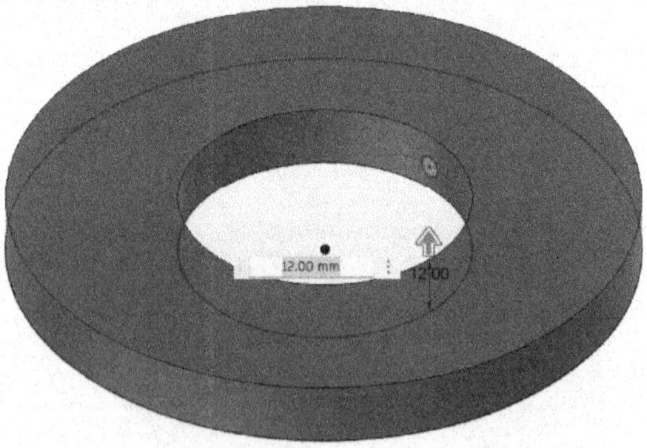

Creating the Counterbore Hole

1. Select **Create Sketch** again, and click directly on the flat bottom face of the newly extruded ring.

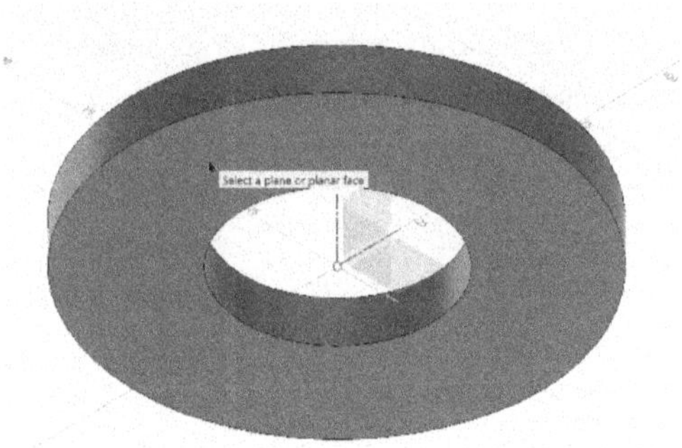

2. Navigate to **Create > Point**.
3. Place a single point directly above the center origin, aligning it with the vertical (Y) axis.
4. Apply a **Vertical/Horizontal** constraint between the new sketch point and the center origin to ensure it stays locked on that vertical line.
5. Press **D** for Sketch Dimension. Click the sketch point, then click the center origin. Enter a vertical distance of **48.00 mm**. The point is now fully constrained.

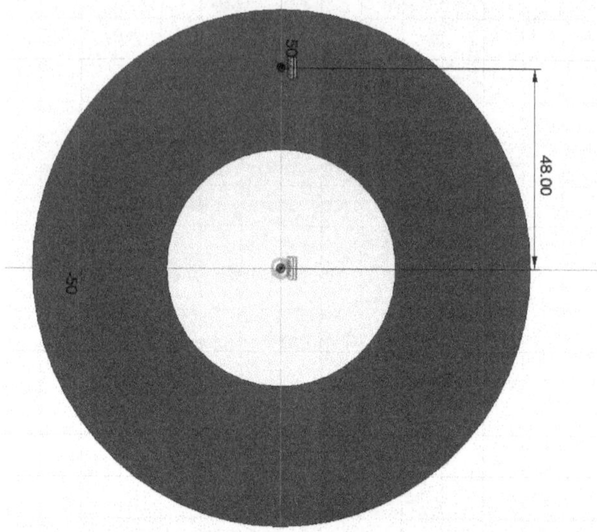

6. Click **Finish Sketch**.
7. Press **H** to activate the **Hole** command.
8. In the **Hole** dialogue box, set **Placement** to **From Sketch** and click the single sketch point you just created.
9. Set the **Extents** dropdown to **All** so the hole cuts entirely through the 12 mm plate.
10. Under **Hole Type**, select the **Counterbore** icon (the middle option).
11. Under **Hole Tap Type**, ensure it is set to **Simple** (the left-most option).
12. In the bottom parameters section, input the following values:
    - **Counterbore Diameter:** 12.00 mm
    - **Counterbore Depth:** 3.00 mm
    - **Lower Hole Diameter:** 7.50 mm

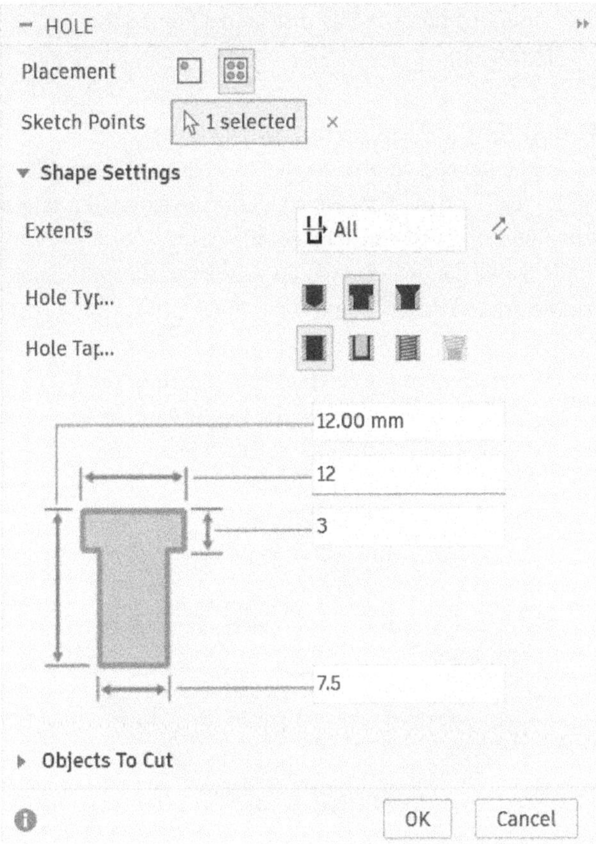

- Verify the red preview cylinder matches your intentions.

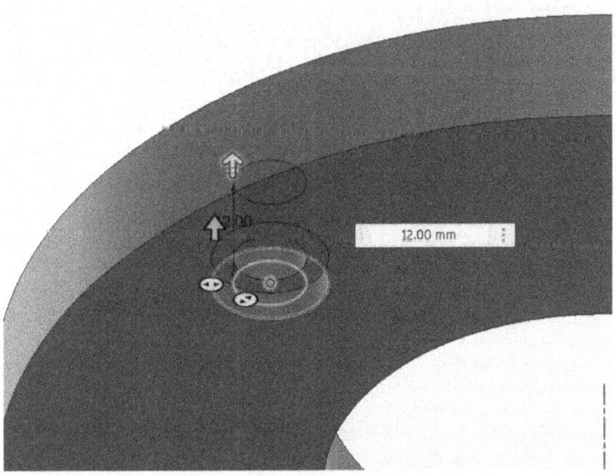

- Click **OK** to complete the feature.

Creating a Circular Pattern

To duplicate the single counterbored hole evenly around the ring, use the **Circular Pattern** tool set to "Features," select the hole as the object, choose the flange's central axis or inner cylindrical face as the center point for rotation, and set the quantity to 8.

1. Navigate to the top ribbon and ensure you are in the **Solid** workspace.
2. Go to the **Create** menu, hover over **Pattern**, and select **Circular Pattern**.

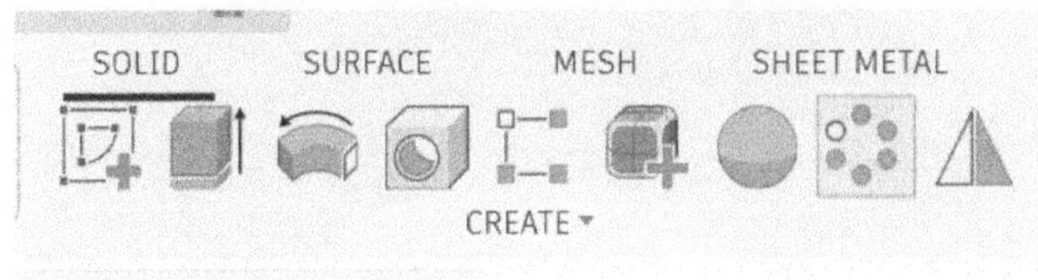

The **Circular Pattern** dialogue box will open on the right side of your screen.

3. In the dialogue box, locate the **Object Type** dropdown and set it to **Features**. This setting allows you to duplicate the hole operation itself, rather than entire solid bodies or raw faces.
4. Ensure the **Objects** selection button is active (highlighted in blue).

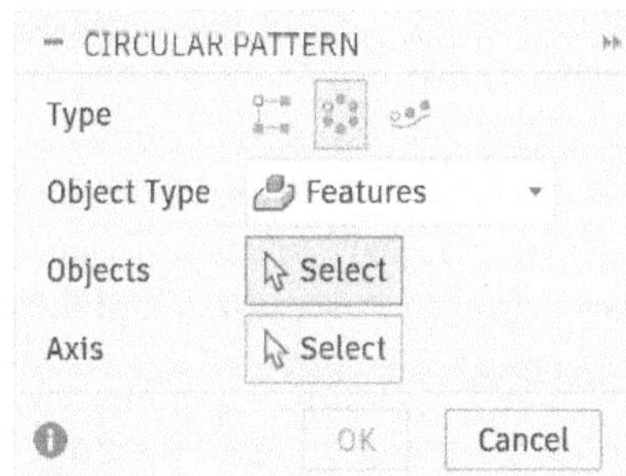

5. Select the counterbored hole you previously created. You can click directly on the hole inside the 3D workspace, or you can click the corresponding **Hole** icon located in your design timeline at the bottom left of the screen.

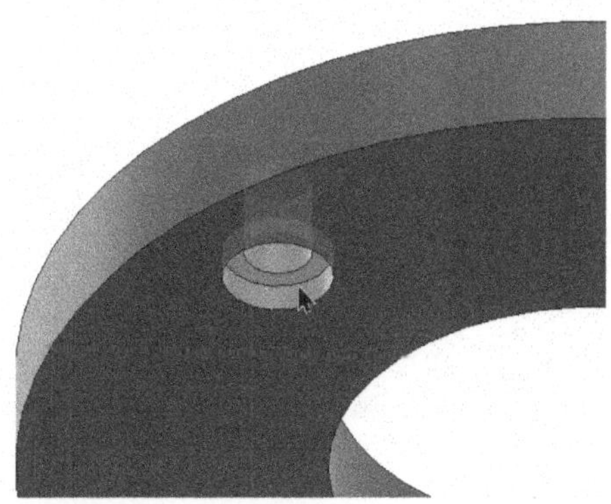

6. In the dialogue box, activate the **Axis** selection button.

7. Click on the central vertical axis, or simply click on the inner cylindrical face of the ring's central opening. Fusion 360 will automatically interpret the center of that cylinder as the rotation point.

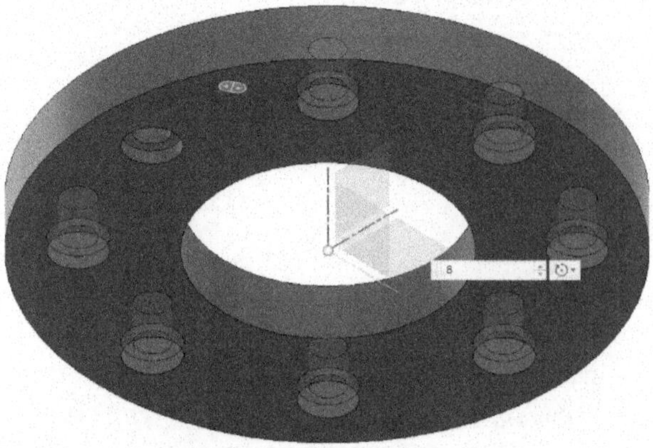

8. Ensure the **Distribution** setting is set to **Full**. This will spread the holes evenly across a complete 360-degree circle.
9. In the **Quantity** input box, enter **8**. The software will display translucent previews of the seven new holes spaced around the flange.
10. Check the **Compute Type** at the bottom of the dialogue box. Leave it set to **Identical** if all holes cut straight through the same flat geometry. If you encounter errors, change it to **Adjust** or **Optimized**.
11. Verify the visual preview is correct.

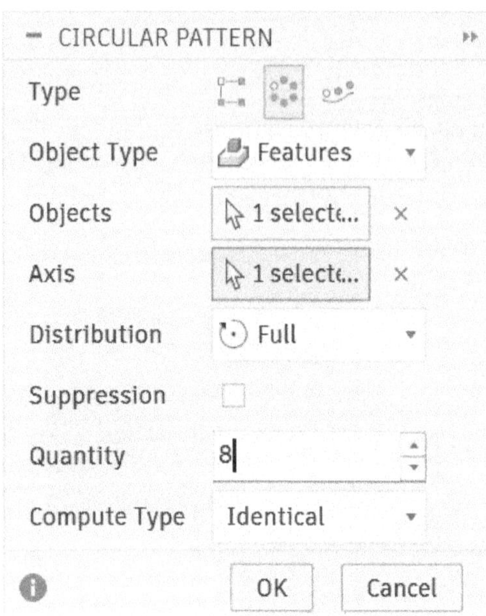

12. Click **OK** to execute the command. The solid flange will update to show all eight identical counterbored mounting holes evenly distributed around the perimeter.

Revolving a Pipe Extension

To create the curved pipe, sketch an angled solid profile ring directly on the flange face, define an external rotation axis line using a dimension, and then use the **Revolve** command set to 40 degrees to sweep the ring profile around that axis into a solid body.

1. Select **Create Sketch** from the **Solid** toolbar.
2. Click directly on the flat top face of the completed flange to set the sketch plane.

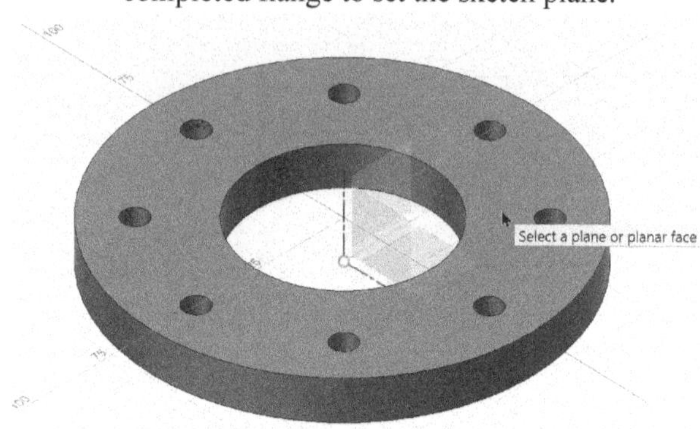

3. Press **P** to open the **Project** dialogue box.
4. Carefully select the inner circular edge of the central opening
5. Click **OK** to complete the projection.
6. Press **C** to activate the **Circle** tool.
7. Select the sketch origin, move the pointer outward and click.
8. Press **D** to activate the **Sketch Dimension** tool.
9. Select the circle, type **69** and press ENTER. This creates the hollow ring profile that will be revolved.
10. While still inside the active sketch, press **L** for the **Line** tool.
11. Move your cursor far to the left of the flange body. Draw a vertical line.
12. Select the line and press **X** to convert it into a dashed construction line.
13. Press **D** for the **Sketch Dimension** tool.
14. Click the central origin point of the flange, then click the vertical construction line. Drag downward and enter a dimension of **113.00 mm**. This sets the exact turning radius for the revolved pipe.
15. Click **Finish Sketch** to exit the 2D environment.

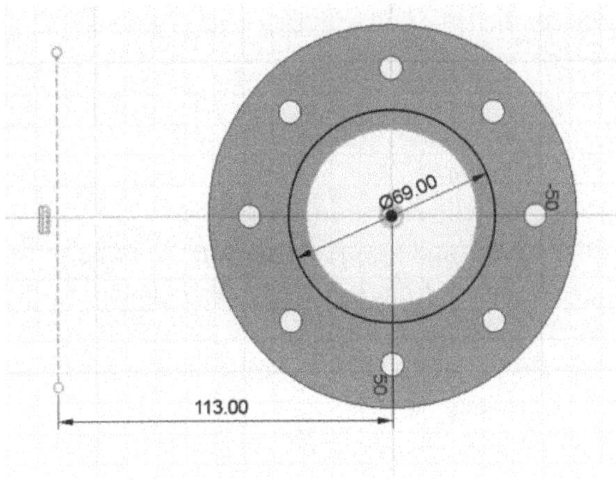

16. Go to the **Solid** workspace ribbon and select **Create > Revolve**.The **Revolve** dialogue box will appear on the right side of the screen.
17. Ensure the **Profile** selection button is active. Click the solid ring area between the inner projected circle and the outer 69.00 mm circle. The selected area will turn blue. Do not select the center hole.

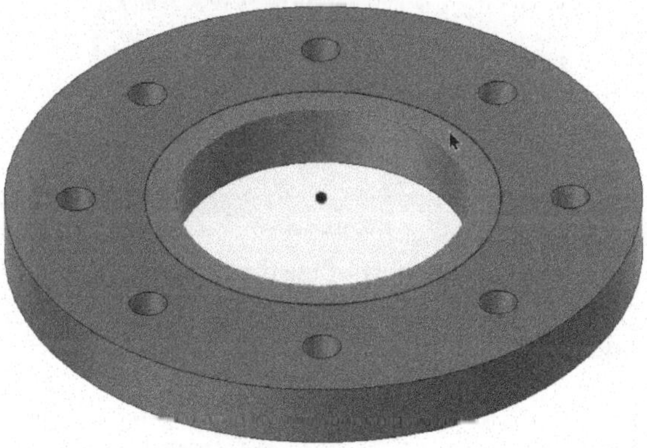

18. Activate the **Axis** selection button in the dialogue menu.
19. Click the construction line located 113.00 mm away from the center. The software will instantly preview a sweep of the profile around that distant axis.

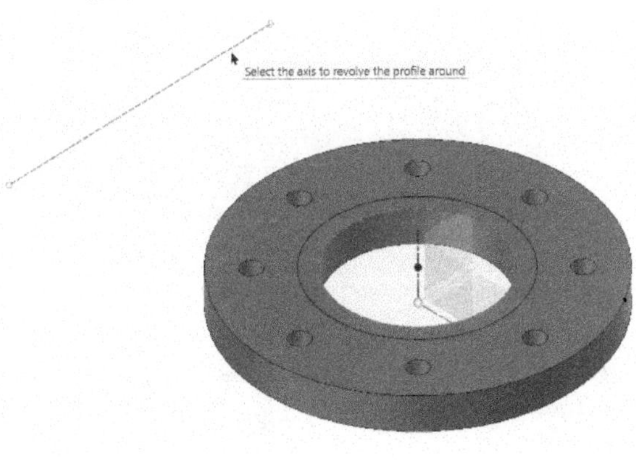

20. In the dialogue box, change the **Angle** parameter to **40 deg**.
21. Ensure the **Operation** is set to **Join** so the new pipe merges physically with the existing flange base.

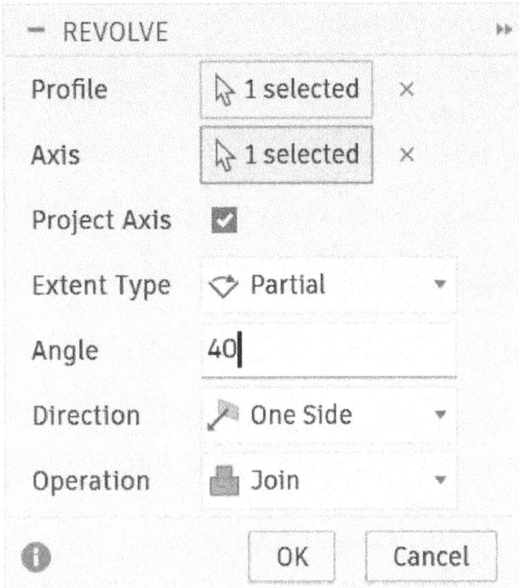

22. Verify the preview shows the pipe curving upward and away at a 40-degree sweep.

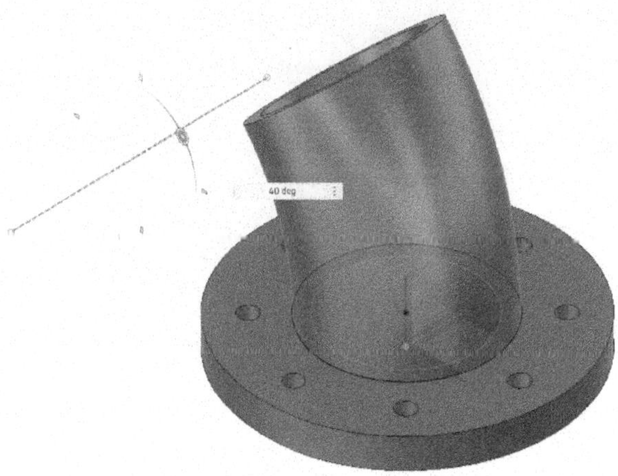

23. Click **OK** to finalize the geometry.

Mirroring the Flange

To duplicate the flange, first generate a symmetrical reference plane between the top and bottom of the pipe using the **Midplane** construction tool. Next, activate the **Mirror** command, select the original flange body (including its holes) as the object, choose the newly created midplane as the mirror plane, and verify the duplicated geometry.

1. Ensure you are in the **Solid** toolbar.
2. Locate the **Construct** dropdown menu in the top ribbon and select **Midplane**.

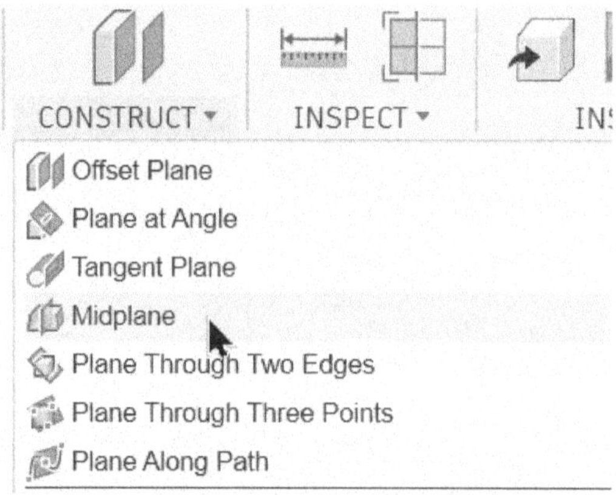

3. The tool requires two faces to calculate a center plane. First, click the flat circular face at the very top of the curved pipe.
4. Click the flat top face of the base flange.

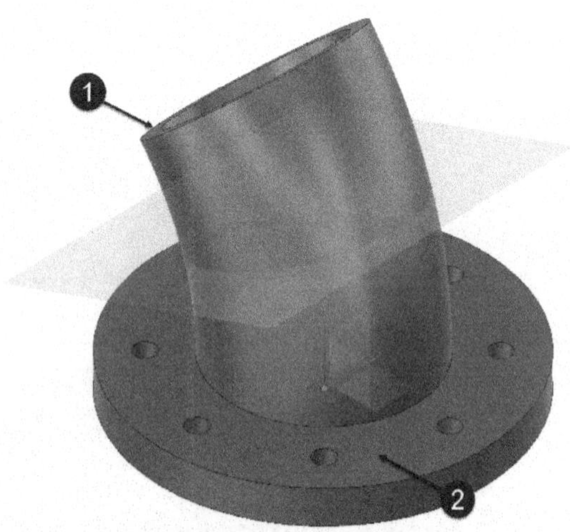

5. An orange translucent plane will immediately appear, cutting perfectly through the center angle of the curved pipe. Click **OK** to generate the plane.
6. Go to the **Create** menu and select the **Mirror** tool.

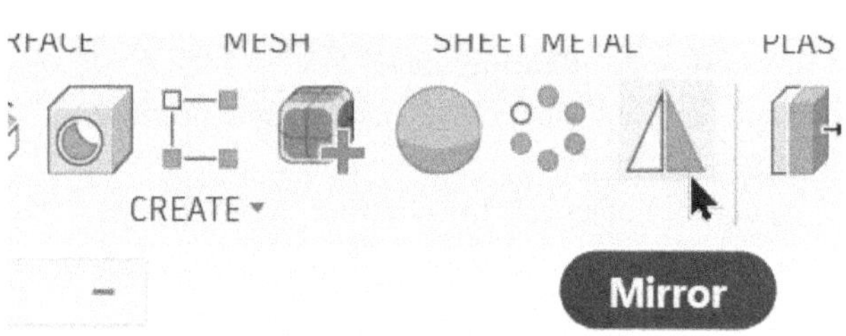

The **Mirror** dialogue box will open on the right side of the screen.

7. In the dialogue box, change the **Object Type** to **Features**.
8. Ensure the **Objects** selection button is active.
9. Click on the solid base flange, hole feature, and circular pattern feature. It will highlight in blue to confirm selection.
10. Activate the **Mirror Plane** selection button in the dialogue menu.
11. Click on the orange construction midplane you created earlier.

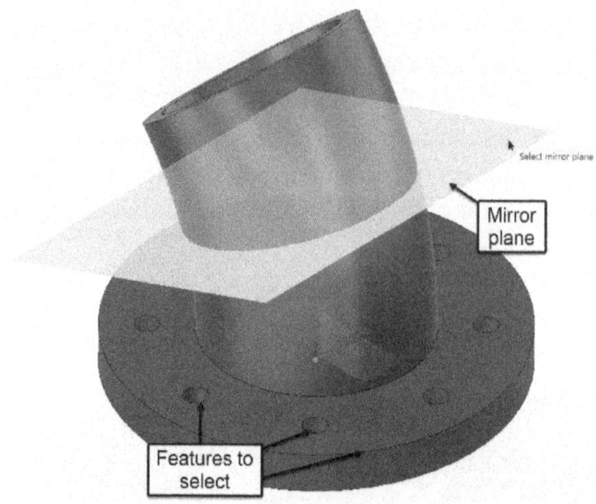

12. A translucent preview of the duplicated flange will appear exactly at the top of the curved pipe, perfectly aligned with the pipe's opening.

13. If the operation setting is available, ensure it is set to **Join** so the new flange merges with the pipe.

14. Click **OK** to execute the command.

15. To clean up your workspace, locate the **Construction** folder in your **Browser** panel on the left side of the screen and click the eye icon next to the midplane to hide it from view.

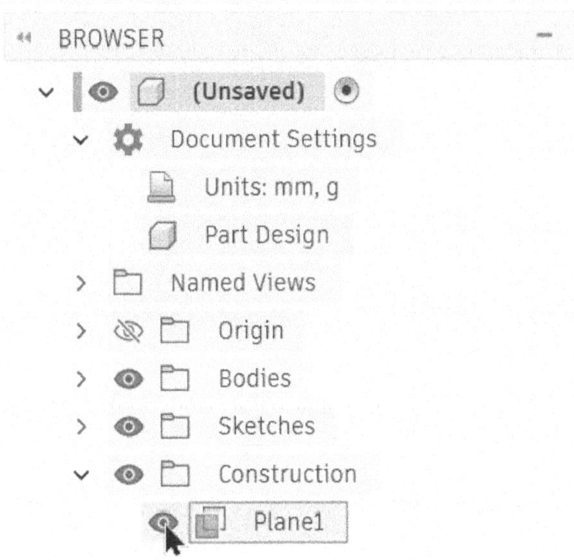

Tutorial 10

In this tutorial, you will create the part shown in figure below.

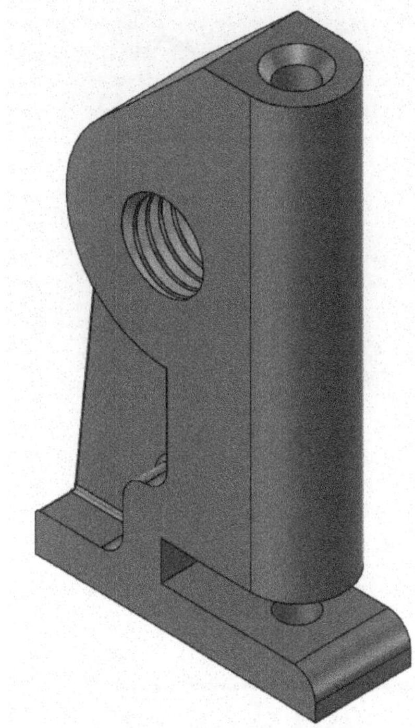

Creating the Base Feature

1. Select **Create Sketch** and choose a YZ plane
2. Press **L** for the **Line** tool.
3. Click on the horizontal axis of the sketch on the left side.
4. Move the cursor vertically upward upto a small distance and click.
5. Move the cursor horizontally toward right and click.
6. Likewise, create the other straight lines. Next press ESC.

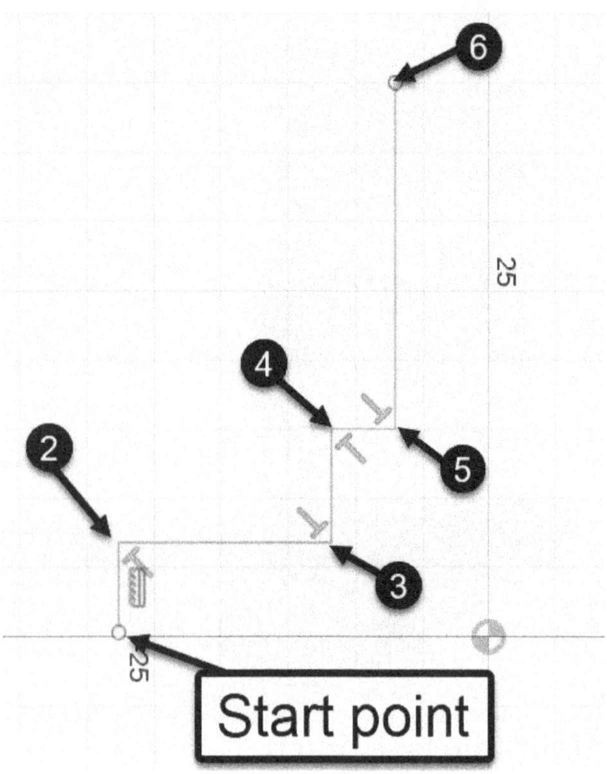

7. Activate the **Line** tool and select the start point of the sketch.
8. Move the cursor toward right horizontally and click.
9. Move the cursor vertically upward up to a small distance and click.
10. Move the cursor horizontally toward left and click.
11. Move the cursor vertically upward up to a small distance and click.
12. Move the cursor horizontally toward right and click.
13. Draw a long vertical line upward.

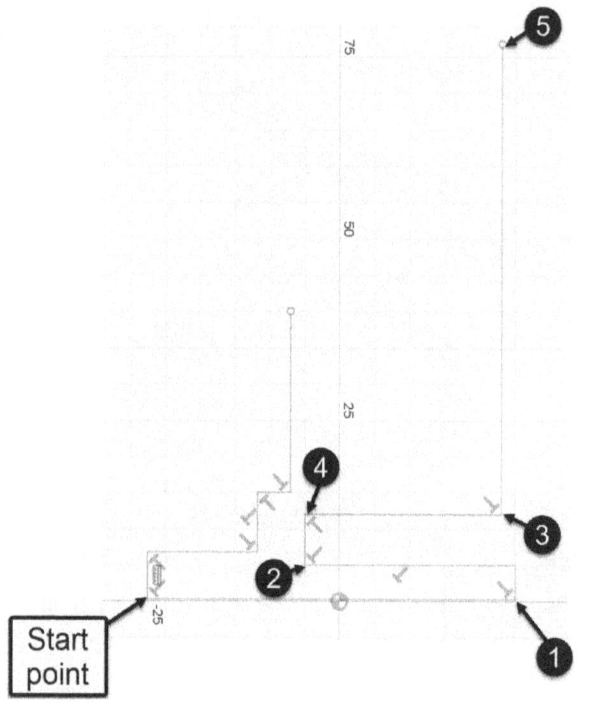

14. Draw a horizontal line left across the top, and a short-angled line pointing diagonally downward and to the left.

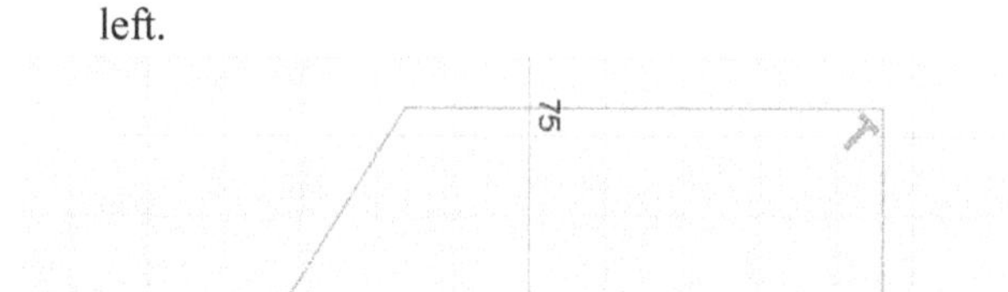

15. Navigate to **Create > Arc > Tangent Arc**.

16. Click the bottom endpoint of the inclined line, then click the top endpoint of the vertical line extending from the bottom steps.

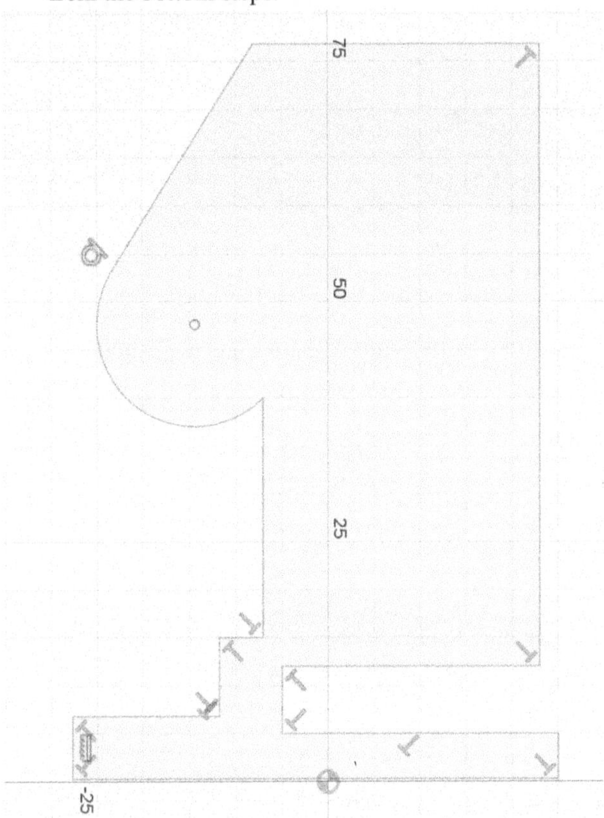

17. Select the **Vertical/Horizontal** constraint tool from the toolbar.
18. Click the center point of the newly drawn arc, then click the bottom endpoint of that same arc. This forces the center of the arc to align perfectly vertically above its connecting point, ensuring a smooth transition.

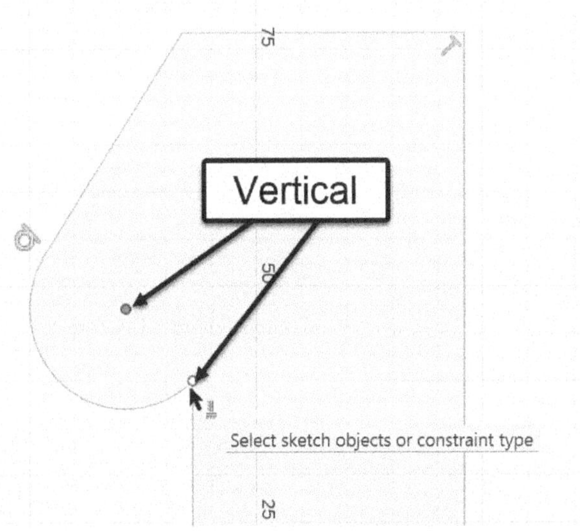

19. Select the **Midpoint** constraint tool on the **Constraints** panel.
20. Click the bottom horizontal line of the entire profile, then click the center origin point of your sketch grid. The entire shape will shift so it is perfectly centered symmetrically over the vertical axis.

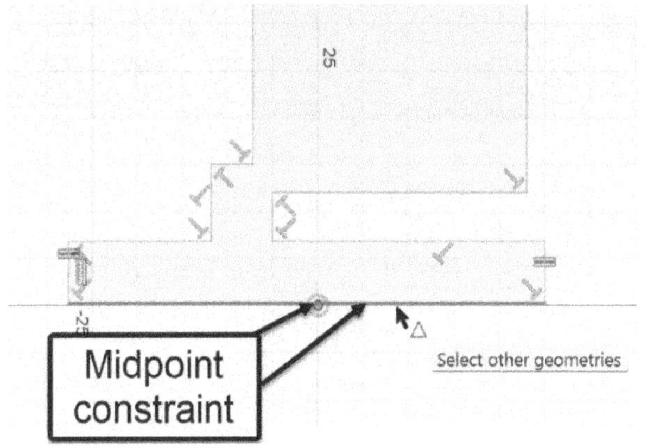

21. Select the **Equal** constraint tool on the **Constraints** panel.
22. Select the two vertical lines at the bottom.

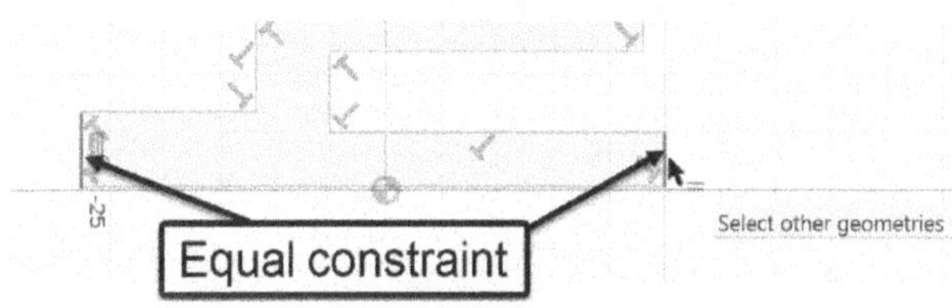

23. Press **D** for the **Sketch Dimension** tool. Apply the following values according to the reference blueprint:
    - Overall bottom width: 45.00 mm

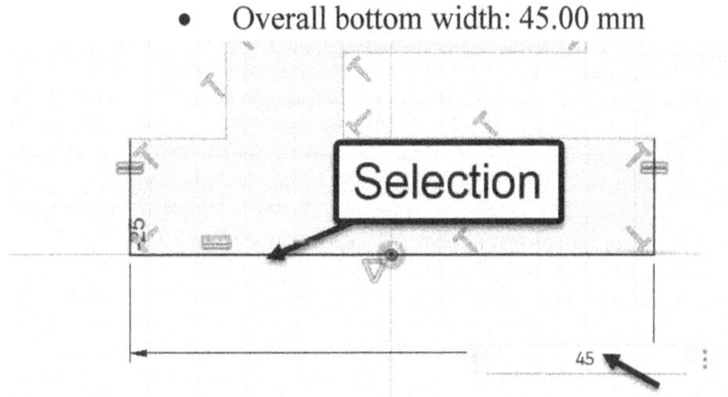

    - Bottom base height: 6.00 mm

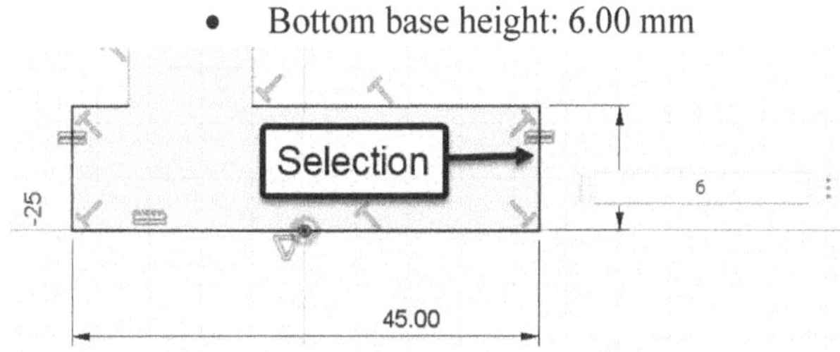

    - Inner base step width: 28.00 mm

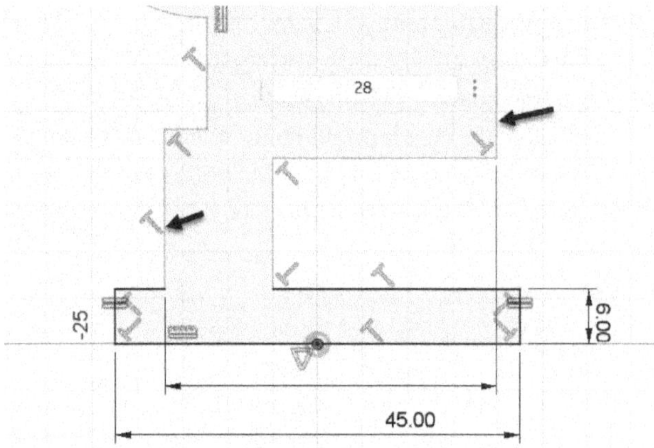

- Base step offset from left: 6.00 mm

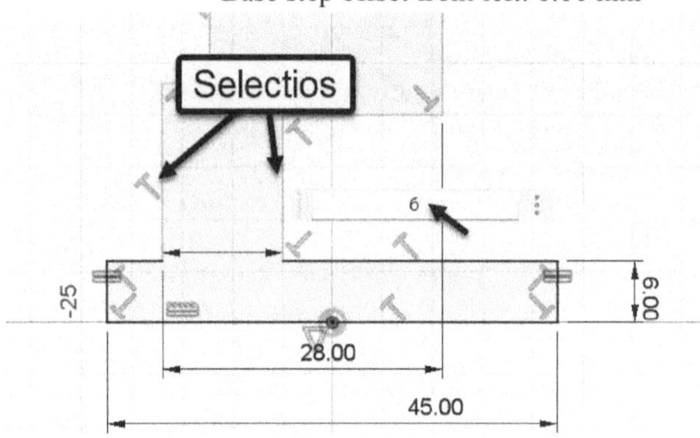

- Step height to inner channel: 6.00 mm

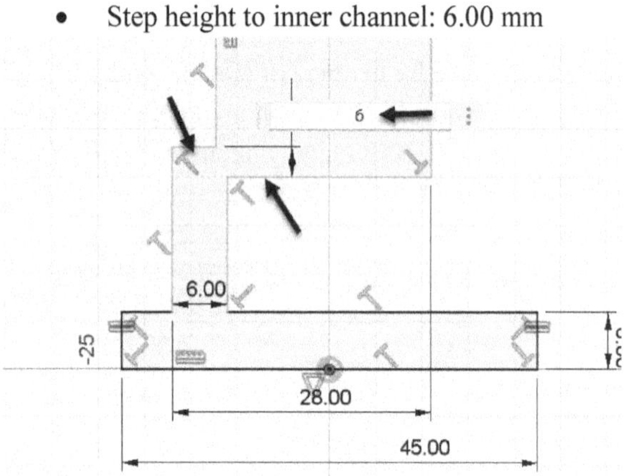

- Inner channel height: 12.00 mm

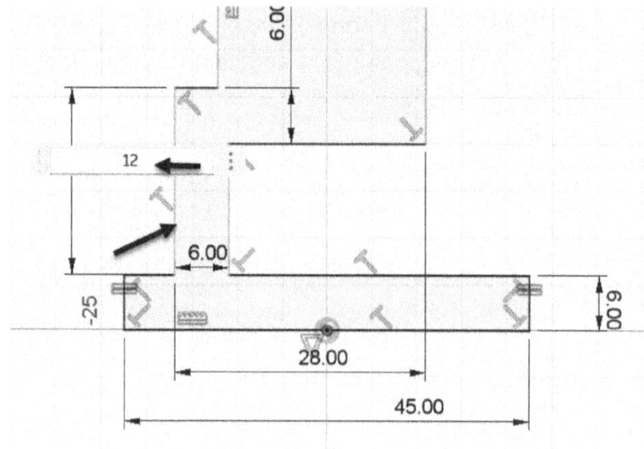

- Height from channel to arc bottom: 45.00 mm

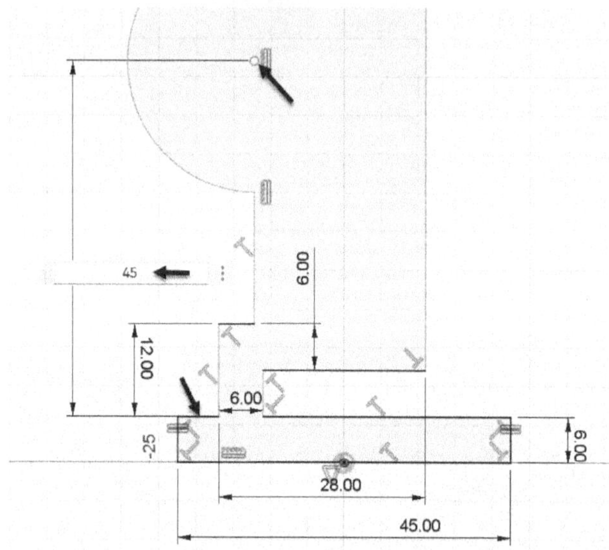

- Click the arc line itself to apply a radial dimension, and enter **R16.00**.

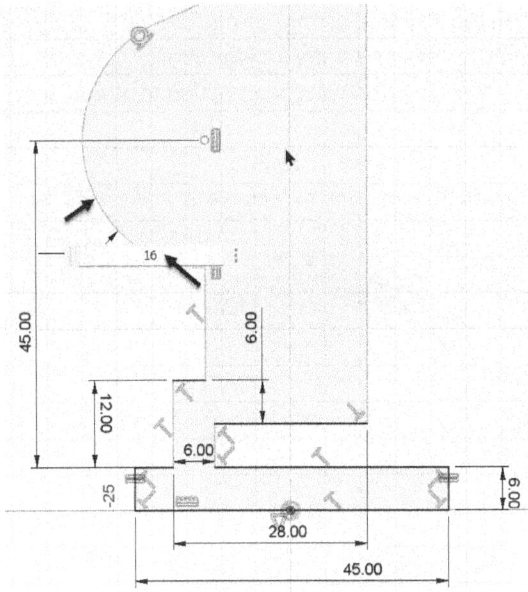

- Top horizontal width: 15.00 mm

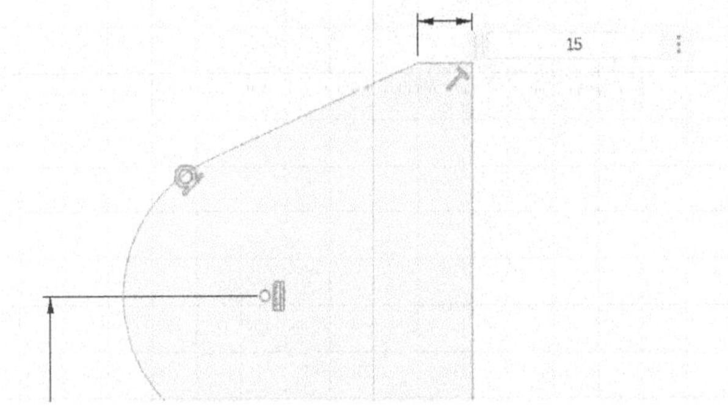

- Click the **vertical straight line** on the right side of the sketch (the reference line from which the width is measured).
- Right-click anywhere in the sketch area.
- From the context menu, select **Pick Circle/Arc Tangent**.

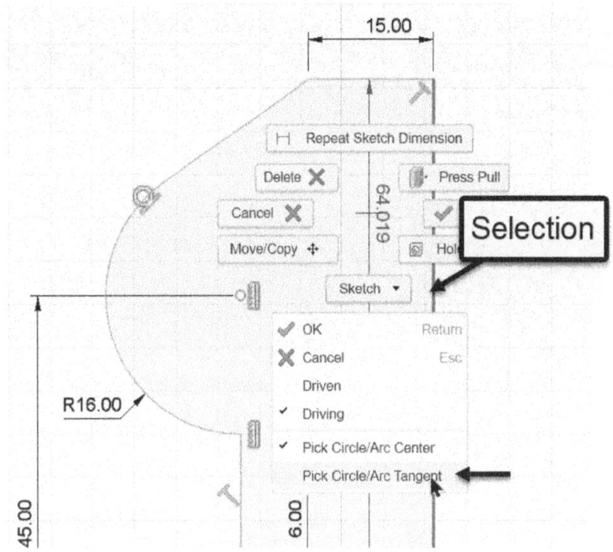

- Click the **arc edge** on the left side of the sketch. Fusion 360 will automatically detect the **tangent point on the arc** that corresponds to the horizontal direction.

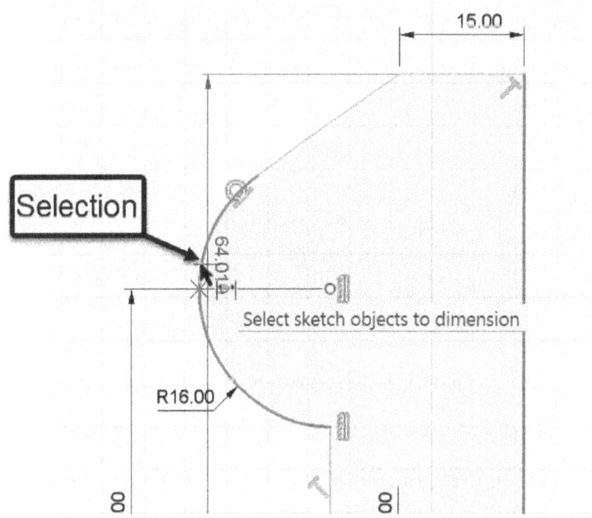

- Move the cursor upward to position the dimension.
- Click to place the dimension line.
- Type the required value (for example **37 mm** as shown in the image).

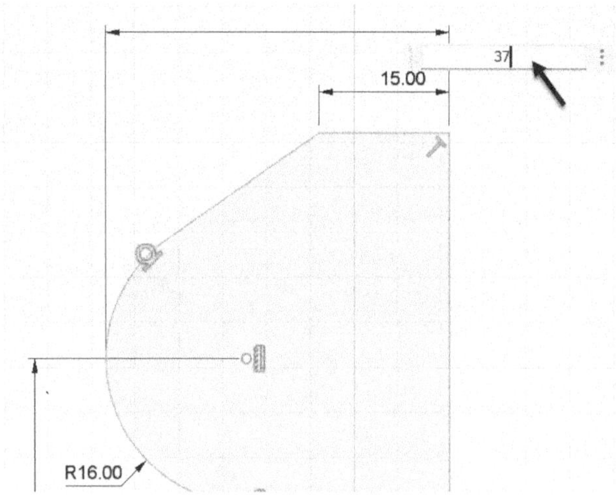

- Right wall recess depth: 3.00 mm
- Overall total height: 78.00 mm

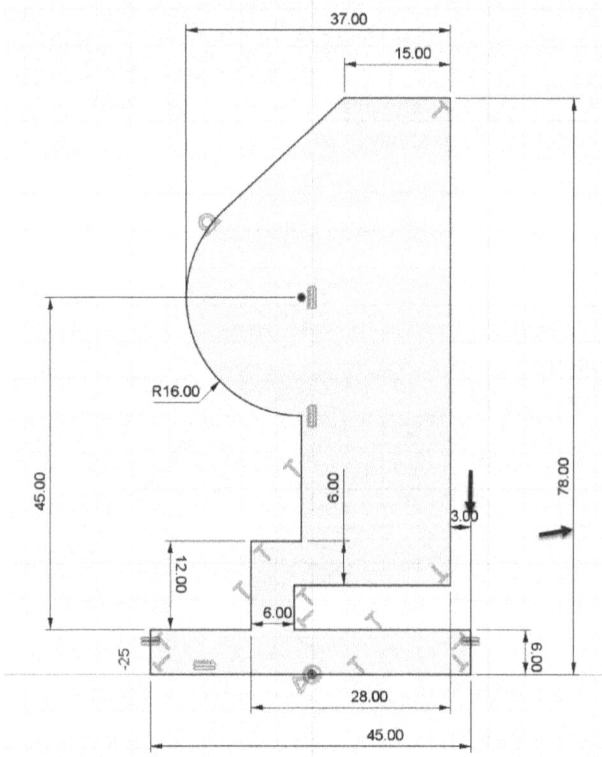

2. Verify that all lines have turned black, indicating the sketch is fully constrained.
3. Click **Finish Sketch**.

Extrude symmetrically

To build this geometry, first extrude the 2D profile symmetrically by 15 mm.

1. Select the **Extrude** tool and click the flat 2D profile you just sketched.
2. In the **Extrude** dialog, change the **Direction** setting to **Symmetric**.
3. Change the **Measurement** option to **Whole Length** (if not already selected).
4. Enter a **Distance** of **15 mm**.
5. Set the **Operation** to **New Body** and click **OK**.

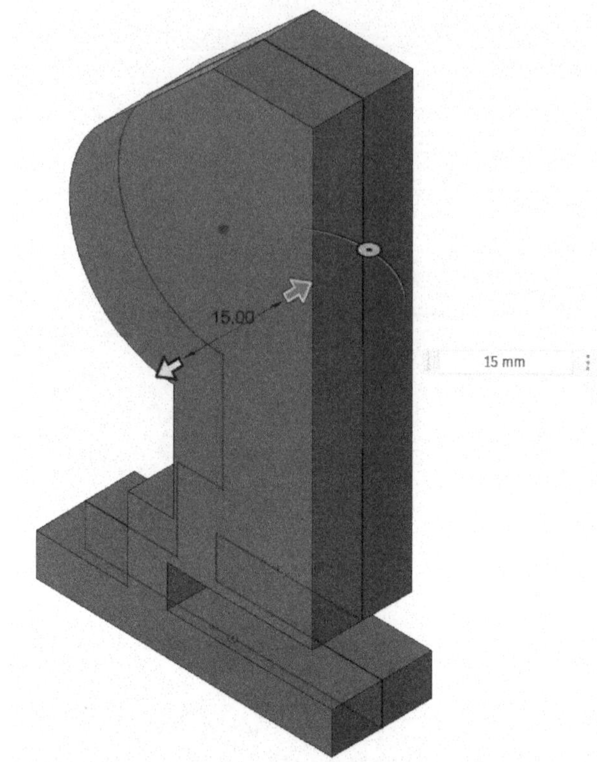

Apply a Full Round Fillet

1. Navigate to the toolbar, open the **Modify** panel menu, and select **Fillet**.
2. In the **Fillet** dialog box, change the **Type** to **Full Round Fillet**.

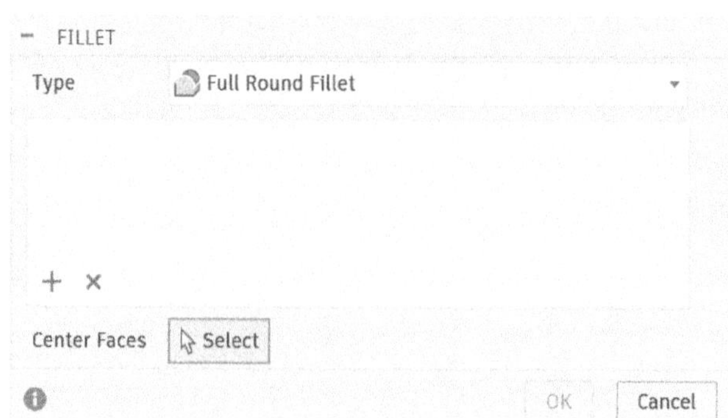

The dialog requires you to select three faces in order.

3. Click the right flat face of the column.The software will instantly consumes and replaces it with a perfect semi-circular dome. Click **OK**.

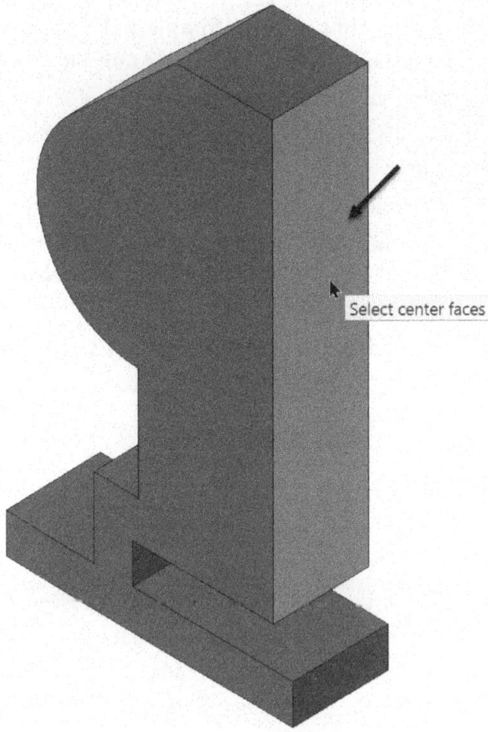

Create the vertical countersunk hole

1. Press **H** for the **Hole** command.
2. For placement, click on the top face of the column. Then, carefully click the circular edge of the dome itself; this acts as a concentric reference, forcing the hole to snap precisely to the center of the arc.

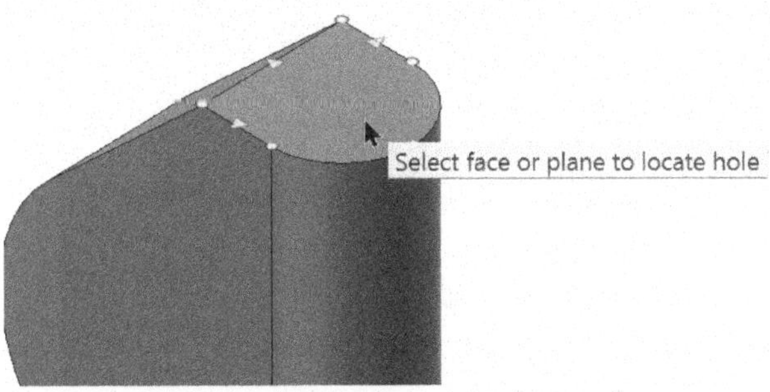

3. Set the **Extents** to **All**.
4. Set the **Hole Type** to **Countersink**. This creates a conical angled opening at the top of the cut so a screw head can sit flush with the surface.
5. Enter the lower hole diameter as **6.00 mm** and the top countersink diameter as **9.00 mm**, with an 82-degree angle. Click **OK**.

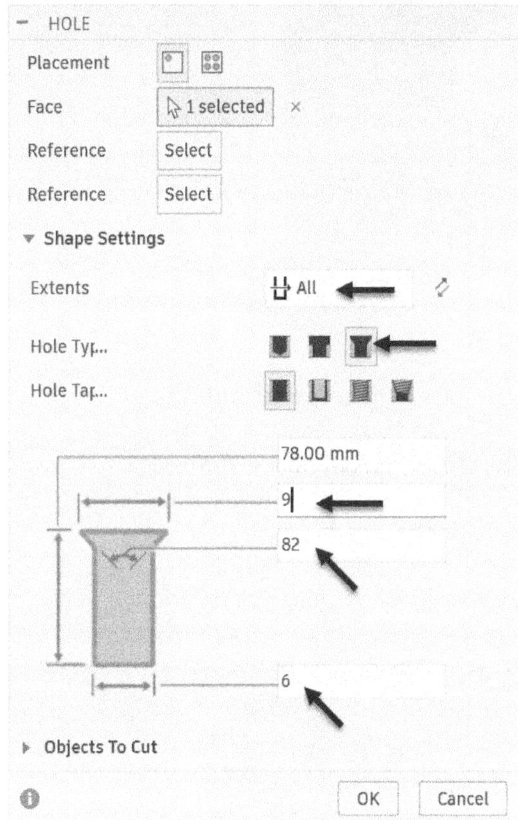

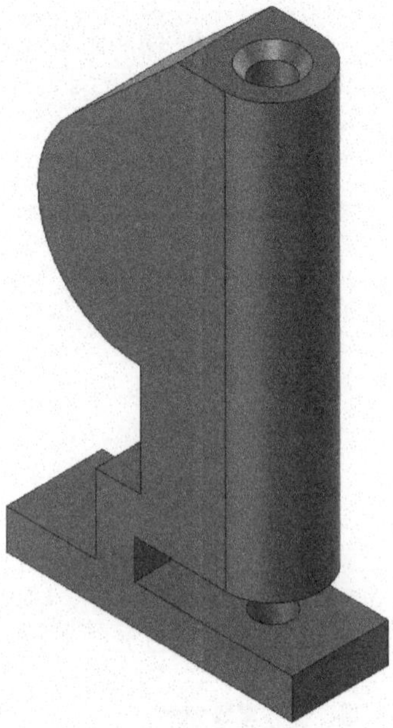

Create the lateral threaded hole

1. Press **H** for the **Hole** command again.
2. Click the large flat front face of the model.
3. To center the hole, click the large circular edge on the front of the bracket to establish a concentric reference. This action automatically locks the center point of the new hole to the exact center axis of the arc.

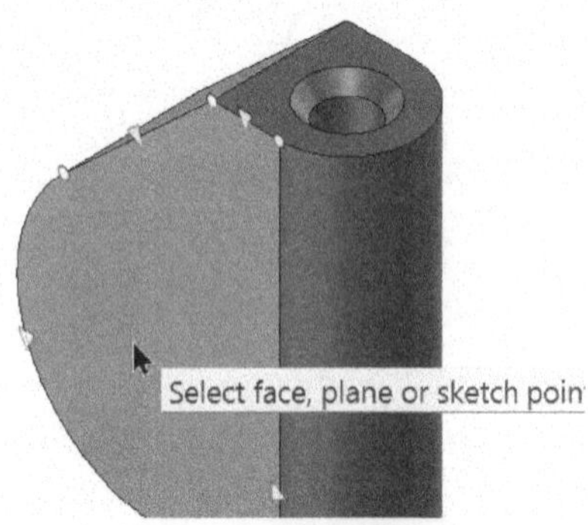

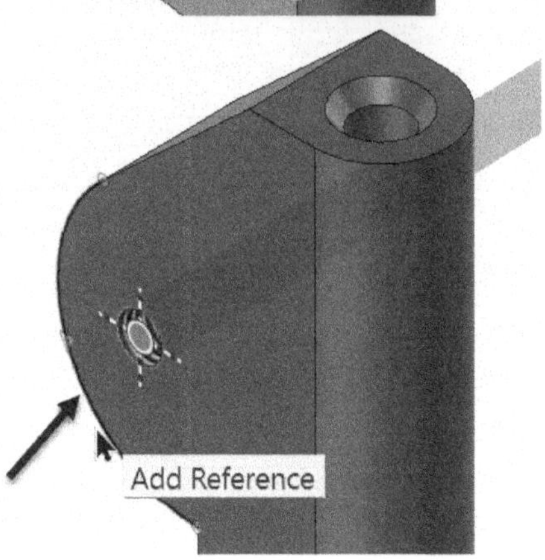

4. Change the **Extents** to **All**. This specific setting instructs the software to cut completely through the solid body regardless of the underlying material thickness.
5. Change the **Hole Type** to **Simple** and change the **Hole Tap Type** to **Tapped**. It tells the software to apply internal machine threads.
6. Specify the thread parameters section at the bottom of the dialog:
   - **Modeled Checkbox**: Check this box so the software computes physical three-dimensional helical cuts instead of applying a flat cosmetic texture.
   - **Thread Type**: Leave this as ISO Metric Profile to use standard international sizing.
   - **Size**: Select 14.0 mm to define the nominal outer diameter of the hole.
   - **Designation**: Select M14x2. The "2" indicates a 2 mm pitch, which is the physical distance between adjacent thread crests.
   - **Class**: Leave this at 6H, which represents a standard, medium-clearance manufacturing tolerance for internal threads.
   - **Direction**: Set to Right Hand for standard tightening behavior

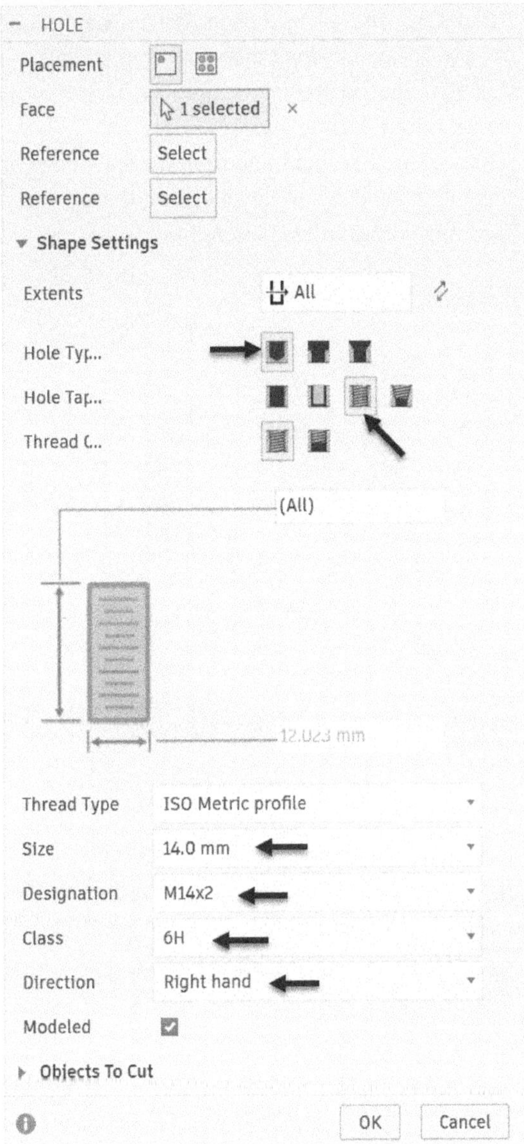

7. Click **OK** to execute the command.

Creating a Rib Feature

To build the structural support, first create a sketch on the vertical midplane and use the **Slice** tool to reveal the internal cross-section. Project the main edges into the sketch, draw a single angled line connecting the top dome to the bottom base using the Tangent constraint, and exit the sketch. Finally, activate the **Rib** command, select the angled line, set a symmetric thickness of 3.5 mm, and flip the direction so the material fills the gap toward the solid body.

1. Select **Create Sketch** from the Solid workspace.

2. Select the origin plane that cuts directly through the symmetrical center of your bracket (the midplane).

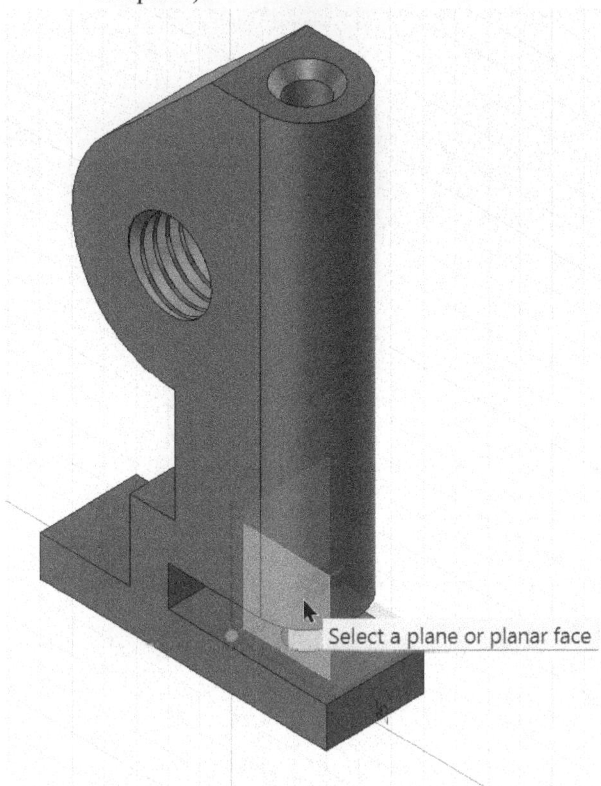

3. Because you are sketching "inside" the existing 3D body, your view may be blocked. Locate the **Sketch Palette** dialog box on the right side of the screen. Check the box labeled **Slice**. This temporarily hides all physical material between the camera and the sketch plane, allowing you to clearly see the internal cross-section where you will be drawing.

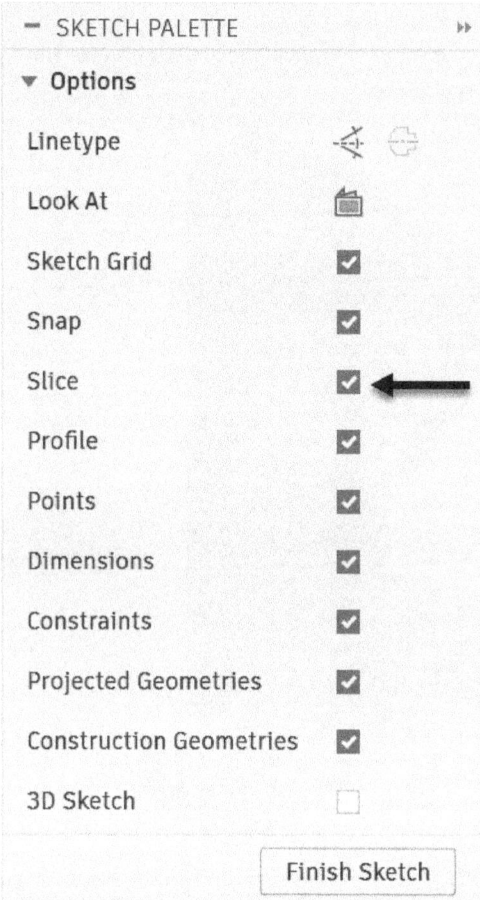

4. Press **P** to activate the **Project** tool. The projection dialog box will appear.
5. Ensure the Selection Filter is set to **Specified Entities**.
6. Click the outer curved edge of the top rounded dome to bring it into your 2D sketch.
7. Click the top horizontal edge of the bottom flat base plate to project it as well.

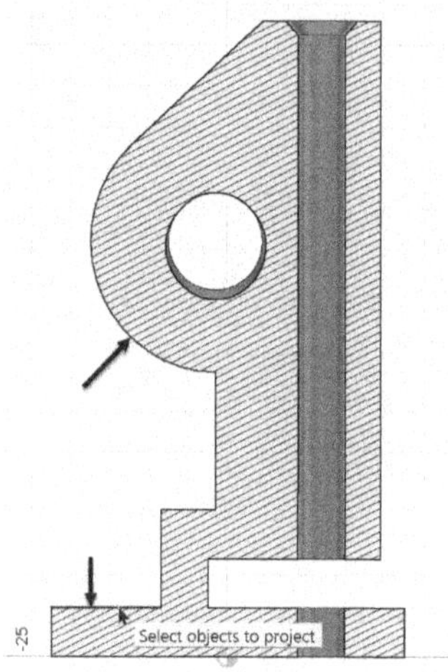

8. Click **OK**. The selected edges will now appear as purple lines, indicating they are parametrically linked to the 3D body.
9. Press **L** for the **Line** tool.
10. Draw a single straight line from the outer edge of the top dome down to the endpoint of the horizontal edge of the bottom base.

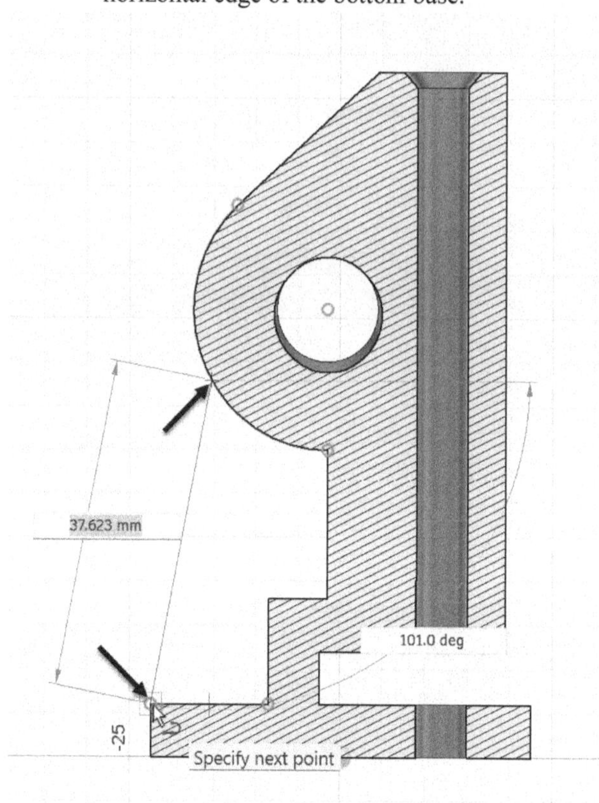

11. To ensure the line transitions smoothly into the top curve, select the **Tangent** constraint from the toolbar.
12. Click the newly drawn line, then click the purple projected curve of the top dome.

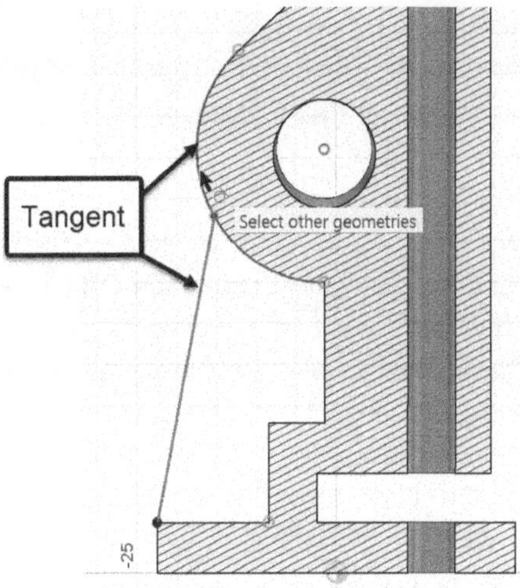

13. To control the bottom location, apply the Coincident constraint between the line and the endpoint of the horizontal edge (if needed).
14. Click **Finish Sketch**. Note that you only drew one single, unclosed line. It is the correct procedure for the Rib tool.

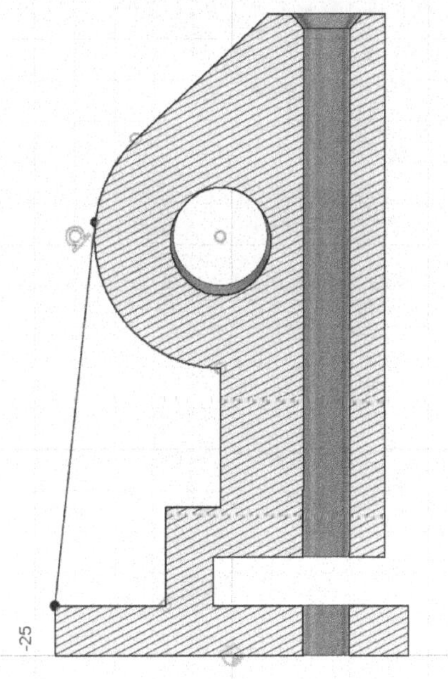

15. Navigate to the **Solid** toolbar, open the **Create** panel menu, and select the **Rib** tool. The **Rib** dialog box will open.

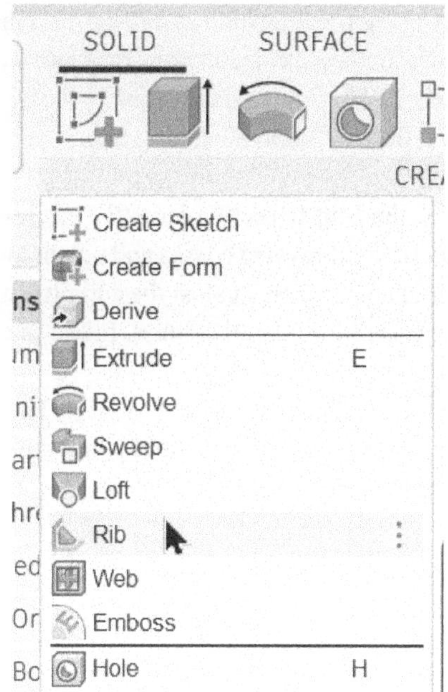

16. For the **Profile**, select the single angled line you just sketched. It will highlight in blue.
17. Set the **Thickness** value to **3.5 mm**.
18. Set the **Thickness Direction** to **Symmetric** (the default icon showing arrows pointing both ways) so the 3.5 mm thickness is split evenly on both sides of the sketch line.

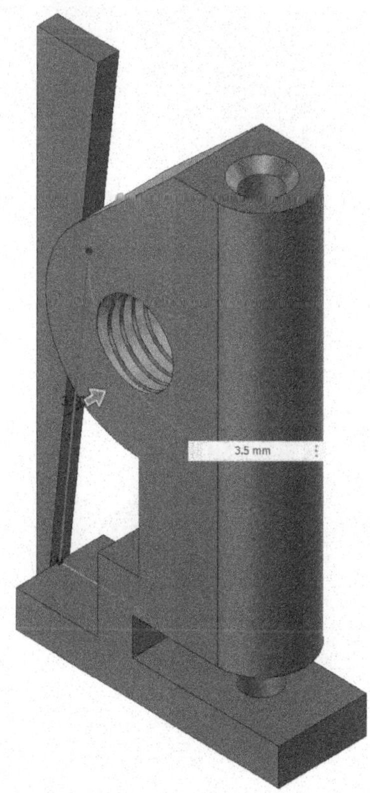

Look closely at the preview in the workspace. If the preview shows material projecting outward into empty space instead of inward toward the column, locate the **Flip Direction** button in the dialog box.

19. Click the **Flip Direction** icon (the arrow). The material will reverse course and automatically terminate perfectly against the complex stepped surfaces of the central column, filling the gap correctly.
20. Verify that the **Extent Type** is set to **To Next**, which forces the rib to naturally hug the contours of the existing body.

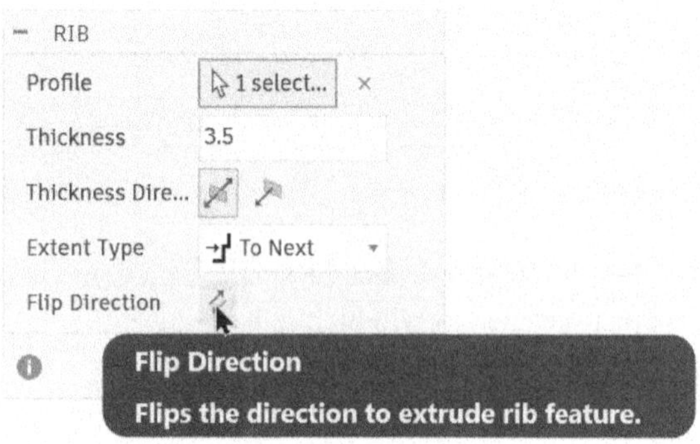

21. Click **OK** to execute the feature.

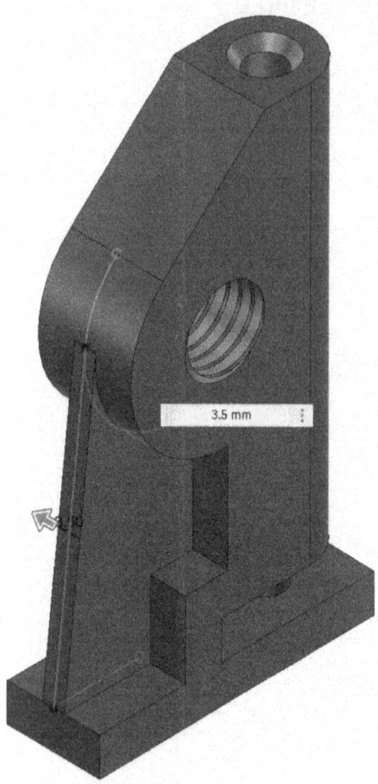

Adding Fillets to the Rib

1. Navigate to the **Solid** toolbar, open the **Modify** panel menu, and select **Fillet**. Alternatively, press the **F** key on your keyboard.
2. The **Fillet** dialog box will open on the right side of the screen.
3. In the **Fillet** dialog box, ensure the **Type** is set to **Fillet** (the standard option, not Full Round).
4. Set the **Radius Type** to **Constant**, which applies a uniform, unchanging curve along the entire length of the selected edge.
5. Select the edges of the model, as shown.

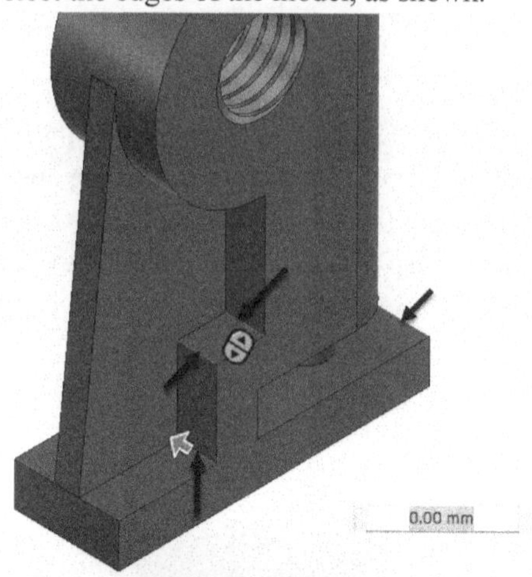

6. Enter a radius value of **3.5** mm and click **OK**.
7. Activate the **Fillet** tool.
8. Zoom in on the area where the newly created 3.5 mm rib intersects with the vertical column and the bottom base. These sharp 90-degree internal corners are known as "stress concentrations" in engineering.
9. Click the specific sharp interior edges that run vertically and horizontally along the base of the rib. The selected lines will highlight in blue.Do not select the flat faces of the rib, only the corner edges.

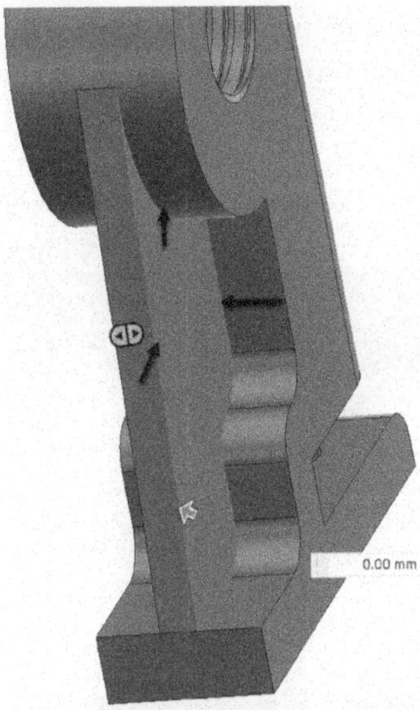

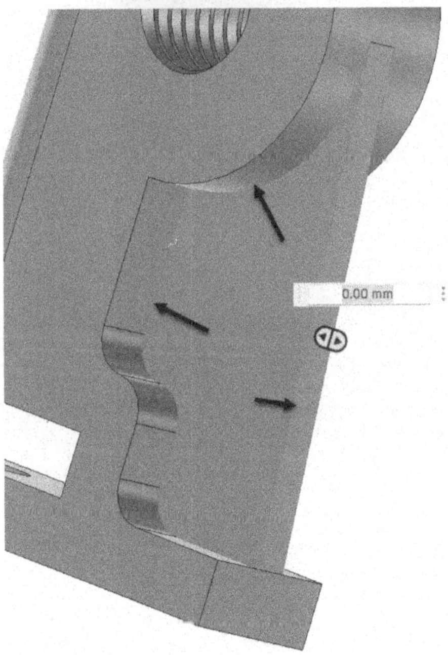

10. Enter a radius value of 0.7.
11. Verify the **Corner Type** is set to its default blending option and click **OK** to finalize the operation.

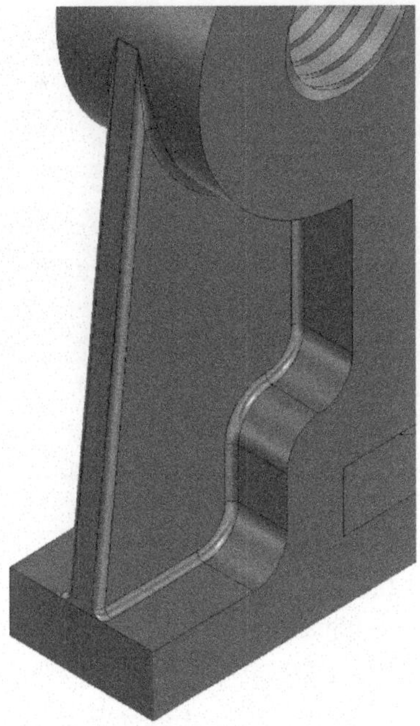

Zoom to the bottom portion of the model where the rib meets the bottom extruded feature. Notice that a surface distortion is caused by a fillet terminating against a sharp, unfilleted boundary. To resolve this, you must edit the existing parametric feature and add the adjacent base edges to a new selection set within the same operation. This forces the software to calculate a simultaneous mathematical blend across all intersecting planes.

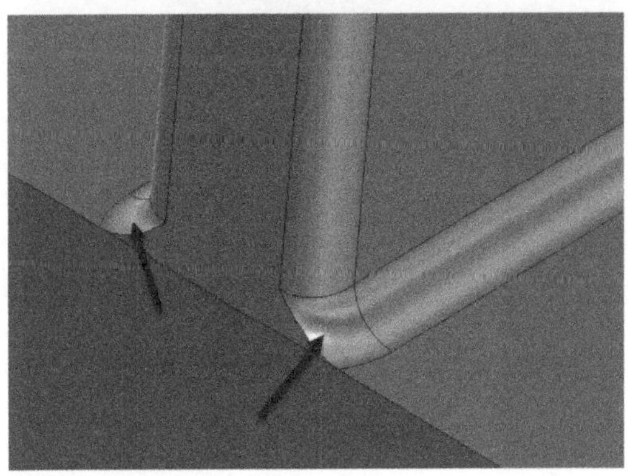

16. Navigate to the parametric timeline located at the bottom of the workspace. Right click the **Fillet** icon corresponding to the problematic geometry and select **Edit Feature** from the context menu.

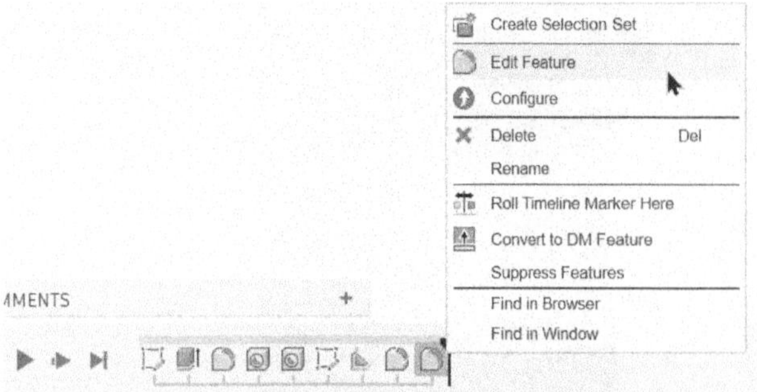

17. Within the **Edit Feature** dialog, click the plus icon (+) labeled Add selection set. This action permits the inclusion of additional geometry under the current command.
18. In the 3D viewing area, select the bare edges of the base component that constitute the sharp corner intersecting your original fillet. The reference image demonstrates selecting the two primary horizontal edges of the main base block.

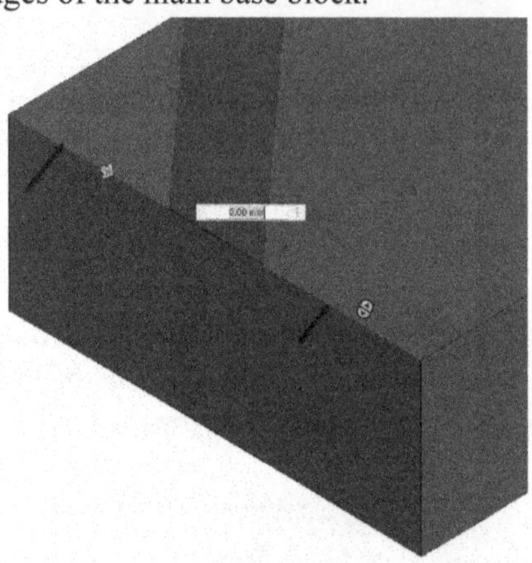

Next you need to input the specified dimension for the new edge selection.

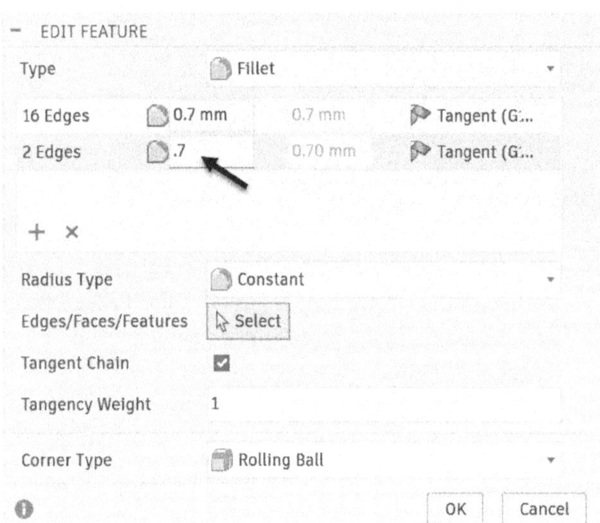

19. To generate the uniform transition depicted, assign a radius of **0.7** identical to the primary fillet parameter.
20. Select **OK** to close the dialog and execute the geometric computation. The application will successfully process a smooth, continuous surface blend across the previously problematic intersection.

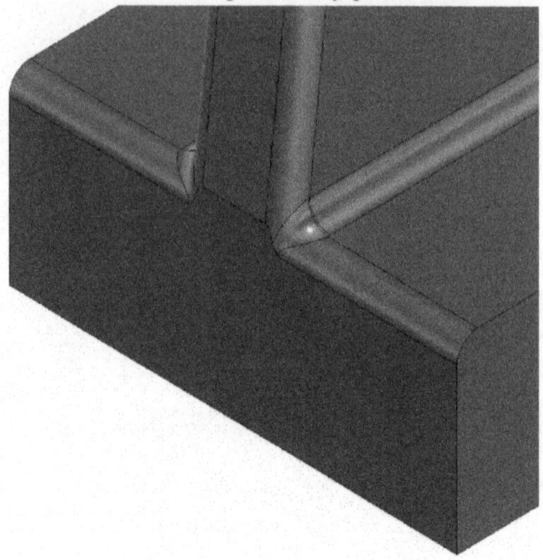

Assembly Modeling

Up to this point, you have modeled individual components in isolation. However, real-world products rarely consist of a single solid piece of material. In this chapter, you will transition from modeling standalone parts to building multi-component mechanical assemblies. You will use the individual components to construct the final mechanical vise assembly. Through this project, you will learn how to bring multiple files together and define how they interact mechanically.

You will focus on applying two core assembly concepts:

Bottom-Up Assembly Structure: You will begin by creating a new, empty design file to act as your main assembly master. Instead of sketching new geometry here, you will use the Data Panel to insert the parts you already saved (like the base bracket, threaded rod, guide pins, and handle). You will learn how to ground the base component so the rest of the assembly has a fixed anchor point in space.

Applying Joints: You cannot simply drag parts next to each other; you must constrain them using Joints. Joints define the physical relationship and allowable motion between two components. You will apply a Rigid Joint to lock the guide pins firmly into the base bracket. You will then apply a Cylindrical Joint to allow the main threaded rod to spin and slide vertically through the top collar, and a Slider Joint to allow the central block to move up and down along the guide pins.

Understanding Degrees of Freedom

When you insert a part into an assembly, it is free to move in any direction (it has six degrees of freedom: three for translation, three for rotation). Your goal is to use Joints to remove the degrees of freedom you do not want. By applying the correct joint types, you create an assembly that behaves exactly like the physical product. When you click and drag the handle of your digital vise, the central block will clamp down, proving your mechanical relationships are correct.

Tutorial 1

In this tutorial, you will create the part shown in figure below.

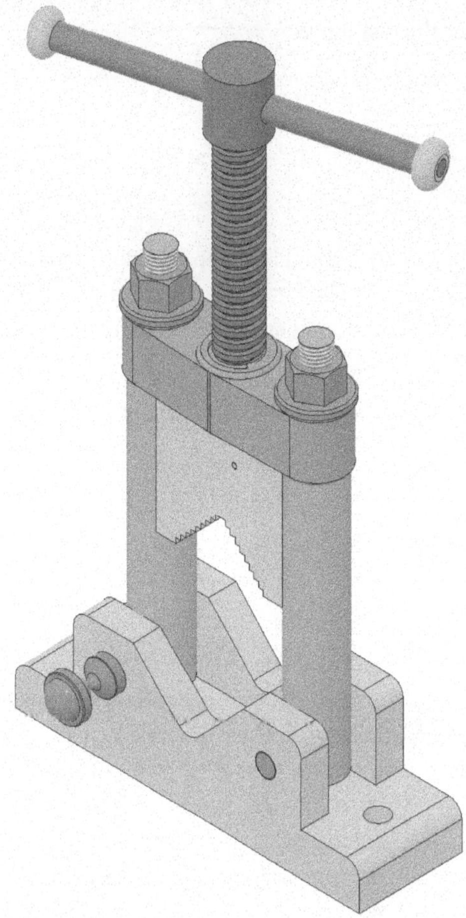

1. Download the Pipe Vise Assembly files from the link:

https://drive.google.com/file/d/1HLkJU-ZPYUZ-aYHH5a2EuZDiPpE8ZnKX/view?usp=sharing

(or) sending us an email to merrickvane99@gmail.com

2. Open **Autodesk Fusion 360**.
3. Navigate to the Data Panel interface. Within the active project directory, locate and click the button labeled **New Folder** positioned near the top right, adjacent to the **Upload** button.

4. A new folder icon will appear with an active text entry field. Enter **Pipe Vise Assembly** for your

directory. Press the Enter key on your keyboard to finalize the text input.

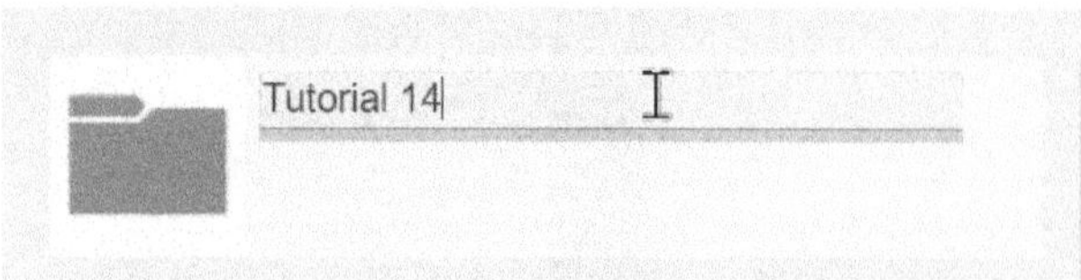

5. Ensure you are located inside the newly created folder directory. Click the prominent blue button labeled **Upload** to initiate the file transfer process.

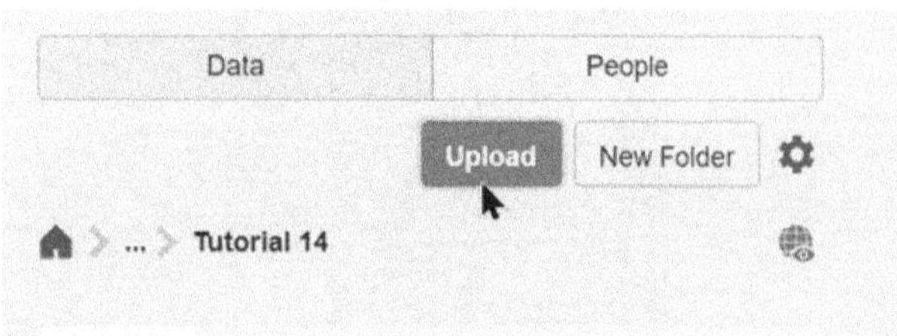

6. The **Upload** dialog window will appear on screen. Verify the **Location** field at the bottom confirms the correct target directory. Click the blue **Select Files** button to browse your local computer storage and choose the downloaded files to import into Fusion 360. Alternatively, you may drag and drop files directly into the designated area within the dialog window.

Starting the Assembly document and Inserting Components

1. Click **File > New** on the Application Bar.
2. Select the **Assembly Design** tile from the available options. Ensure the Unit System is appropriately configured (e.g., millimeter, gram) before clicking the **Create New** button situated in the lower right corner.

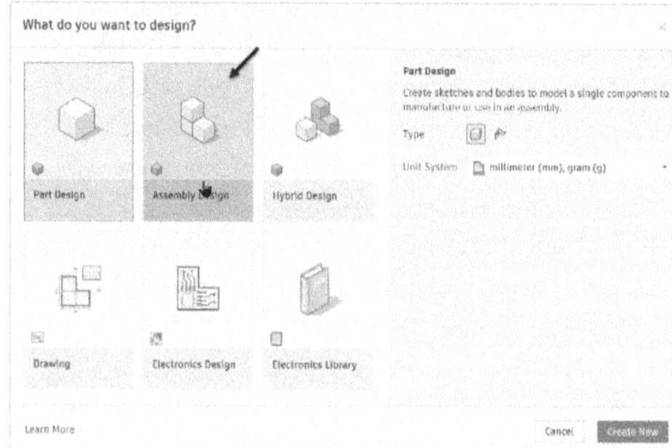

3. Within the newly created assembly workspace, navigate to the main toolbar at the top of the interface.
4. Click the **Insert Component** icon on the **Insert** Panel of the **Assembly** toolbar, represented by a chain link symbol, and click it to open the insertion dialog.The "**Insert Component**" window will display the contents of your current project directory.

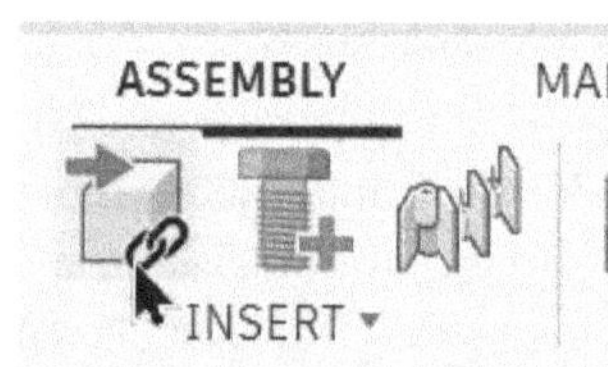

5. Navigate to the Tutorial 14 folder.
6. Select the **Fixed Jaw** file from the list.

7. Click the **Insert** button to place the geometry into the workspace. Upon insertion, the **Initial Position**

dialog will appear, alongside a 3D manipulator overlaid on the component.

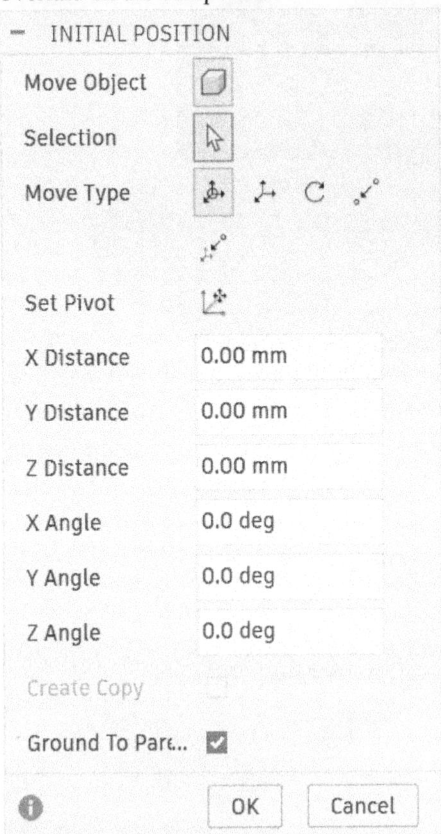

8. Review the X, Y, and Z coordinate values. If the default origin placement is correct, check the **Ground To Parent** option. This checkbox restricts all degrees of freedom for the inserted component relative to its parent assembly. Selecting this option fixes the component in space exactly where it is placed upon insertion.

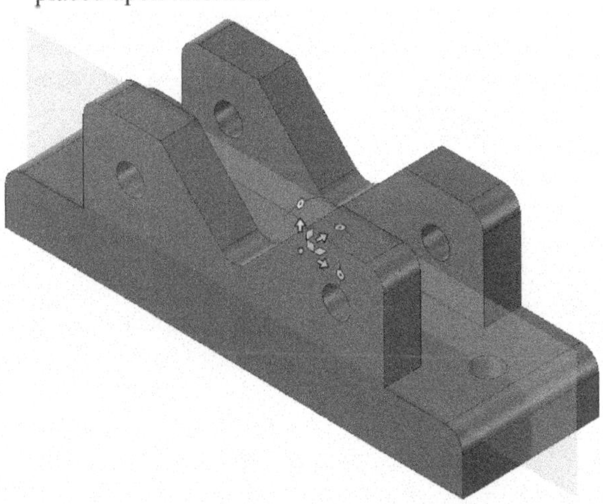

9. Click the **OK** button to finalize the operation and anchor the component.

Inserting and positioning the second Component

1. On the main toolbar under the **Assembly** tab, click the **Insert** icon.
2. In the **Insert Component** dialog, navigate the file list and select **Mounting Shaft**.

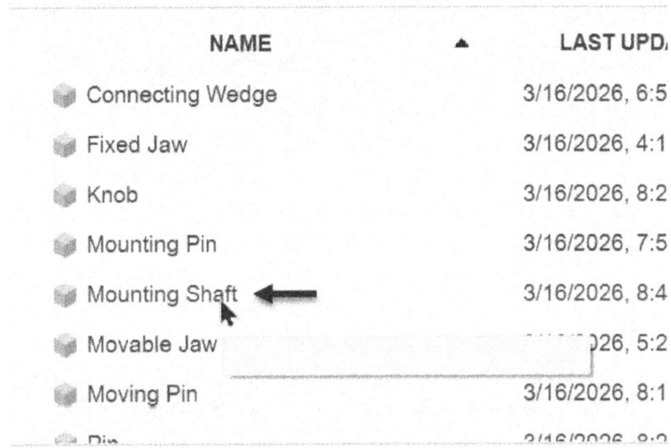

3. Click the **Insert** button to place the component into the workspace. The **Initial Position** dialog will appear on the right side of the screen.
4. In the 3D workspace, locate the directional arrows on the manipulator tool attached to the new component.
5. Click and drag the appropriate arrow to move the component.

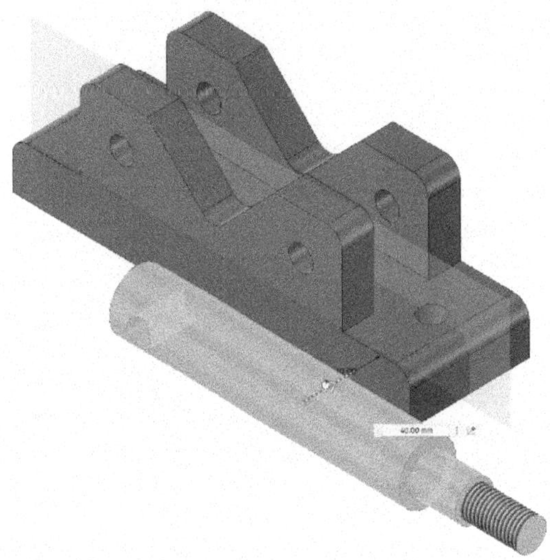

6. Click **OK** at the bottom right corner of the Initial Position dialog to confirm the placement.

Applying Component Constraints

1. On the **Assembly** toolbar, locate the **Relationships** panel and click the **Constrain Components** tool.

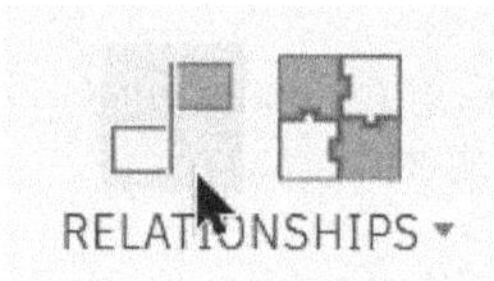

The **Constrain Components** dialog will appear. The Type option defines the primary geometric relationship. The default **Type** shown is **Align**, which aligns two faces or axes.

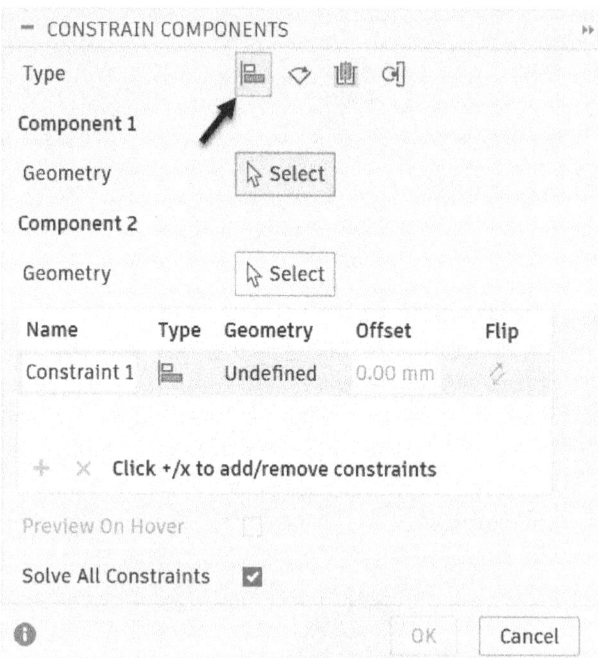

2. In the 3D workspace, click the internal cylindrical face of the fixed jaw to define the **Component 1** Geometry.

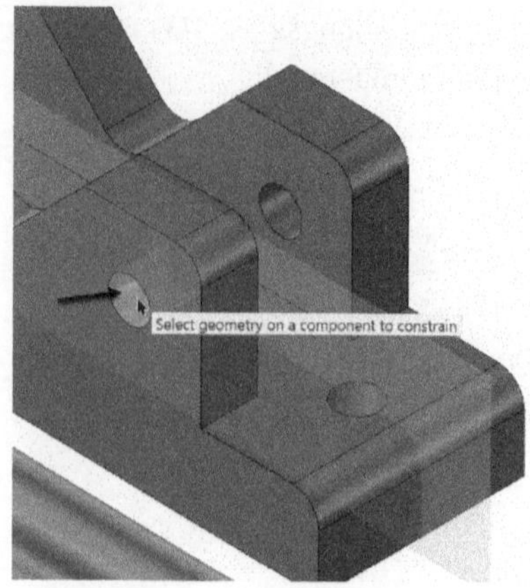

3. Click on the hole of the mounting shaft to define the **Component 2** Geometry. The software will calculate the primary **Align** constraint, aligning the central axes of the two cylindrical selections.

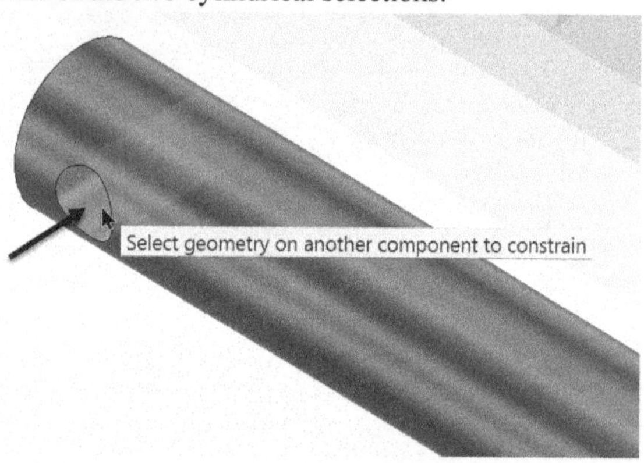

4. In the **Constrain Components** dialog, locate the plus icon (+) near the bottom of the list area. Click this icon to add an additional constraint.

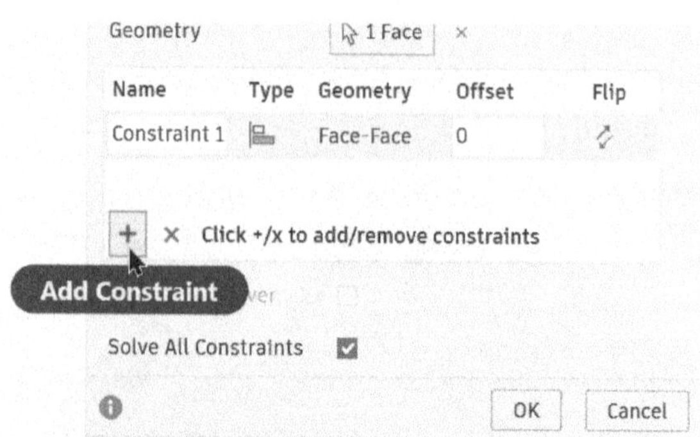

5. For the new constraint, change the **Type** option to the **Center**. This option centers one component between two faces of another component.

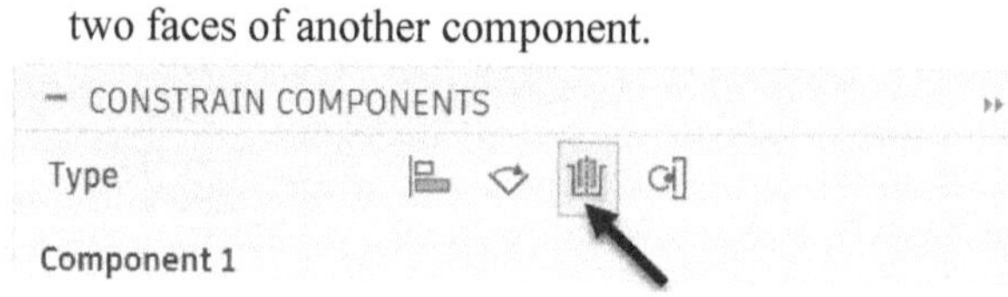

6. Click the first inner vertical face of the upright fixed jaw.

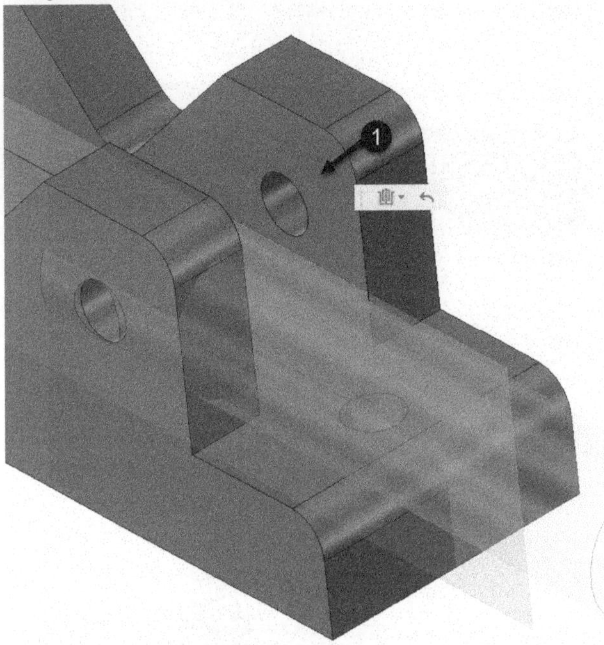

7. Rotate the view if necessary and click the opposing inner vertical face of the fixed jaw.

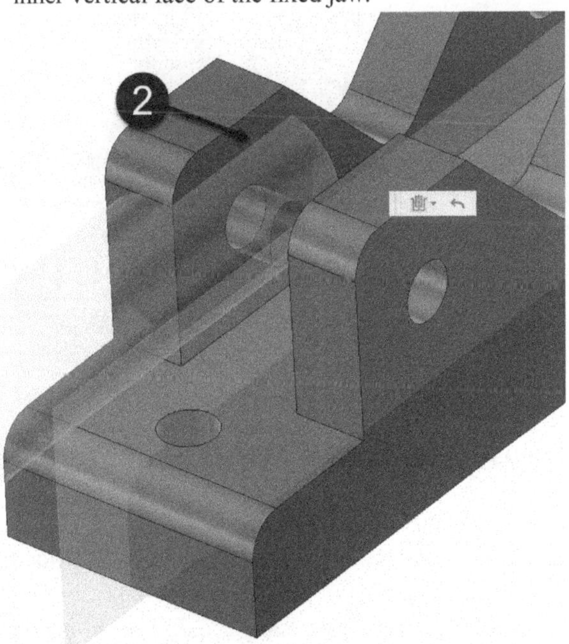

The dialog will now prompt you to select the target geometry. Locate the mounting shaft component in the workspace.

8. Click the main outer cylindrical face of the mounting shaft.

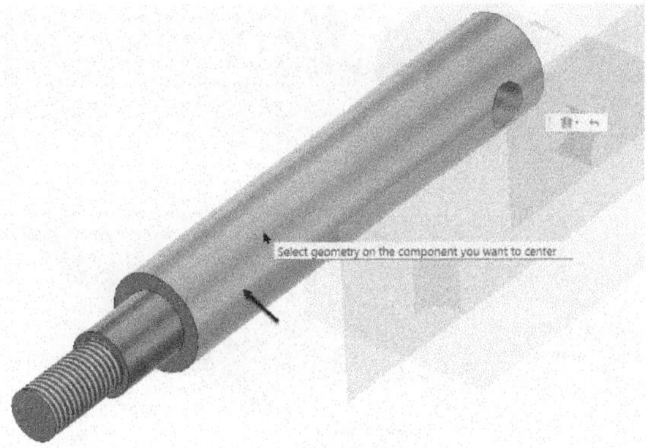

9. The software will instantly calculate the midpoint between the first two selected faces and move the shaft to align centrally.

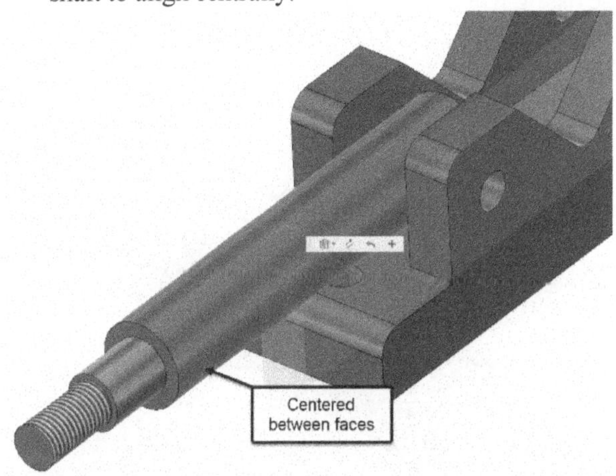

10. In the **Constrain Components** dialog, click the plus icon (+) near the bottom of the list area to add an additional constraint.
11. In the **Constrain Components** dialog, locate the Type options at the top.
12. Click the **Angle** icon. This option positions selected geometry with a relative angle between them.

13. Click the flat, top horizontal face of fixed jaw.

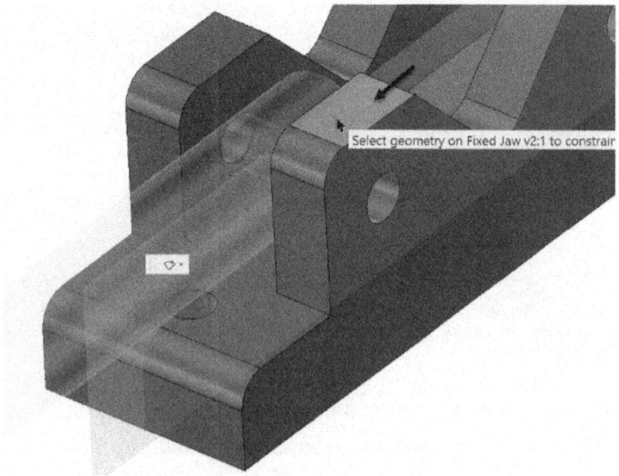

The dialog will advance to Component 2. Locate the vertical mounting shaft in the workspace.

14. Click the flat, circular end face of the shaft.

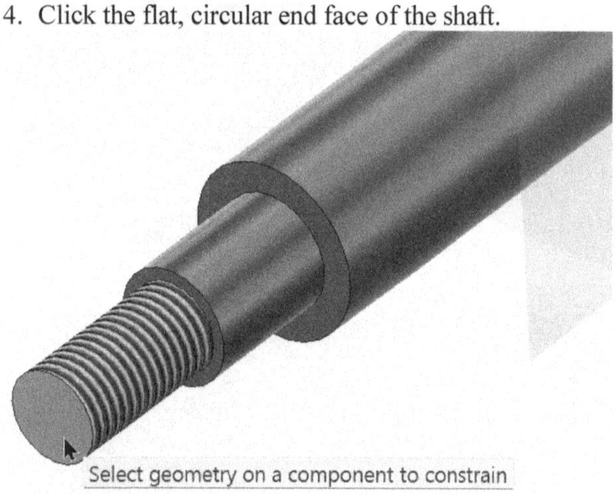

15. Review the constraint table at the bottom of the dialog box. This table lists all active relationships between the two components.
16. Locate the row for the newly created Angle constraint, shown as Constraint 3.
17. If the shaft is oriented upside down, locate the **Flip** icon at the far right of the constraint row.
18. Click the Flip icon. This action flips the orientation of the selected geometry. The shaft will invert to the correct upright position.

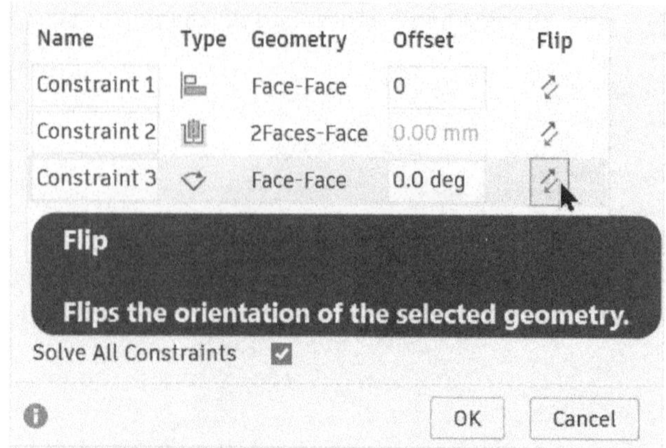

19. Verify the numerical offset value in the table is set to 0.0 deg.
20. Click **OK** to confirm the final placement.

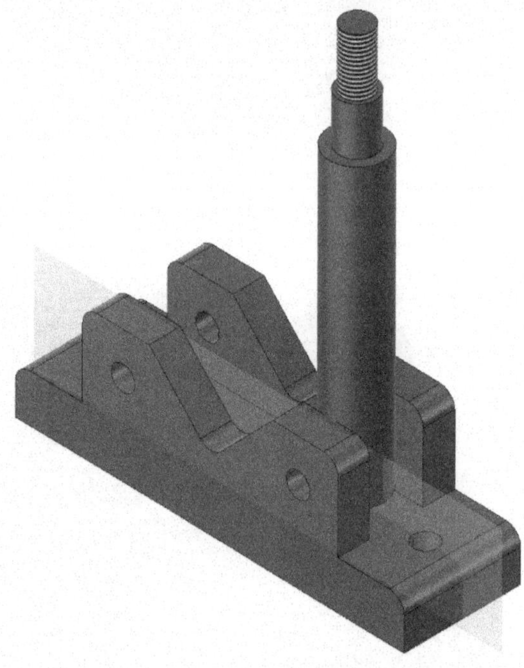

Inserting the Second Mounting Shaft

1. On the Assembly toolbar under the Insert panel, click the Insert icon.
2. In the **Insert Component** dialog, select the Mounting Shaft file from your project folder.
3. Click the **Insert** button to place the second instance of the component into the workspace.
4. Use the **Initial Position** dialog to drag the new shaft roughly near the empty second hole on the base component, then click **OK**.
5. On the main toolbar, click the **Constrain Components** tool.
6. Repeat the constraint process applied to the first shaft. Begin by applying a **Align** constraint between

the outer cylindrical face of the new shaft and the inner cylindrical face of the empty hole on the base component.

7. Click the plus icon to add the **Center** constraint within the same dialog.
8. Apply the **Angle** constraint between the flat top face of the new shaft and the top flat face of the base component to set the vertical position.
9. Verify the second shaft is fully constrained and oriented identically to the first.
10. Click **OK** to confirm the final placement.

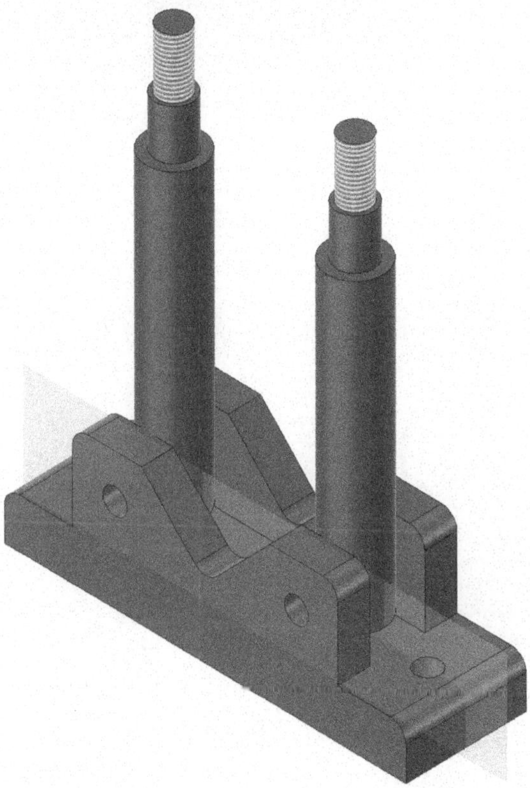

Inserting and Constraining the Connecting Wedge

1. Open the Data Panel on the left side of the workspace to view your project files.
2. Locate the file named **Connecting Wedge** within the list.
3. Right click the file name and select **Insert into Current Design**. This specific option imports the external part directly into your active assembly environment. The **Initial Position** dialog will appear.

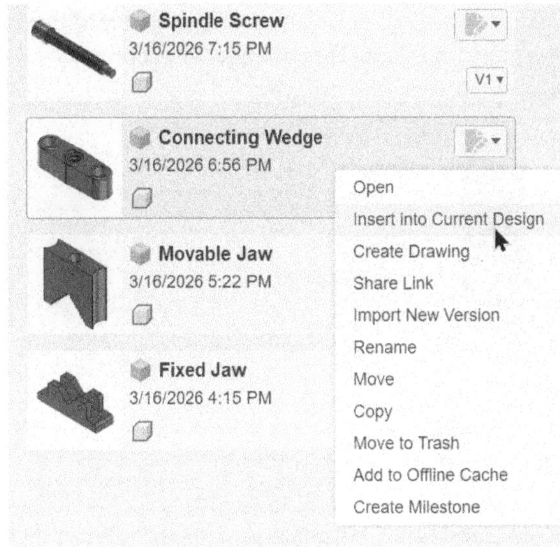

4. Drag the graphical arrows in the 3D workspace to move the wedge roughly into the empty space, then click **OK**.

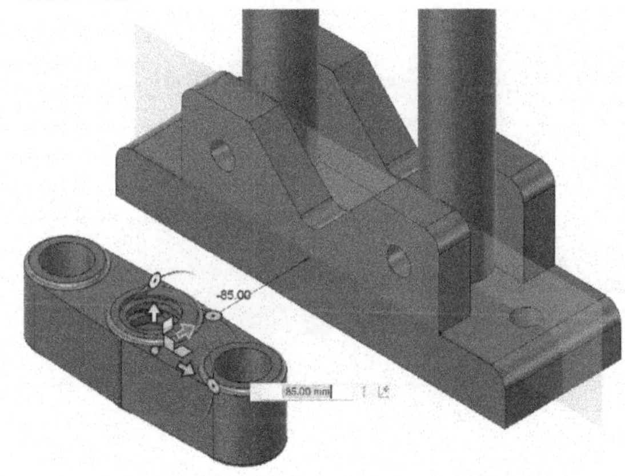

5. On the **Assembly** toolbar, click **Relationships** panel > **Constrain Components** tool to open the dialog box.
6. In the 3D workspace, click the inner cylindrical face of the first hole located on the wedge.

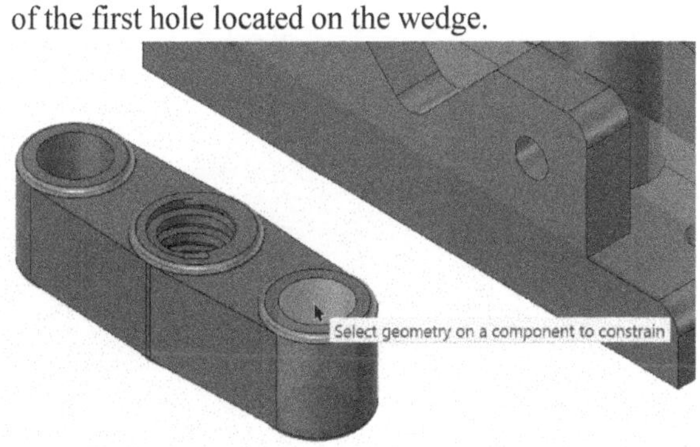

7. Next, click the upper smooth cylindrical face of the first mounting shaft. The software will apply a primary alignment to the axes.

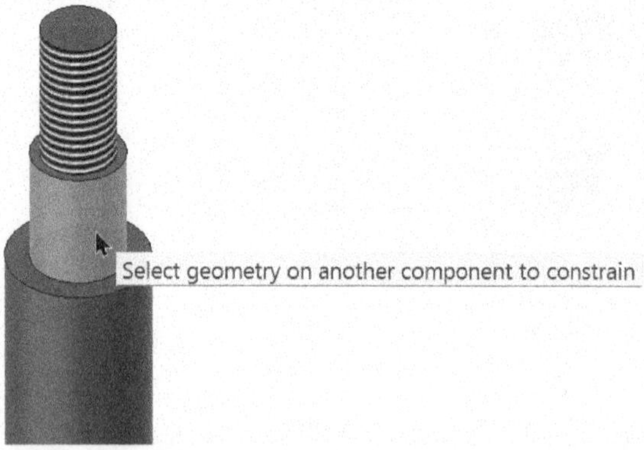

8. In the **Constrain Components** dialog box, locate and click the plus icon to add a second constraint row. This **Add Constraint** option allows you to build multiple geometric relationships before finalizing the command.

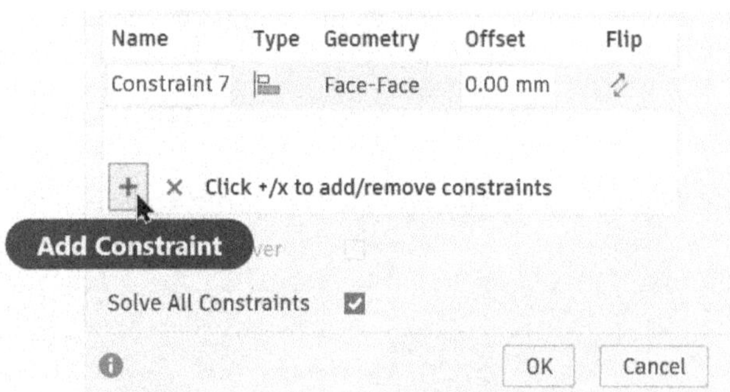

9. Click the inner cylindrical face of the second hole on the wedge.

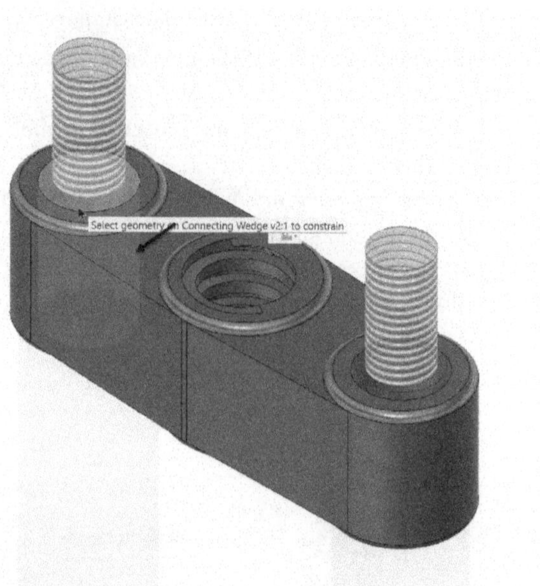

10. Click the upper smooth cylindrical face of the second mounting shaft.

11. Click **OK** at the bottom right corner of the dialog box to execute the calculation and secure the component in place.
12. In the 3D workspace, click and hold the left mouse button on the solid body of the wedge component.
13. Drag the wedge upward along the shafts to create clear visual separation between the parts.
14. Release the mouse button.

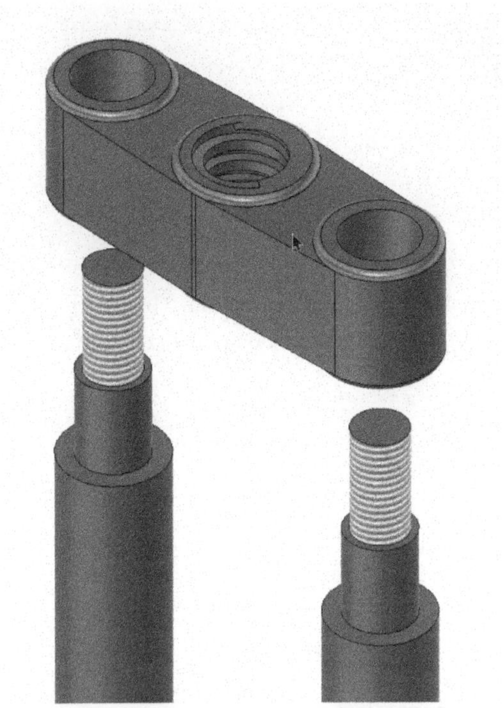

15. Manipulate the camera view to observe the newly exposed underside of the wedge component.
16. On the **Assembly** toolbar, click the **Constrain Components** tool if the dialog is not already active.
17. Click the flat bottom face of the wedge.

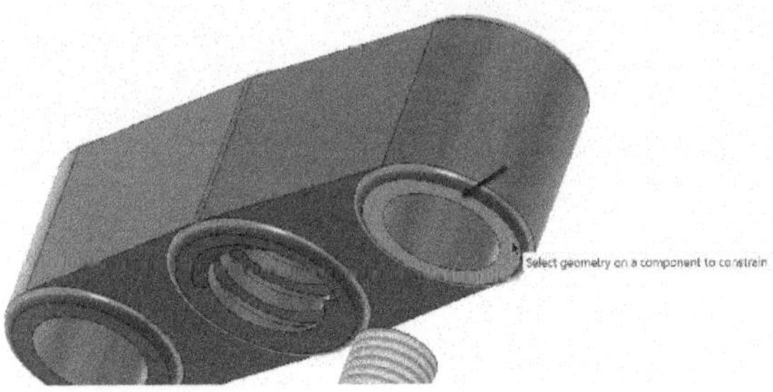

18. Rotate the camera view to observe the vertical mounting shafts.
19. Click the flat horizontal shoulder face located on the middle section of the first mounting shaft.

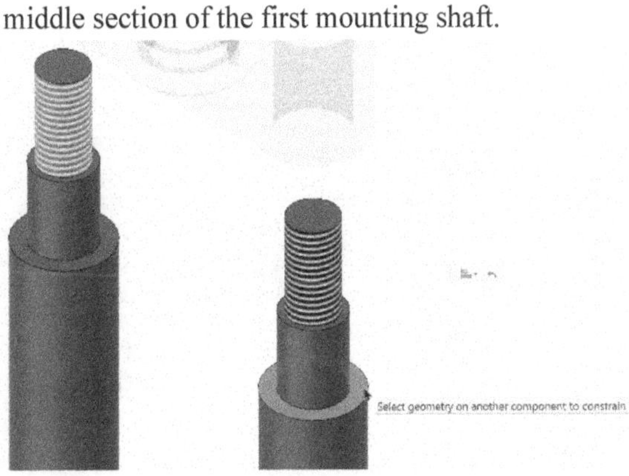

20. The software will apply a planar constraint, dropping the wedge down to rest directly on the shaft shoulder.
21. Review the constraint table in the dialog box. Locate the Offset input field next to the newly created constraint.Verify the Offset value is set to 0.00 mm to ensure a flush contact surface.The Offset option allows you to define an exact numerical gap between the selected faces if a clearance is required.

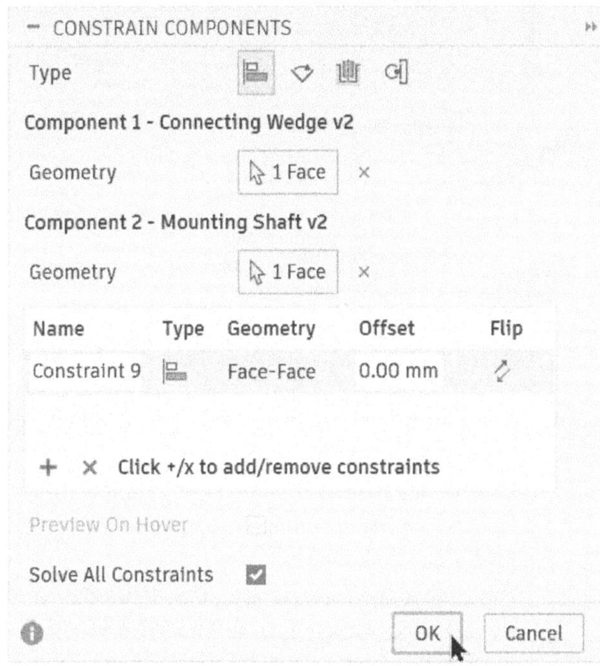

22. Click **OK** at the bottom right corner of the dialog box to execute the calculation and secure the component in its final position.

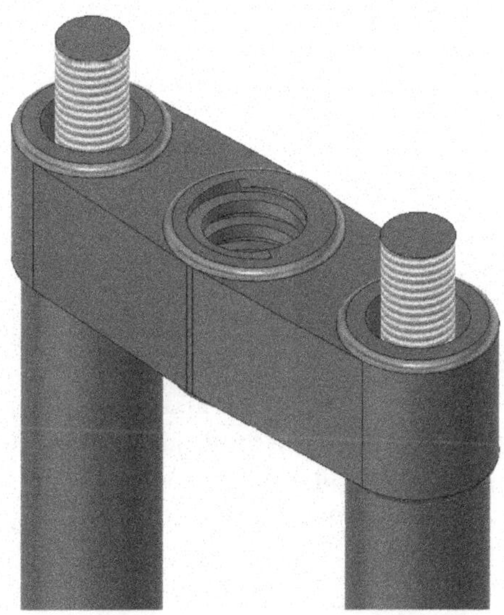

Inserting and Joining the Mounting Pin

1. Open the Data Panel on the left side of the workspace to view your project files.
2. Locate the file named Mounting Pin.
3. Right click the file name and select **Insert into Current Design**.

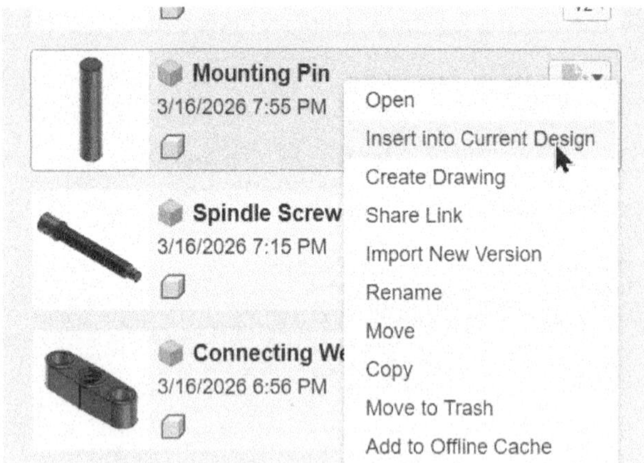

4. The **Initial Position** dialog will appear alongside an on-screen manipulator.
5. Drag the directional arrow to move the pin away from the center origin point to ensure clear visibility. Click OK.
6. Navigate to the **Assembly** toolbar. Click the Relationships panel menu drop-down and select the **Joint** tool, or press the J key on your keyboard.

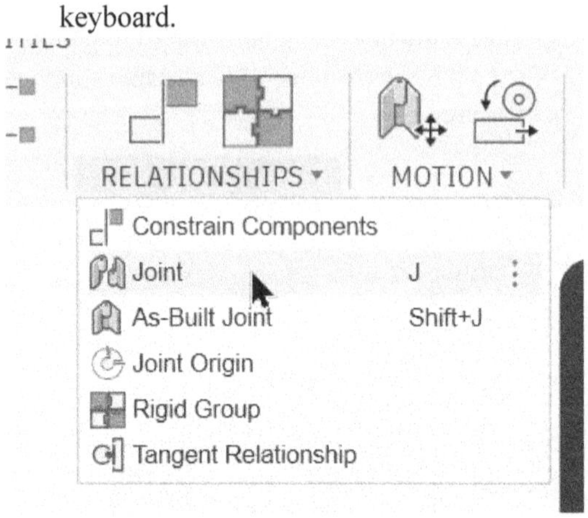

7. The **Joint** dialog box will open. Locate the **Motion** tab at the top of the dialog and verify the **Type** is set to **Rigid**. A **Rigid** joint lock all spatial movement between the selected origins.

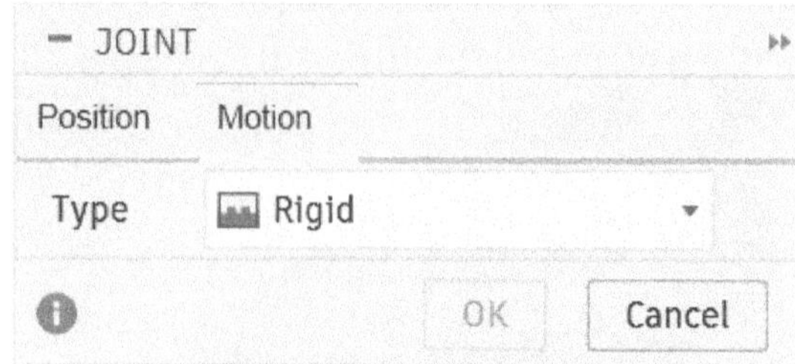

8. Switch back to the **Position** tab. The dialog prompts you to define Component 1.

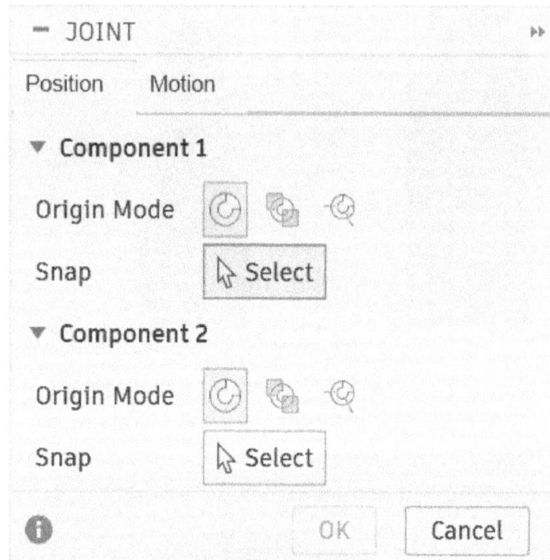

9. Hover your cursor over the flat top face of the newly inserted Mounting Pin.
10. A graphical disc will appear representing the joint origin. Select the top circular edge to define the Component 1 Snap selection.The dialog will automatically advance to Component 2.

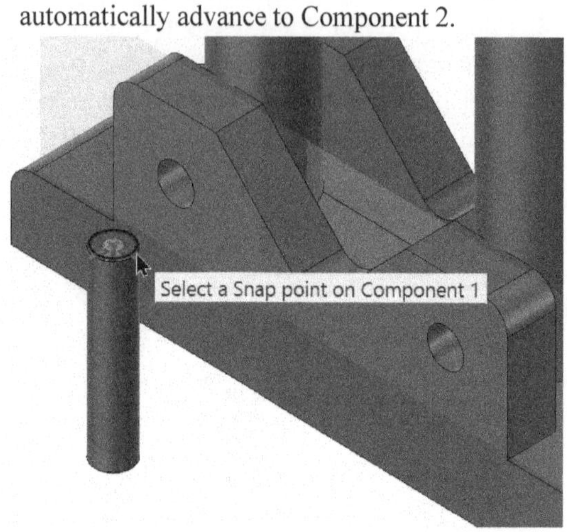

11. Hover your cursor over the small horizontal hole located on the outer side of the base bracket.

12. Click the circular edge of the hole to define the Component 2 Snap selection.

The pin will visually move to align the two selected origins. If the pin is protruding outward horizontally instead of seating inward, locate the on-screen manipulator next to the aligned joint.

13. Click the **Flip** icon, represented by two opposing arrows. This flips the component over the joint origin. The pin will reverse direction and seat properly into the base.

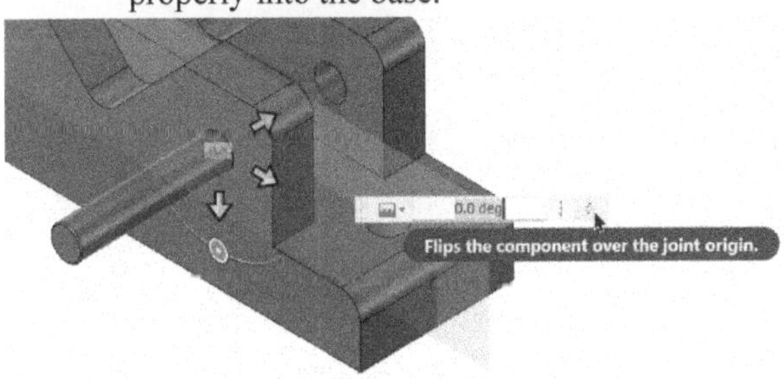

14. Click **OK** at the bottom right corner of the dialog box to finalize the Joint operation.

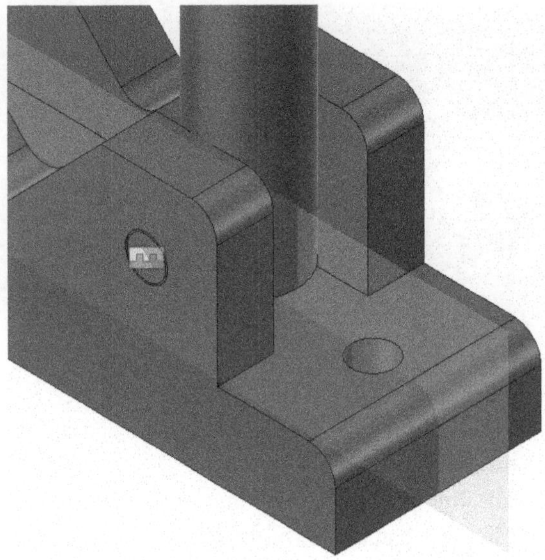

Inserting and Joining the Moving Pin

1. Open the Data Panel on the left side of the workspace to view your project files.
2. Locate the file named **Moving Pin** within the list.
3. Right click the file name and select **Insert into Current Design**.

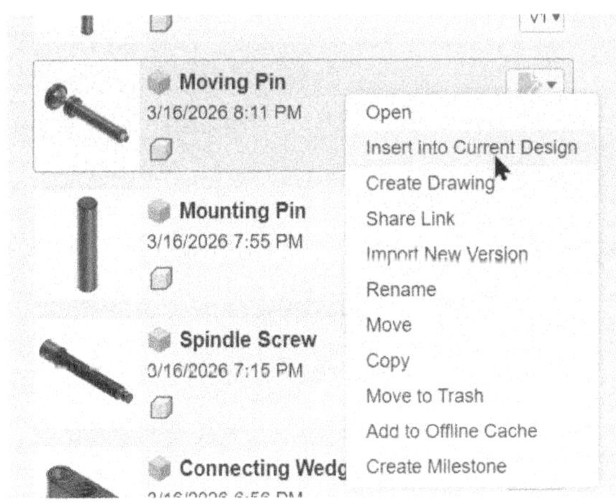

4. Drag the directional arrow to move the pin away from the base to ensure clear visibility. Click **OK**.

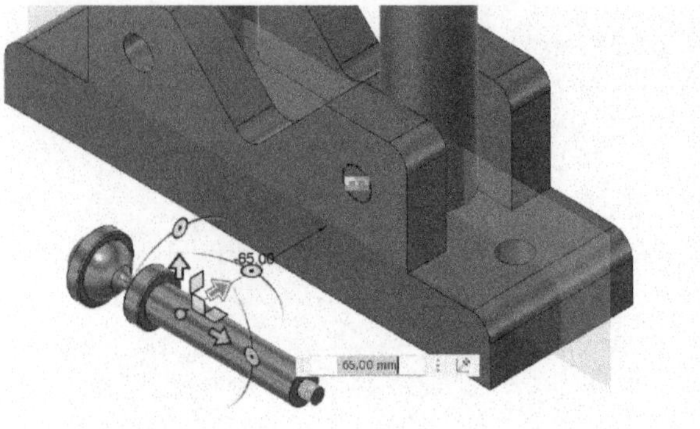

5. Navigate to the **Assembly** toolbar. Click the **Relationships** panel menu drop down and select the **Joint** tool.
6. The **Joint** dialog box will open. Locate the **Motion** tab at the top of the dialog and verify the **Type** is set to **Rigid**.
7. Switch back to the **Position** tab. The dialog prompts you to define Component 1.
8. Hover your cursor over the inner cylindrical section of the Moving Pin, specifically near the flat vertical shoulder where the shaft diameter increases.
9. Select the circular edge to define the Component 1 Snap selection. The dialog will advance to Component 2.

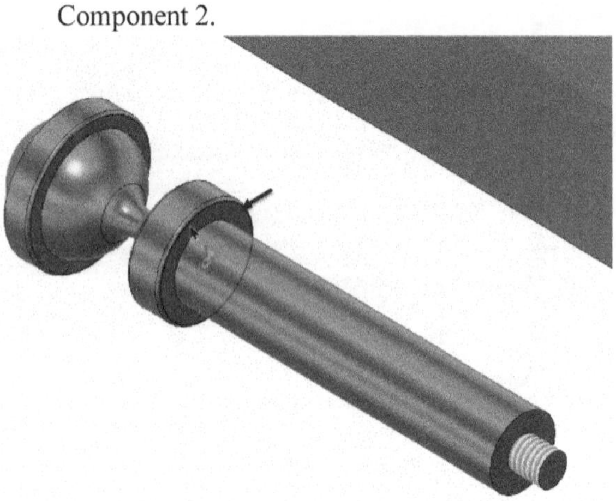

10. Hover your cursor over the large horizontal hole located on the outer side of the base bracket.
11. Click the circular edge of the hole to define the Component 2 Snap selection.The pin will visually move to align the two selected origins.

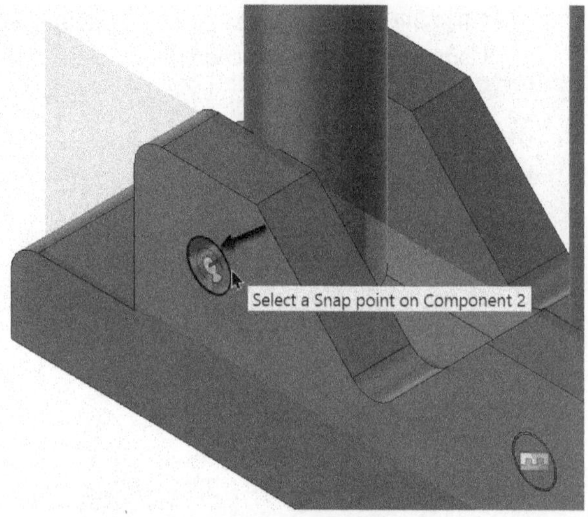

12. Review the **Alignment** section within the **Joint** dialog box.

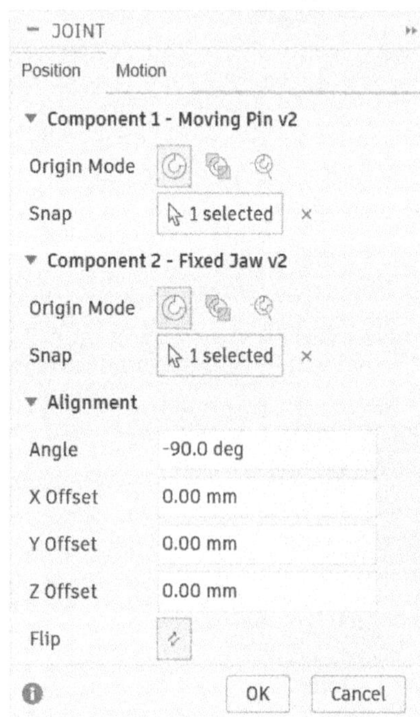

13. Click **OK** at the bottom right corner of the dialog box to finalize the Joint operation.

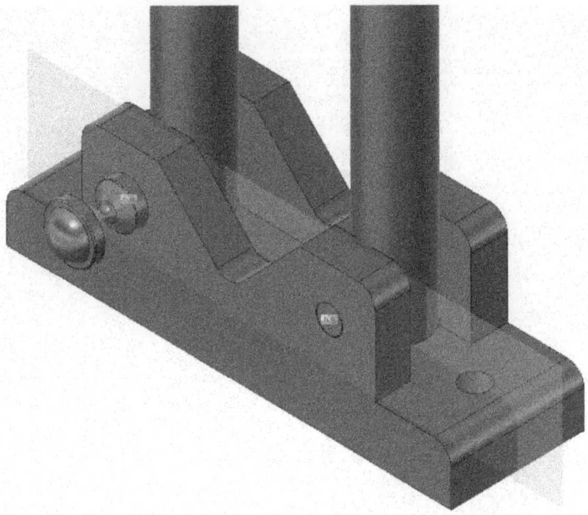

Modifying Components with Edit In Place

1. In the 3D workspace, locate the first vertical Mounting Shaft.
2. Right click any face of the shaft component and select **Find in Browser** from the context menu. This option automatically expands the assembly tree and highlights the exact node for that specific part.

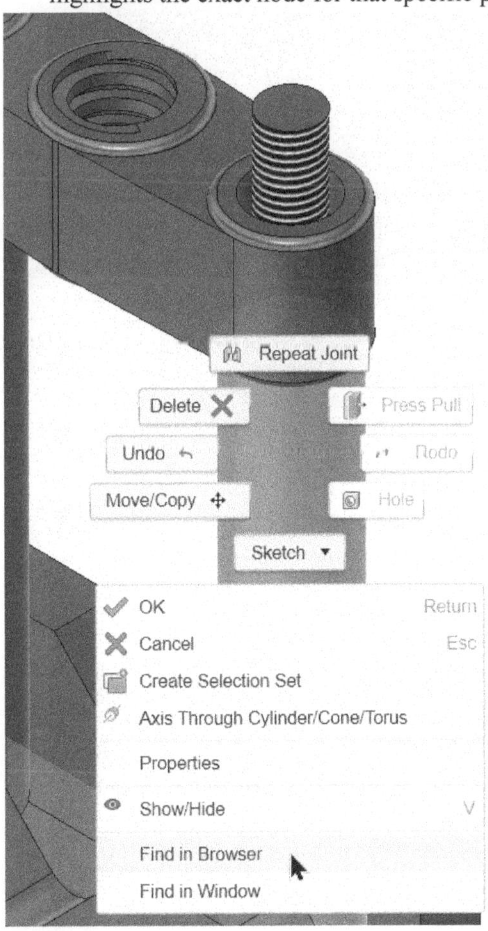

3. In the Browser on the left side of the screen, right click the highlighted component node named Mounting Shaft.
4. Select the **Edit In Place** tool, indicated by a pencil icon.

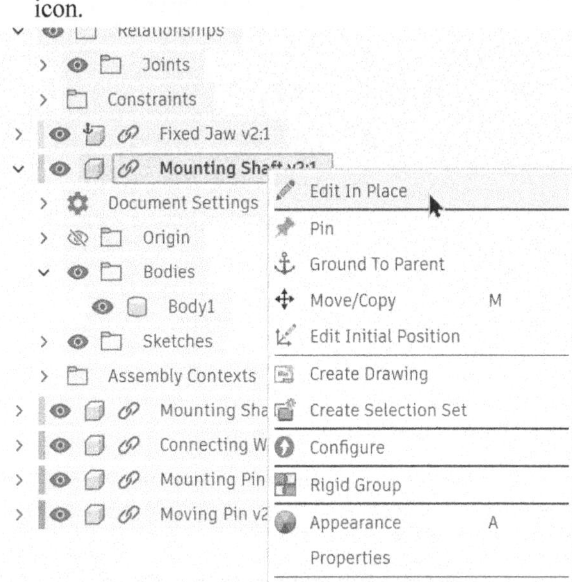

5. An information dialog titled Associative Edit in Place will appear. This dialog states that references to other components will be captured in an **Assembly Context**.

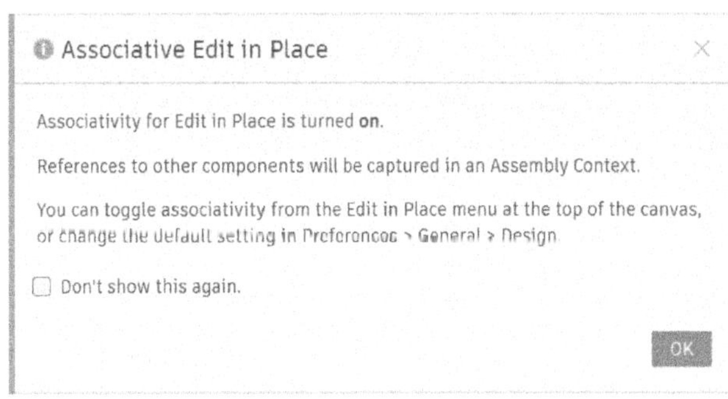

6. Click the blue **OK** button to dismiss the dialog and activate the edit mode. The parent assembly parts will become transparent.
7. Navigate to the parametric timeline at the bottom left of the workspace.
8. Right click the icon representing the original base sketch of the shaft.
9. Select **Edit Sketch** from the menu.

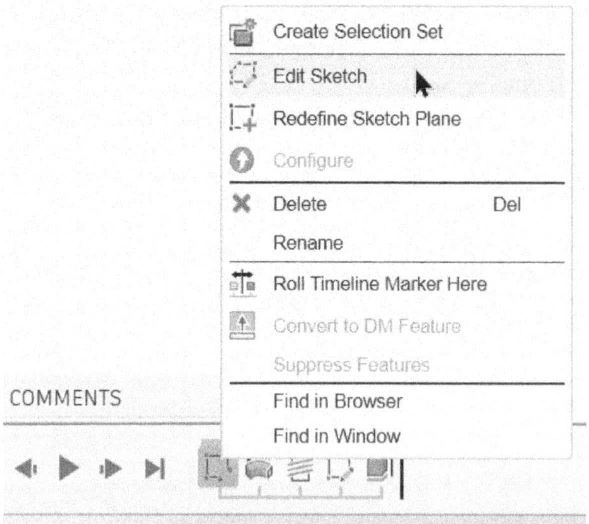

10. The 2D sketch grid will overlay the workspace. Locate the specific horizontal linear dimension controlling the length of the smooth middle section, located just below the top threaded section. Find the dimension currently set to 25 mm.
11. Double click the numeric text of the dimension to activate the input box.
12. Type 35 to increase the length. Press the Enter key to confirm the new value.

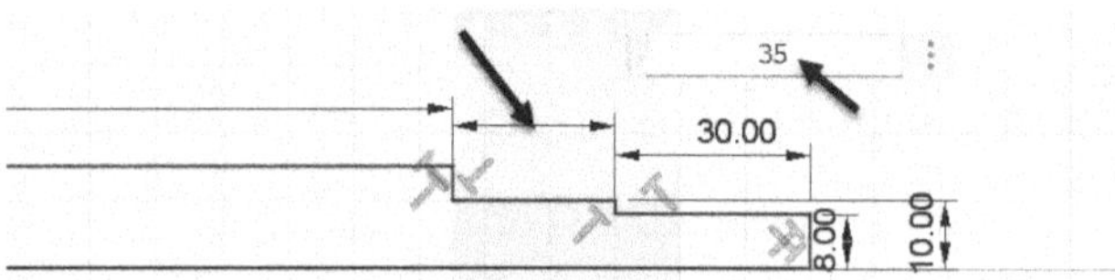

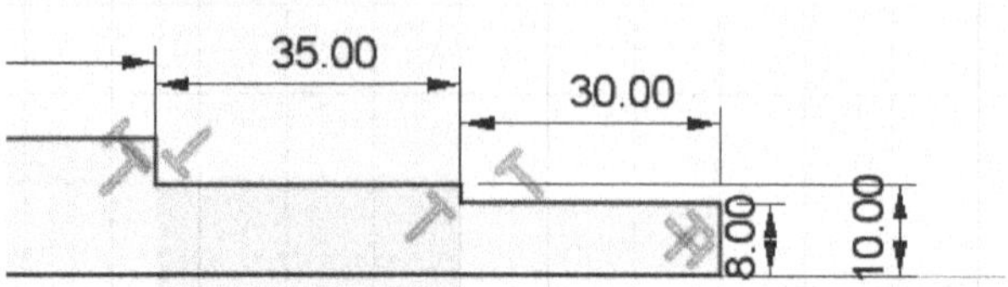

13. On the main toolbar, click the green **Finish Sketch** icon. The 3D body of the shaft will update to reflect the longer dimension.
14. Navigate back to the main toolbar at the top of the interface.
15. Locate and click the **Finish Edit In Place** icon, indicated by a green checkmark next to a pencil symbol. This ends the active session and returns you to the context of the parent design.

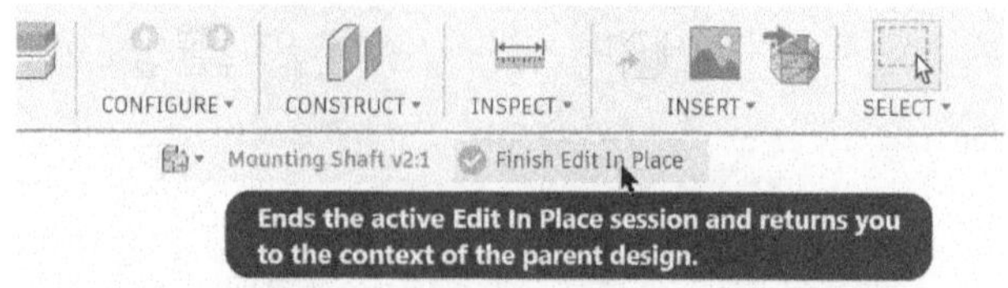

16. The transparency will fade, and the entire assembly will update to accommodate the modified shaft geometry

Applying a Cylindrical Joint with Limits

1. Open the Data Panel, right click the **Spindle Screw**, and select **Insert into Current Design**.

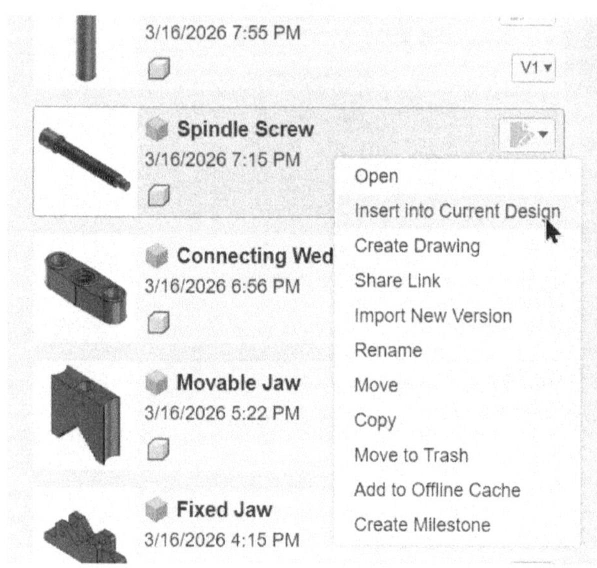

2. Navigate to the **Assembly** toolbar. Click the **Relationships** panel drop down and select the **Joint** tool.

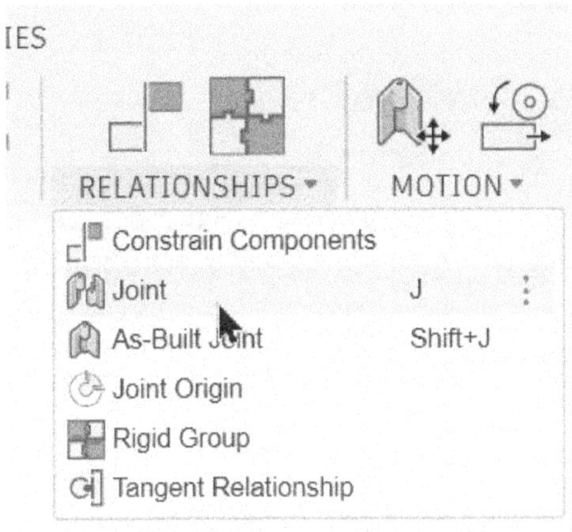

3. Hover your cursor over the lower section of the Spindle screw, just above the flat bottom tip.
4. Click the circular edge where the shaft diameter transitions. This sets the Component 1 Snap selection.

5. Zoom to bottom portion of the Connecting Wedge to define Component 2.
6. Hover your cursor over the large central threaded hole on the bottom face of the wedge.
7. Click the circular edge to set the Component 2 Snap selection. The screw will move to align with the hole.

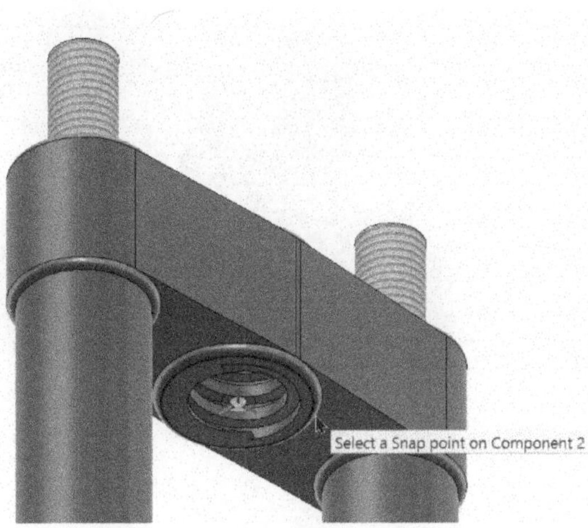

8. Within the **Joint** dialog box, switch to the **Motion** tab at the top.
9. Click the **Type** drop down menu and select **Cylindrical**. This option permits simultaneous linear translation and rotation.
10. Verify the **Axis** drop down menu is set to the **Z Axis**. This aligns the movement vertically. The **Joint Motion Limits** section within the dialog restricts how far the component can physically travel.
11. Check the box next to **Minimum**. Input negative **80** in the corresponding numeric field. This allows the screw to travel 80 millimeters downward.
12. Check the box next to **Maximum**. Verify the value is set to 0.00 mm. This prevents the screw from backing out above its origin point.

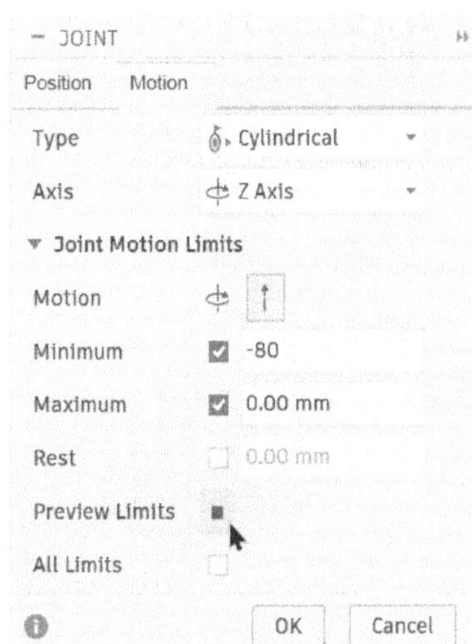

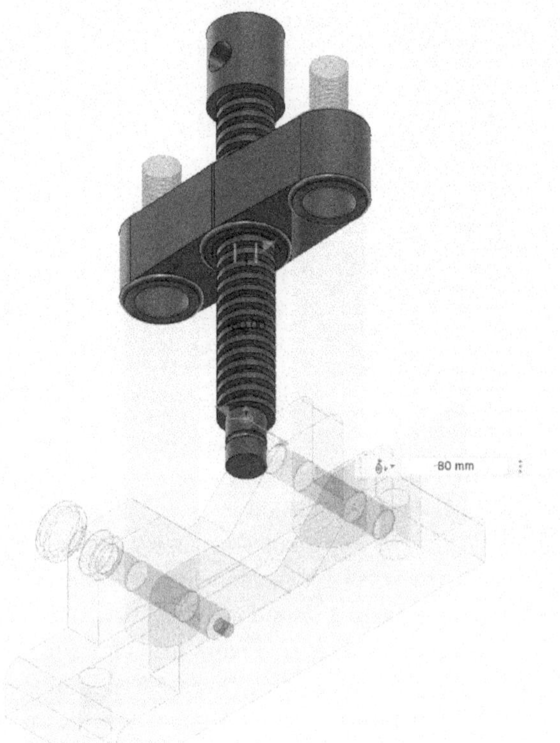

13. Click **OK** at the bottom right corner to finalize the command and calculate the mechanical limits.

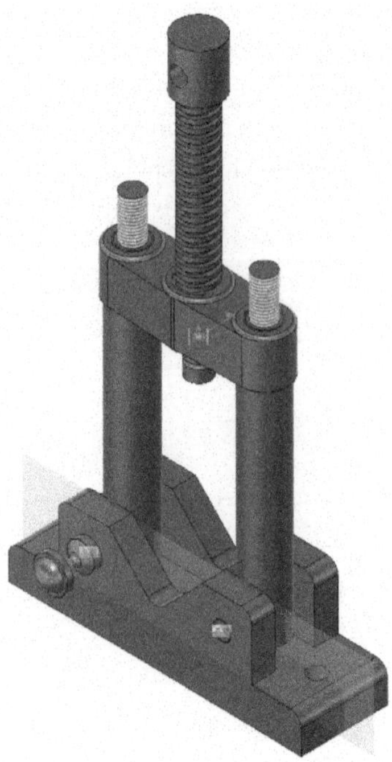

14. Open the Data Panel on the left side of the Fusion interface to locate the Movable Jaw.
15. Drag the part file directly into the active 3D workspace.

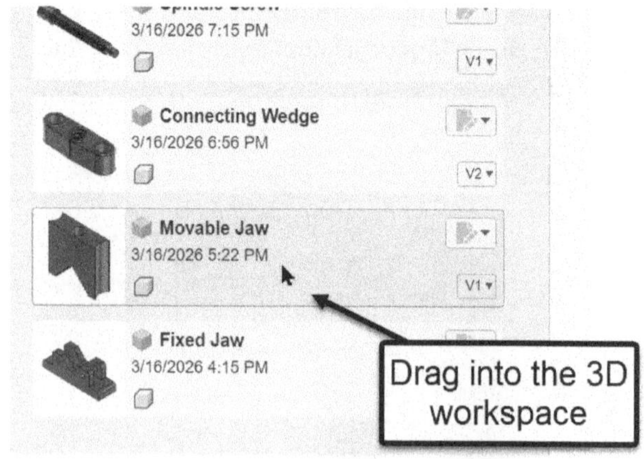

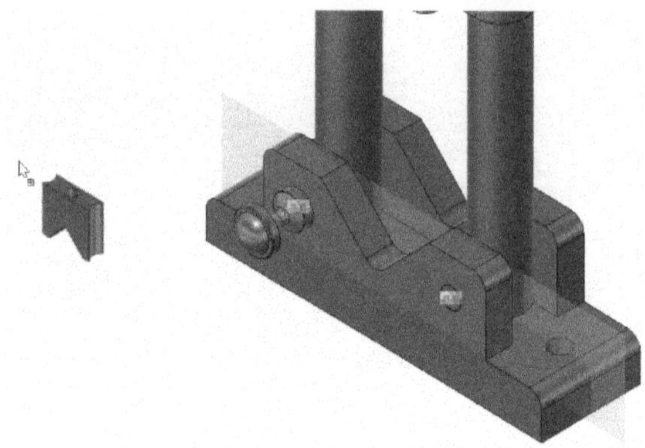

16. Drag the component so the component becomes visible in the canvas.
17. Navigate to the **Assembly** toolbar and select the **Relationships** panel > **Constrain Components** tool to open the dialog box on the right side of the screen.
6. Click a cylindrical face on your inserted part.

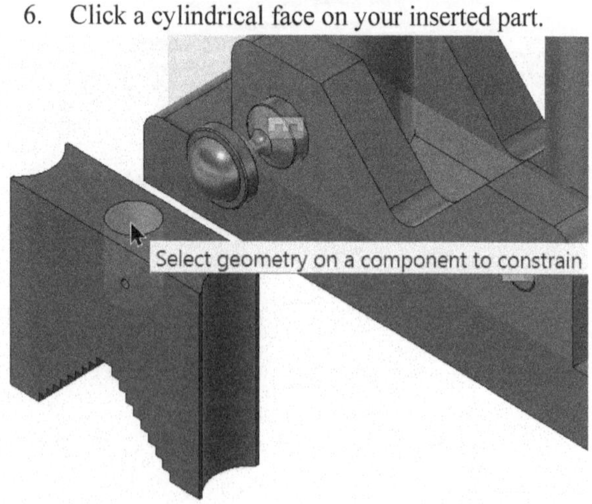

9. Click the cylinder on the Spindle Screw, as shown.

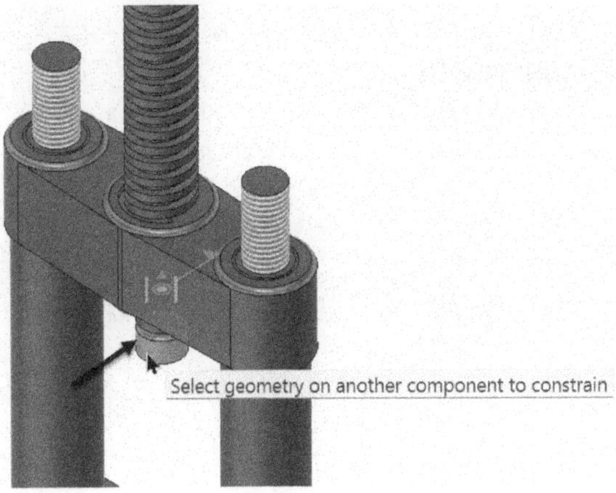

Evaluate the visual preview in the canvas to ensure the part faces the correct direction. Click the **Flip** option in the dialog box to reverse the alignment of the active constraint row if the spatial orientation is backwards.

10. Click the plus icon labeled **Add Constraint** to generate a new row in the dialog table. Use this icon to define a secondary positional relationship without closing the active command, which helps fully secure the component.

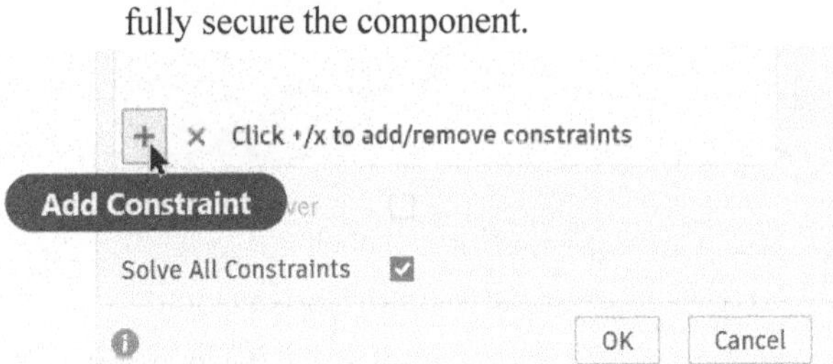

11. Select the top flat face of the Movable Jaw for the first half of this new relationship.

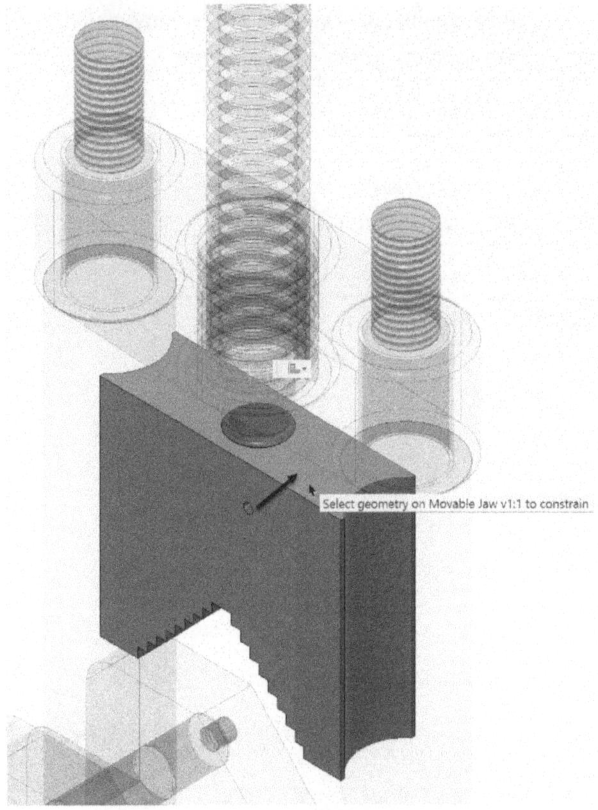

12. Select the horizontal flat mating face on the Spindle Screw for the second half of the relationship.

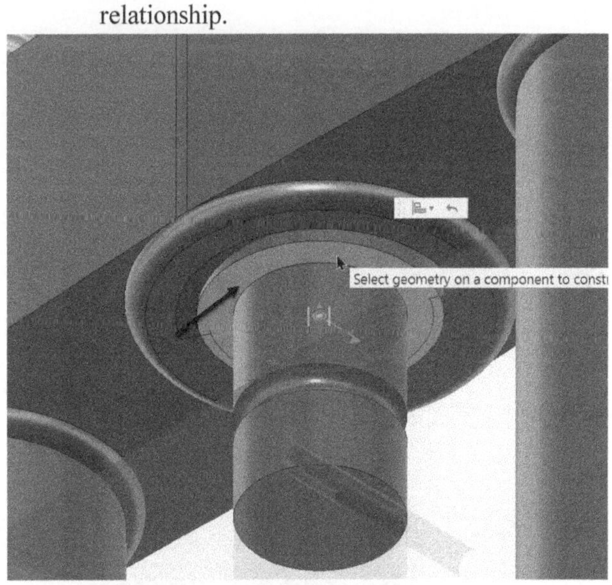

13. Verify in the dialog box that both rows list a Type of Face Face, which instructs the software to align the selected flat surfaces perfectly together.
14. Verify that the **Offset** value is exactly 0.00 mm to ensure the selected flat faces sit completely

flush against one another without any added distance.

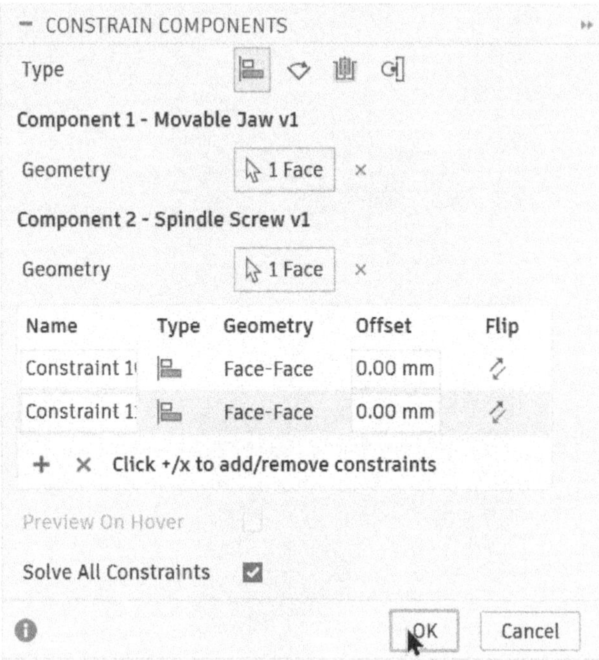

20. Click the **OK** button to accept the configuration, apply the constraints to the assembly, and close the tool.

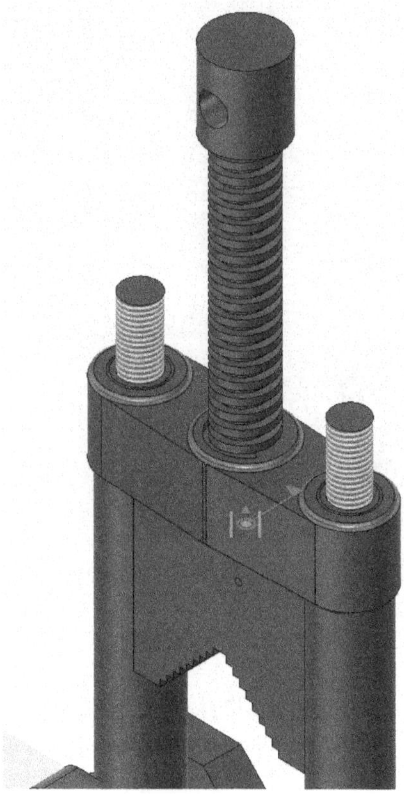

Inserting the Pin

1. Open the Data Panel to locate your parts and drag the Pin component into the 3D workspace.

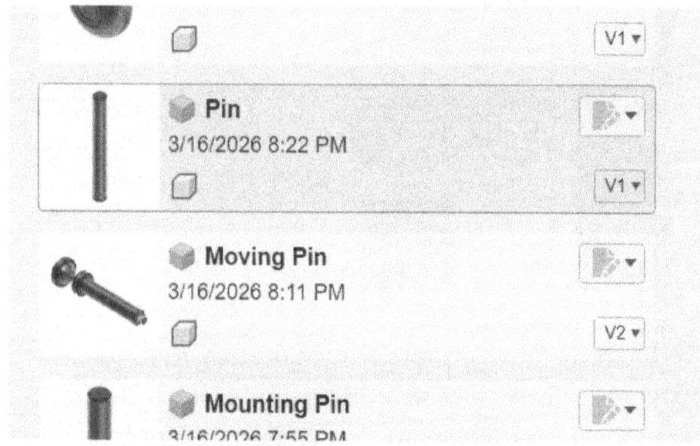

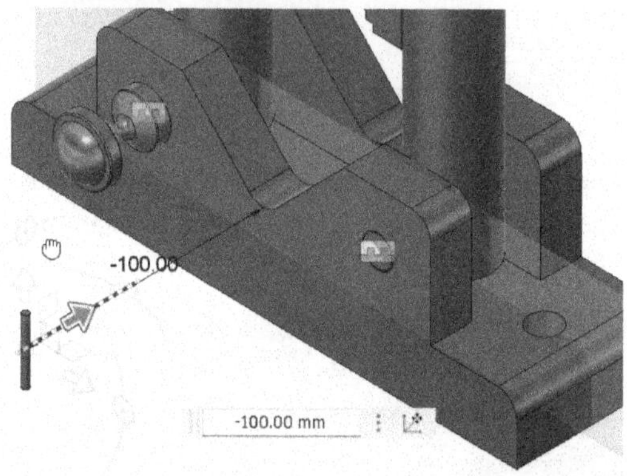

2. Navigate to the toolbar and click the **Assemble** tab > **Relationships** panel > **Joint** command to open the dialog box and start the process, or press the J key on your keyboard.
3. Hover your cursor over the top circular edge of the Pin until a disk icon appears, indicating an available joint origin.
4. Click the top circular edge to lock in your first selection.

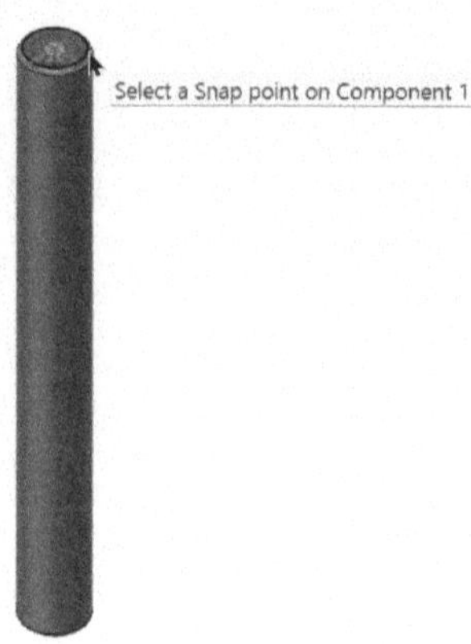

5. Hover your cursor over the destination hole on the Movable Jaw part and click the cicular edge of the hole to establish the connection.

6. On the Joint dialog box, click the **Motion** tab and set the **Type** menu to **Rigid**, which instructs the software to lock the two components together completely without allowing any rotation or sliding motion.

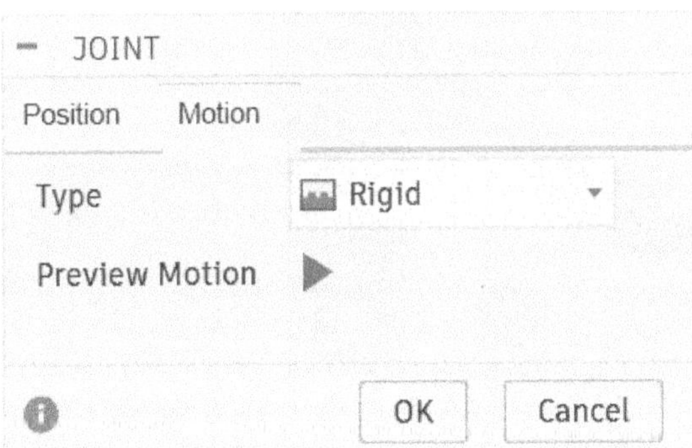

7. Check the alignment of the pin in the 3D canvas and click the **Position** tab, and then the **Flip** icon in the dialog box if the pin points outward instead of going inside the hole.

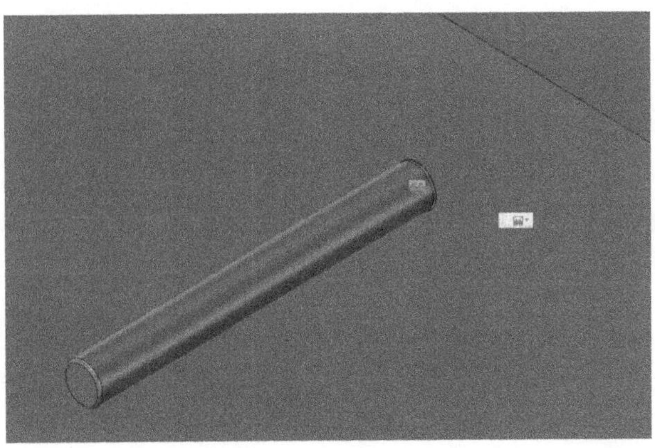

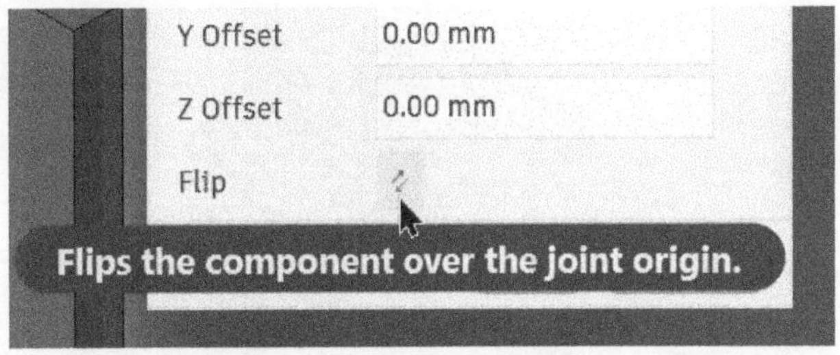

8. Review the Y Offset and Z Offset fields, which allow you to type specific numerical values to shift the pin away from the exact snap point.

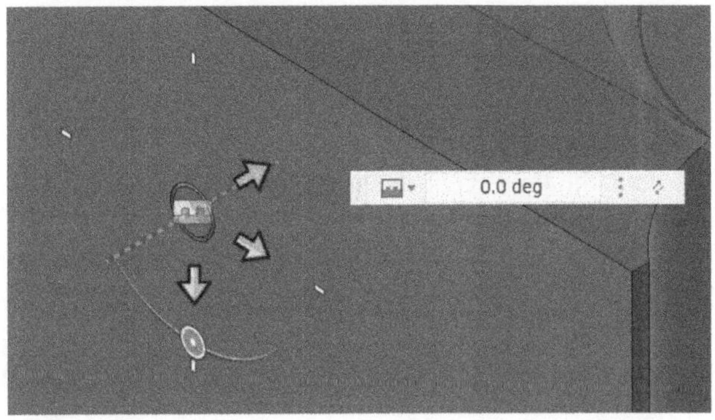

9. Keep these offset values at 0.00 mm to ensure the pin sits flush against the hole edge and click the **OK** button to finalize the operation.

Inserting the Turning Shaft

1. Locate the **Turning Shaft** component in the Data Panel on the left side of the screen and insert it into the active 3D workspace.

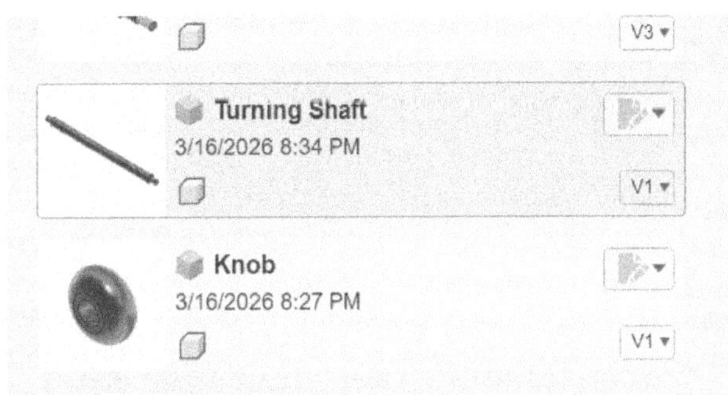

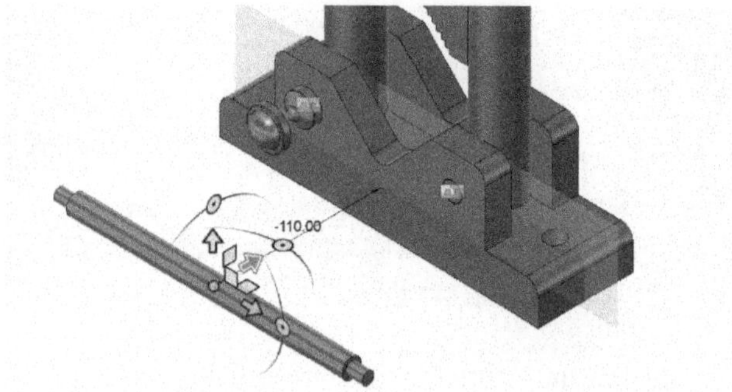

2. Navigate to the Toolbar at the top of the interface, click **Assemble > Relationships** panel > **Joint** tool to launch the dialog box.
3. Hover your cursor over the cylindrical face of the Turning Shaft until the joint origin disk appears.
4. Press and hold the CTRL key on your keyboard to lock the joint origin selection exclusively to that specific cylindrical face.
5. Keep holding the CTRL key, move your cursor to the center snap point on the shaft, and click to confirm your first selection.

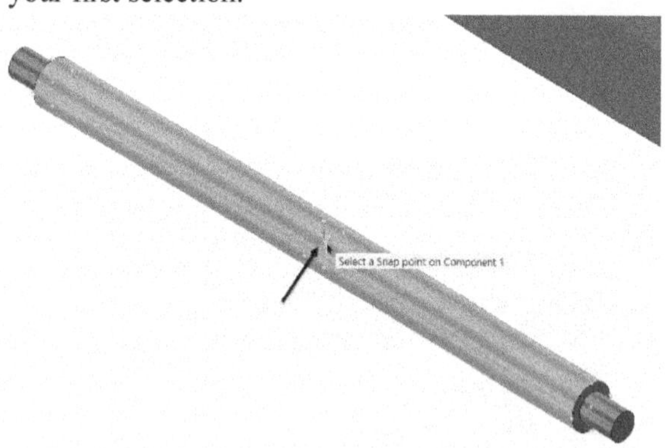

6. Hover your cursor inside the horizontal hole located at the top of the vertical spindle screw part.
7. Press and hold the CTRL key.
8. Click the center snap point inside that hole to establish the connection between the two components.

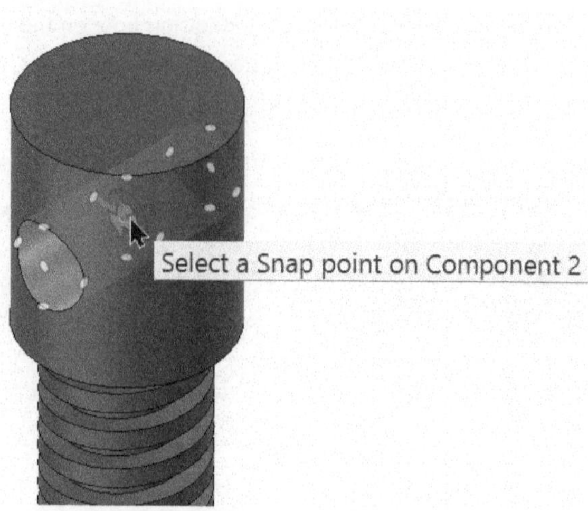

9. Review the **Joint** dialog box and verify that the **Type** is set to **Rigid**, which completely locks the components together.

10. Click the **OK** button in the dialog box to finish the operation and apply the locked joint.

Inserting the Knob

1. Locate the Knob component in the Data Panel on the left side of the screen and drag it into the active 3D workspace.

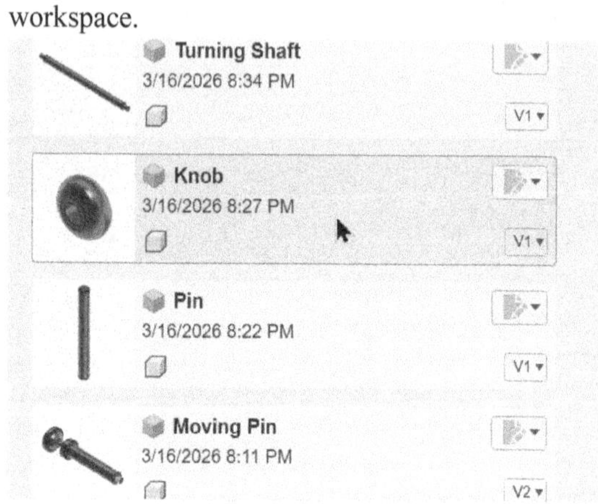

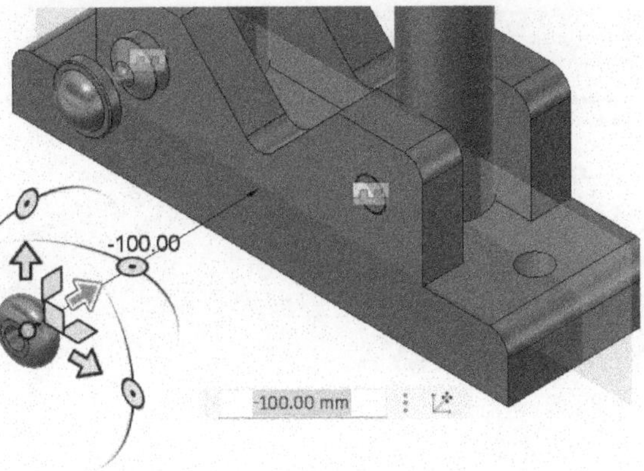

2. Navigate to the Toolbar at the top of the interface, click **Assemble > Relationships** panel > **Joint** tool
3. Hover your cursor over the flat circular base of the Knob and click the circular edge to register your first selection.

4. Hover your cursor over the flat end of the Turning Shaft and click the circular edge to establish the physical connection between the two parts.

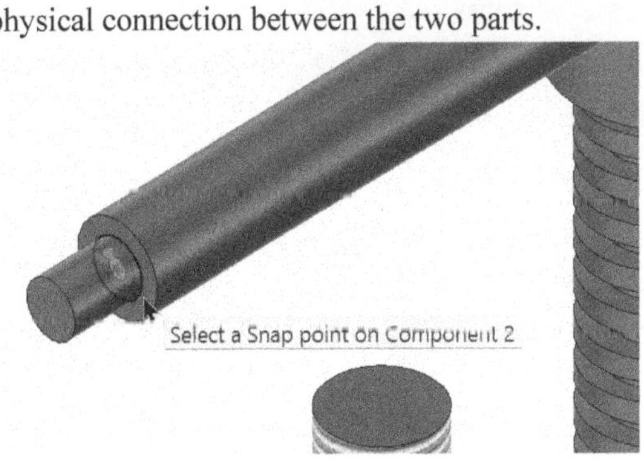

5. Click the **Flip** icon to flip the component correctly over the joint origin.

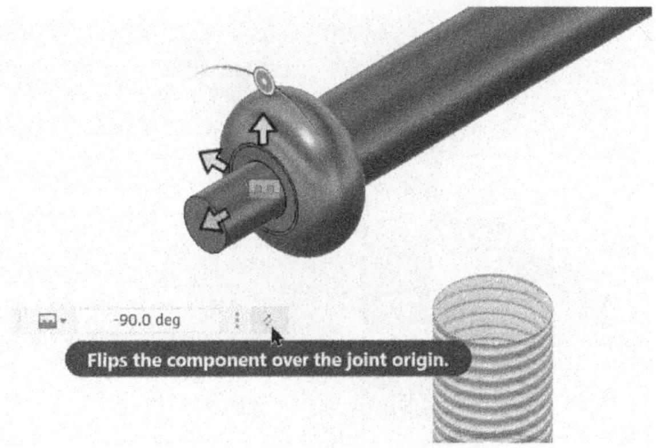

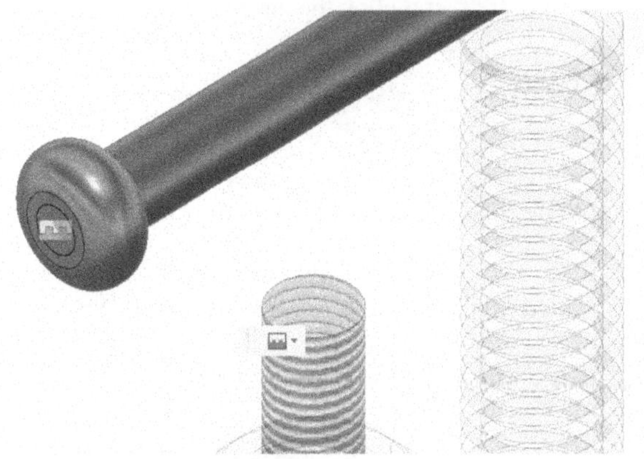

6. Click the **OK** button in the dialog box to finish the operation and apply the locked joint.
7. Navigate to the Toolbar at the top of the interface, click **Assemble > Insert** panel > **Duplicate With Joints**.
8. Review the warning dialog box titled Capture or revert component positions. Click the **Revert Position** button. This action returns any freely moved parts to their officially recorded locations to ensure parametric accuracy.

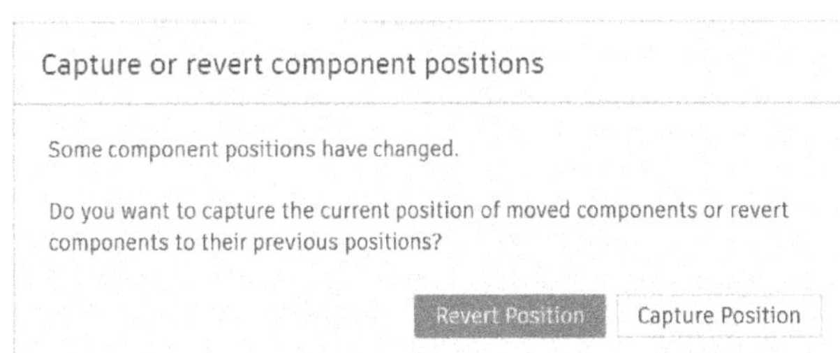

9. Click the newly attached Knob component directly in the 3D workspace.

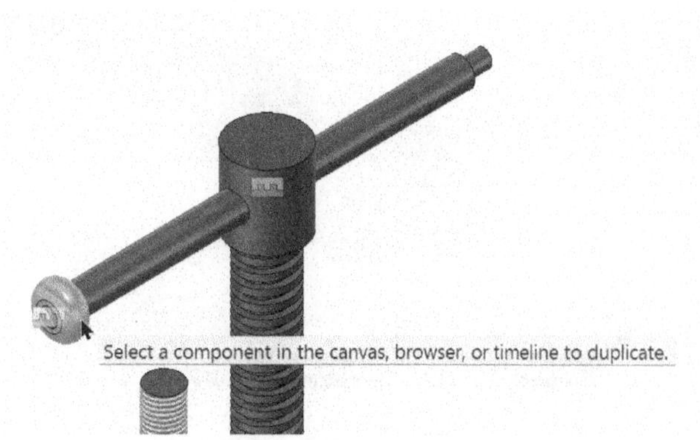

10. Move your cursor to the opposite, empty end of the Turning Shaft and click the circular edge.

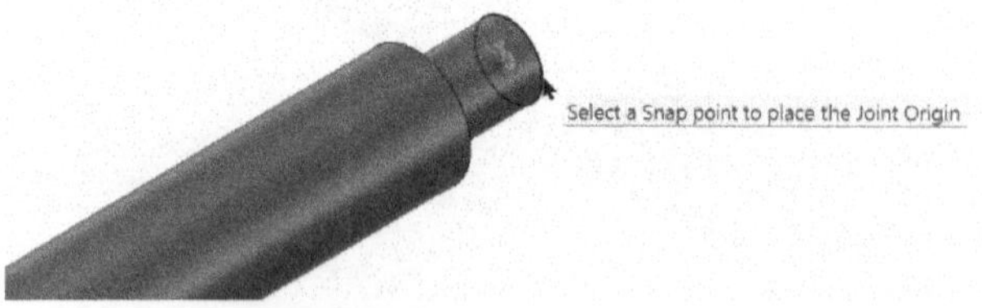

11. Verify that the Components field displays exactly one selected item and the Origin Mode is set to Snap.

12. Click the **OK** button at the bottom of the dialog box to generate an exact copy of the Knob with the identical negative 90.0 degree joint constraint already applied.

Inserting Fasteners

1. On the Toolbar, click the **Assembly** tab, open the **Insert** drop down menu, and click **Insert Fastener** to launch the configuration dialog box.

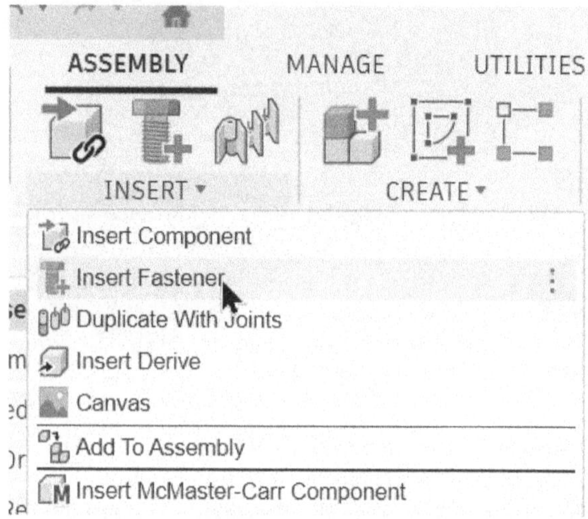

2. In the **Insert Fastener** dialog box, verify the top filter is set to **ISO / All units**.
3. Navigate through the library folders by clicking **Nuts**, then **Flanged Hex**, and finally select the **Hex Weld Nut With Flange** option.

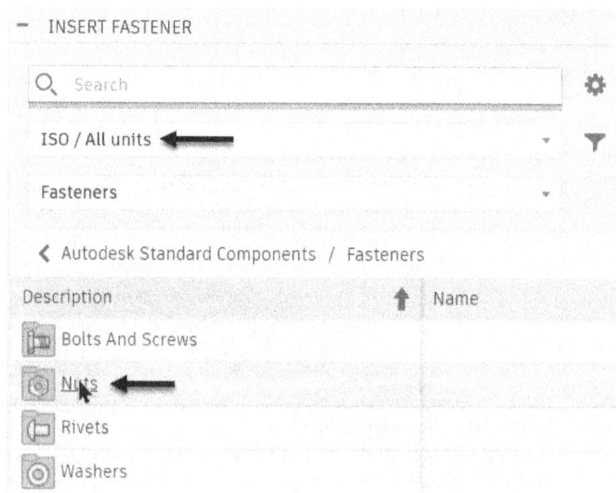

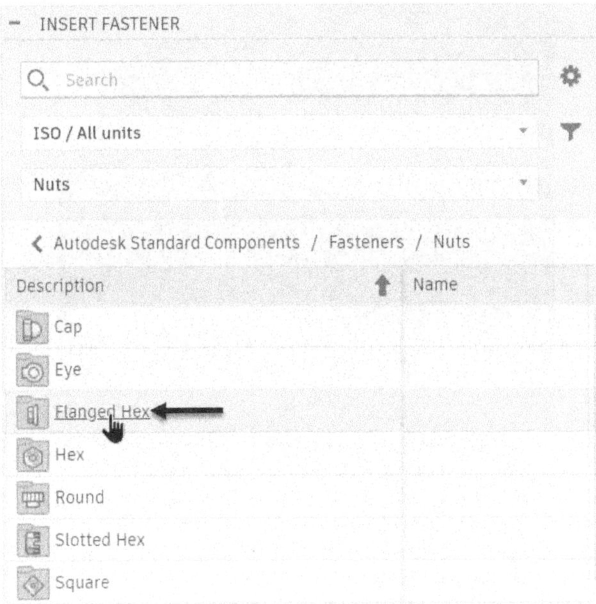

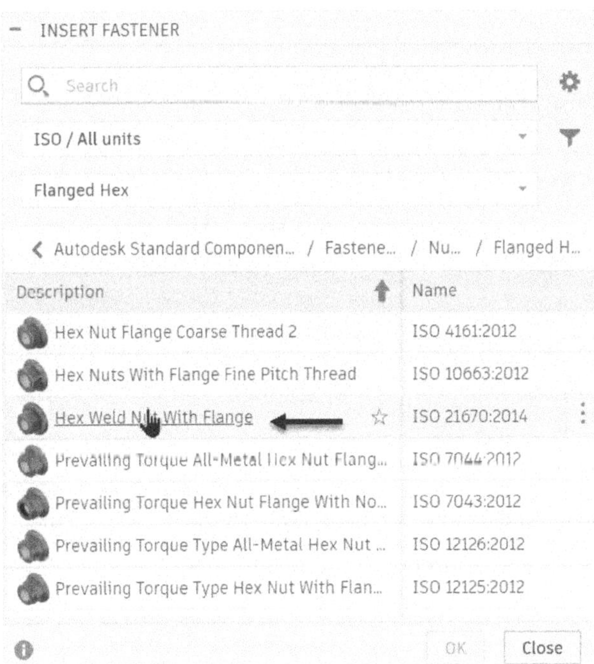

4. In the graphics window, move your cursor to the top of the vertical threaded rod.
5. Click the top cylindrical face. The **Position** option in the dialog box registers this selection to dictate the central axis of your fastener.

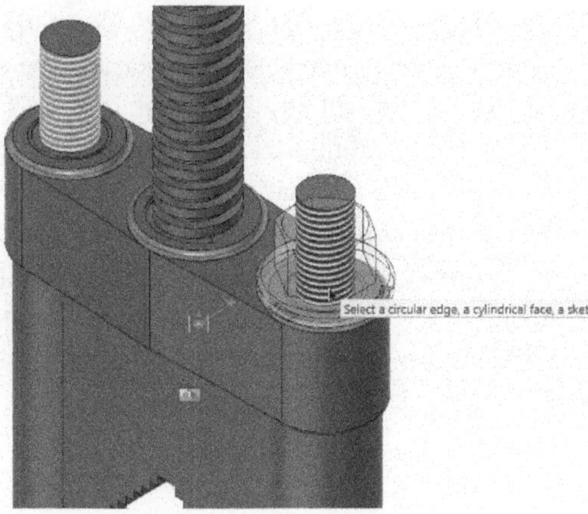

6. Move your cursor to the flat top face of the black block located directly below the threads.
7. Click that flat face. The **Secondary Geometry** option uses this selection to determine exactly where the base of the nut will physically rest.

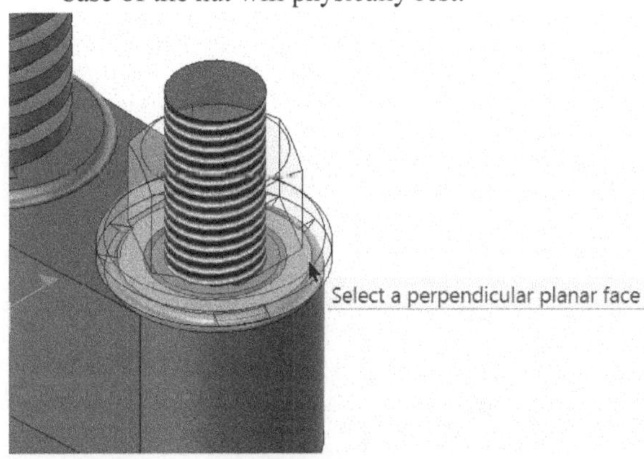

8. Move your cursor to the top of the second vertical threaded rod and click its top circular edge to manually add it to your selection. The **Position** option in the dialog box will now read 2 selected.

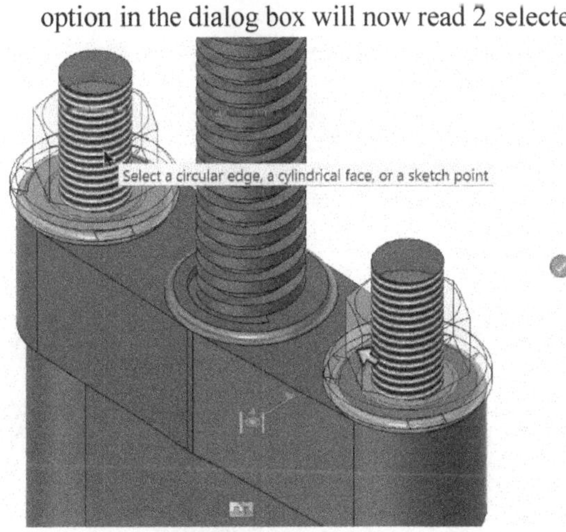

9. Move your cursor to the flat top face of the black block located directly below the threads.

10. Click that flat face. The Secondary Geometry option uses this selection to determine exactly where the base of the nut will physically rest.
11. Verify the **Nominal Size** is set to Auto. This allows the software to automatically calculate the correct M16 thread size based on your chosen circular edge.
12. Click **Create and continue** at the bottom of the dialog box. This button applies your current nuts to the assembly while keeping the tool open for additional hardware placement.

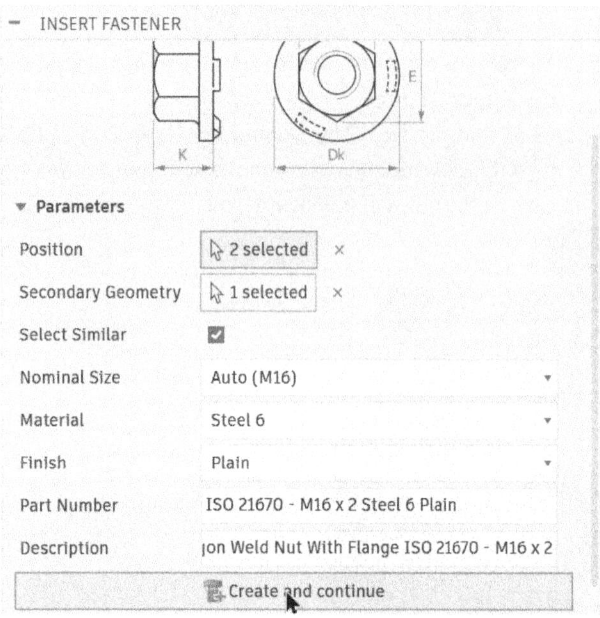

13. In the graphics window, locate the horizontal threaded rod passing through the Fixed jack.
14. Click the cylindrical face of that horizontal rod for the new **Position** selection.

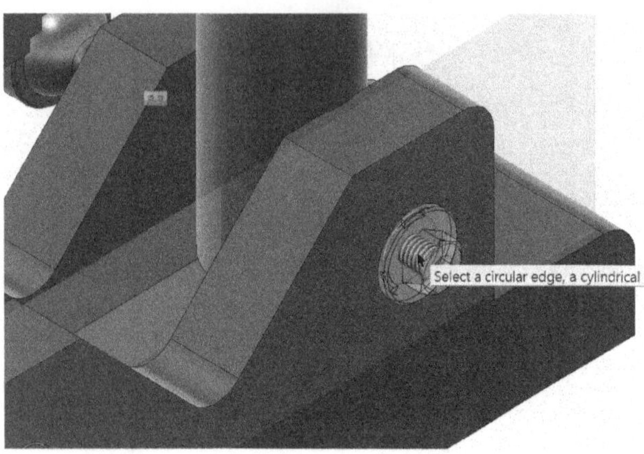

15. Click the vertical flat face of the yellow block for the new **Secondary Geometry** selection.

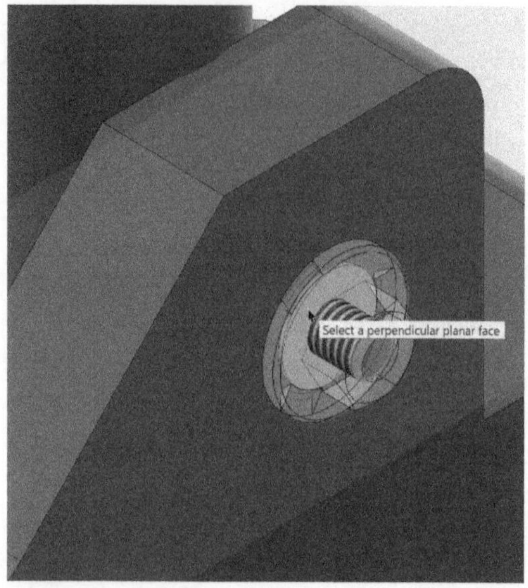

16. Click **OK** at the bottom of the dialog box to place this final M6 nut and completely close the tool.

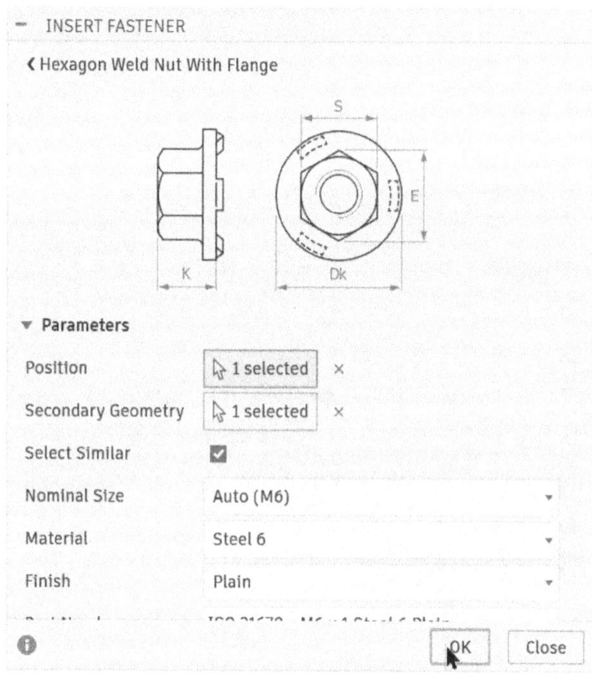

Animating the Joint Relationships

1. In the Browser on the left side of the screen, click the arrow next to the **Relationships** folder to expand it.
2. Click the arrow next to the **Joint**s folder to reveal the complete list of applied assembly connections.
3. Locate the specific joint you want to evaluate, such as the connection labeled Cylindrical 7.
4. Right click that specific joint to open the context menu.

5. Review the available options and note the functional difference. The Animate Joint option moves only your selected connection and ignores all other parts. The **Animate Joint Relationships** option evaluates all connected components and moves the entire mechanical assembly realistically.
6. Click **Animate Joint Relationships**.

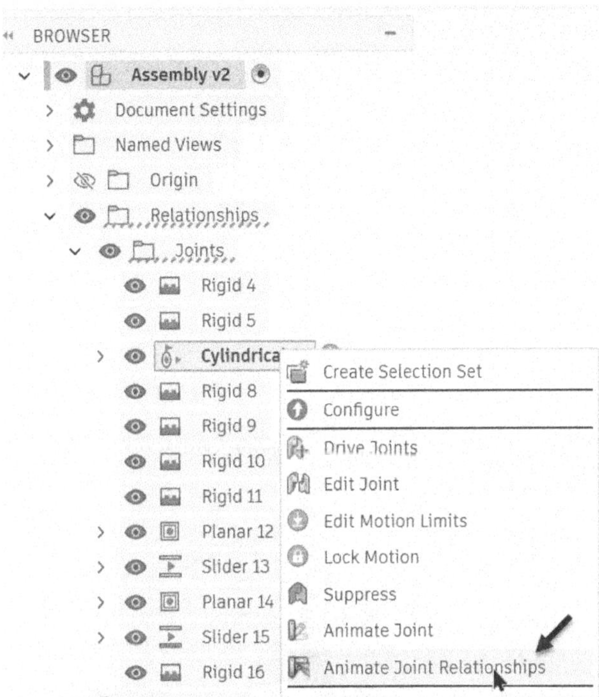

7. Observe the graphics window. The software will automatically drive the selected Cylindrical joint through its defined degrees of freedom, causing the spindle screw to rotate and translate up and down while the connected jaws react accordingly.

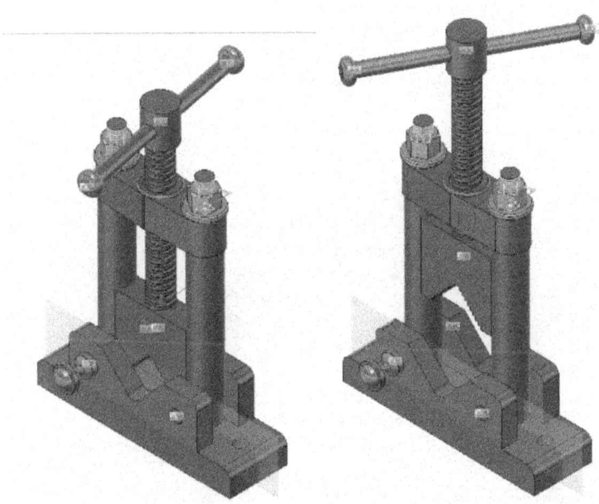

8. Press the **Escape** key on your keyboard or click anywhere in the graphics window to stop the continuous playback.

Accessing the Bill of Materials

Accessing and customizing the Bill of Materials directly inside the assembly environment.

1. Navigate to the Toolbar in your active workspace and locate the Modify panel.
2. Click the icon displaying a spreadsheet graphic to launch the **Bill of Materials**.

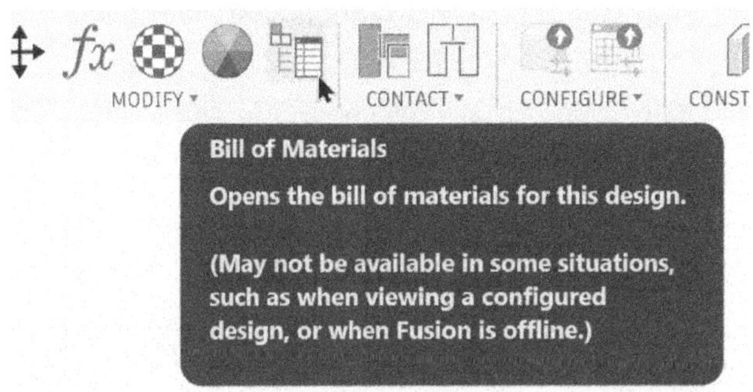

3. Observe the full parts list that appears on the screen. The software automatically scans your design file and compiles every individual component into a structured hierarchy.

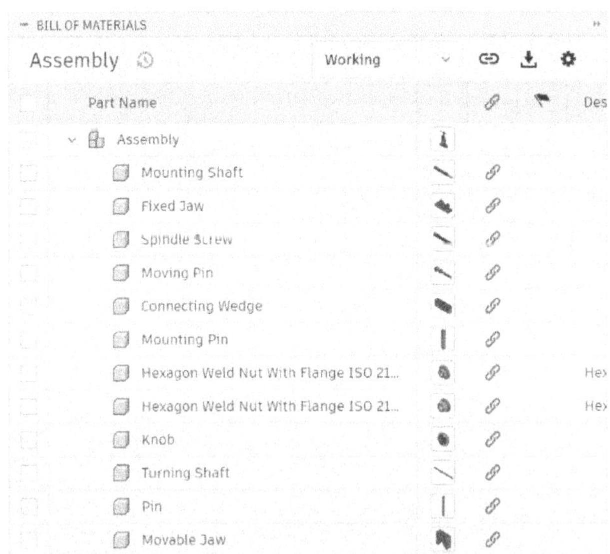

Configuring the Data

1. Review the top menu bar of the Bill of Materials window and ensure the drop down menu is set to

Working rather than Released, which allows you to view the current active state of your design.

2. Click the gear icon located in the top right corner of the **Bill of Materials** window to open the **Column Settings** menu.
3. Review the list of available data categories divided into **General** and **Manage** sections.
4. Check the box next to specific categories like Quantity, Material Name, or Part Number to instruct the software to extract and display that exact data for every component in your list.
5. Uncheck any boxes for data you do not need, such as **Lifecycle** or Milestone, to keep your spreadsheet clean and focused on manufacturing.
6. Click the **Reset Order** button at the top of the settings menu if you want to revert your column arrangement back to the factory defaults.

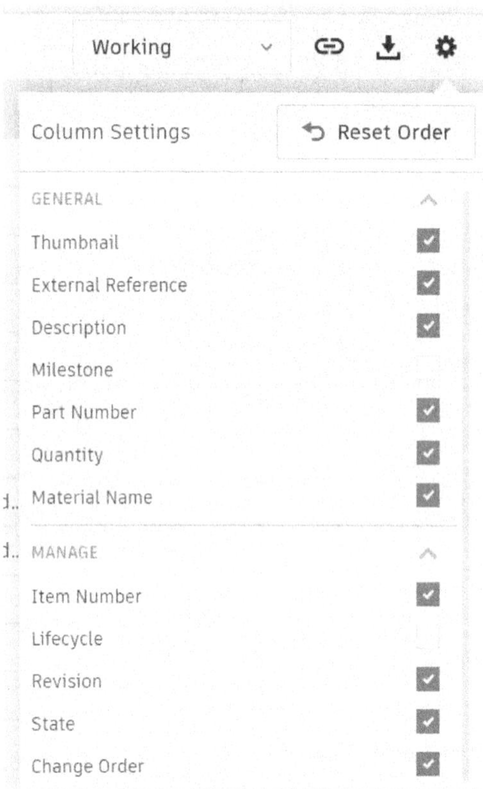

Exporting the Spreadsheet

1. Click the icon showing a downward arrow pointing into a horizontal line, located next to the gear icon at the top of the window.
2. Use this export function to save your customized spreadsheet locally as a CSV or XLS file, allowing you to open the exact parts list in Microsoft Excel or other external business software.

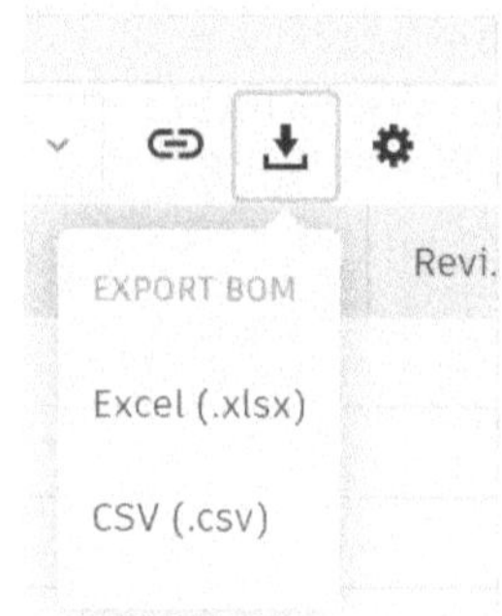

3. Click the **Close** button at the bottom of the window to exit the tool and return to your modeling canvas.
4. Save and close the assembly file.

Tutorial 2

In this tutorial, you will create the exploded animation of the assembly created in Tutorial 1.

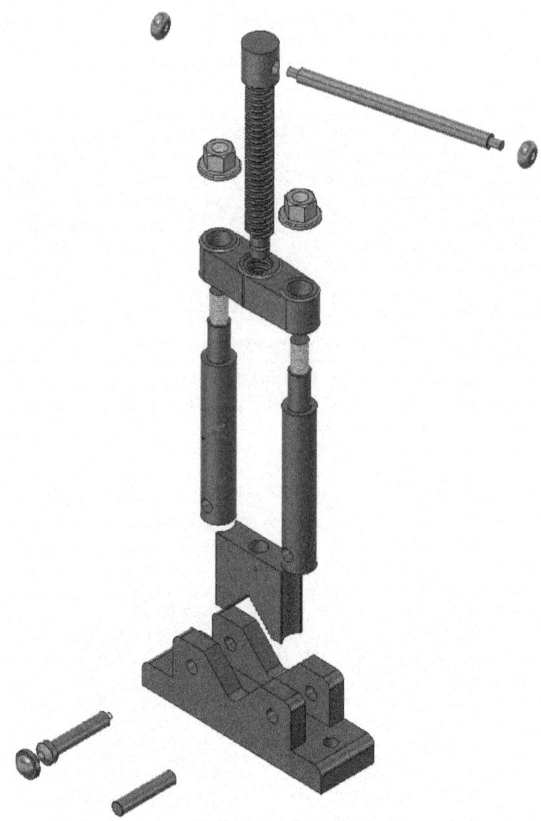

Creating an exploded view in Autodesk Fusion 360 requires transitioning from the standard **Design** environment into the **Animation** workspace, where you can safely pull components apart without permanently altering your original assembly.

Automatic Explosion

1. Navigate to the top left corner of the interface and click the **Workspace** menu to reveal the drop-down list.
2. Select **Animation** from the list to switch to the dedicated workspace for generating exploded diagrams.

3. Locate the Browser on the left side of the screen and click the top level assembly name to select all components simultaneously.

4. Navigate to the Toolbar, click the Transform menu, and select **Auto Explode: All Levels**, or press the U key on your keyboard.

5. Drag the **Explosion Scale** slider in the dialog box to adjust the physical distance between the separated parts.

6. Click the icon showing staggered horizontal bars next to the slider to open the drop-down menu and select **Sequential Explosion** if you want the timeline to record the parts separating one by one.

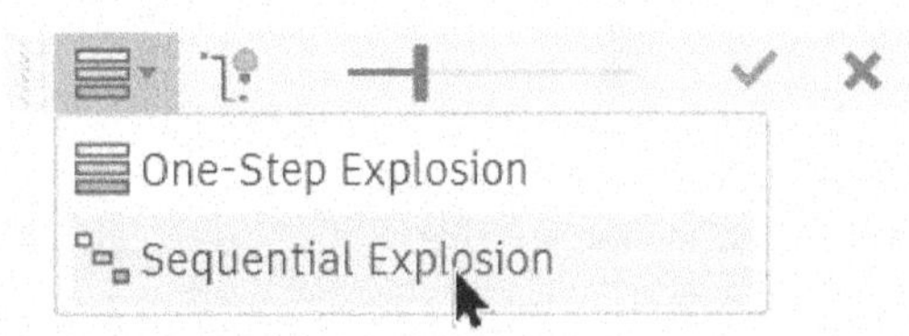

Choose **One Step Explosion** if you want the parts to separate together as a single action.

7. Click **OK** to apply the automatic transformation.

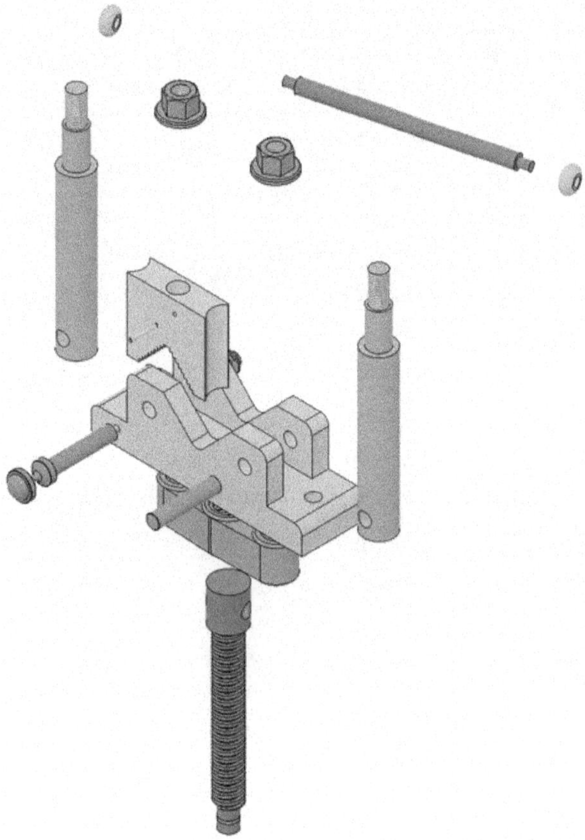

Other Transform commands

1. In the Browser on the left side of the screen, click the top-level assembly.

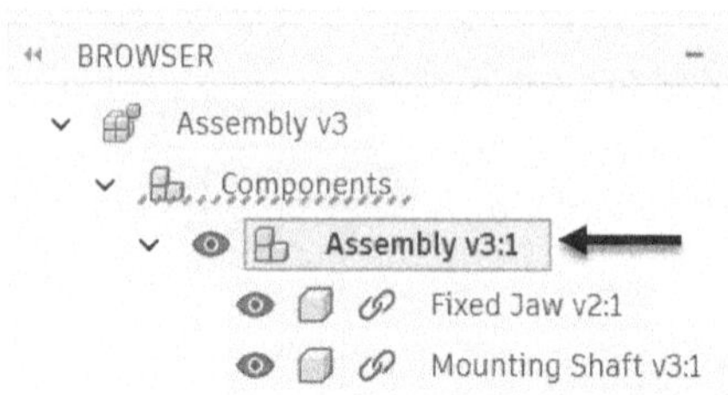

2. On the Toolbar, click **Transform**, then click **Restore Home** if you want all exploded components to return to their original assembled positions.

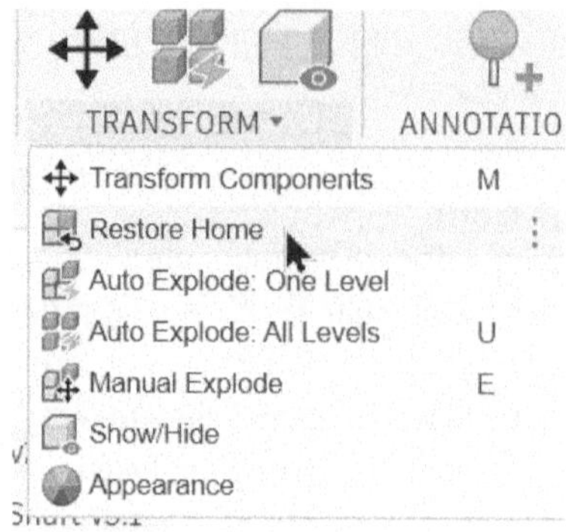

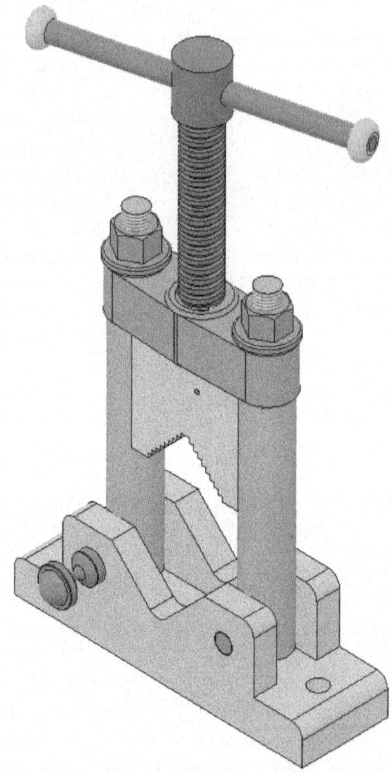

Use **Restore Home** when you need to reset the view quickly before creating a new explode sequence or checking the fully assembled model again.

If your design contains subassemblies, navigate to the Toolbar, click Transform, and select **Auto Explode: One Level** to handle grouped parts differently.

This alternative command separates only the major structural groups from each other, ensuring the internal parts of any subassembly remain connected as a single block instead of exploding into individual pieces.

Manual Explosion

Navigate to the top left area of the interface next to the save icon, click the small downward arrow next to the

Undo button to open the command history list, and select **Undo Auto Explode: All Levels**.

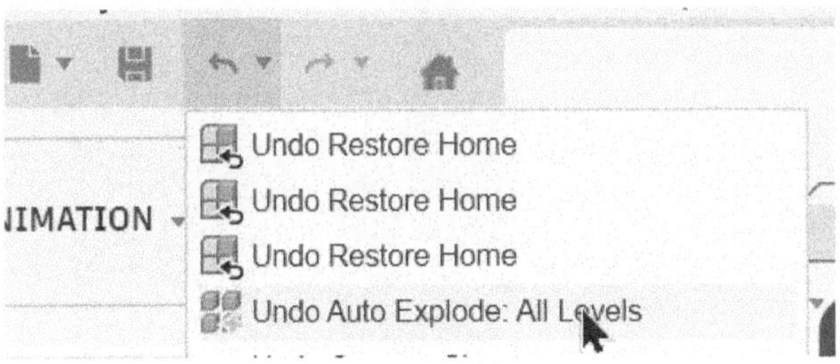

1. Navigate to the Toolbar, click the **Transform** panel, and select **Manual Explode** to open the configuration dialog box.
2. In the graphics window, click on the movable pin, as shown.
3. Observe the cluster of directional arrows that instantly surrounds your selected component.
4. Click the specific arrow that points in the forward direction. This action locks the explosion path and turns that single arrow blue.

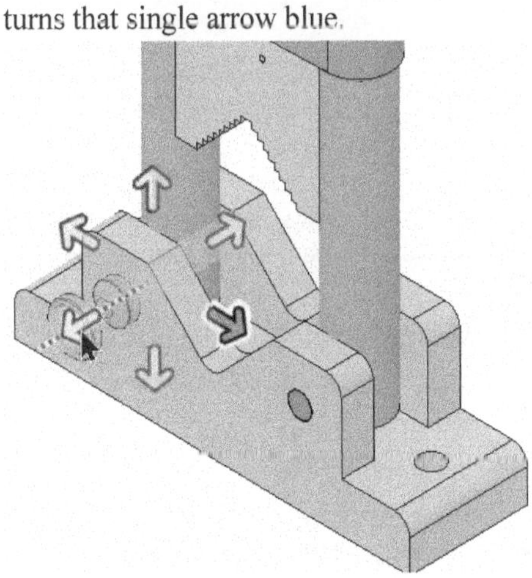

5. Look at the floating control box and drag the Explosion Scale slider to push the selected component outward along your chosen blue axis.

6. Click the green check mark in the floating control box to lock the movable pin in its new location.

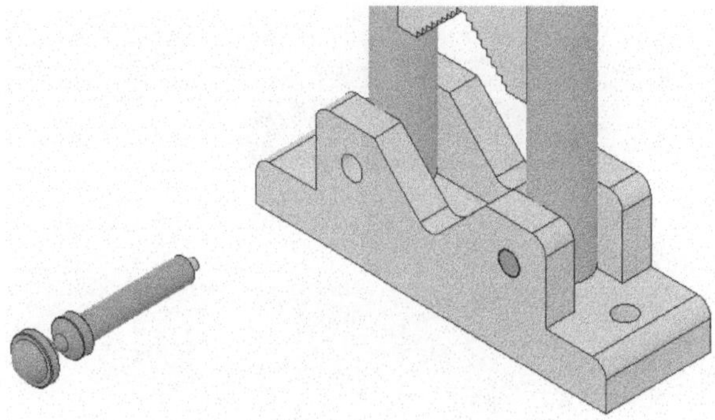

7. Navigate to the Toolbar, click the **Transform** panel, and select **Manual Explode** to open the configuration dialog box.
8. Click the Mounting pin located on the right side of the yellow base block.

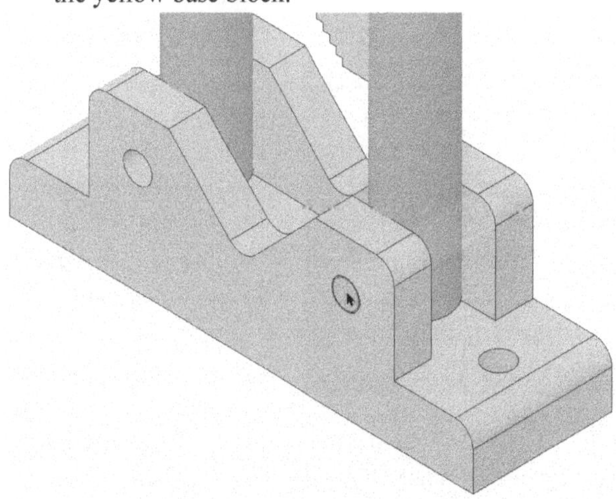

9. Select the forward directional arrow for this new part to lock its travel path.

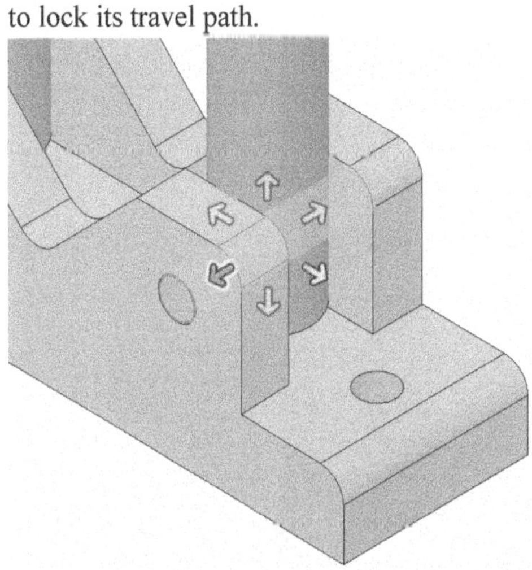

10. Drag the **Explosion Scale** slider again to push the pink pin out of the assembly.

11. Click the green check mark to confirm this second movement.

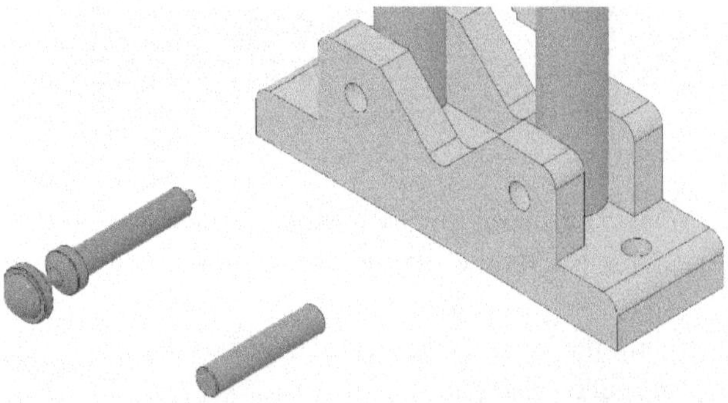

Transform Components

In Earlier sections, you have used the Auto Explode and Manual Explode tool to explode the components. The **Auto Explode** algorithmically pushes all parts outward, which works for basic shapes but often causes visual overlaps. **Manual Explode** allows pulling parts along a single straight arrow using a visual scale slider, but it lacks the ability to rotate objects or input exact measurements.

Now, choose the **Transform Components** tool to achieve exact numerical placement and full spatial control.

1. Click and drag a selection box from right to left over the components above the fixed jaw to select them simultaneously.

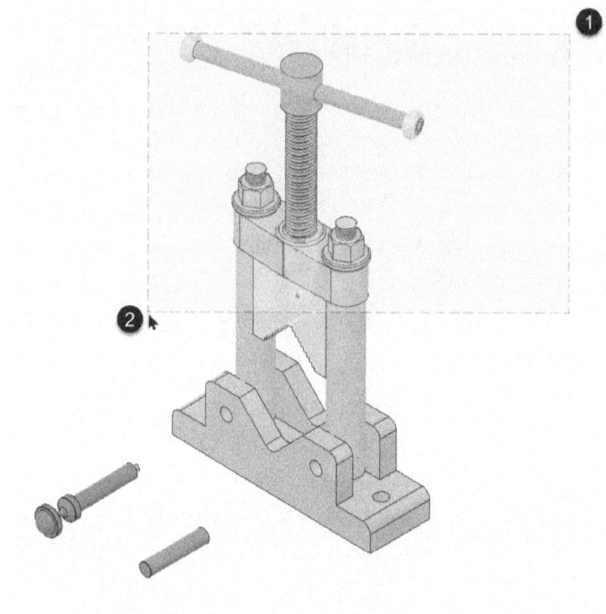

2. Navigate to the Toolbar, click the **Transform** panel, and select **Transform Components**, or press the **M** key on your keyboard to open the configuration dialog box.

3. Observe the triad manipulator that appears at the calculated center point of your selected components. Unlike the **Manual Explode** tool which only provides a single straight directional arrow, this advanced triad features arrows for linear movement and curved lines for rotational movement.
4. Click and drag the vertical blue arrow pointing upward to manually slide the selected group straight up along the Z axis.
5. Type exactly negative 150.00 mm directly into the floating coordinate box or the Z Distance field in the dialog box. This specific numerical input provides absolute precision, avoiding the random algorithmic placement of Auto Explode and the visual guesswork of the Manual Explode slider.

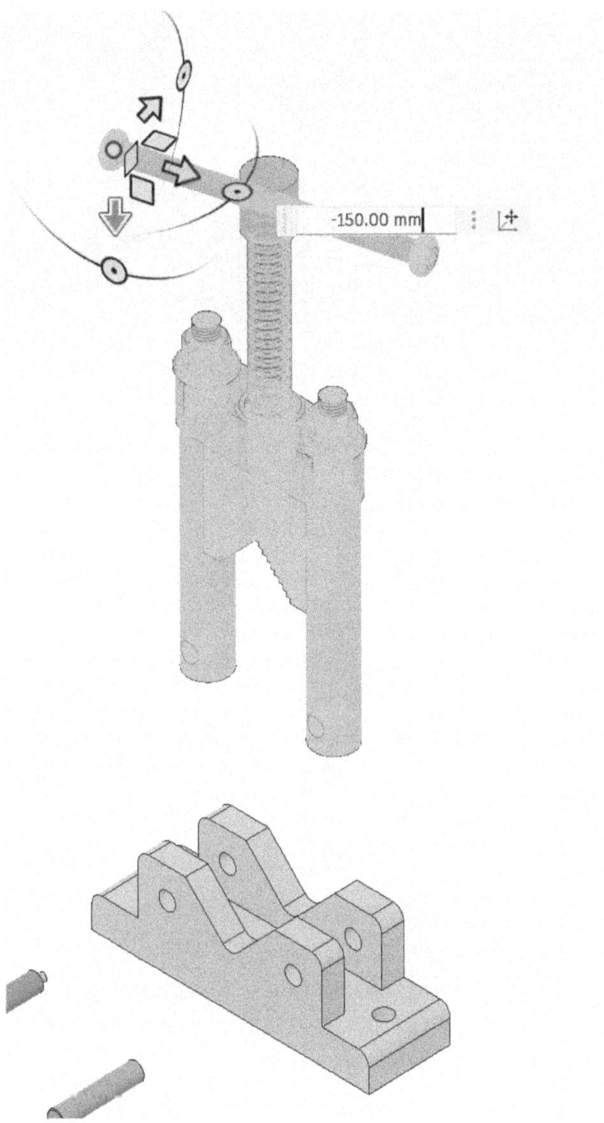

6. Verify that the **Trail Visibility** checkbox is unchecked in the dialog box so the software avoids drawing dashed lines that connect the moved parts back to their original origin points.
7. Click in the 3D workspace to deselect the selections.
8. Click the pin inside the movable jaw.

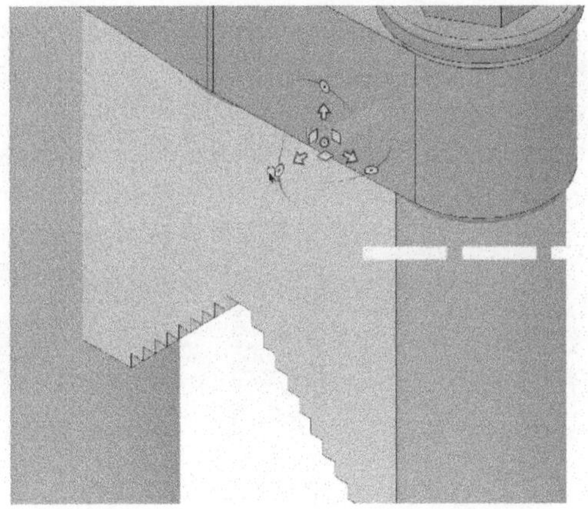

9. Click and drag the arrow pointing forward on the triad to slide the pin in the forward direction.

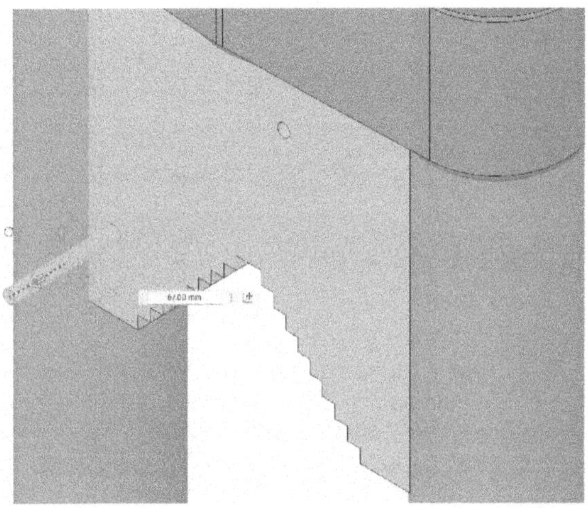

10. Click in the 3D workspace to deselect the selection.
11. Click the movable jaw piece in the graphics window.

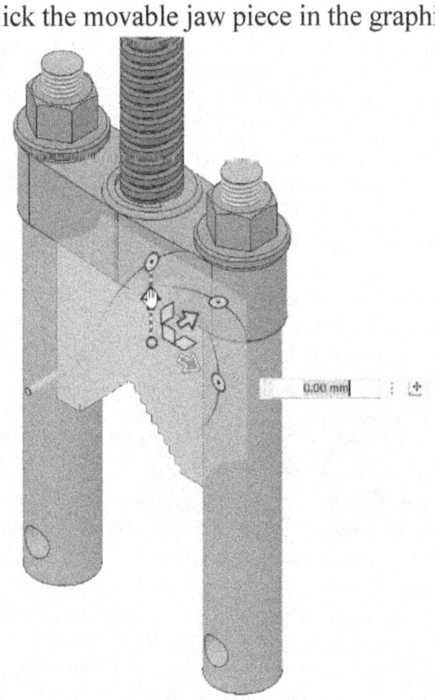

12. Click and drag the vertical blue arrow on the triad to slide the jaw straight downward.
13. Type negative 160.00 mm into the floating Z Distance coordinate box to set the exact downward position.

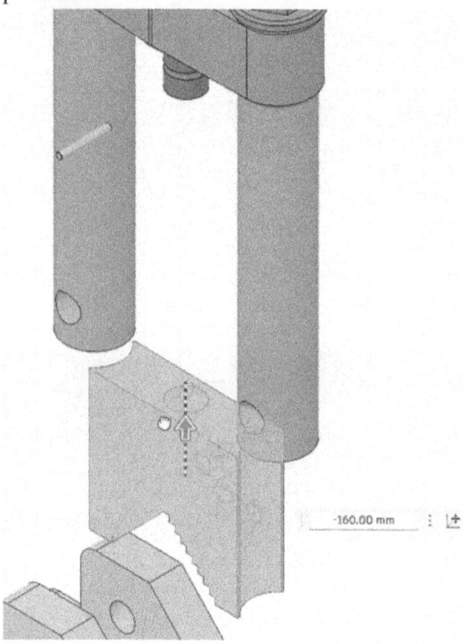

14. Click in the 3D workspace.
15. Click the empty space in the top right area of the graphics window and drag your cursor down to the bottom left area to form a selection box. Ensure the box touches the spindle screw, turning shaft, and knobs.

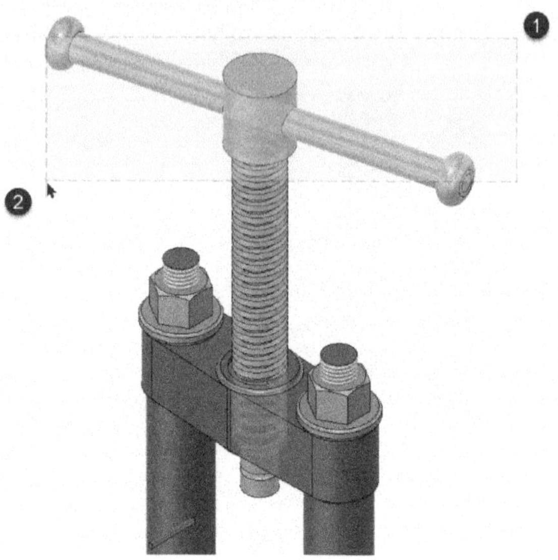

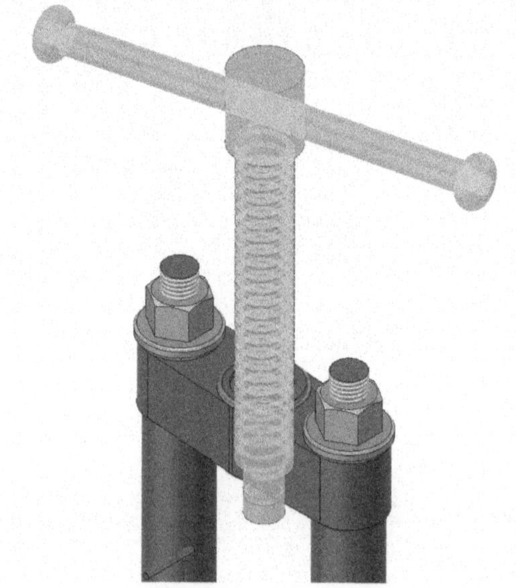

16. Click and drag the straight arrow aligned with the central axis of the spindle screw upward, then release it when the value reaches -150.

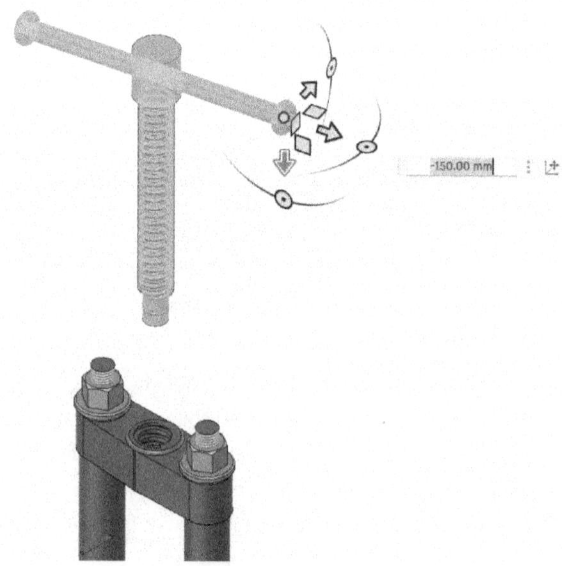

17. Click in the 3D workspace.
18. Press and hold the CTRL key and click the turning shaft, and right knob.
19. Click and drag the straight arrow pointing to right, then release it when the value reaches -130.

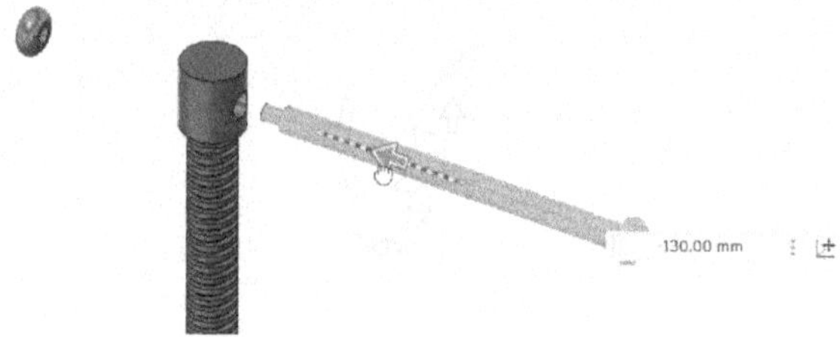

20. Click the remaining right knob in the graphics window to select it.
21. Click and drag the straight arrow pointing outward to the right side of the screen.
22. Type exactly 30.00 mm into the distance box to pull the knob further away from the central spindle screw.

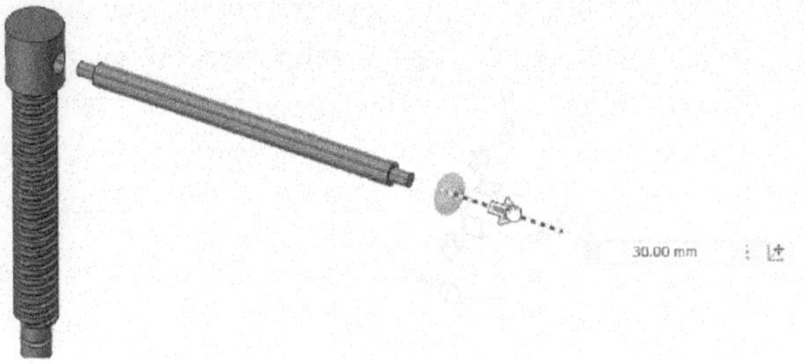

23. Press and hold the CTRL key and click the left and right flanged nut in the graphics window to select it. Observe the triad manipulator that appears directly on that individual part.

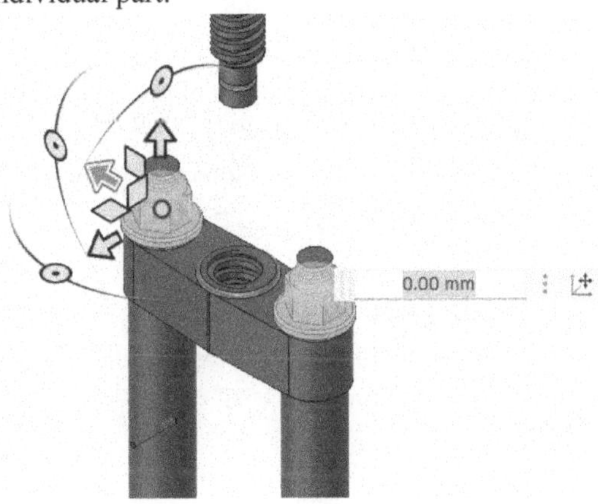

24. Click and drag the vertical arrow pointing upward to slide both nuts straight up along the Z axis simultaneously.
25. Type exactly 150.00 mm directly into the floating coordinate distance box to define a precise vertical separation distance.

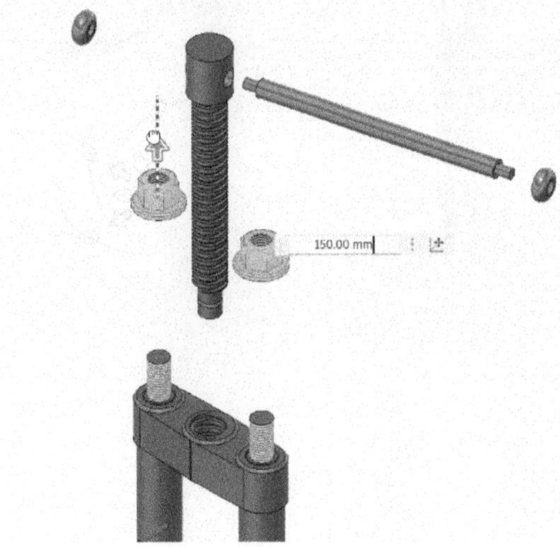

26. Click in the 3D workspace.
27. Click the connecting wedge block located directly below the vertical spindle threads in the graphics window.

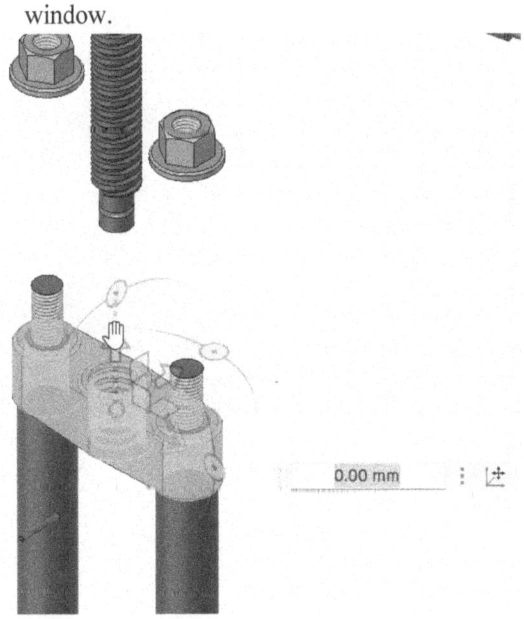

28. Click and drag the vertical arrow pointing upward on the triad manipulator to slide the wedge block straight up along the Z axis.
29. Type exactly 80.00 mm into the floating coordinate distance box to set the final vertical position.

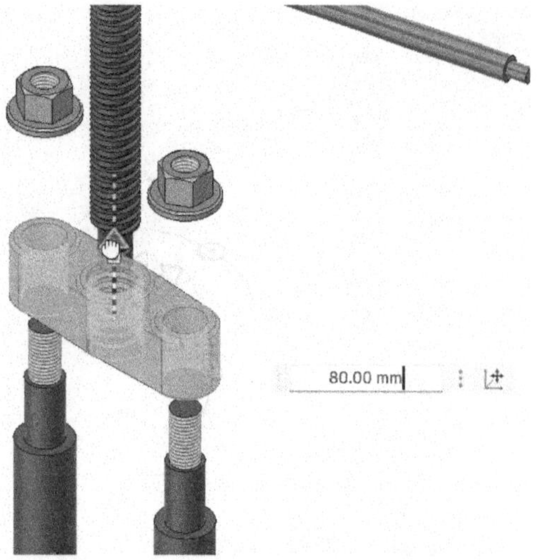

30. Click **OK** in the dialog box to finish the command and lock the placement of the connecting wedge.

Managing the Timeline and Camera

Locate the Animation Timeline panel running across the bottom of your workspace.

Observe the list of individual components on the left side of the panel, such as the Moving Pin and the Hexagon Weld Nut. The colored blocks next to these names represent the specific physical movements you recorded previously.

You can click and drag the edges of any individual block to adjust the duration of that specific movement.

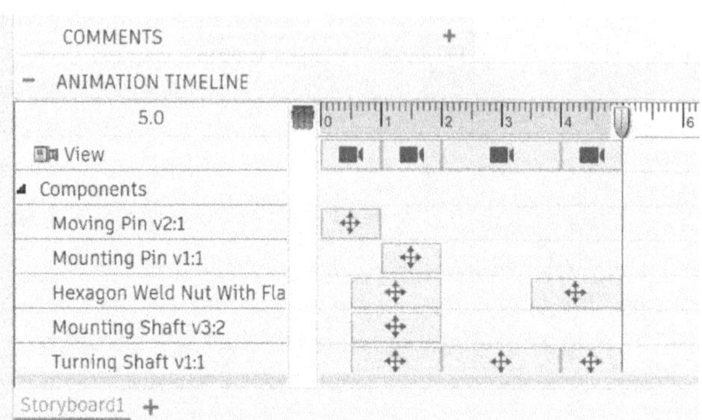

1. Look at the top Toolbar and verify that the **View** icon displays a small red dot. This dot indicates the software is actively recording your camera perspective

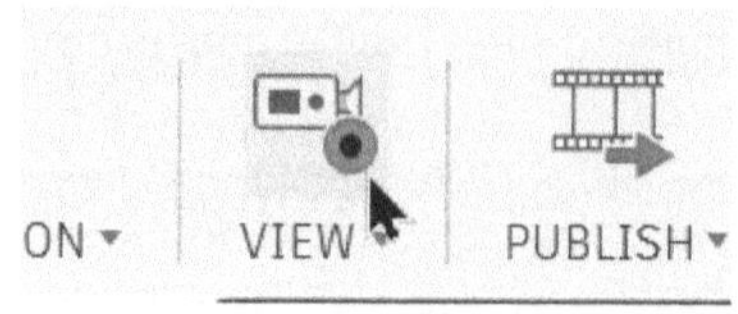

2. Click and drag the vertical grey playhead marker
3. Locate the cluster of playback control buttons in the bottom right corner of the timeline panel.
4. Click the first button on the left, which looks like a vertical line next to a left pointing arrow, to instantly jump the playhead back to the 0.0 second start line.

5. Click the center **Play** button, which looks like a right pointing triangle, to watch your recorded sequence run in real time. The software will move the parts and shift the camera exactly as indicated by the blocks on the timeline.
6. Click the **Play** button a second time to pause the sequence if you spot an error.

Publishing the Video

1. Navigate to the Toolbar and click the **Publish** icon, which features a film strip and a blue arrow.

2. Review the floating dialog box that appears and select **Current Storyboard** from the Video Scope section.
3. Select your desired visual quality from the **Video Resolution** section.

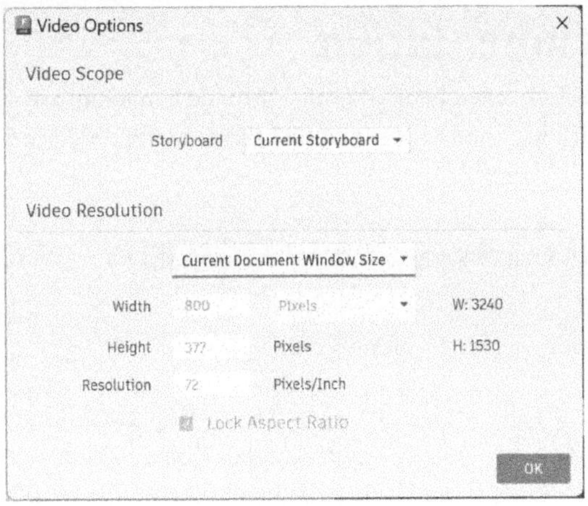

4. Click **OK.** Next, browse to the desired location on your computer and click **Save** on the **Save As** window. The software will render your timeline into a standard video file suitable for sharing.
5. Save and close the design file.

2D Drafting and Documentation

Creating a 3D model is the first phase of the design process. To manufacture a product, you must provide a machinist with formal, two-dimensional engineering documents. In this chapter, you will use the Drawing workspace to extract precise 2D manufacturing data from your existing 3D files.

You will use the fixed jaw component and the completed vise assembly to generate two standard drawing sheets.

You will execute two distinct documentations:

Detailing a Single Part: You will create a dedicated drawing sheet specifically for the fixed jaw. You will place a primary Base View to anchor the layout, generate standard orthographic views (Top, Front, and Right), and position a 3D isometric view for reference. You will then apply linear dimensions, angular measurements, and hole callouts directly to the profile edges to define the physical boundaries required for machining.

Documenting the Master Assembly: You will generate a separate drawing for the complete mechanical vise. Instead of dimensioning part geometry, you will place an exploded view to illustrate how the components fit together. You will generate an automated Bill of Materials (BOM) table to list every component, material specification, and required quantity. You will then apply the Balloon tool to tag each part in the view with an index number matching the BOM.

Parametric Drawing Updates

Your 2D drawing files maintain a parametric link to the source 3D models. If you modify the geometry of the fixed jaw in the Design workspace, you do not need to recreate the 2D sheet. You update the original 3D file, save the changes, and click the Update icon in the Drawing workspace. The software will automatically recalculate the views, adjust the dimension values, and update the BOM to match the new geometry.

Tutorial 1

In this tutorial, you will create the drawing view of the Fixed jaw component used in the assembly created in Pipe Vise Assembly.

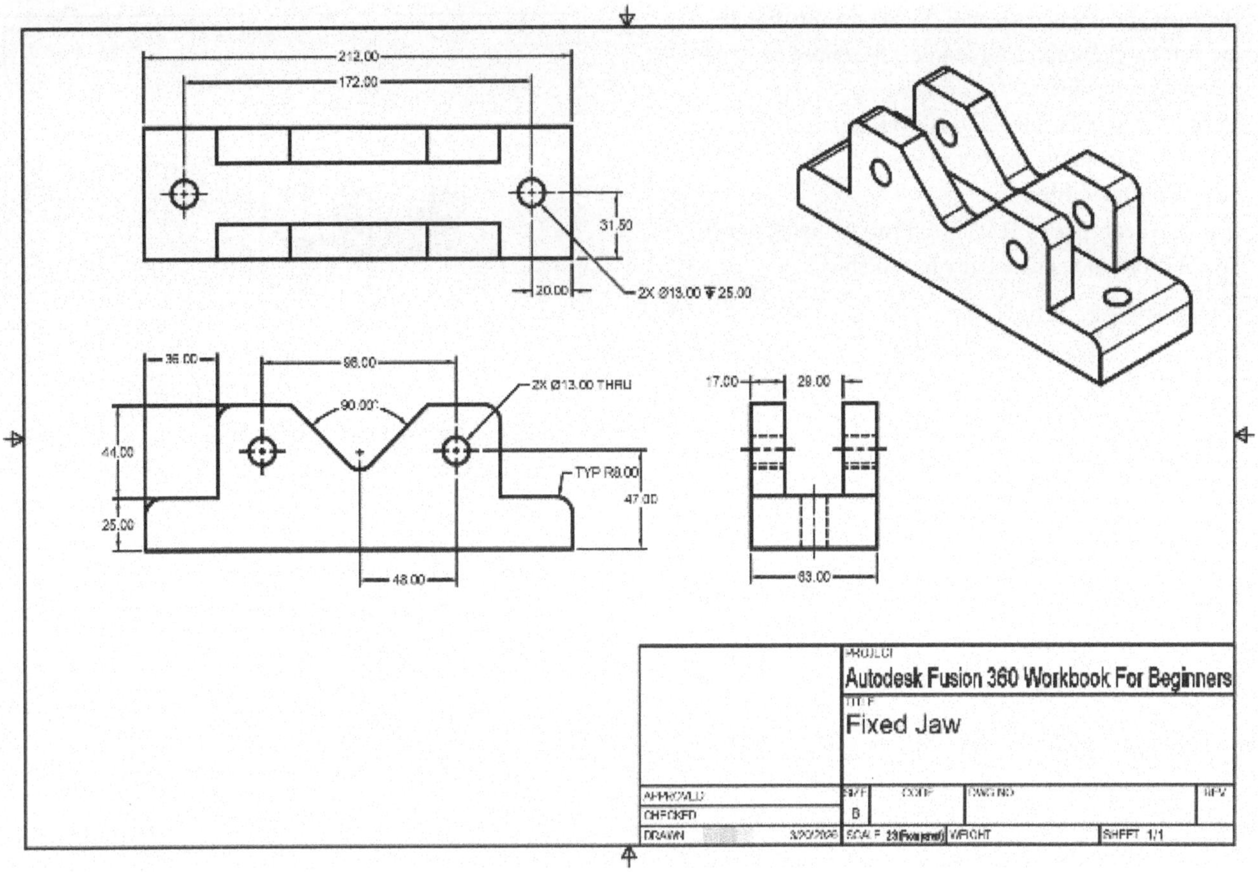

The Drawing workspace in Autodesk Fusion 360 provides a dedicated 2D environment specifically built for generating formal manufacturing documentation. Unlike the 3D canvas, this workspace utilizes flat sheets to display scaled orthographic projections, detailed part dimensions, and standardized text layouts to ensure correct fabrication.

Creating the Drawing File

1. Click the grid icon in the top left corner of the interface to open the Data Panel.
2. Locate the specific **Fixed Jaw** component file in your project folder and double click it to open it in its own active **Design** workspace.

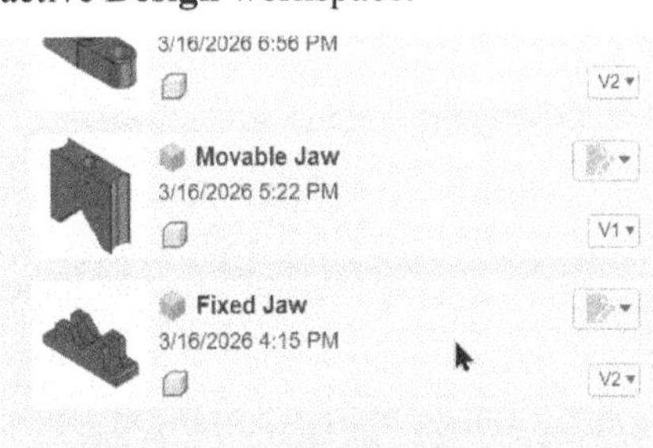

3. Navigate to the top left corner of the interface and click the Workspace menu.
4. Hover your cursor over the **Drawing** option and click **From Design**.

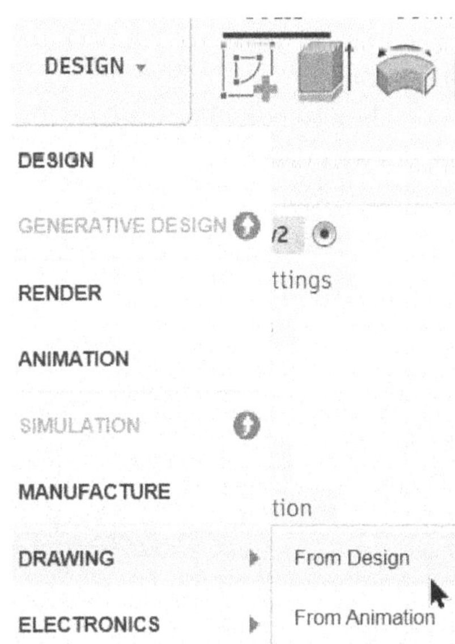

5. Review the floating **Create Drawing** dialog box.

Because you opened the individual part file directly, the software automatically targets the entire contents of this specific file for the drawing.

6. Verify the Standard is set to **ASME** to match the title block format shown in your image.
7. Set the **Units** to **mm**.
8. Set the **Sheet Size** to **B** (17in x 11in) to match the layout proportions listed in your title block.

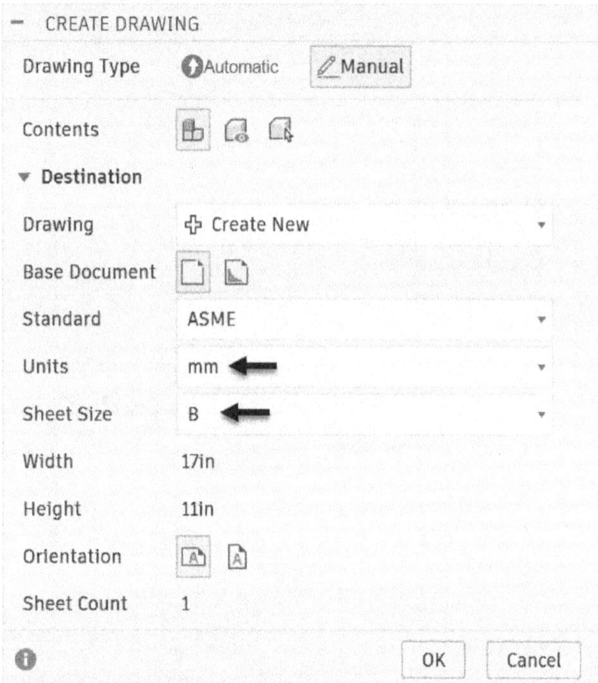

9. Click **OK** to confirm the settings and load the new 2D workspace.

Placing the Base View

1. Observe that the **Base View** tool is automatically active as soon as the new sheet loads, and a floating outline of your part is following your cursor.
2. Click the empty space on the middle left side of the white sheet to place the view exactly where shown in the reference image.

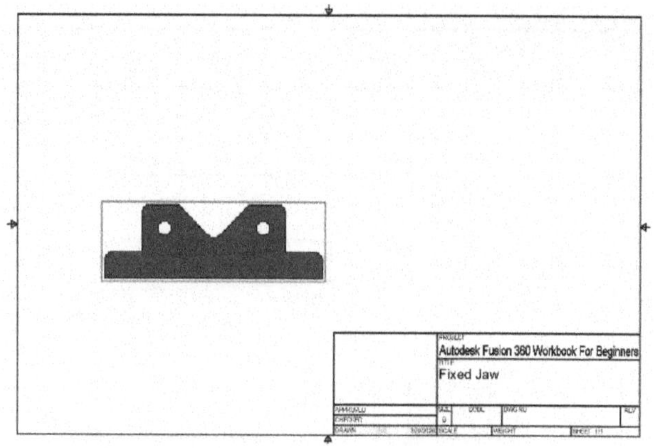

3. Review the **Drawing View** dialog box that appears.
4. Set the **Orientation** to **Front** to display the wide, flat profile of the jaw.
5. Select **Visible Edges** in the **Style** section to configure the software to render the part using standard technical outlines without solid color fills.
6. Ensure the **Scale** is set to **2:3**.

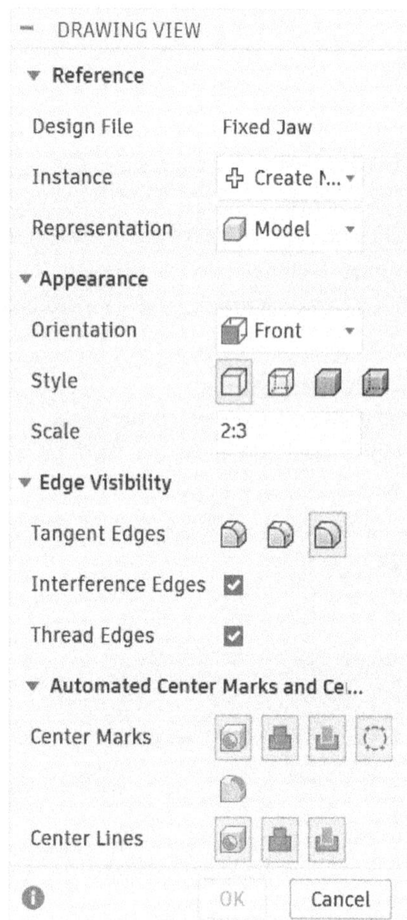

7. Click **OK** to lock the view onto the sheet.

Placing the Projected Views

The **Projected View** tool generates additional orthographic and isometric representations automatically derived from your original Base View.

1. Navigate to the Toolbar, open the **Create** menu, and select **Projected View** to activate the command.

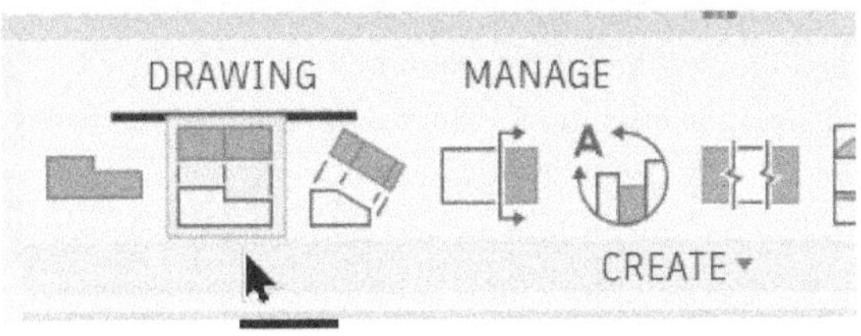

2. Click directly on the Front base view you placed previously, which selects it as the parent geometry for the new projections.
3. Move your cursor straight up from the base view to generate a preview of the top profile.
4. Click the empty space near the top of the sheet to lock the placement of the Top view.

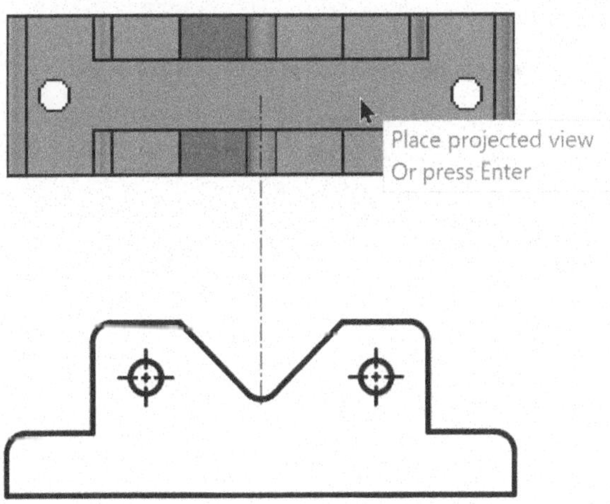

5. Move your cursor straight to the right of the Front base view to generate a side profile preview.
6. Click the empty space to place the Right Side view.

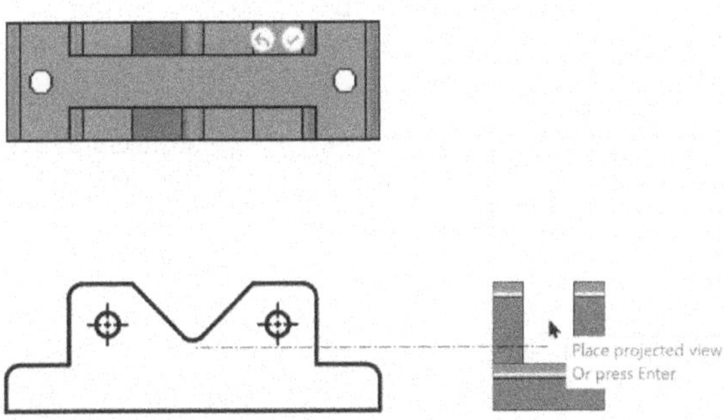

7. Move your cursor diagonally to the upper right corner of the sheet to generate a 3D isometric representation.
8. Click the empty space to place the Isometric view.

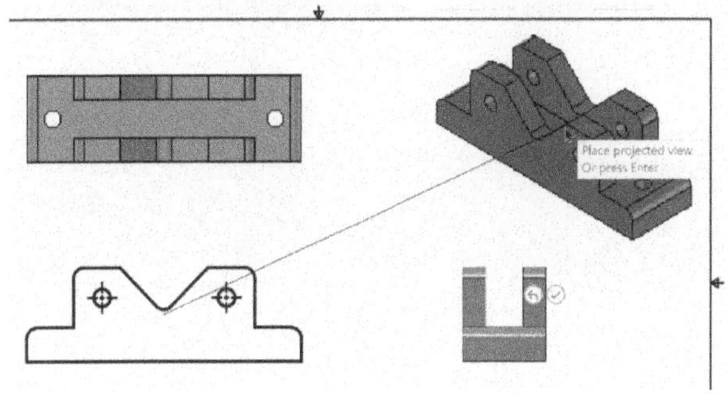

9. Click the green check mark floating near the cursor, or press the Enter key on your keyboard, to generate the final line work and completely close the tool.

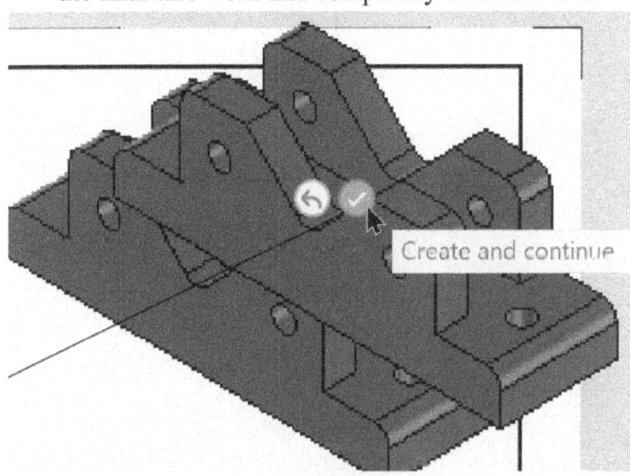

Modifying the Right View

1. Observe that all new projected views automatically inherited the standard line style from the parent base view.
2. Right click directly on the newly created Right view and select **Edit View** from the context menu to reopen the configuration dialog box specifically for that component.

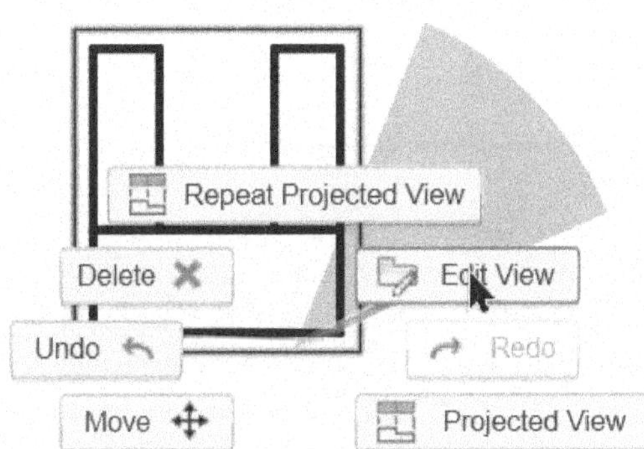

3. Click the **Style** options in the dialog box and select **Visible and Hidden Edges**. This specific setting

forces the software to draw dashed lines representing the internal hole and the stepped geometry that are otherwise hidden from that specific viewing angle.

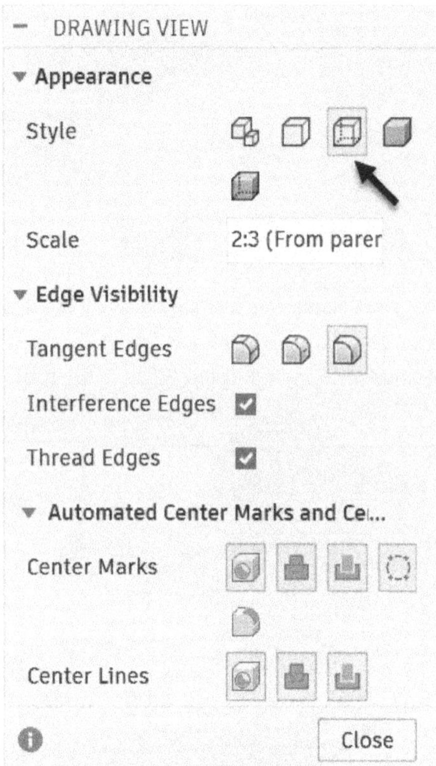

4. Click **Close** in the dialog box to finish the configuration and apply the dashed lines to the Right view.

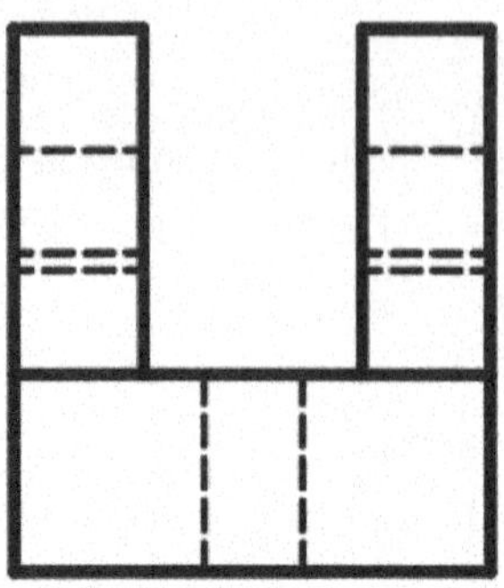

Placing the Initial Linear Dimension

The Drawing workspace provides specialized tools to accurately annotate your 2D views for manufacturing. The **Dimension** tool handles basic horizontal and vertical distances, while the **Chain Dimension** tool links multiple measurements together in a clean, continuous line from a single starting point to save space and maintain strict alignment.

1. Navigate to the Toolbar and click the **Dimension** icon, or press the **D** key on your keyboard.

2. Click the bottom left corner endpoint of the jaw profile, then click on the horizontal edge of the first step directly above it.
3. Move your cursor outward to the left and click the empty space to place the 25.00 vertical measurement.

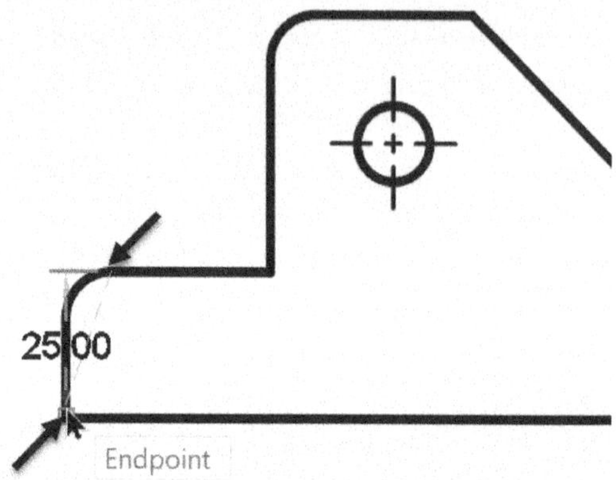

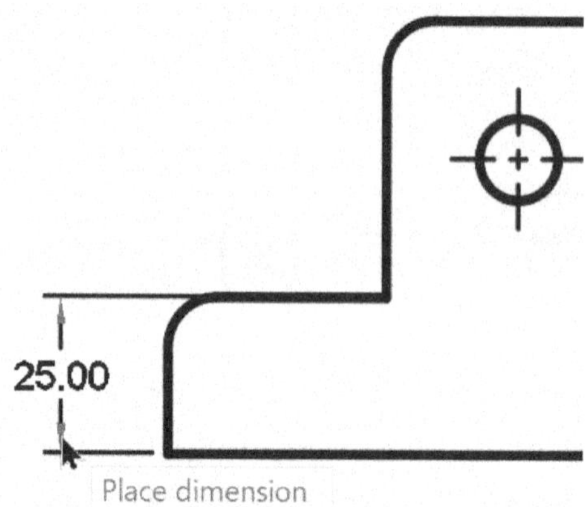

Using the Chain Dimension Tool

1. Navigate back to the Toolbar, open the **Dimensions** drop down menu, and select **Chain Dimension**. This specific tool requires an existing measurement to act as a baseline.

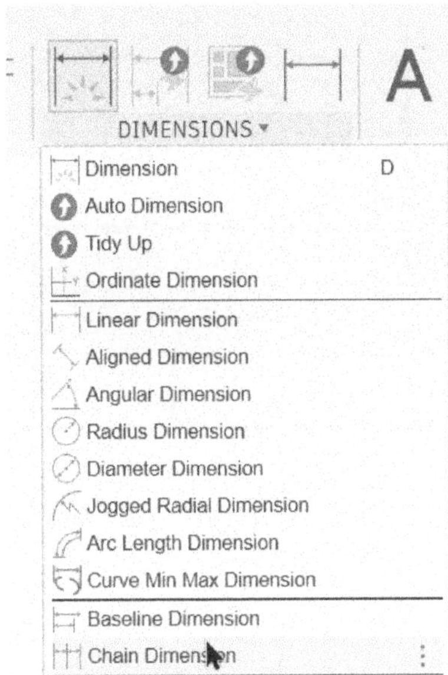

2. Click the 25.00 dimension you just created to establish it as your starting reference.
3. Click the top left corner endpoint of the jaw profile. The software automatically calculates the next distance and stacks the 44.00 dimension perfectly in line with your base measurement.

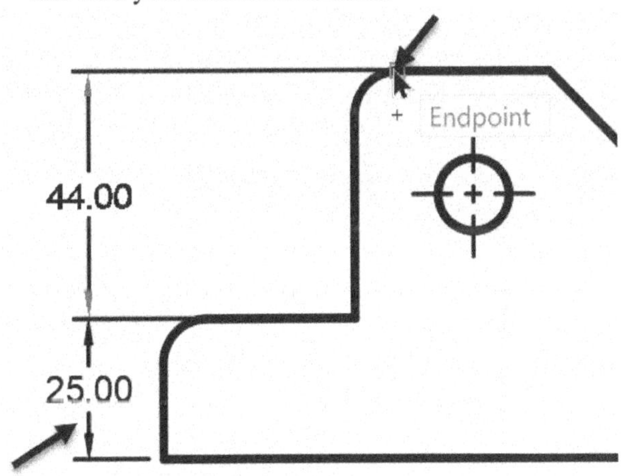

4. Click the green check mark labeled **OK** in the floating dialog box to lock the chain and close the tool.

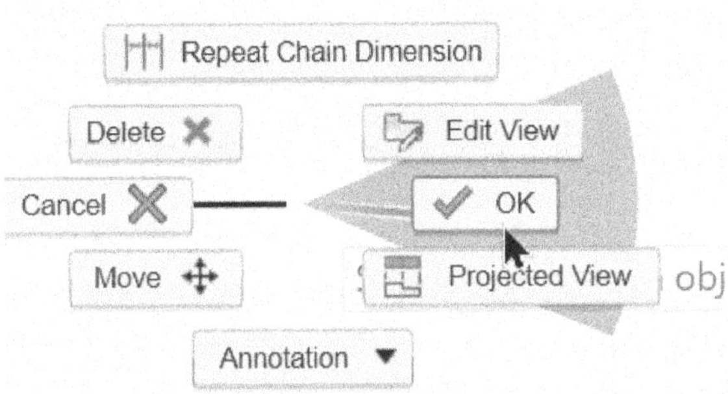

Placing Additional Linear Dimensions

1. Press the D key on your keyboard to reactivate the standard **Dimension** tool.
2. Click the center mark of the left hole, then click the bottom horizontal edge of the part.
3. Move your cursor to the right side of the hole and click to place the 47.00 vertical dimension.

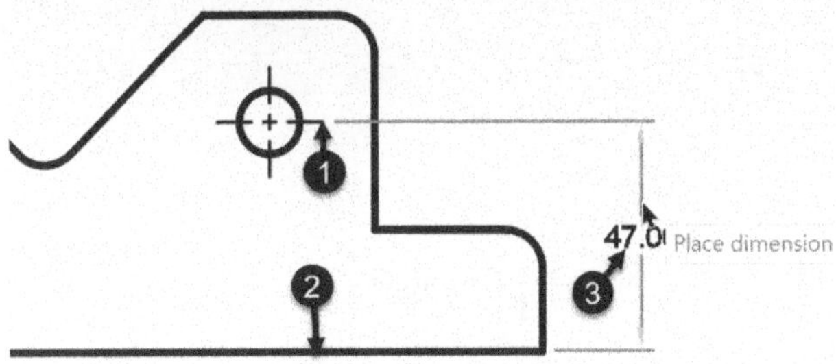

4. Click the center mark of the left hole again, then click the center mark of the right hole.
5. Move your cursor straight up above the part and click to place the 96.00 horizontal distance.

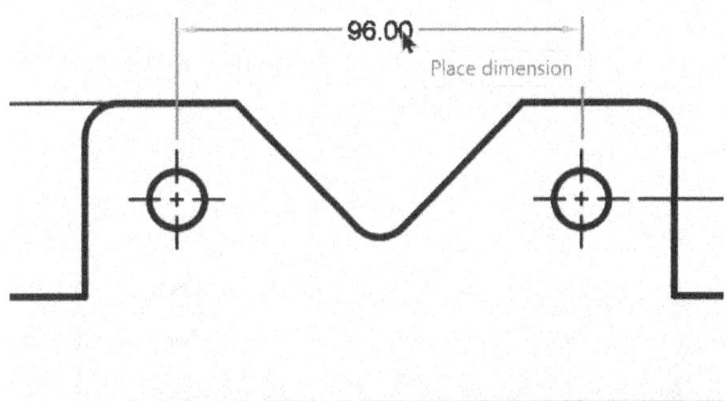

6. Click the far left vertical edge of the part, click the vertical edge, and click above the part to place the 36.00 horizontal dimension.

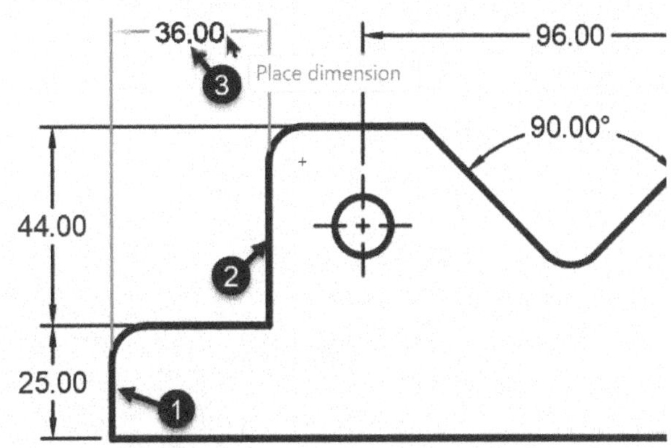

Adding Angular Dimensions and Hole Callouts

1. Open the **Dimensions** drop down menu and select

Angular Dimension to measure the central V notch.

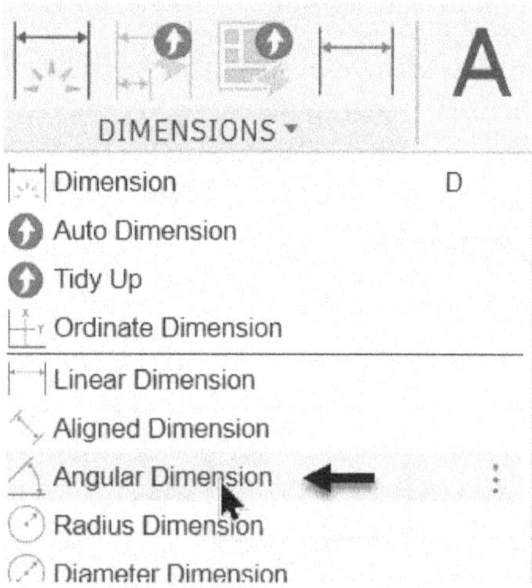

2. Click the left angled line, then click the right-angled line.
3. Move your cursor upward between the two selected lines and click to place the 90.00 degree angle label.

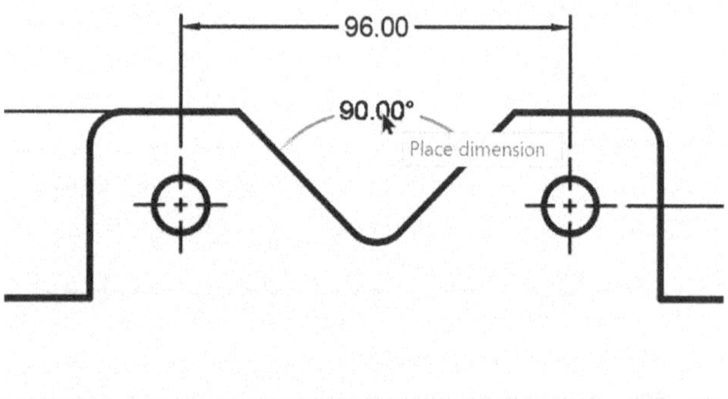

4. On the toolbar, click **Text** panel > **Hole and Thread Callout** to formally document the manufacturing requirements for the circular cutouts.
5. Click the circular edge of right hole and move your cursor outward to place the generated text leader. The software automatically extracts and displays the exact diameter and depth data directly from the physical properties of your 3D model.

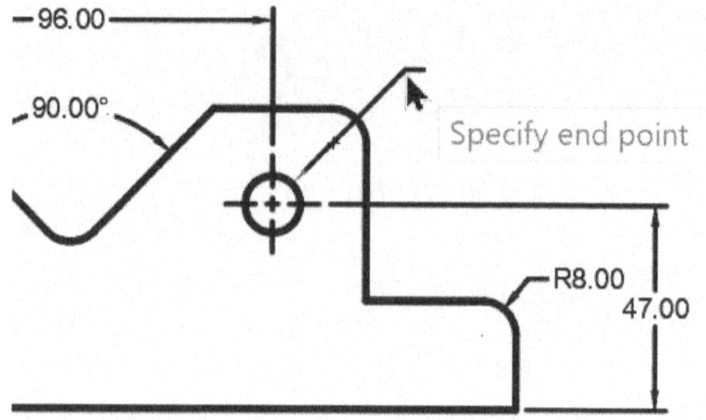

6. Click **OK** on the **Note** dialog.

Modifying the Callout Text

The automated **Hole and Thread Callout** tool extracts exact parameters directly from your 3D model, but you can manually edit this text to meet specific shop floor requirements or drafting standards.

1. Double click the existing hole callout text in the graphics window to launch the Text dialog box.
2. Observe the active text field hovering directly over the part, which initially displays the fully automated parameter string.
3. Click and drag your cursor to highlight the downward pointing depth symbol and the 25.00 numerical value.

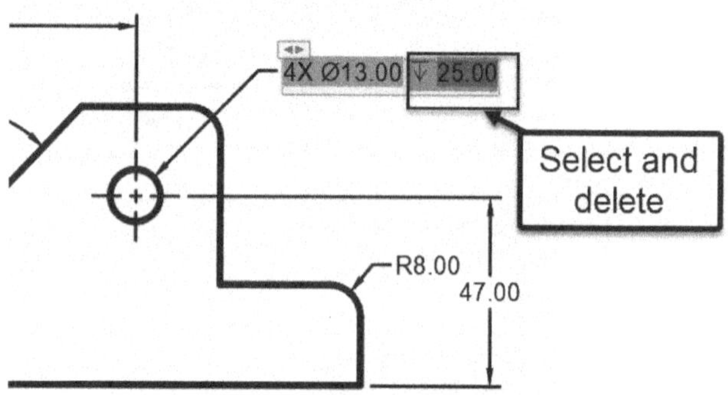

4. Press the Delete key on your keyboard to completely remove that specific depth information from the callout.
5. Type the word THRU to explicitly state that the drill path passes completely through the physical material.
6. Click and drag your cursor to highlight the 4X quantity prefix located at the very beginning of the text string.

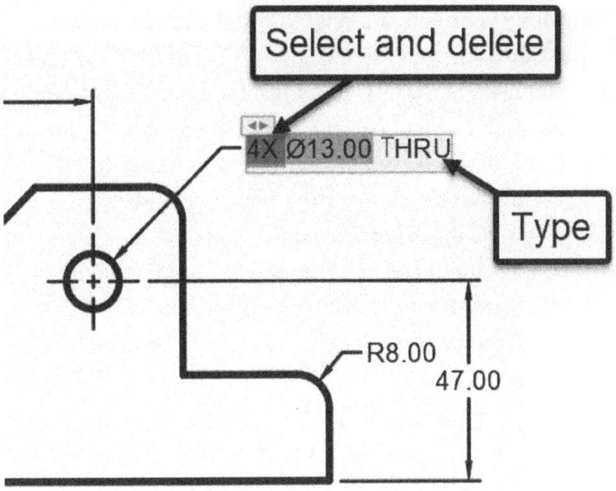

7. Type 2X to replace the highlighted prefix and manually update the documented hole quantity.

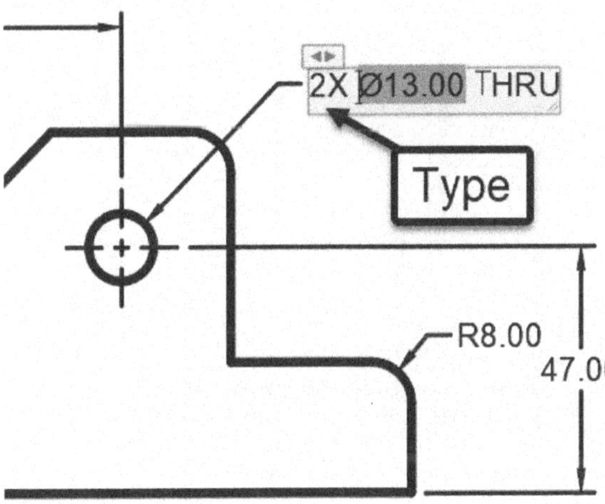

8. Review the floating text box to ensure it reads exactly 2X followed by the diameter symbol, 13.00, and THRU.

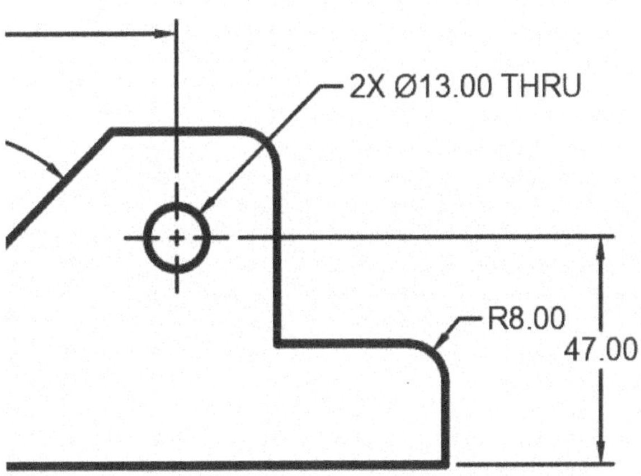

9. Review the Text dialog box on the right side of the screen and click the **Close** button at the bottom to lock your manual edits and finish the command.
10. Navigate to the Toolbar and click the **Dimension** icon, or press the **D** key on your keyboard.
11. Click the top endpoint of the center mark belonging to the left hole, then click the top endpoint of the center mark belonging to the right hole in the Top view.
12. Move your cursor straight up and click in the empty space to place the 172.00 horizontal dimension.

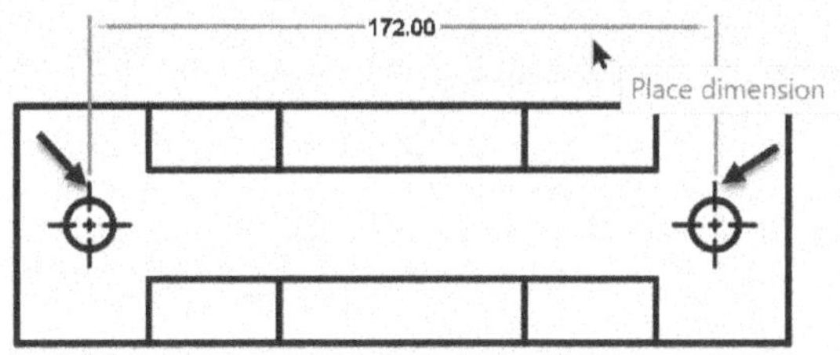

13. Click the far-left vertical edge of the Top view, then click the far right vertical edge.
14. Move your cursor upward above the previous measurement and click to place the 212.00 overall length dimension.

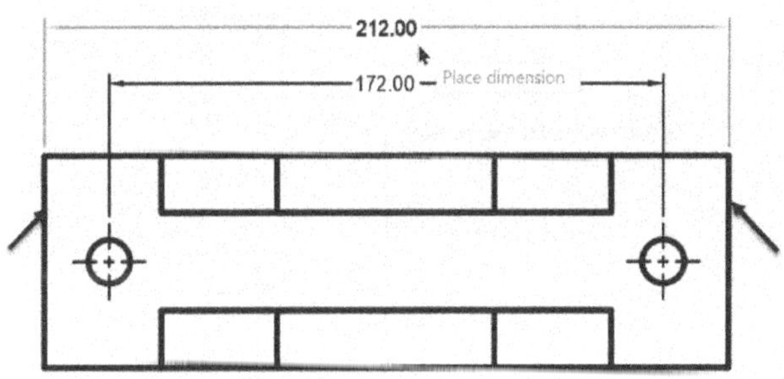

15. Press the **D** key on your keyboard.
16. Click the bottom horizontal edge of the top view and then click the center mark of the circular hole.
17. Move your cursor to the right side of the part and click to place the 31.50 vertical dimension.

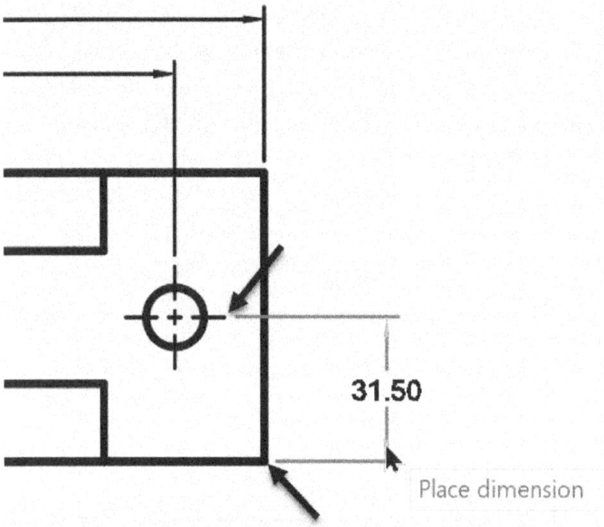

18. Click the bottom horizontal edge of the Right view, move your cursor straight down, and click to place the 63.00 overall width dimension.

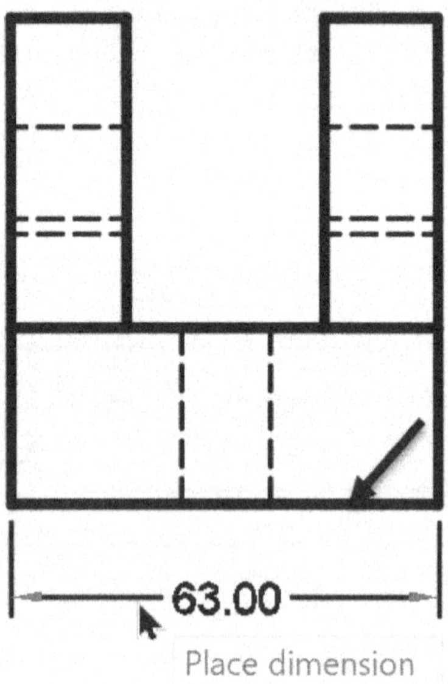

19. Click the top horizontal edge of the left vertical prong.

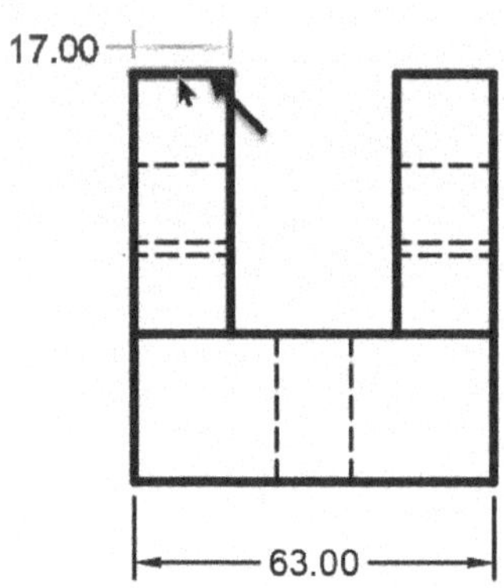

20. Move your cursor straight up and click to place the 17.00 horizontal dimension.
21. Navigate to the Toolbar, open the **Dimensions** drop down menu, and select **Chain Dimension**.
22. Click the 17.00 dimension you just created to establish it as your starting reference base.
23. Click the inner vertical edge located on the right side of the central cutout. The software automatically calculates the next distance and stacks the 29.00 dimension perfectly in line with your base measurement.
24. Click the green check mark labeled **OK** in the floating dialog box to lock the chain and close the tool.

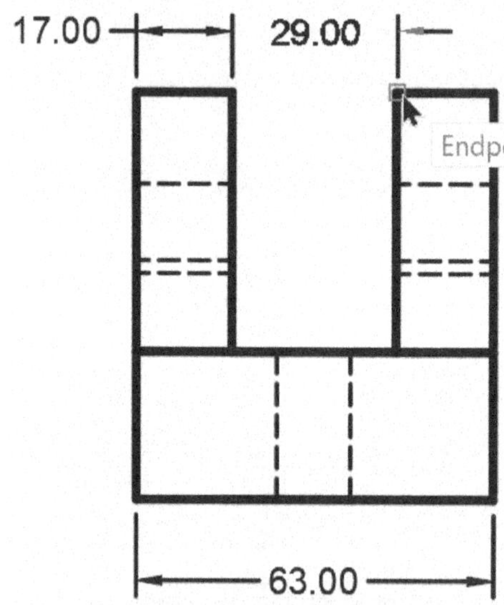

Applying a Dimension Break

1. Navigate to the Toolbar, on the Text panel, select **Hole and Thread Callout**.
2. Locate the top view and click the circular hole.
3. Move your cursor diagonally downward and to the right, dragging the leader line away from the main geometry.
4. Click the empty space to place the automated text, which automatically reads 2X for the quantity, the diameter symbol followed by 13.00, and the depth symbol followed by 25.00.

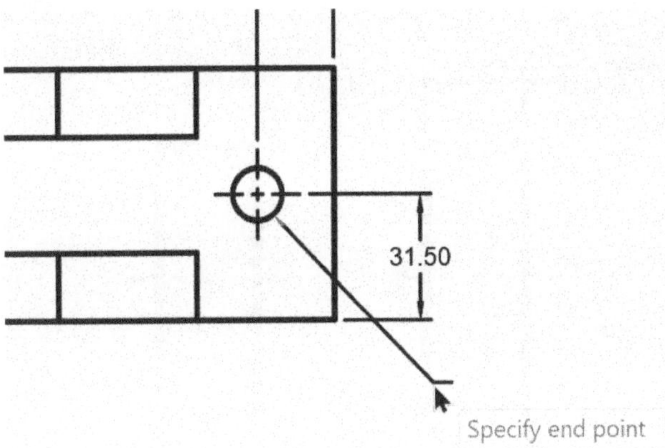

Observe the area where the diagonal leader line of your hole callout physically crosses the horizontal extension line of the newly placed 31.50 dimension.

5. Navigate to the Toolbar, open the **Dimensions** drop down menu, and select **Dimension Break**.

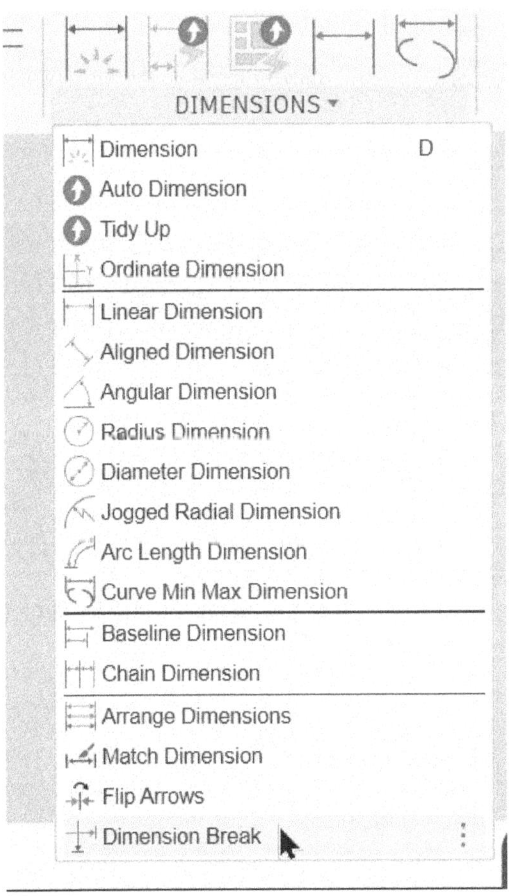

6. Click the diagonal leader line of the hole callout in the graphics window to select it.

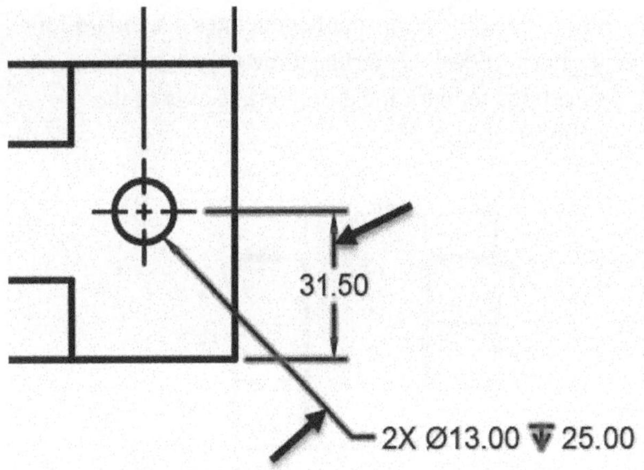

7. Click **OK** in the floating dialog box to apply the modification, which generates a clean visual gap exactly where the two lines cross.

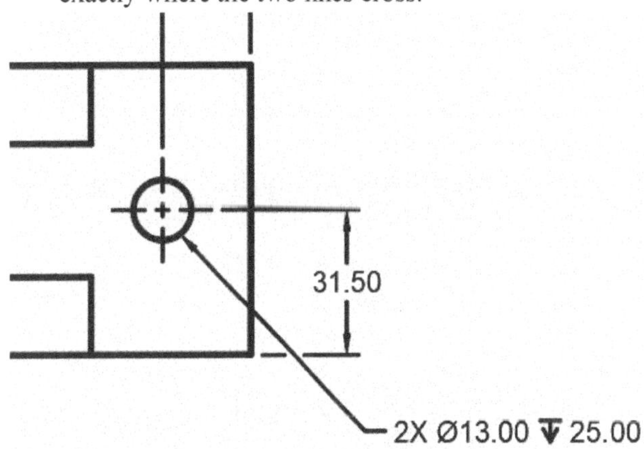

Adding Centerlines

The **Geometry** panel in the Drawing workspace contains specialized tools like **Centerline** and **Center Mark** to correctly define the central axes of cylindrical features according to strict engineering standards. These drafting symbols provide precise snapping points for dimensions.

1. Navigate to the Toolbar, locate the **Geometry** panel, and click the **Centerline** icon.

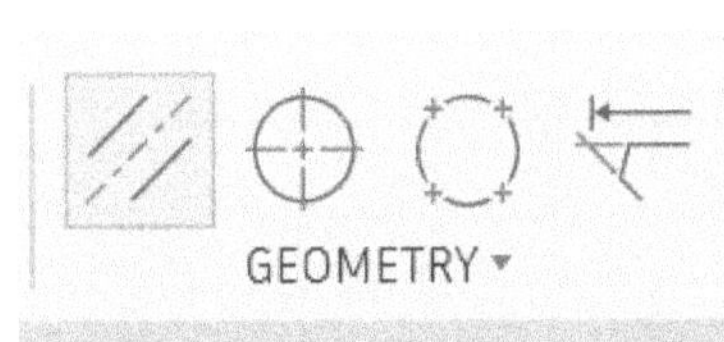

2. Focus on the righ view and locate the two vertical dashed lines representing the hidden walls of the central hole.
3. Click the left dashed line, then click the right dashed

line. The software instantly generates a standard long dash, short dash centerline directly between your selections to mark the exact middle axis of the cylindrical feature.

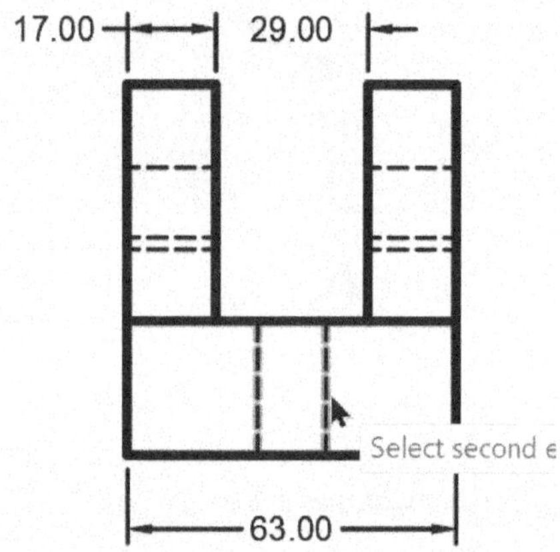

4. Move to the top left area of the Right view and click the two horizontal dashed lines representing the upper horizontal hole.
5. Click the two horizontal dashed lines located directly beneath them representing the lower horizontal hole.
6. Move to the top right area of the Right view and click the corresponding pairs of horizontal dashed lines to generate the final two centerlines on that side.

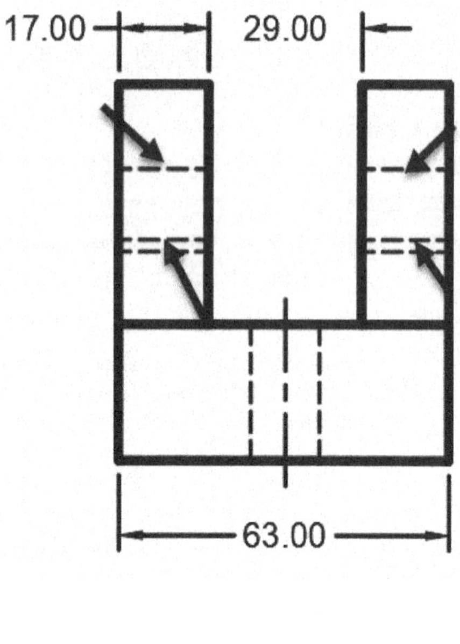

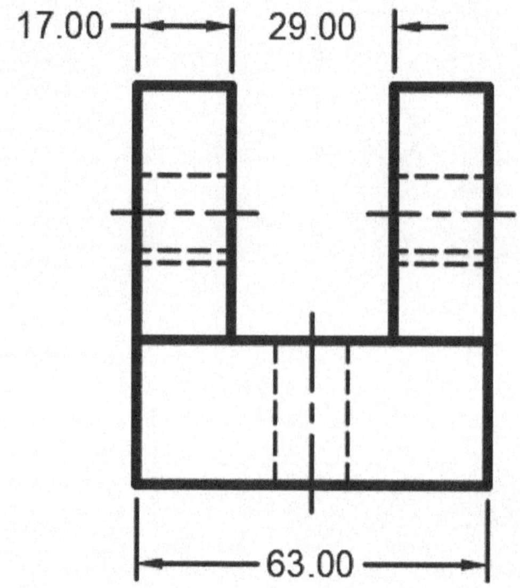

7. Press the Escape key on your keyboard to exit the **Centerline** tool.
8. Navigate to the Toolbar, locate the **Geometry** panel, and click the **Center Mark** icon.

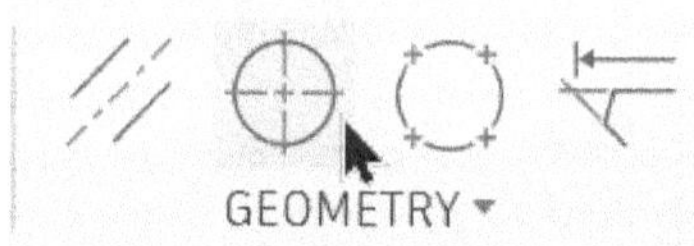

9. Focus on the large Front view located in the center of the sheet.

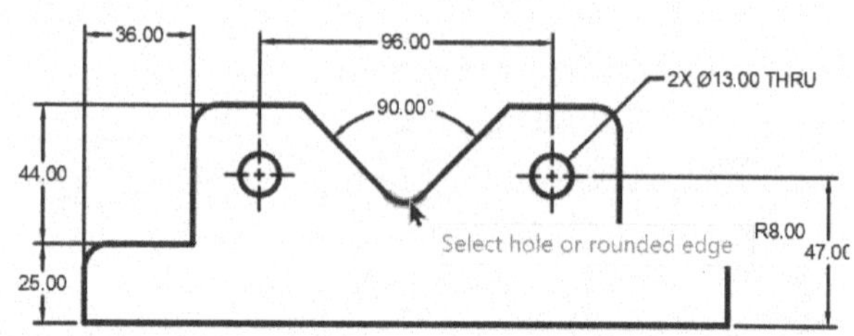

10. Click the curved edge of the rounded fillet located at the very bottom of the central V-notch.

    Observe the standard crosshair symbol that immediately appears in the empty space above the curve, officially marking the exact geometric center of that specific radius.

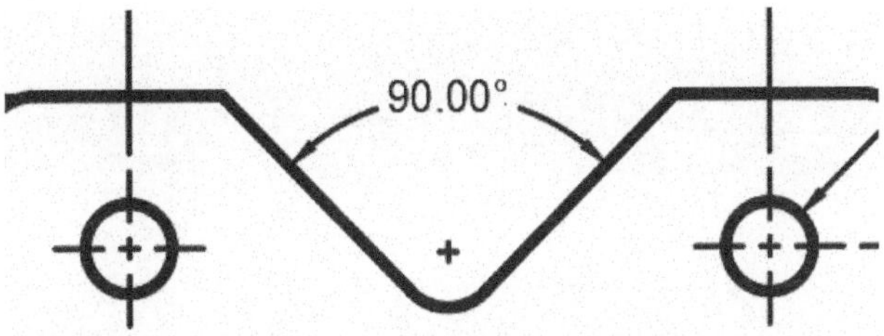

11. Press the Escape key on your keyboard to exit the **Center Mark** tool.

Dimensioning from Centerlines

1. Navigate to the Toolbar and click the **Dimension** icon, or press the **D** key on your keyboard.
2. Focus on the large Front view located in the center of the sheet.
3. Click the central crosshair of the center mark belonging to the right hole.
4. Click the center mark located exactly in the middle of the rounded fillet at the bottom of the V-notch, as shown by the cursor tooltip in your reference image.
5. Move your cursor straight down below the part and click to place the 48.00 horizontal dimension.

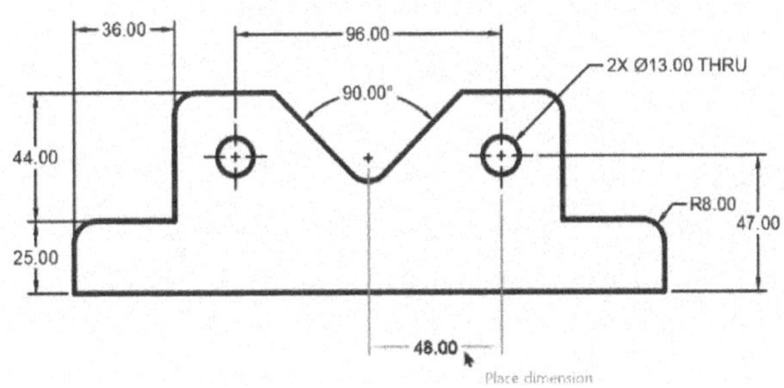

6. Focus on the top view.
7. Click the far right vertical edge of the top view, then click the center mark of the right hole.
8. Move your cursor downward and to the right, and click to place the 20.00 horizontal dimension to specify the edge distance.

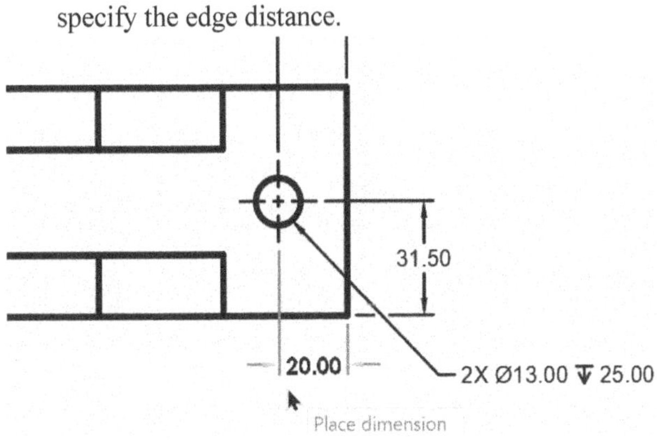

Modifying the Dimension Text

In engineering drawings, the abbreviation TYP stands for Typical, indicating that the specified measurement applies to all visually identical features across the part unless noted otherwise. Adding this text to the single radius dimension informs the manufacturer that all the rounded corners on the base share the exact same R8.00 measurement.

1. Locate the R8.00 radius dimension you placed on the bottom right fillet of the Front view.
2. Double click directly on the R8.00 text to open the inline editing box.
3. Observe the highlighted parameter inside the editing box, which represents the automated dimension value.
4. Click your cursor inside the text box at the very beginning of the string, placing it immediately before the R character.
5. Type the letters TYP followed by a single space.

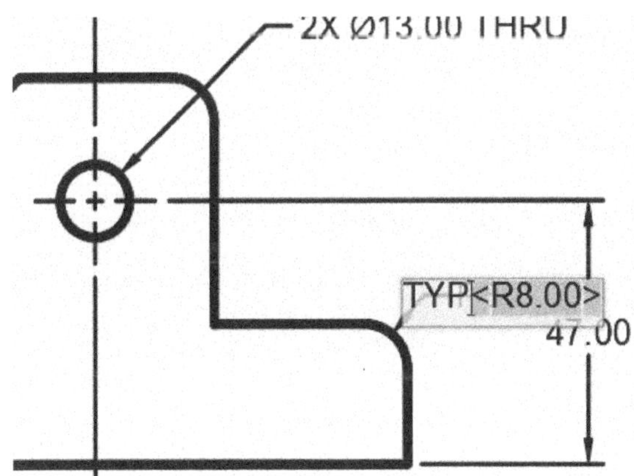

6. Ensure the text string now reads exactly TYP before the automated value.
7. Click your cursor anywhere in the empty graphics window, or press the Enter key on your keyboard, to lock the manual edit and close the text box
8. Save and close the drawing file.

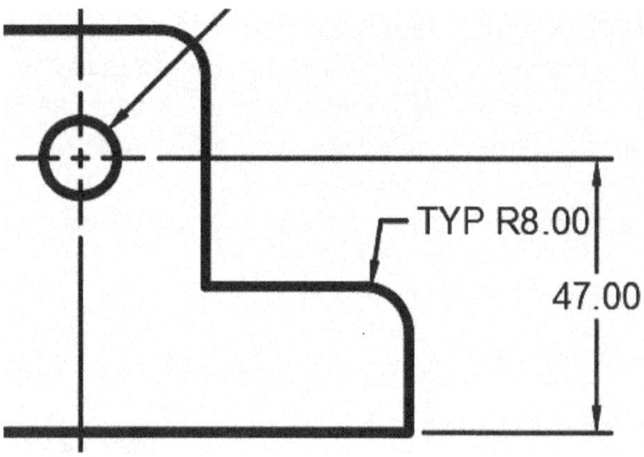

Tutorial 2

In this tutorial, you will create the assembly drawing of the Pipe Vise assembly.

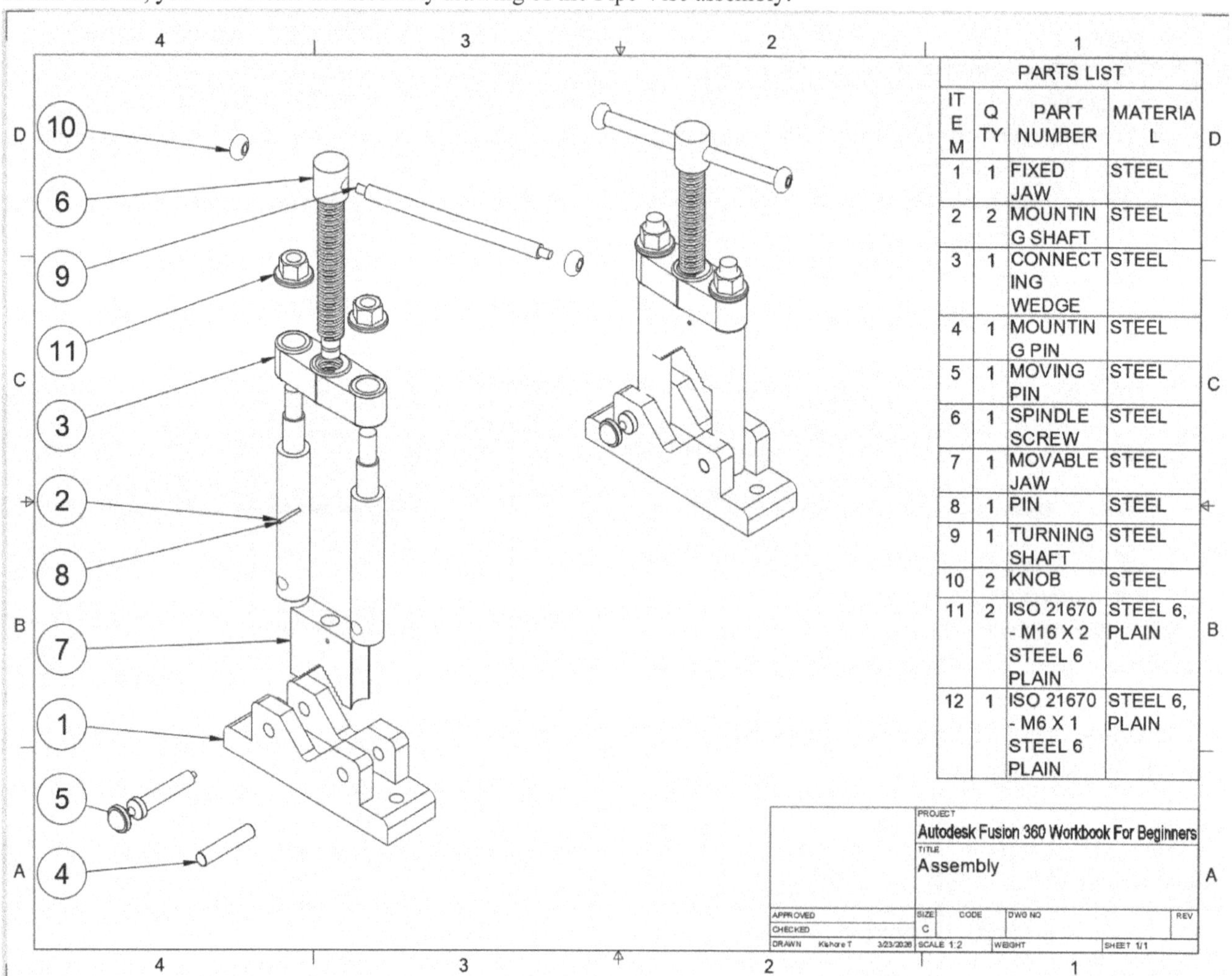

PARTS LIST

ITEM	QTY	PART NUMBER	MATERIAL
1	1	FIXED JAW	STEEL
2	2	MOUNTING SHAFT	STEEL
3	1	CONNECTING WEDGE	STEEL
4	1	MOUNTING PIN	STEEL
5	1	MOVING PIN	STEEL
6	1	SPINDLE SCREW	STEEL
7	1	MOVABLE JAW	STEEL
8	1	PIN	STEEL
9	1	TURNING SHAFT	STEEL
10	2	KNOB	STEEL
11	2	ISO 21670 - M16 X 2 STEEL 6 PLAIN	STEEL 6, PLAIN
12	1	ISO 21670 - M6 X 1 STEEL 6 PLAIN	STEEL 6, PLAIN

Initiate Drawing from the Data Panel

1. Open the **Data Panel** on the left side of the Fusion 360 interface.
2. Locate your design file created in Tutorial 14.
3. Right-click the **Assembly** file and select **Create Drawing** from the context menu. This action targets the entire external file for 2D documentation.

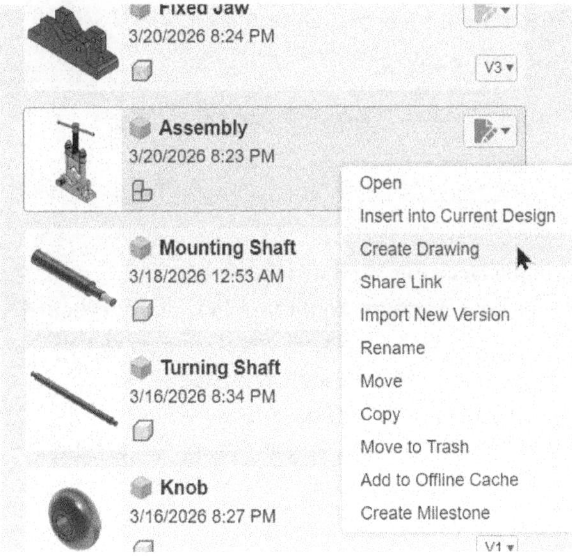

Configure the Create Drawing Dialog

Once the command executes, the **Create Drawing** dialog appears. Set the parameters exactly as follows to establish the sheet foundation.

1. **Drawing Type:** Select **Manual**. This requires the user to place views individually rather than automating the layout.
2. **Destination - Drawing:** Select **Create New**.
3. **Standard:** Select **ASME** (American Society of Mechanical Engineers drafting standards).
4. **Units:** Select **mm** (millimeters).
5. **Sheet Size:** Select **C**. The dialog will lock the dimensions to **Width 22in** and **Height 17in**.
6. Click **OK** to generate the drawing and enter the Drawing Workspace.

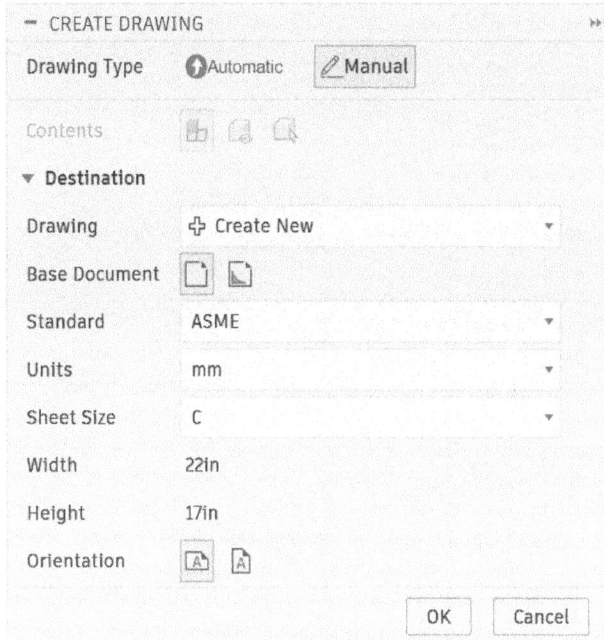

Place the Primary Assembled Base View

The **Drawing View** dialog opens automatically, attaching a preview to your cursor. Configure the assembled state:

1. **Representation:** Leave as **Model**. This pulls the standard, unexploded geometric state.
2. **Orientation:** Set to **HOME** for the default isometric angle.
3. **Style:** Select the first icon, **Visible Edges**.
4. **Scale:** Set to **1:2** to reduce the model to half scale.
5. **Edge Visibility:** Select the first icon for **Tangent Edges** (displays full length transitions between curved faces). Check the boxes for **Interference Edges** and **Thread Edges**.

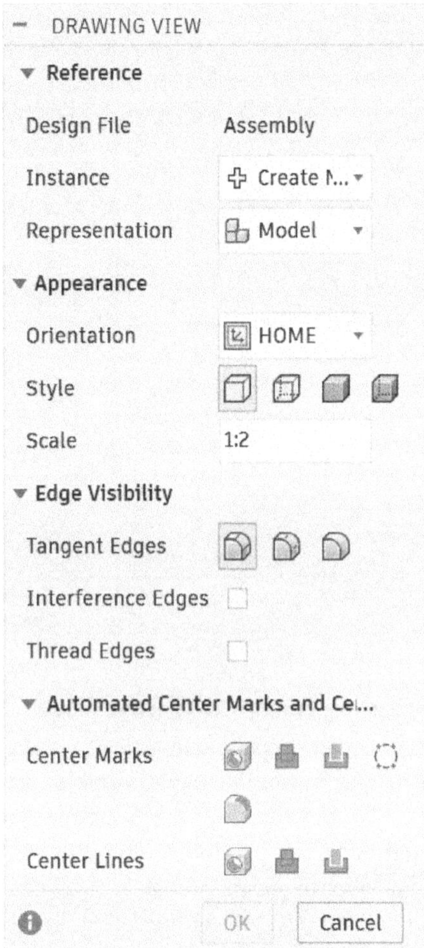

6. Click in the top center portion of canvas to **Place base view**, then click **OK**.

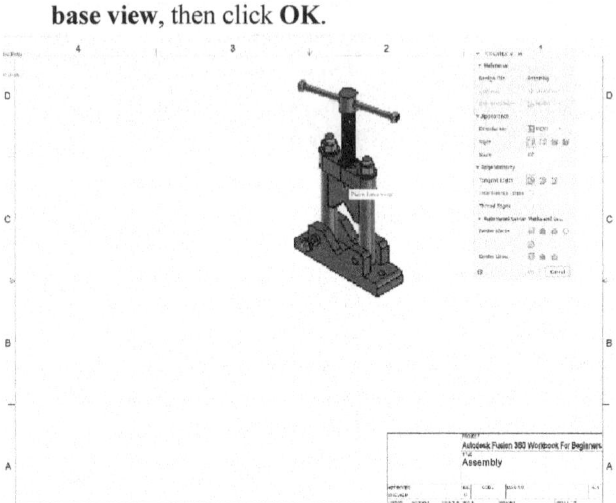

Place the Exploded Base View

To document the individual components, you must place a second view referencing an animation sequence.

1. Click **Base View** from the toolbar.

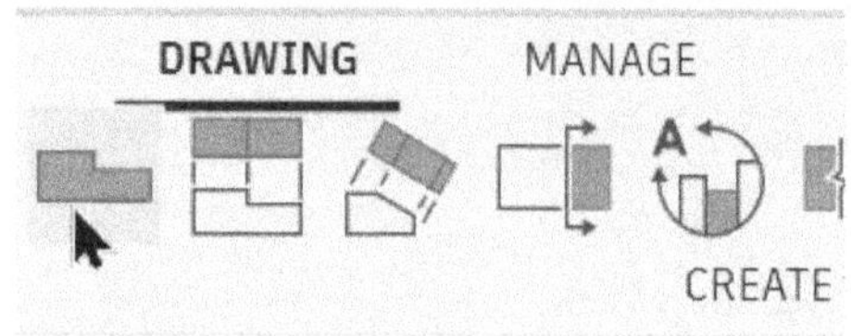

2. In the **Drawing View** dialog, change **Representation** from Model to **Storyboard**. This extracts the exploded visual state previously defined in the Animation workspace.
3. **Orientation:** Set to **HOME**.
4. **Style:** Select the second icon, **Visible and Hidden Edges**. This creates a standard wireframe technical drawing without color shading.
5. **Scale:** Set to **1:2**.

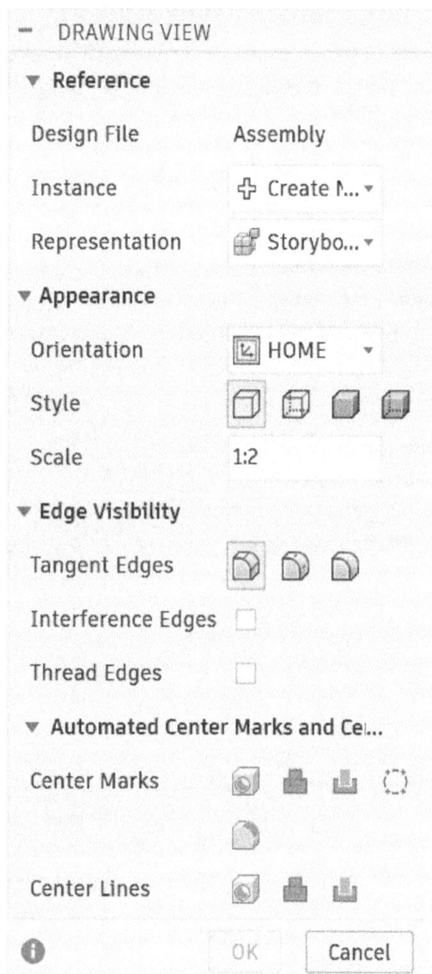

6. Click the canvas to the left of the assembled view to place this second exploded view, then click **OK**.

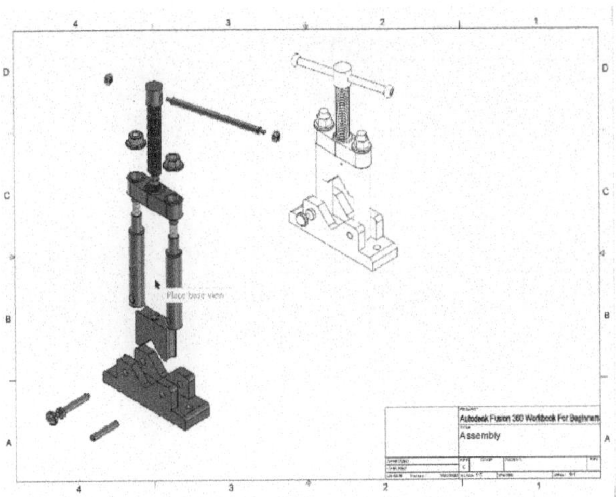

Generate and Place the Parts List Table

1. Navigate to the **Tables** panel on the toolbar and select **Table**.

2. In the **Table** dialog, configure the following options:
   - **Type:** Select **Parts List**.
   - **Structure:** Select **First Level**. This ensures only primary, top-level components are itemized, preventing the table from detailing individual sub-assembly hardware.
   - **Auto Balloon:** Leave this checked.

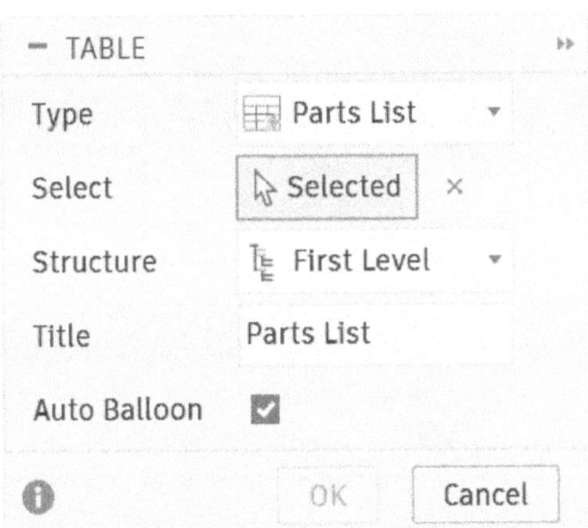

3. The **Select** button will be active. Click directly on the exploded drawing view in the canvas to link the structural metadata to that specific visual representation.
4. Move your cursor to the top right corner of the drawing border and click to place the table. The table will automatically extract and populate the ITEM, QTY, PART NUMBER, and MATERIAL columns for all 12 main components.

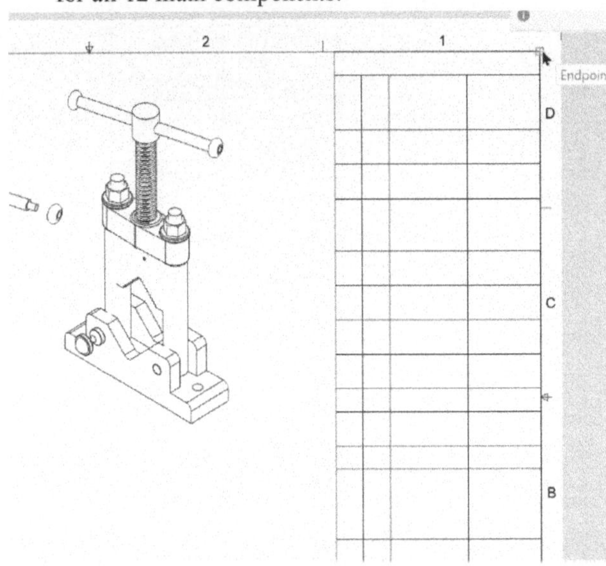

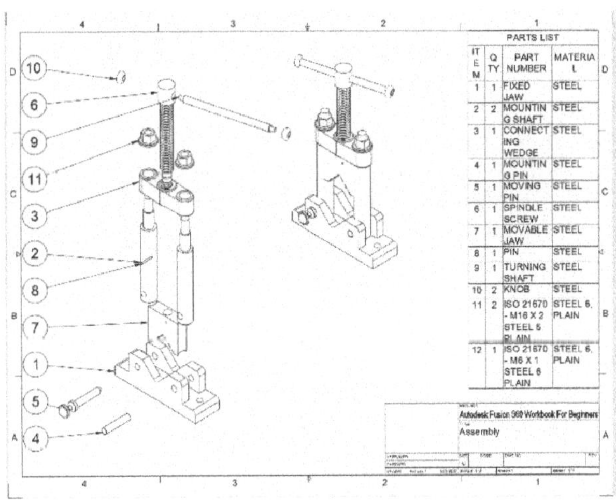

Modify the Parts List Table via Selection Grips

1. **Activate Table Grips:** Single-click anywhere on the placed Parts List table. The table will highlight, and several gray selection grips (small squares and triangles) will appear along its bounding box and column borders.

PARTS LIST			
ITEM	QTY	PART NUMBER	MATERIAL
1	1	FIXED JAW	STEEL
2	2	MOUNTING SHAFT	STEEL
3	1	CONNECTING WEDGE	STEEL
4	1	MOUNTING PIN	STEEL
5	1	MOVING PIN	STEEL
6	1	SPINDLE SCREW	STEEL
7	1	MOVABLE JAW	STEEL
8	1	PIN	STEEL
9	1	TURNING SHAFT	STEEL
10	2	KNOB	STEEL
11	2	ISO 21670 - M16 X 2 STEEL 6 PLAIN	STEEL 6, PLAIN
12	1	ISO 21670 - M6 X 1 STEEL 6 PLAIN	STEEL 6, PLAIN

2. **Reposition and Snap the Table**

- Locate the primary anchor grip at the top-right corner of the table.

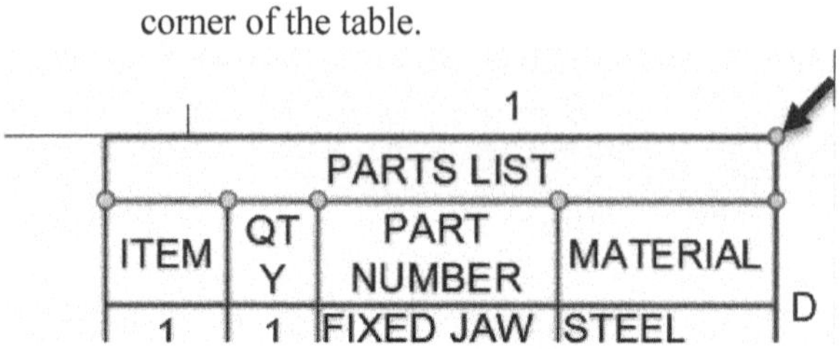

- Click and hold this anchor grip.
- Drag the table to the desired location on the sheet. To ensure alignment, drag the grip toward the inner perimeter of the drawing border or the top edge of the Title Block until the software's geometric snapping engages, then release the mouse button to lock it in place.

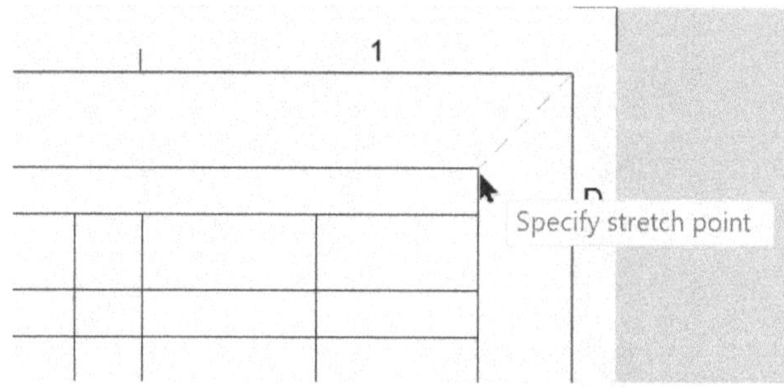

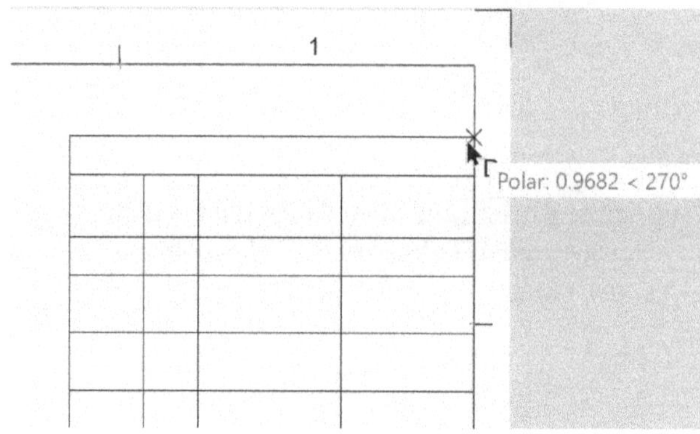

3. **Resize Column Widths:**
   - To resolve text wrapping (e.g., in the "PART NUMBER" column), hover your cursor over the selection grip located directly on the vertical line separating two column headers.
   - Click and hold the grip.

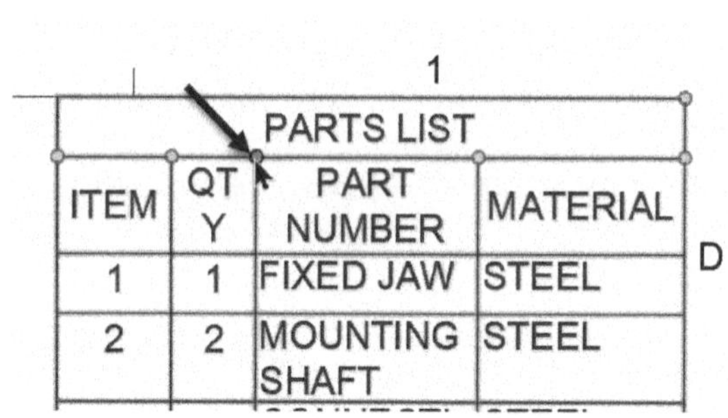

   - Drag your cursor horizontally to the left or right to expand or contract the column width. Release the mouse button once the text fits on a single line. The overall table width will automatically adjust to accommodate the new column dimension.

PARTS LIST			
ITEM	QTY	PART NUMBER	MATERIAL
1	1	FIXED JAW	STEEL
2	2	MOUNTING SHAFT	STEEL

4. **Split the Table Layout (If Necessary):**
   - If the assembly contains too many components to fit vertically above the title block, locate the triangular directional grip at the bottom-center of the table.

8	1	PIN	STEEL
9	1	TURNING SHAFT	STEEL
10	2	KNOB	STEEL
11	2	ISO 21670 - M16 X 2 STEEL 6 PLAIN	STEEL 6, PLAIN
12	1	ISO 21670 - M6 X 1 STEEL 6 PLAIN	STEEL 6, PLAIN

   - Click and drag this grip upward. This action splits the parts list dynamically, wrapping the lower rows into a new, parallel table segment adjacent to the original list.

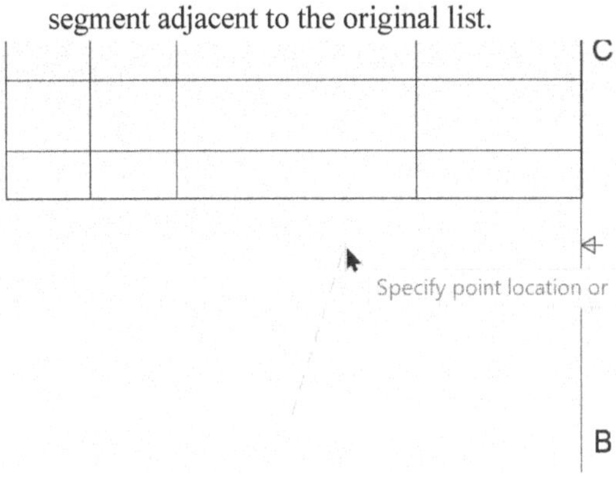

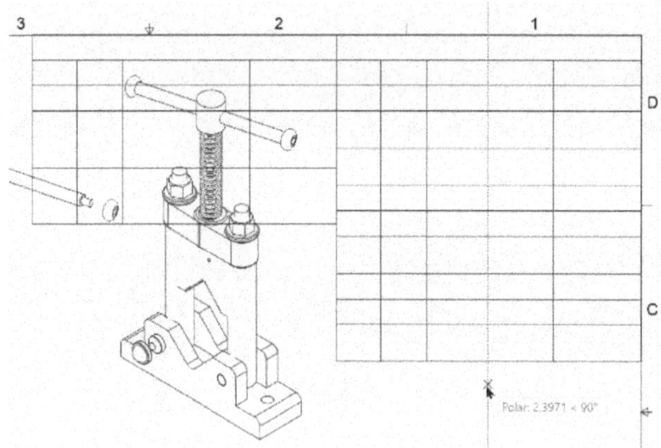

5. Save and close the drawing file.

9 788199 428935

Printed at Repro India Ltd.